THE HUMANISTIC TRADITION

THIRD EDITION

4 Faith, Reason, and Power in the Early Modern World

THE HUMANISTIC TRADITION

THIRD EDITION

4 Faith, Reason, and Power in the Early Modern World

Gloria K. Fiero

New York   St. Louis   San Francisco   Auckland   Bogotá   Caracas
Lisbon   London   Madrid   Mexico City   Milan   Montreal   New Delhi
San Juan   Singapore   Sydney   Tokyo   Toronto

McGraw-Hill

*A Division of The **McGraw·Hill** Companies*

THE HUMANISTIC TRADITION, BOOK 4

Copyright © 1998 by The McGraw-Hill Companies, Inc.
Previous editions © 1995, 1992 by William C. Brown Communications, Inc.
All rights reserved. Except as permitted under the United States Copyright Act
of 1976, no part of this publication may be reproduced or distributed in any
form or by any means, or stored in a data base or retrieval system, without
the prior written permission of the publisher.

Permissions Acknowledgments appear on page 169,
and on this page by reference.

Library of Congress Catalog Card Number: 97–071268

ISBN 0–697–34071–6

Editorial Director *Phillip Butcher*
Senior Sponsoring Editor *Cynthia Ward*
Director of Marketing *Margaret Metz*
National Sales Manager *Jerry Arni*

This book was designed and produced by
CALMANN & KING LTD
71 Great Russell Street, London WC1B 3BN

Editor *Ursula Payne*
Designer *Karen Osborne*
Cover Designer *Karen Stafford*
Timeline Designer *Richard Foenander*
Picture Researcher *Carrie Haines*
Maps by Oxford Illustrators Ltd.

Developmental Editing by M. J. Kelly for McGraw-Hill

Typeset by Fakenham Photosetting, Norfolk
Printed in Hong Kong

10 9 8 7 6 5 4 3 2 1

http://www.mhhe.com

Front cover
Main image: Marie-Louise-Elisabeth Vigée-Lebrun, detail of *Marie Antoinette*,
1788. Oil on canvas, full image 12 ft. 1½ in. × 6 ft. 3½ in. Musée de Versailles.
Giraudon/Art Resource, New York.
Insets: (top) Charles-Henri-Joseph Cordier, detail of *African in Algerian Costume*,
ca. 1856–1857. Bronze and onyx, complete sculpture 37¾ × 26 × 14 in.
Musée d'Orsay, Paris. Photo: © R.M.N., Paris.
(center) Marisol Escobar, detail of *Women and Dog*, 1964. Wood, plaster, synthetic
polymer, and miscellaneous items, full assemblage 72¼ × 73 × 30¹⁵⁄₁₆ in.
Collection of the Whitney Museum of American Art, New York. Purchase, with
funds from the Friends of the Whitney Museum of American Art (64.17 a–g).
Photo: Robert E. Mates, N.J. © Marisol Escobar/DACS, London VAGA, New York 1997.
(bottom) Toshusai Sharaku, *Bust Portrait of the Actor Segawa Tomisaburo as
Yadorigi, the Wife of Ogishi Kurando*, 1794–1795. Woodblock print, 14½ × 9¼ in.
Photograph © 1997, The Art Institute of Chicago, All Rights Reserved.
Clarence Buckingham Collection, 1928.1056.

Frontispiece
Pieter de Hooch, detail of *A Dutch Courtyard*, 1658–1660. Oil on canvas,
full image 26¾ × 23 in. © 1998 Board of Trustees, National Gallery of Art,
Washington, D.C. Andrew W. Mellon Collection.

Series Contents

BOOK

1

The First Civilizations and the Classical Legacy

PART I PREHISTORY AND THE FIRST CIVILIZATIONS
1 Prehistory and the Birth of Civilization: People and Nature
2 Ancient Civilizations: People and the Gods
3 Ancient Civilizations: People and the Social Order

PART II THE CLASSICAL LEGACY
4 Humanism, Individualism, and the Greek Community
5 Greek Philosophy: The Speculative Leap
6 The Classical Style
7 Bipolar Empires: Rome and Han China

BOOK

2

Medieval Europe and the World Beyond

PART I THE SHAPING OF THE MIDDLE AGES
8 A Flowering of Faith: Christianity and Buddhism
9 The Language of Faith: Symbolism and the Arts
10 The Islamic World: Religion and Culture

PART II THE MEDIEVAL WEST
11 Patterns of Medieval Life
12 Christianity and the Medieval Mind
13 The Medieval Synthesis in the Arts

PART III THE WORLD BEYOND THE WEST
14 Asian Civilizations: The Artistic Record

BOOK

3

The European Renaissance, the Reformation, and Global Encounter

PART I THE AGE OF THE RENAISSANCE
15 Adversity and Challenge: The Fourteenth-Century Transition
16 Classical Humanism in the Age of the Renaissance
17 Renaissance Artists: Disciples of Nature, Masters of Invention

PART II A BRAVE NEW WORLD
18 Protest and Reform: The Waning of the Old Order
19 Africa, the Americas, and Cross-Cultural Encounter

BOOK

4

Faith, Reason, and Power in the Early Modern World

PART I THE AGE OF THE BAROQUE
20 The Catholic Reformation and the Baroque Style
21 The Baroque in the Protestant North
22 The Scientific Revolution and the New Learning
23 Absolute Power and the Aristocratic Style

PART II THE AGE OF THE ENLIGHTENMENT
24 The Promise of Reason
25 The Limits of Reason
26 Eighteenth-Century Art, Music, and Society

BOOK

5

Romanticism, Realism, and the Nineteenth-Century World

PART I THE ROMANTIC ERA
27 The Romantic View of Nature
28 The Romantic Hero
29 The Romantic Style in Art and Music

PART II REALISM AND THE MODERNIST TURN
30 Industry, Empire, and the Realist Style
31 The Move Toward Modernism

BOOK

6

The Global Village of the Twentieth Century

PART I THE TRIUMPH OF MODERNISM
32 The Modernist Assault
33 The Freudian Revolution
34 Total War, Totalitarianism, and the Arts
35 The Quest for Meaning

PART II THE POSTMODERN TURN
36 Identity and Liberation
37 The Arts in the Information Age

Book 4
Contents

Preface   *ix*

Timeline   *xiv*

Summary of the Renaissance and the Reformation   *xvi*
  Classical Humanism   *xvi*
  Renaissance Artists   *xvi*
  Shattering the Old Order: Protest and Reform   *1*

PART I
The Age of the Baroque   *3*

20 The Catholic Reformation and the Baroque Style   5

The Catholic Reformation   *5*
READING 4.1 From Loyola's *Spiritual Exercises*   *6*
Catholicism's Global Reach   *7*
Literature and the Catholic Reformation   *7*
READING 4.2 From Saint Teresa's *Visions*   *9*
READING 4.3 From Crashaw's *The Flaming Heart*   *9*
The Visual Arts and the Catholic Reformation   *9*
  Mannerist Painting   *9*
  Baroque Painting   *14*
  Baroque Sculpture in Italy   *17*
  Baroque Architecture in Italy   *18*
Baroque Music   *24*
  The Genius of Gabrieli   *24*
  Monteverdi and the Birth of Opera   *24*
Summary   *25*
  Glossary   *26*
  Suggestions for Reading   *26*
  Music Listening Selections   *26*

21 The Baroque in the Protestant North   27

The Rise of the English Commonwealth   *27*
The King James Bible   *29*
READING 4.4 From the Douay Bible, 1609, and the
  King James Bible, 1611   *29*
English Literature of the Seventeenth Century   *29*
  John Donne   *29*
READING 4.5 From Donne's *Meditation 17*   *29*
READING 4.6 From Donne's *Holy Sonnets*   *30*
  The Genius of John Milton   *31*
READING 4.7 From Milton's *Paradise Lost*   *32*
The London of Christopher Wren   *34*
Rembrandt and Protestant Devotionalism   *35*
The Music of the Protestant North   *38*
  Handel and the English Oratorio   *38*
  Bach and Religious Music   *39*
Summary   *40*
  Glossary   *41*
  Suggestions for Reading   *41*
  Music Listening Selections   *41*

22 The Scientific Revolution and the New Learning   42

The Scientific Revolution   *42*
  Kepler and Galileo   *42*
The New Learning   *44*
  Bacon and the Empirical Method   *44*
READING 4.8 From Bacon's *Novum Organum*   *44*
READING 4.9 From Bacon's *Of Studies*   *46*
  Descartes and the Birth of Modern Philosophy   *47*

READING 4.10 From Descartes' *Discourse on Method* (Part IV) *47*
Religion and the New Learning *48*
Locke and the Culmination of the Empirical Tradition *49*
READING 4.11 From Locke's *Essay Concerning Human Understanding* *49*
Newton's Scientific Synthesis *50*
The Impact of the Scientific Revolution on Art *51*
Northern Baroque Painting *51*
Vermeer and Dutch Painting *54*
Dutch Portraiture *56*
Baroque Instrumental Music *58*
Summary *59*
Glossary *60*
Suggestions for Reading *60*
Music Listening Selections *60*

23 Absolute Power and the Aristocratic Style *61*

The Aristocratic Style in France *63*
Louis XIV and French Absolutism *63*
Versailles: Symbol of Royal Absolutism *63*
Louis as Patron of the Arts *69*
Poussin and the Academic Style in Painting *71*
The Aristocratic Portrait *72*
The Aristocratic Style in Europe *73*
Velásquez, Rubens, and van Dyck *73*
Music and Dance at the Court of Louis XIV *75*
Neoclassicism and French Literature *76*
READING 4.12 From La Rochefoucauld's *Maxims* *76*
Molière's Human Comedy *77*
READING 4.13 From Molière's *Le Bourgeois Gentilhomme* *77*
Absolute Power and the Aristocratic Style Beyond Europe *82*
The Aristocratic Style in India *84*
The Patronage of Jahangir and Shah Jahan *85*
The Aristocratic Style in China: The Ming and Manchu Dynasties *88*
The Forbidden City *90*
Imperial Patronage of the Arts *90*
Chinese Literature and the Theater Arts *92*
The Aristocratic Style in Japan *92*
Summary *95*
Glossary *95*
Suggestions for Reading *95*

PART II

The Age of the Enlightenment *97*

24 The Promise of Reason *98*

The Political Theories of Hobbes and Locke *98*
READING 4.14 From Hobbes' *Leviathan* *99*
Locke's Government of the People *100*
READING 4.15 From Locke's *Of Civil Government* *101*
The Influence of Locke on Montesquieu and Jefferson *102*
READING 4.16 From Jefferson's Declaration of Independence *102*
Adam Smith and the Birth of Economic Theory *103*
READING 4.17 From Smith's *An Inquiry into the Nature and Causes of the Wealth of Nations* *103*
The *Philosophes* *104*
Diderot and the *Encyclopédie* *105*
READING 4.18 From the *Encyclopédie* *107*
The Encyclopedic Cast of Mind *108*
The Crusade for Progress *108*
READING 4.19 From Condorcet's *Sketch for a Historical Picture of the Progress of the Human Mind* *109*
The Journalistic Essay and the Birth of the Modern Novel *110*
Pope: Poet of the Age of Reason *110*
READING 4.20 From Pope's *Essay on Man* *111*
Summary *112*
Glossary *112*
Suggestions for Reading *112*

25 The Limits of Reason *113*

The Transatlantic Slave Trade *113*
READING 4.21 From Equiano's *Travels* *114*
Satire: Weapon of the Enlightenment *117*
The Satires of Jonathan Swift *117*
READING 4.22 From Swift's *A Modest Proposal* *117*
Voltaire and *Candide* *119*
READING 4.23 From Voltaire's *Candide* *121*
Satire in Chinese Literature *129*
READING 4.24 From Li Ruzhen's *Flowers in the Mirror* *130*
The Visual Satires of William Hogarth *131*

Rousseau's Revolt Against Reason   *133*
READING 4.25 From Rousseau's *Discourse on the Origin of
    Inequality among Men*   *134*
Kant's Mind/World Revolution   *135*
The Revolutions of the Late Eighteenth Century   *136*
Summary   *138*
    Glossary   *138*
    Suggestions for Reading   *138*

26   Eighteenth-Century Art,
     Music, and Society   *139*

The Rococo Style   *139*
    Rococo Painting in France   *143*
    Rococo Sculpture   *147*
Eighteenth-Century French Genre Painting   *148*
Eighteenth-Century Neoclassicism   *150*
    Neoclassical Architecture   *152*
    Neoclassicism in America   *154*
    Neoclassical Sculpture   *157*
    Neoclassical Painting and Politics: The Art of
        David   *158*
    Ingres and the Neoclassical Line   *160*
    Neoclassicism under Napoleon   *160*
Eighteenth-Century Western Music   *162*
    Rococo Music   *162*
    Classical Music   *162*
    The Birth of the Orchestra   *163*
    Classical Instrumental Compositions   *164*
    The Development of the Classical Style: Haydn   *165*
    The Genius of Mozart   *165*
Summary   *167*
    Glossary   *168*
    Suggestions for Reading   *168*
    Music Listening Selections   *168*

Selected General Bibliography   *169*
        Books in Series   *169*

            Credits   *169*

            Index   *170*

MUSIC LISTENING SELECTIONS

Cassette II Selections 1 to 10
Gabrieli, Motet, "In Ecclesiis," 1615, excerpt   *24*
Monteverdi, *Orfeo*, Aria, "Vi recorda, o boschi
    ombrosi," 1607   *25*
Handel, *Messiah*, "Hallelujah Chorus," 1742   *39*
Bach, Cantata No. 80, "Ein feste Burg ist unser Gott"
    ("A Mighty Fortress is Our God"), Chorale,
    1724   *40*
Vivaldi, *The Four Seasons*, "Spring," Concerto in E
    Major, Op. 8, No. 1, first movement, 1725   *59*
Bach, Brandenburg Concerto No. 4 in G Major,
    first movement, 1721   *59*
Bach, *The Art of Fugue*, Canon in the 12th,
    1749–1750   *59*
Couperin, Ordre No. 22, "Le Croc-en-jambe,"
    1730   *162*
Haydn, Symphony No. 94 in G Major, "Surprise,"
    second movement, 1791   *165*
Mozart, Serenade No. 3 in G Major, K.525,
    "Eine kleine Nachtmusik," first movement,
    1787   *165*

MAPS

22.1 The Intellectual Revolution of the Seventeenth
    and Eighteenth Centuries in Western Europe   *46*
23.1 Empires in the Late Sixteenth and Early
    Seventeenth Centuries   *61*

Preface

"It's the most curious thing I ever saw in all my life!"exclaimed Lewis Carroll's Alice in Wonderland, as she watched the Cheshire Cat slowly disappear, leaving only the outline of a broad smile. "I've often seen a cat without a grin, but a grin without a cat!" A student who encounters an ancient Greek epic, a Yoruba mask, or a Mozart opera—lacking any context for these works— might be equally baffled. It may be helpful, therefore, to begin by explaining how the artifacts (the "grin") of the humanistic tradition relate to the larger and more elusive phenomenon (the "cat") of human culture.

The Humanistic Tradition and the Humanities

In its broadest sense, the term *humanistic tradition* refers to humankind's cultural legacy—the sum total of the significant ideas and achievements handed down from generation to generation. This tradition is the product of responses to conditions that have confronted all people throughout history. Since the beginnings of life on earth, human beings have tried to ensure their own survival by achieving harmony with nature. They have attempted to come to terms with the inevitable realities of disease and death. They have endeavored to establish ways of living collectively and communally. And they have persisted in the desire to understand themselves and their place in the universe. In response to these ever-present and universal challenges—*survival, communality,* and *self-knowledge*—human beings have created and transmitted the tools of science and technology, social and cultural institutions, religious and philosophic systems, and various forms of personal expression, the sum total of which we call culture.

Even the most ambitious survey cannot assess all manifestations of the humanistic tradition. This book therefore focuses on the creative legacy referred to collectively as *the humanities*: literature, philosophy, history (in its literary dimension), architecture, the visual arts (including photography and film), music, and dance. Selected examples from each of these disciplines constitute our *primary sources*. Primary sources (that is, works original to the age that produced them) provide firsthand evidence of human inventiveness and ingenuity. The primary sources in this text have been chosen on the basis of their authority, their beauty, and their enduring value. They are, simply stated, the great works of their time and, in some cases, of all time. Universal in their appeal, they have been transmitted from generation to generation. Such works are, as well, the landmark examples of a specific time and place: They offer insight into the ideas and values of the society in which they were produced. The drawings of Leonardo da Vinci, for example, reveal a passionate determination to understand the operations and functions of nature. And while Leonardo's talents far exceeded those of the average individual of his time, his achievements may be viewed as a mirror of the robust curiosity that characterized his time and place—the age of the Renaissance in Italy. *The Humanistic Tradition* surveys such landmark works, but joins "the grin" to "the cat" by examining them within their political, economic, and social contexts.

The Humanistic Tradition explores a living legacy. History confirms that the humanities are integral forms of a given culture's values, ambitions, and beliefs. Poetry, painting, philosophy, and music are not, generally speaking, products of unstructured leisure or indulgent individuality; rather, they are tangible expressions of the human quest for the good (one might even say the "complete") life. Throughout history, these forms of expression have served the domains of the sacred, the ceremonial, and the communal. And even in the waning days of the twentieth century, as many time-honored traditions have come under assault, the arts retain their power to awaken our imagination in the quest for survival, communality, and self-knowledge.

The Scope of the Humanistic Tradition

The humanistic tradition is not the exclusive achievement of any one geographic region, race, or class of human beings. For that reason, this text assumes a global and multicultural rather than exclusively Western perspective. At the same time, Western contributions are emphasized, first, because the audience for these books is predominantly Western, but also because in recent centuries the West has exercised a dominant influence on the course and substance of global history. Clearly, the humanistic tradition belongs to all of humankind, and the best way to understand the Western contribution to that tradition is to examine it in the arena of world culture.

As a survey, *The Humanistic Tradition* cannot provide an exhaustive analysis of our creative legacy. The critical reader will discover many gaps. Some aspects of culture that receive extended examination in traditional Western humanities surveys have been pared down to make room for the too often neglected contributions of Islam, Africa, and Asia. This book is necessarily selective—it omits many major figures and treats others only briefly. Primary sources are arranged, for the most part, chronologically, but they are presented as manifestations of *the informing ideas of the age* in which they were produced. The intent is to examine the evidence of the humanistic tradition thematically and topically, rather than to compile a series of mini-histories of the individual arts.

Studying the Humanistic Tradition

To study the creative record is to engage in a dialogue with the past, one that brings us face to face with the values of our ancestors, and, ultimately, with our own. This dialogue is (or should be) a source of personal revelation and delight; like Alice in Wonderland, our strange, new encounters will be enriched according to the degree of curiosity and patience we bring to them. Just as lasting friendships with special people are cultivated by extended familiarity, so our appreciation of a painting, a play, or a symphony depends on close attention and repeated contact. There are no shortcuts to the study of the humanistic tradition, but there are some techniques that may be helpful. It should be useful, for instance, to approach each primary source from the triple perspective of its *text*, its *context*, and its *subtext*.

The Text: The *text* of any primary source refers to its *medium* (that is, what it is made of), its *form* (its outward shape), and its *content* (the subject it describes). All literature, for example, whether intended to be spoken or read, depends on the medium of words—the American poet Robert Frost once defined literature as "performance in words." Literary form varies according to the manner in which words are arranged. So poetry, which shares with music and dance rhythmic organization, may be distinguished from prose, which normally lacks regular rhythmic pattern. The main purpose of prose is to convey information, to narrate, and to describe; poetry, by its freedom from conventional patterns of grammar, provides unique opportunities for the expression of intense emotions. Philosophy (the search for truth through reasoned analysis) and history (the record of the past) make use of prose to analyze and communicate ideas and information. In literature, as in most kinds of expression, content and form are usually interrelated. The subject matter or the form of a literary work determines its *genre*. For instance, a long narrative poem recounting the adventures of a hero constitutes an *epic*, while a formal, dignified speech in praise of a person or thing constitutes a *eulogy*.

The visual arts—painting, sculpture, architecture, and photography—employ a wide variety of media, such as wood, clay, colored pigments, marble, granite, steel, and (more recently) plastic, neon, film, and computers. The form or outward shape of a work of art depends on the manner in which the artist manipulates the formal elements of color, line, texture, and space. Unlike words, these formal elements lack denotative meaning. The artist may manipulate form to describe and interpret the visible world (as in such genres as portraiture and landscape painting); to generate fantastic and imaginative kinds of imagery; or to create imagery that is nonrepresentational—without identifiable subject matter. In general, however, the visual arts are spatial, that is, they operate and are apprehended in space.

The medium of music is sound. Like literature, music is durational: It unfolds over the period of time in which it occurs. The formal elements of music are melody, rhythm, harmony, and tone color—elements that also characterize the oral life of literature. As with the visual arts, the formal elements of music are without symbolic content, but while literature, painting, and sculpture may imitate or describe nature, music is almost always nonrepresentational—it rarely has meaning beyond the sound itself. For that reason, music is the most difficult of the arts to describe in words. It is also (in the view of some) the most affective of the arts. Dance, the artform that makes the human body itself a medium of expression, resembles music in that it is temporal and performance-oriented. Like music, dance exploits rhythm as a formal tool, but, like painting and sculpture, it unfolds in space as well as time.

In analyzing the text of a work of literature, art, or music, we ask how its formal elements contribute to its meaning and affective power. We examine the ways in which the artist manipulates medium and form to achieve a characteristic manner of execution and expression that we call *style*. And we try to determine the extent to which a style reflects the personal vision of the artist and the larger vision of his or her time and place. Comparing the styles of various artworks from a single era, we may discover that they share certain defining features and characteristics. Similarities (both formal and stylistic) between, for instance, golden age Greek temples and Greek tragedies, between Chinese lyric poems and landscape paintings, and between postmodern fiction and pop sculpture, prompt us to seek the unifying moral and aesthetic values of the cultures in which they were produced.

The Context: We use the word *context* to describe the historical and cultural environment. To determine the context, we ask: In what time and place did the artifact originate? How did it function within the society in which it was created? Was the purpose of the piece decorative, didactic, magical, propagandistic? Did it serve the religious or political needs of the community? Sometimes our answers to these questions are mere guesses. Nevertheless, understanding the function of an artifact often serves to clarify the nature of its form (and vice versa). For instance, much of the literature produced prior to the fifteenth century was spoken or sung rather than read; for that reason, such literature tends to feature repetition and rhyme, devices that facilitate memorization. We can assume that literary works embellished with frequent repetitions, such as the *Epic of Gilgamesh* and the Hebrew Bible, were products of an oral tradition. Determining the original function of an artwork also permits us to assess its significance in its own time and place: The paintings on the walls of Paleolithic caves, which are among the most compelling animal illustrations in the history of world art, are not "artworks" in the modern sense of the term but, rather, magical signs that accompanied hunting rituals, the performance of which was essential to the survival of the community. Understanding the relationship between text and context is one of the principal concerns of any inquiry into the humanistic tradition.

The Subtext: The *subtext* of the literary or artistic object refers to its secondary and implied meanings. The subtext embraces the emotional or intellectual messages embedded in, or implied by, a work of art. The epic poems of the ancient Greeks, for instance, which glorify prowess and physical courage in battle, suggest that such virtues are exclusively male. The state portraits of the seventeenth-century French ruler Louis XIV carry the subtext of unassailable and absolute power. In our own century, Andy Warhol's serial adaptations of soup cans and Coca-Cola bottles offer wry commentary on the supermarket mentality of postmodern American culture. Identifying the implicit message of an artwork helps us to determine the values and customs of the age in which it was produced and to assess those values against others.

Beyond *The Humanistic Tradition*

This book offers only small, enticing samples from an enormous cultural buffet. To dine more fully, students are encouraged to go beyond the sampling presented at this table; and for the most sumptuous feasting, nothing can substitute for first-hand experience. Students, therefore, should make every effort to supplement this book with visits to art museums and galleries, concert halls, theaters, and libraries. *The Humanistic Tradition* is designed for students who may or may not be able to read music, but who surely are able to cultivate an appreciation of music in performance. The clefs that appear in the text refer to the forty-five Music Listening Selections found on two accompanying cassettes,

available from the publishers. Lists of suggestions for further reading are included at the end of each chapter, while a selected general bibliography of humanities resources appears at the end of each book.

The Third Edition

On the threshold of the new millennium, this third edition of *The Humanistic Tradition* brings increased attention to the theme of global cross-cultural encounter and, in particular, to the interaction of the West with the cultures of Islam, East Asia, and Africa. In this connection, literary selections by Ibn Battuta, Shen Fu, Iqbal, and other non-Western writers have been added. New Western readings include selections from the works of Hernán Cortés, Jonathan Swift, Mary Shelley, Ralph Waldo Emerson, Alice Walker, Malcolm X, and Seamus Heaney. Japanese theater, the transatlantic slave trade, Islamic literature, and contemporary computer art are among the topics that receive expanded treatment in this edition.

The third edition also features two new study aids, both of which are designed to facilitate an appreciation of the arts in relation to their time and place: *Science and Technology Boxes*, which appear throughout the chapters, list key scientific and technological developments that have directly or indirectly affected the history of culture. *Locator Maps* (keyed to the map that appears on p. xii) assist readers in linking specific cultural events with the geographic region in which they occurred. This edition also expands on the number of color illustrations and large color maps, renumbers the Readings by book, and updates the Suggestions for Reading and Selected General Bibliography. Finally, in the transcription of the Chinese language, the older Wade-Giles system has been replaced by the more modern Hanyu Pinyin.

A Note to Instructors

The key to successful classroom use of *The Humanistic Tradition* is *selectivity*. Although students may be assigned to read whole chapters that focus on a topic or theme, as well as complete works that supplement the abridged readings, the classroom should be the stage for a selective treatment of a single example or a set of examples. The organization of this textbook is designed to emphasize themes that cut across geographic boundaries—themes whose universal significance prompts students to evaluate and compare rather than simply memorize and repeat lists of names and places. In an effort to assist readers in achieving global cultural literacy, every effort has been made to resist isolating (or "ghettoizing") individual cultures and to avoid the inevitable biases we bring to our evaluation of relatively unfamiliar cultures.

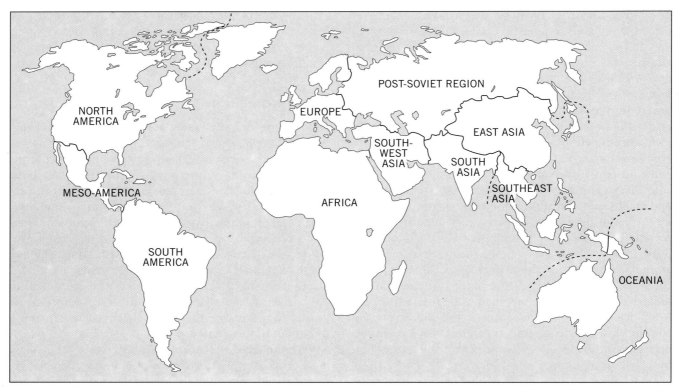

Keymap Indicating Areas Shown as White Highlights on the Locator Maps.

Acknowledgments

Writing *The Humanistic Tradition* has been an exercise in humility. Without the assistance of learned friends and colleagues, assembling a book of this breadth would have been an impossible task. James H. Dormon read all parts of the manuscript and made extensive and substantive editorial suggestions; as his colleague, best friend, and wife, I am most deeply indebted to him. I owe thanks to the following faculty members of the University of Southwestern Louisiana: for literature, Allen David Barry, Darrell Bourque, C. Harry Bruder, John W. Fiero, Emilio F. Garcia, Doris Meriwether, and Patricia K. Rickels; for history, Ora-Wes S. Cady, John Moore, Bradley Pollack, and Thomas D. Schoonover; for philosophy, Steve Giambrone and Robert T. Kirkpatrick; for geography, Tim Reilly; for the sciences, Mark Konikoff and John R. Meriwether; and for music, James Burke and Robert F. Schmalz.

The following readers and viewers generously shared their insights in matters of content and style: Michael K. Aakhus (University of Southern Indiana), Vaughan B. Baker (University of Southwestern Louisiana), Katherine Charlton (Mt. San Antonio Community College), Bessie Chronaki (Central Piedmont Community College), Debora A. Drehen (Florida Community College—Jacksonville), Paula Drewek (Macomb Community College), William C. Gentry (Henderson State University), Kenneth Ganza (Colby College), Ellen Hofman (Highline Community College), Burton Raffel (University of Southwestern Louisiana), Frank La Rosa (San Diego City College), George Rogers (Stonehill College), Douglas P. Sjoquist (Lansing Community College), Howard V. Starks (Southeastern Oklahoma State University), Ann Wakefield (Academy of the Sacred Heart—Grand Coteau), Sylvia White (Florida Community College—Jacksonville), and Audrey Wilson (Florida State University).

In the preparation of the third edition, I have benefited from the suggestions and comments generously offered by numerous readers, only some of whom are listed below. Rodney D. Boyd (Collin County Community College), Arnold Bradford (Northern Virginia Community College), Patricia L. Brace (Southwest State University), Orville V. Clark (University of Wisconsin—Green Bay), Carolyn Copeland (Bethune Cookman), Susan Cornett (St. Petersburg Junior College—Tarpon Center), Anthony M. Coyne (University of North Carolina), Kenneth Ganza (Colby College), Margaret Hasselman (Virginia Polytechnic Institute and State University), Victor Hébert (Fayetteville State University), Ellen Hofmann (Highline Community College), Enid Housty (Hampton University), Mabel Khawaja (Hampton University), James W. Mock (University of Central Oklahoma), Lewis Parkhill (East Central University), Joseph G. Rahme (University of Michigan—

Flint), David Simmons (Brevard Community College), J. Paul De Vierville (St. Phillip's College), Bertha L. Wise (Oklahoma City Community College), and Jon Young (Fayetteville State University). I am grateful to Julia Girouard, who provided research assistance for the third edition, to Professor Timothy Reilly, who kindly helped with the Locator Keymap, and to Professor Sabruta Dasgupta (University of Southwestern Louisiana), who generously assisted in the preparation of the Science and Technology Boxes in books 4 and 5.

The burden of preparing the third edition has been lightened by the assistance of M. J. Kelly, Developmental Editor, and by the editorial vigilance of Ursula Payne at Calmann & King.

SUPPLEMENTS FOR THE INSTRUCTOR AND THE STUDENT

A number of useful supplements are available to instructors and students using *The Humanistic Tradition*. Please contact your sales representative or call 1-800-338-5371 to obtain these resources, or to ask for further details.

Audiocassettes
Two ninety-minute audiocassettes containing a total of forty-five musical selections have been designed exclusively for use with *The Humanistic Tradition*. Cassette One corresponds to the music listening selections discussed in books 1–3 and Cassette Two contains the music in books 4–6. Each selection on the cassettes is discussed in the text and includes a voice introduction for easier location. Instructors may obtain copies of the cassettes for classroom use by calling 1-800-338-5371. Individual cassettes may be purchased separately; however, upon the request of instructors who place book orders, Cassette One or Two can be packaged with any of the six texts, so that students may use the musical examples *along with* the text.

Slide Sets
A set of fifty book-specific slides is available to adopters of *The Humanistic Tradition*. These slides have been especially selected to include many of the less well-known images in the books, and will be a useful complement to your present slide resources. A larger set of two hundred book-specific slides is available for purchase from Sandak, Inc. For further information, please contact Sandak, 180 Harvard Avenue, Stamford, CT 06902 (phone 1-800-343-2806, fax 203-967-2445).

Instructor's Resource Manual
The Instructor's Resource Manual is designed to assist instructors as they plan and prepare for classes. Course outlines and sample syllabuses for both semester and quarter systems are included. The chapter summaries emphasize key themes and topics that give focus to the primary source readings. The study questions for each chapter may be removed and copied as handouts for student discussion or written assignments. A Test Item File follows each chapter along with a correlation list that directs instructors to the appropriate music examples, slides, transparencies, and software sections of the other supplements. A list of suggested videotapes, recordings, videodiscs, and their suppliers is included.

MicroTest III
The questions in the Test Item File are available on MicroTest III, a powerful but easy-to-use test generating program. MicroTest is available for DOS, Windows, and Macintosh personal computers. With MicroTest, an instructor can easily select the questions from the Test Item File and print a test and answer key. You can customize questions, headings, and instructions and add or import questions of your own.

Humanities Transparencies
A set of seventy-one acetate transparencies is available with *The Humanistic Tradition*. These show examples of art concepts, architectural styles, art media, maps, musical notation, musical styles, and musical elements.

Culture 3.0 CD-ROM
Culture 3.0 CD-ROM is a unique Macintosh reference tool that emphasizes the interaction of varied disciplines. It contains 40 historical maps, 120 signature melodies, 50,000 hypertext links, and 170 essays on topics ranging from Greek gods and goddesses to the Cold War. Thirty-two CultureGrids are arranged chronologically from the biblical era to the twentieth century, organizing people, places, and events by country, discipline, and generation. (*Culture 2.0* is also available in a seven-disk set for Mac and IBM.)

Student Study Guides, Volumes 1 and 2
Written by Gloria K. Fiero, two new Student Study Guides are now available to help students gain a better understanding of subjects found in *The Humanistic Tradition*. Volume 1 accompanies books 1–3 and Volume 2 accompanies books 4–6. Each chapter contains: a Chapter Objective; a Chapter Outline; Key Terms, Names, and Dates; Vocabulary Building; Multiple Choice Questions; and Essay Questions. Many chapters also contain a Visual/Spatial Exercise and Bonus Material. At the end of each Part, Synthesis material helps students draw together ideas from a set of chapters.

The Art Historian CD-ROM, Volumes 1 and 2
This flexible two-volume series on dual platform (Mac and Windows) CD-ROMs is designed to supplement introductory level art history education. Volume 1 covers ancient and medieval art, and Volume 2 covers Renaissance to modern art. The images included on the CD were gathered from over three hundred museums, galleries, and private collections throughout the world, and the text and test questions were written by current scholars from universities across the United States. With *The Art Historian*, students may listen to multimedia presentations, review full-color high-resolution images, and test their knowledge with flashcards and essay questions. *The Art Historian* is flexible, allowing students to take notes, compare two images on the screen at the same time, and create personalized collections of images for study and review. With *The Art Historian*, we place the power of multimedia *and* art at your fingertips.

	To 1550	1600	1625	1650	1675

WORLD EVENTS

CATHOLIC REFORMATION
Loyola founds Jesuit order 1530
Council of Trent reaffirms
Catholic doctrine

Copernicus: heliocentric theory
Vesalius: *Anatomy*

——————— THIRTY YEARS' WAR ———————

SCIENTIFIC REVOLUTION
Kepler records planetary movements
Galileo perfects telescope
Camera obscura
Mathematics and experimentation

THE AGE OF ABSOLUTISM

Louis XIV of France

French Royal Academy of
Language and Literature

Elizabeth I of — James I — Charles I — Civil War — English Commonwealth
England
Cromwell
Royal Society of London for
Improving Natural Knowledge
Fire of London 1666

—— SAFAVID EMPIRE/Shah Abbas ——

—— OTTOMAN EMPIRE/Suleiman ——

India: MOGUL EMPIRE/Akbar — Jahangir — Shah Jahan
Persian culture and language
imported into India

China: —— MING DYNASTY —— QING (MANCHU DYNASTY) ——

Japan: —— TOKUGAWA DYNASTY: Tokugawa Shogunate ——
Edo becomes capital 1616 Japan expels all Europeans 1637

LITERATURE AND PHILOSOPHY

Loyola: *Spiritual Exercises*

Council of Trent: *Index Expurgatorius*

Teresa of Avila: autobiography

Grotius: *On the Law of War and Peace*

Descartes: *Discourse on Method*

Crashaw: *The Flaming Heart*

La Rochefoucauld: maxims
Pascal: *Pensées*

Racine: *Phaedra*

King James Bible

Donne: meditations and sonnets

Bacon: *Novum Organum*

First weekly newspaper published in London

Milton: *Paradise Lost*
Spinoza: *Ethics*

Hobbes: *Leviathan*

Safavid poetry

Ming drama and poetry

Kabuki theater emerges around 1650

Basho: *haiku*

VISUAL ARTS AND ARCHITECTURE

— MANNERISM — — THE BAROQUE STYLE —

Michelangelo: *Last Judgment*
Parmigianino: *Madonna*
Tintoretto: *Last Supper*
El Greco: *Agony in the Garden*
Vignola and della Porta: *Il Gesù*

Caravaggio: *Supper at Emmaus*

Bernini: *Ecstasy of Saint Teresa*; *Baldacchino* and colonnade, Saint Peter's, Rome
Borromini: San Carlo

Poussin: *Arcadian Shepherds*
Lorrain: landscapes

Le Vau and Mansart: Versailles
Perrault: Louvre
Girardon: *Apollo*

Rembrandt: *Return of the Prodigal Son*

Van Dyck: *Charles I*
Rubens: *Rape of Daughters of Leucippus*

Velásquez: *Las Meninas*
de Heem: *Still Life*

Hals and Leyster: Dutch portraits
de Hooch: *Dutch Courtyard*
ter Borch: *Suitor's Visit*
Vermeer: *View of Delft*

Ottoman court painting and metalcraft

Safavid carpets
Bichitr: Mogul court painters
Imperial Mosque at Isfahan

Shajahanabad
Taj Mahal

Red Fort at Delhi

Ming porcelains and silks

Forbidden City at Beijing

MUSIC AND DANCE

Palestrina: Pope Marcellus Mass
Gabrieli: polychoral style; "In Ecclesiis"

Victoria: church music

Chromatic scale

Violin, viola, cello, organ, and harpsicord perfected

First opera house in Venice, 1637
Monteverdi: *Orfeo*

Lully: French opera

Minuet

Modern oboe invented

1700	1725	1750	1775	1800

Dutch Republic

Lavoisier: *Treatise on Chemistry*

Newton: *Principia Mathematica*

INDUSTRIAL REVOLUTION

Flying shuttle — Spinning jenny — Watt: steam engine — Power loom

Winckelmann: *History of Ancient Art*

Louis XV — Louis XVI — French Revolution begins 1789
Declaration of the Rights of Man and Citizen

Excavations at Herculaneum

Glorious Revolution
William and Mary
Bill of Rights

American Revolution begins 1775
Jefferson: Declaration of Independence

Decline of Ottoman Empire

Decline of Mogul Empire

THE AGE OF THE ENLIGHTENMENT

Molière: *Le Bourgeois Gentilhomme*

Montesquieu: *Spirit of the Laws*

Diderot: *Encyclopédie*
Voltaire: *Candide*

Rousseau: *Discourse; Social Contract; Emile*

Condorcet: *Progress of the Human Mind*

Locke: *Essay Concerning Human Understanding; Of Civil Government*

Leibniz: "philosophical optimism"

Gay: *Beggar's Opera*

European novel: Richardson, Fielding

Equiano: *Travels*
Johnson: *Dictionary*
Gibbon: *Decline and Fall of the Roman Empire*

Kant: *Critique of Pure Reason*

Addison and Steele: *Tatler* and *Spectator*

Swift: *Gulliver's Travels; A Modest Proposal*
Pope: *Essay on Man*

Zen Buddhist revival in Japan

Cao Xueqin: *Dream of the Red Chamber*

Li Ju-chen: *Flowers in the Mirror*

THE ROCOCO STYLE

Watteau: *Departure from Cythera*

Fischer: Church of Ottobeuren, Bavaria
Vigée-Lebrun: portraits
Fragonard: *The Swing*
Boucher: *Venus Consoling Love*

Clodion: *Intoxication*

Rigaud: *Louis XIV*

THE NEOCLASSICAL STYLE

Pozzo: *Saint Ignatius*

French genre
Greuze: *Village Betrothal*
Chardin: *Kitchen Maid*

Soufflot: Sainte Geneviève

Canova: *Venus*
Ingres: *Grande Odalisque*
David: *The Oath of the Horatii*
Vignon: La Madeleine

Wren: Saint Paul's

Hogarth: *Marriage Contract*
Gibbs: London churches

Wedgwood
Adam: Kedleston Hall, England
Houdon: *Voltaire; Diderot; Jefferson; Washington*

Chalgrin: Arch of Triumph
Jefferson: University of Virginia

Korin: Japanese painted screens

Japanese woodblock prints
Chinoiserie

Feuillet: choreographic notation
Couperin: suites; *Art of Playing Clavecin*

Vivaldi: *Four Seasons*; concerto grosso

Haydn: "Father of the Symphony"; string quartets

Piano invented

Handel: oratorio; *Messiah*
J.S. Bach: cantata; *Passion According to Saint Matthew*; *Brandenburg Concertos; Art of Fugue*

Stamitz: Mannheim orchestra; orchestral scores

Mozart: "Eine kleine Nachtmusik"; *Marriage of Figaro*

Chinese opera

Summary of the Renaissance and the Reformation

The following paragraphs provide an overview of the Renaissance and Reformation, the two movements that ushered in the modern era in the West. This summary of fifteenth- and sixteenth-century culture (dealt with in detail in Book 3) offers some background to the materials contained in books 4, 5, and 6, which deal with the modern era in a global context.

Classical Humanism

The effort to recover, edit, and study ancient Greek and Latin manuscripts, a movement known as classical humanism, first occurred in fourteenth-century Italy, where it marked the beginnings of the Renaissance. This revival of Greco-Roman culture was to spread throughout Western Europe over the following three hundred years. Petrarch, known as the father of humanism, provided the model for Renaissance scholarship and education. He promoted the study of the classic Greek and Latin writers, especially Cicero, encouraged textual criticism, and wrote introspective and passionate sonnets that were revered and imitated for centuries to come.

The city of Florence was the unrivaled center of classical humanism in the first 150 years of the Renaissance. A thriving commercial and financial center dominated by a well-to-do middle class, Florence found political and cultural leadership in such wealthy and sophisticated families as the Medici. Classical humanism helped to cultivate a sense of civic pride, a new respect for oral and written eloquence, and a set of personal values that sustained the ambitions of the rising merchant class.

Fifteenth-century humanists carried on Petrarch's quest to recover the classical past. Ficino translated the entire body of Plato's writings, while Pico's investigations in Hebrew and Arabic led him to believe that the world's great minds shared a single, universal truth. Pico's *Oration on the Dignity of Man* proclaimed the centrality of humankind and defended the unlimited freedom of the individual within the universal scheme.

Renaissance humanists cultivated the idea of the good life. Following Alberti's maxim, "A man can do anything he wants," they applied the moral precepts of the classical past to such contemporary pursuits as diplomacy, politics, and the arts. While Petrarch and his peers were concerned primarily with the recovery of classical manuscripts and the production of critical editions, Alberti, Castiglione, and Machiavelli eagerly infused scholarship with action. Allying their scrutiny of the past to an empirical study of the present, they fostered a heroic ideal of the individual that surpassed all classical models. For Alberti, wealth and authority proceeded from the exercise of *virtù*; for Castiglione, the superior breed of human being was identical with *l'uomo universale*, the well-rounded person; for Machiavelli, only a ruthless master of power politics could ensure the survival of the state. Alberti, Castiglione, and Machiavelli were representative of the larger group of Renaissance humanists who asserted the human capacity for self-knowledge and exalted the role of the individual in the secular world. Their views shaped the modern character of the humanistic tradition in the European West.

Renaissance Artists

Most significant about the artists of the Renaissance is that they were disciples of nature: They brought a scientific curiosity to the study of the natural world and untiringly investigated its operations. Such Early Renaissance artists as Donatello, Pollaiuolo, Masaccio, and Brunelleschi studied the mechanics of the human body, the effects of light on material substances, and the physical appearance of objects in three-dimensional space. At the same time, Renaissance artists were masters of invention: They perfected the technique of oil painting, formulated the laws of perspective, and applied the principles of classical art to the representation of Christian and contemporary subjects. Patronized by a wealthy European middle class, they revived such this-worldly genres as portraiture and gave new attention to the nude body as an object of natural beauty.

The art of the High Renaissance marks the culmination of a hundred-year effort to wed the techniques of naturalistic representation to classical ideals of proportion and harmony. Leonardo da Vinci, the quintessential artist-scientist, tried to reconcile empirical experience with basic principles of balance and order. The compositions of Raphael, with their monumental scale and unity of design, became standards by which Western paintings would be judged for many centuries. The multitalented Michelangelo brought a heroic idealism to the treatment of traditional Christian and classical themes. In Venice, Titian's painterly handling of the reclining female nude represented a new and more sensuous naturalism. In architecture, the centrally planned buildings of Bramante and Palladio fulfilled the quest of such Early Renaissance architects as Brunelleschi and Alberti for an architecture of harmony, balance, and clarity.

The Renaissance produced an equally splendid flowering in music, especially among Franco-Flemish composers. Secular compositions began to outnumber religious ones. The techniques of imitation and word painting infused both religious and secular music with homogeneity and increased expressiveness. Printed sheet music helped to popularize the madrigal and other secular, vernacular song forms. Instrumental music and dance now emerged as independent genres. Like their classical predecessors, Renaissance artists placed human concerns and feelings at the center of a harmonious universe. Such optimism, combined with intellectual curiosity and increasing worldliness, fueled the early modern era in the West.

Shattering the Old Order: Protest and Reform

The sixteenth century was a time of rapid change marked by growing secularism, advancing technology, and European geographic expansion. It was also an age of profound religious and social upheaval. Northern humanists led by Erasmus of Rotterdam made critical studies of early Christian literature and urged a return to the teachings of Jesus and the early church fathers. Demands for church reform went hand in hand with the revival of early Christian writings to culminate in the Protestant Reformation.

Aided by Gutenberg's printing press, Martin Luther contested the authority of the Church of Rome. He held that Scripture was the sole basis for religious interpretation and emphasized the idea of salvation through faith in God's grace rather than through good works. As Lutheranism and other Protestant sects proliferated throughout Europe, the unity of medieval Christendom was shattered.

The music and the art of the Northern Renaissance reflect the mood of religious reform. In music, the Lutheran chorale became the vehicle of Protestant piety. In art, the increasing demand for illustrated devotional literature and private devotional art stimulated the production of woodcuts and metal engravings. The works of Dürer and Grünewald exhibit the Northern Renaissance passion for realistic detail and graphic expression, while the fantastic imagery of Hieronymous Bosch suggests a pessimistic and typically Northern concern with sin and death. Bosch's preoccupation with the palpable forces of evil found its counterpart in the witch-hunts of the sixteenth century. In painting, too, such secular subjects as portraiture, landscapes, and scenes of everyday life mirrored the tastes of a growing middle-class audience for an unidealized record of the visual world.

Northern Renaissance writers took a generally skeptical and pessimistic view of human nature. Erasmus, More, Cervantes, and Rabelais lampooned individual and societal failings and described the ruling influence of folly in all aspects of human conduct. In France, Montaigne devised the essay as an intimate form of rational reflection. The most powerful form of literary expression to evolve in the late sixteenth century, however, was secular drama. In the hands of William Shakespeare, drama became the ultimate expression of the sixteenth-century quest to examine the human personality in its secular and spiritual dimensions. Shakespeare's tragedies (as opposed, for instance, to Montaigne's essays) reveal the human condition through overt action, rather than through private reflection.

By the end of the sixteenth century, national loyalties, religious fanaticism, and commercial rivalries had splintered the European community, rendering ever more complex the society of the West. And yet, on the threshold of modernity, the challenges to the human condition—economic survival, communality, self-knowledge, and the inevitability of death—were no less pressing than they had been two thousand years earlier. If the technology of the sixteenth century was more sophisticated than that of ancient times—giving human beings greater control over nature than ever before—it also provided more devastating weapons of war and destruction. In the centuries to come, the humanistic tradition would be shaped and reshaped by changing historical circumstances and the creative imagination of indomitable humankind.

PART

I

THE AGE OF
THE BAROQUE

The period between approximately 1600 and 1800 was an age of contradictions. In Western Europe, deeply felt, even mystical religious sentiment vied with the rise of science and rational methods of scientific investigation. Newly developed theories of constitutional government contended with firmly entrenched claims to divine right among "absolute" rulers—monarchs who recognized no legal limitations to their authority. The rising wealth of a small segment of the population failed to offset widespread poverty and old aristocratic privilege. In Asia, as well, the seventeenth and eighteenth centuries brought major changes: Muslim rulers united the primarily Hindu peoples of India and proceeded to establish the glorious Mogul dynasty. The Ming emperors of China, who governed an empire larger than any other in the world, fell to Mongol (Manchu) tribes in the early seventeenth century. These foreign rulers secured internal stability through rigid control of Chinese culture.

The early modern era witnessed the beginnings of the European state system and the establishment of the fundamental political, economic, and cultural norms of European and, by extension, American life. Rival religious claims following the Protestant Reformation complicated the scramble for land and power among European states. The first half of the seventeenth century witnessed the Thirty Years' War and other devastating conflicts between Catholics and Protestants. In 1648, however, by the terms of the Treaty of Westphalia, which ended the Thirty Years' War, the principle of national sovereignty was firmly established in the West: By that principle, each European state would exercise independent and supreme authority over its own territories and inhabitants.

In the economic arena, the prosperity of the sixteenth century was followed by marked decline in the seventeenth. Nevertheless, after 1660, commercial capitalism and the production of manufactured goods flourished in the West, where economic growth was tied to a pattern of global commerce. Asia, Africa, and the Americas—lucrative markets for European goods—were frontiers for European traders. And as global perceptions widened, Europeans realized that the "Old World" could no longer live in isolation.

In the West, the years between 1600 and 1750 were closely associated with a style known as "the baroque." Characterized by dramatic expression, theatrical spectacle, and spatial grandeur, the baroque became the hallmark of an age of exuberant expansion. The style also reflected the new, dynamic view of the universe as set forth by proponents of the Scientific Revolution. The baroque encompassed various phases: In Italy, it mirrored the intensely religious mood of the Catholic Reformation; in Northern Europe, it reflected the intimate spirit of Protestant devotionalism as well as the reliance on sensory experience associated with the New Science; and among authoritarian regimes throughout Europe and Asia, it worked to glorify secular power and wealth.

The age of the baroque was fueled by the human ambition to master nature on a colossal scale. This ambition—inspired perhaps by a more detached and

(opposite) Andrea Pozzo, detail of *Apotheosis of Saint Ignatius* showing allegorical figure of America, 1691. Fresco. Nave ceiling, Sant'Ignazio, Rome. Scala, Florence.

objective view of the self in relation to the world—is as evident in Galileo's efforts to understand and explain the operations of nature as it is in Louis XIV's attempts to exert unlimited power over vast territories and peoples. A similar kind of energy is apparent in the complexities of a Bach fugue, the cosmic scope of Milton's *Paradise Lost*, the spectacle of early Italian opera, the panoramic sweep of Dutch landscape paintings, the splendor of the royal palaces at Versailles, Delhi, and Peking, and the efforts of Ming and Manchu emperors to collect and copy all of China's literary classics.

Chapter 20, "The Catholic Reformation and the Baroque Style," examines the Catholic and Counter Reformations as inspiration for the arts of seventeenth-century Italy and Spain. Major topics include the literary contributions of Ignatius Loyola and Saint Teresa, the sculpture of Bernini, the paintings of El Greco and Caravaggio, the music of Palestrina and Gabrieli, and the rise of European opera. Chapter 21, "The Baroque in the Protestant North," explores selected examples of seventeenth- and early eighteenth-century Northern European literature, art, and music. The poetry of Donne and Milton, the art of Rembrandt, and the vocal music of Handel and Bach are examined as evidence of an essentially different religious sensibility from that of Catholic Europe, but one that shared the baroque taste for grandeur and dramatic expression.

Chapter 22, "The Scientific Revolution and the New Learning," investigates the ways in which advances in the sciences and the rise of early modern philosophy contributed to the formation of modern Western culture. The search for new modes of rational investigation in the writings of Bacon, Descartes, and Locke; the development of an empirically precise style of painting among the artists of the North Netherlands; and the birth of pure instrumental music are central, complementary themes in this chapter. Finally, chapter 23, "Absolute Power and the Aristocratic Style," focuses on the phenomenon of political absolutism in Western Europe and Asia and its influence on the arts. Under King Louis XIV of France, as among the Safavid Persians, the Moguls of India, the Ming and Manchu emperors of China, and the Tokugawa shoguns in Japan, there emerged an aristocratic style that aimed to glorify the majesty and power of the ruler. The chapter surveys the cult of majesty in France, the palace at Versailles, and the rise of academic neoclassicism, whose influence is still felt in our own time. It also includes selections from a fine Molière comedy that captures the spirit of seventeenth-century French society. Beyond Europe, the aristocratic style is embodied in the Taj Mahal and other glorious monuments of Mogul India, in the Forbidden City of imperial China, and in the elegant arts of Japanese society.

20
The Catholic Reformation and the Baroque Style

The Protestant Reformation created a religious upheaval unlike any other within the history of Western Christianity. Luther's criticism of the Roman Catholic Church had encouraged religious devotion free of papal authority and had prepared the way for the rise of other Protestant sects (chapter 18). The rival religious beliefs that fragmented Western Europe quickly accelerated into armed combat. The Thirty Years' War (1618–1648), which ended with the establishment of Protestantism throughout most of Northern Europe, caused the death of some five million Christians. During the early sixteenth century, as Protestant sects began to lure increasing numbers of Christians away from Roman Catholicism, the Church undertook a program of internal reform and reorganization known as the Catholic Reformation. Further, by the 1540s, in an effort to win back to Catholicism those who had strayed to Protestantism, the Church launched the evangelical campaign known as the Counter-Reformation. These two interdependent movements gradually introduced a more militant form of Catholicism to all parts of the world. They also encouraged intensely personalized expressions of religious sentiment, particularly in Spain, Italy, and Latin America. In the arts, a vigorous new style—the *baroque*—became the vehicle for this new, more dynamic outpouring of religious fervor.

The Catholic Reformation

In the face of the Protestant challenge, the Roman Catholic Church pursued a path that ensured its survival in the modern world. Between 1540 and 1565 churchmen undertook papal and monastic reforms that eliminated corruption and restored Catholicism to many parts of Europe. The impetus for renewal came largely from fervent Spanish Catholics, the most notable of whom was Ignatius Loyola (1491–1556). A soldier in the army of King Charles I of Spain (the Holy Roman emperor Charles V), Loyola brought to Catholicism the same iron will he had exercised on the battlefield. After his right leg was fractured by a French cannonball at the siege of Pamplona, Loyola became a religious teacher and a hermit, traveling lame and barefoot to Jerusalem in an effort to convert Muslims to Christianity. In the 1530s he founded the Society of Jesus, the most important of the many new monastic orders associated with the Catholic Reformation. The Society of Jesus, or Jesuits, followed Loyola in calling for a militant return to fundamental Catholic dogma and the strict enforcement of traditional Church teachings. In addition to the monastic vows of celibacy, poverty, and obedience, the Jesuits took an oath of allegiance to the pope, whom they served as soldiers of Christ.

Under Loyola's leadership, the Jesuit order became the most influential missionary society of early modern times. Rigorously trained, its members acted as preachers, confessors, and teachers—leaders in educational reform and moral discipline. Throughout Europe, members of the newly formed order worked as missionaries to win back those who had strayed from "Mother Church." With the aid of the Inquisition (see chapter 12), the Jesuits were fairly successful in stamping out Protestantism in much of France, Southern Germany, and other parts of Europe. But their reach extended further: As pioneers in learning the languages and customs of India, China, and Japan, the Jesuits were the prime intermediaries between Europe and Asia from the sixteenth through the nineteenth century. In the Americas, which became prime targets for Jesuit activity, missionaries mastered Native American tribal languages and proceeded to convert thousands to Roman Catholicism. Their success in Mexico, Central and South America has stamped these parts of the world with a distinctive cultural character.

The Jesuit order was a fascinating amalgam of two elements—mysticism and militant religious zeal. The first emphasized the personal and intuitive experience of God, while the second involved an attitude of unquestioned submission to the Church as the absolute source of truth. These two aspects of Jesuit thinking—mysticism and militancy—are reflected in Loyola's influential handbook, the *Spiritual Exercises*, published in 1548. In his introductory observations, Loyola explains that the spiritual exercises should do for the soul what such physical exercises as running and walking do for the body. As aids to the development of perfect spiritual discipline, these devotional exercises—each of which should occupy a full hour's time—engage the body in perfecting the soul. For example, in the Fifth Exercise, a meditation on Hell, each of the five senses is summoned to heighten the mystical experience:

> FIRST POINT: This will be to *see* in imagination the vast fires, and the souls enclosed, as it were, in bodies of fire.
> SECOND POINT: To *hear* the wailing, the howling, cries, and blasphemies against Christ our Lord and against His saints.
> THIRD POINT: With the sense of *smell* to perceive the smoke, the sulphur, the filth, and corruption.
> FOURTH POINT: To *taste* the bitterness of tears, sadness, and remorse of conscience.
> FIFTH POINT: With the sense of *touch* to feel the flames which envelop and burn the souls.

Loyola also insists on an unswerving commitment to traditional Church teachings. Among the "rules for thinking with the Church" is Loyola's advice that Christians put aside all judgments of their own and remain obedient to the "holy Mother, the hierarchical Church."

READING 4.1
From Loyola's *Spiritual Exercises*

THE FOLLOWING RULES SHOULD BE OBSERVED TO FOSTER THE TRUE ATTITUDE OF MIND WE OUGHT TO HAVE IN THE CHURCH MILITANT.

1 We must put aside all judgment of our own, and keep the mind ever ready and prompt to obey in all things the true Spouse of Christ our Lord, our holy Mother, the hierarchical Church.

2 We should praise sacramental confession, the yearly reception of the Most Blessed Sacrament, and praise more highly monthly reception, and still more weekly Communion, provided requisite and proper dispositions are present.

3 We ought to praise the frequent hearing of Mass, the singing of hymns, psalmody, and long prayers whether in the church or outside; likewise, the hours arranged at fixed times for the whole Divine Office, for every kind of prayer, and for the canonical hours.[1]

4 We must praise highly religious life, virginity, and continency; and matrimony ought not be praised as much as any of these.

5 We should praise vows of religion, obedience, poverty, chastity, and vows to perform other works . . . conducive to perfection. . . .

6 We should show our esteem for the relics of the saints by venerating them and praying to the saints. We should praise visits to the Station Churches,[2] pilgrimages, indulgences, jubilees,[3] crusade indults,[4] and the lighting of candles in churches.

7 We must praise the regulations of the Church with regard to fast and abstinence. . . . We should praise works of penance, not only those that are interior but also those that are exterior.

8 We ought to praise not only the building and adornment of churches, but also images and veneration of them according to the subject they represent.

9 Finally, we must praise all the commandments of the Church, and be on the alert to find reasons to defend them, and by no means in order to criticize them. . . .

13 If we wish to proceed securely in all things, we must hold fast to the following principle: What seems to me white, I will believe black if the hierarchical Church so defines. For I must be convinced that in Christ our Lord, the bridegroom, and in His spouse the Church, only one Spirit holds sway, which governs and rules for the salvation of souls. For it is by the same Spirit and Lord who gave the Ten Commandments that our holy Mother Church is ruled and governed.

———————◆———————

Loyola's affirmation of Roman Catholic doctrine anticipated the actions of the Council of Trent, the general church council that met three times between 1545 and 1563. The Council of Trent reconfirmed all seven of the sacraments and asserted the absolute and infallible leadership of the pope. It also set clear guidelines for the elimination of abuses among members of the clergy and encouraged the regeneration of intellectual life within Catholic monasteries. Church leaders revived the activities of the Inquisition and established the *Index Expurgatorius*, a list of books judged heretical and therefore forbidden to Catholic readers. The Catholic Reformation supported a broadly based Catholicism that emphasized the direct and intuitive—hence, mystical—experience of God. And although the Church of Rome would never again reassume the universal authority it had enjoyed during the Middle Ages, its internal reforms and its efforts to rekindle the faith restored its dignity in the minds and hearts of its followers.

---

[1]The eight times of the day appointed for special devotions; see chapters 9 and 15.

[2]Churches with images representing the stages of Christ's Passion.
[3]A time of special solemnity, ordinarily every twenty-five years, proclaimed by the pope; also, special indulgences granted during that time. The jubilee principle is based on a biblical injunction to free slaves, return land to its original owners, and leave fields untilled once every fifty years (Leviticus 25).
[4]Church indulgences granted to Christian Crusaders.

Catholicism's Global Reach

The evangelical activities of the Jesuits and other religious orders were widespread, but not uniformly successful. In China, where European traders were regarded as "ocean devils," the Catholic missionaries assumed a cordial relationship with the intellectual classes and succeeded in converting a number of Chinese scholars. By the eighteenth century, however, disputes between the Jesuits and the Dominicans over the veneration of Confucius (aggravated by papal condemnation of Confucian rites in 1744) weakened Catholic influence. The first Jesuit missionaries in Japan diligently mastered the Japanese language. Although they admired and respected many aspects of Tokugawa culture (see chapter 23), they found disfavor among Japanese Buddhists, who viewed all Christians as potentially subversive to the social order. By 1606, following decades of disruption caused by European efforts to win trading privileges in Japan, the Japanese outlawed Christianity. The country expelled almost all Western foreigners from Japanese soil by 1624, after a wave of brutal persecutions of both European Christians and Japanese converts to Catholicism.

Christian evangelism in the Americas proved to be an entirely different story. In sixteenth-century Latin America, where Spanish political authority went largely unchallenged, Catholicism went hand in hand with colonization. The arrival of the Jesuits in Mexico in 1571 followed that of the Augustinians, the Dominicans, and the Franciscans in a vast program of Christianization. Just as the convergence of Europeans and Indians came to produce a unique new "Latin American" population, so the blend of European Catholic and native religious traditions produced a unique synthesis in the culture of Mexico. A formidable example of this creolizing phenomenon, and one that testifies to the powerful religious impact of Catholicism, is the Miracle of the Virgin of Guadalupe: In 1531, ten years after the conquest of Mexico by Cortés, on the site of a former shrine to the Aztec mother-goddess, a dark-skinned Virgin Mary appeared in a vision before a simple Mexican peasant. The legend of this miraculous apparition of the Mother of God, commemorated in hundreds of carved and painted images (Figure 20.1), became the basis for the most important religious cult in Mexican history: the cult of the Virgin of Guadalupe. The colonial cult of Guadalupe worships the Virgin in the traditional medieval guise of mother, intercessor, and protector, but it also exalts her as the symbol of Mexican national consciousness. At her shrine—the goal of thousands of pilgrims each year—and at hundreds of chapels throughout Mexico, the faithful pay homage to the Virgin, who is shown standing on a crescent moon, surrounded by a corona of sunrays and angels bearing the

Figure 20.1 Shrine of the Virgin of Guadalupe, the New Basilica of the Virgin of Guadalupe, Mexico City, Mexico.

colors of the Mexican flag. The significance of the Virgin of Guadalupe as a Christian devotional image, enthusiastically promoted by the Jesuits beginning in the late sixteeth century, and her widespread popularity as protectress of Mexico have persisted even into modern times: In 1910, she was made an honorary general of the Mexican Revolution.

Literature and the Catholic Reformation

The passionate mysticism of the Catholic Reformation infused the arts of the sixteenth and seventeenth centuries. In literature, there appeared a new emphasis on heightened spirituality and on personal visionary experience acquired by way of the senses. One of the most colorful personalities to emerge in forging the new language of mysticism was the Spanish Carmelite nun

Teresa of Avila (1515–1582), who was canonized in 1622. Teresa's activities in founding religious houses and in defending groups of Carmelites, who symbolized their humility by going without shoes, took her all over Spain and earned her the nickname "the roving nun." It was not until she was almost forty years old that her life as a visionary began. Teresa's visions, including the one described in the following autobiographical excerpt, marry sensory experience to spiritual contemplation. They address, moreover, the intriguing kinship between physical suffering and psychic bliss and between divine and erotic fulfillment. For Saint Teresa, love is the inspiration for oneness with God. The language by which the saint describes that union is charged with passion, for instance, when she relates how God's flaming arrow leaves her "completely afire."

Figure 20.2 Gianlorenzo Bernini, *The Ecstasy of Saint Teresa*, 1645–1652. Marble, height of group 11 ft. 6 in. Altar of Cornaro Chapel, Santa Maria della Vittoria, Rome. Scala, Florence.

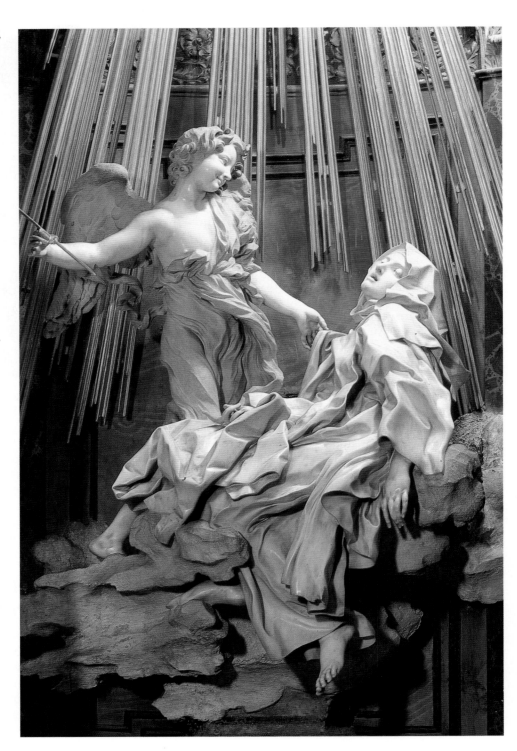

READING 4.2
From Saint Teresa's *Visions*

It pleased the Lord that I should sometimes see the following vision. I would see beside me, on my left hand, an angel in bodily form—a type of vision which I am not in the habit of seeing, except very rarely. Though I often see representations of angels, my visions of them are of the type which I first mentioned. It pleased the Lord that I should see this angel in the following way. He was not tall, but short, and very beautiful, his face so aflame that he appeared to be one of the highest types of angel who seem to be all afire. They must be those who are called cherubim: they do not tell me their names but I am well aware that there is a great difference between certain angels and others, and between these and others still, of a kind that I could not possibly explain. In his hands I saw a long golden spear and at the end of the iron tip I seemed to see a point of fire. With this he seemed to pierce my heart several times so that it penetrated to my entrails. When he drew it out, I thought he was drawing them out with it and he left me completely afire with a great love for God. The pain was so sharp that it made me utter several moans; and so excessive was the sweetness caused me by this intense pain that one can never wish to lose it, nor will one's soul be content with anything less than God. It is not bodily pain, but spiritual, though the body has a share in it—indeed, a great share. So sweet are the colloquies of love which pass between the soul and God that if anyone thinks I am lying I beseech God, in His goodness, to give him the same experience.

1

10

20

The sensuous tone of Teresa's visions enriched much of the religious verse of the seventeenth century, including that of her Spanish contemporaries, Saint John of the Cross (1542–1591), also a Carmelite, and Luis de Góngora y Argote (1561–1637). Similarly, in the poetry of devout English Catholics such as Richard Crashaw (1613–1649), the language of religious ecstasy swells with brooding desire.

Born into a Protestant family, Crashaw converted to Catholicism early in life. His religious poems, written in Latin and English, reflect the dual influence of Loyola's meditations and Teresa's visions. At least two of his most lyrical pieces are dedicated to Saint Teresa: *A Hymn to the Name and Honor of the Admirable Saint Teresa* and *The Flaming Heart, upon the Book and Picture of the Seraphical Saint Teresa, as She Is Usually Expressed with a Seraphim beside Her*. The latter poem suggests that Crashaw was familiar with Bernini's sculpted version of Teresa's vision before it was publicly unveiled in Rome (Figure **20.2**). Representative of this visionary sensibility, the last sixteen lines of *The Flaming Heart*, reproduced in Reading 4.3, are rhapsodic in their intense expression of personal emotion. Erasing boundaries

between erotic and spiritual love, Crashaw pleads that Teresa ravish his soul, even as she has been ravished by God.

READING 4.3
From Crashaw's *The Flaming Heart*

. . . .

O thou undaunted daughter of desires!
By all thou dower of lights and fires;
By all the eagle in thee, all the dove;
By all thy lives and deaths of love;
By thy large draughts of intellectual day,
And by thy thirsts of love more large than they;
By all thy brim-filled bowls of fierce desire,
By thy last morning's draught of liquid fire;
By the full kingdom of that final kiss
That seized thy parting soul, and sealed thee His;
By all the heavens thou hast in Him,
Fair sister of the seraphim,
By all of Him we have in thee;
Leave nothing of myself in me!
Let me so read thy life that I
Unto all life of mine may die.

The Visual Arts and the Catholic Reformation
Mannerist Painting

The religious zeal of the Catholic reformers inspired a tremendous surge of artistic activity, especially in Italy and Spain. In Venice and Rome, the centers of Italian cultural life, the art of the High Renaissance underwent radical transformation: The clearly defined, symmetrical compositions of High Renaissance painters and the decorum and dignity of the grand style (see chapter 17) gave way to *mannerism*, a style marked by spatial complexity, artificiality, and affectation. Mannerist artists brought a new psychological intensity to visual expression. Their paintings mirrored the self-conscious spirituality and the profound insecurities of an age of religious wars and political rivalry.

The mannerist style is already evident in *The Last Judgment* that the sixty-year-old Michelangelo (see chapter 17) painted on the east wall of the Sistine Chapel (Figure **20.3**). Between 1534 and 1541, only a few years after the armies of the Holy Roman Empire had sacked the city of Rome, Michelangelo returned to the chapel whose ceiling he had painted some twenty years earlier with the optimistic vision of salvation. Now, in a mood of brooding pessimism, the aging genius filled the altar wall with agonized, writhing figures that press dramatically against one another. Surrounding the wrathful Christ are the Christian martyrs, who carry the instruments of their torture, and throngs of the resurrected—originally depicted nude but later, in the wake of Catholic reform, draped to hide their genitals. Reflecting the anxieties of his day, Michelangelo has replaced the classically proportioned figures, calm balance, and spatial clarity of High Renaissance painting with a more troubled vision of salvation.

The traits of the mannerist style can be seen best in the *Madonna of the Long Neck* (Figure **20.4**) by Parmigianino (1503–1540). In this work the traditional subject of Madonna and Child is given a new mood of theatricality (compare Raphael's *Alba Madonna*; see chapter 17). Perched precariously above a courtyard adorned with a column that supports no superstructure, the unnaturally elongated Mother of God—her spidery

Figure 20.3 (opposite) Michelangelo Buonarroti, *The Last Judgment* (after restoration), 1536–1540. Fresco, 48 ft. × 44 ft. Altar wall, Sistine Chapel, Vatican, Rome. Nippon Television, Tokyo.

Figure 20.4 (right) Parmigianino, *Madonna of the Long Neck*, 1534–1540. Oil on panel, 7 ft. 1 in. × 4 ft. 4 in. Uffizi Gallery, Florence. Scala/Art Resource, New York.

fingers affectedly touching her breast—gazes at the oversized Christ child, who seems to slip lifelessly off her lap. Onlookers press into the ambiguous space from the left, while a small figure (perhaps a prophet) at the bottom right corner of the canvas draws our eye into distant space. Cool coloring and an overall smoky hue make the painting seem even more contrived and artificial, yet, by its very contrivance, unforgettable.

The degree to which the mannerists rejected the guiding principles of High Renaissance painting is nowhere better illustrated than by a comparison of *The Last Supper* (Figure 20.5) by the Venetian artist Jacopo Tintoretto (1518–1594) with the fresco of the same subject by Leonardo da Vinci (see chapter 17) executed approximately a century earlier (Figure 20.6). In his rendering of the sacred event, Tintoretto renounces the

Figure 20.5 Jacopo Tintoretto, *The Last Supper*, 1592–1594. Oil on canvas, 12 ft. × 18 ft. 8 in. San Giorgio Maggiore, Venice. Scala, Florence.

symmetry and geometric clarity of Leonardo's composition. The receding lines of the table and the floor in Tintoretto's painting place the viewer above the scene and draw the eye toward a vanishing point that lies in a distant and uncertain space beyond the bounds of the canvas. The even texture of Leonardo's fresco gives way in Tintoretto's canvas to vaporous contrasts of dark and light, produced by a smoking oil lamp. Clouds of angels flutter spectrally at the ceiling, and phosphorescent halos seem to electrify the figures of the apostles. At the most concentrated burst of light, the Savior is pictured distributing bread and wine to the disciples. While Leonardo focuses on the human element of the Last Supper—the moment when Jesus acknowledges his impending betrayal—Tintoretto illustrates the super-human and miraculous moment when Jesus initiates the sacrament by which the bread and wine become his flesh and blood. Yet Tintoretto sets the miracle amidst

Figure 20.6 Leonardo da Vinci, *The Last Supper*, ca. 1485–1498. Mural: oil and tempera on plaster, 14 ft. 5 in × 28 ft. Refectory, Santa Maria delle Grazie, Milan. Scala/Art Resource, New York.

the ordinary activities of household servants, who occupy the entire right-hand portion of the picture.

The mannerist passion for pictorial intensity was most vividly realized in the paintings of Domenikos Theotokopoulos, generally known (because of his Greek origins) as El Greco (1541–1614). A master painter who worked in Italy and Spain in the service of the Church and the devout Philip II, El Greco preferred the dramatic grace of Tintoretto to the more muscular vitality of Michelangelo. With the inward eye of a mystic, he produced visionary canvases marked by bold distortions of form, dissonant colors, and a daring handling of space. His figures, elongated and flamelike, and often highlighted by ghostly whites and yellow-grays, seem to radiate halos of light—auras that symbolize the luminous power of divine revelation. In *The Agony in the Garden*, the moment of Jesus' final submission to the divine will, El Greco created a moonlit landscape in which clouds, rocks, and fabrics billow and swell with mysterious energy (Figure **20.7**). Below the tempestuous sky, Judas (lower right) leads the arresting officers to the Garden of Gethsemane. The sleeping apostles, tucked away in a cocoonlike envelope, violate rational space: They are too small in relation to the oversized image of Jesus and the angel that hovers above. El Greco's ambiguous spatial fields, which often include multiple vanishing points, his acrid greens and acid yellows, and his "painterly" techniques—his brushstrokes remain engagingly visible on the surface of the canvas— all contribute to the creation of a highly personal and, by our standards, "modern" style that captured the mystical fervor of the new Catholicism.

Figure 20.7 El Greco, *The Agony in the Garden*, ca. 1585–1586. Oil on canvas, 3 ft. 4¼ in. × 3 ft. 8¾ in. Courtesy of the Toledo Museum of Art, Toledo, Ohio. Purchased with funds from the Libbey Endowment, Gift of Edward Drummond Libbey.

Baroque Painting

If mannerism was the vehicle of the Counter-Reformation mysticism, the *baroque style* conveyed the dynamic spirit of an entire age. Derived from the Portuguese word *barocco*, which describes the irregularly shaped pearls commonly featured in ornamental European decoration, the term *baroque* is associated with such features as ornateness, spatial grandeur, and theatrical flamboyance. In painting, the baroque style is characterized by asymmetric compositions, strong contrasts of light and dark, and bold, illusionistic effects.

The baroque style originated in Italy and came to dominate artistic production in the years between 1600 and 1750 throughout Europe and in those parts of the Americas colonized by Spain. Italian baroque artists worked to increase the dramatic expressiveness of religious subject matter in order to give viewers the sense that they were participating in the action of the scene. They tried to copy nature faithfully and without idealization. Such was the ambition of the North Italian artist Michelangelo Merisi, known as Caravaggio (1573–1610). The leading Italian painter of the seventeenth century, Caravaggio flouted Renaissance artistic

conventions, even as he flouted the law—he was arrested for violent acts that ranged from throwing a plate of artichokes in the face of a tavern keeper to armed assault and murder. In his paintings, Caravaggio renounced the grand style of the High Renaissance, which called for dignity, decorum, and the idealization of figures and setting. Rather, he recreated the early Christian past as though its major events were occurring in the local taverns and streets of sixteenth-century Italy. Caravaggio dramatized these events with strong contrasts of light and dark that give his figures a sculptural presence. A golden light bathes Christ and his disciples in *The Supper at Emmaus* (Figure **20.8**); Caravaggio "spotlights" Jesus at the moment when, raising his hand to bless the bread, he is recognized as the Christ (Luke 24:30–31). Caravaggio further underscores the moment of recognition by means of vigorous theatrical gestures. Christ's right arm, painted at angles to the picture plane by means of a perspective device known as **foreshortening**, seems to project sharply toward the beholders, as if to bless them as well as the bread. At the moment of recognition, the disciple at the right flings his arms outward along a diagonal axis, while the figure at the left grips the arm of his chair as though to rise in

Figure 20.8 Caravaggio, *The Supper at Emmaus*, ca. 1600. Oil on canvas, 4 ft. 7 in. × 6 ft. 5½ in. National Gallery, London.

Figure 20.9 Caravaggio,
The Crucifixion of Saint Peter,
1601. Oil on canvas,
7 ft. 6 in. × 5 ft. 9 in.
Santa Maria del Popolo, Rome.
Scala, Florence.

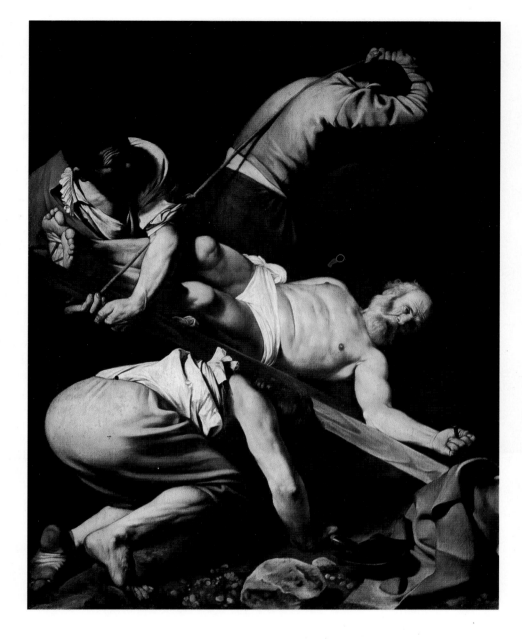

astonishment. Unlike the visionary El Greco, Caravaggio brought sacred subjects down to earth with an almost cameralike naturalism. Where El Greco's saints and martyrs are ethereal, Caravaggio's are solid, substantive, and often quite ordinary. Their strong physical presence and frank homeliness eliminate the psychological distance between viewer and subject, even as they challenge Renaissance conventions of beauty.

Caravaggio organized traditional religious compositions with unprecedented theatrical power and daring. In *The Crucifixion of Saint Peter* (Figure **20.9**), he arranged the figures in a tense, off-centered pinwheel that catches the eccentricity of Saint Peter's torment (he was crucified upside down). The saint's powerful physique is belied by the expression of vulnerability on his aging face. By placing the vigorously modeled figures close to the viewer and illuminating them against a darkened background, Caravaggio "stages" the action so that it seems to take place within the viewer's space—a space whose cruel light reveals such banal details as the executioner's dirty feet. True to the ideals of the Catholic Reformation, Caravaggio's paintings appealed to the senses rather than to the intellect, but they also introduced into European art a new and vigorously lifelike realization of the natural world.

Caravaggio's powerful style had considerable impact throughout Europe, but his most talented follower was born in Rome: Artemisia Gentileschi (1593–1653) was the daughter of a highly esteemed painter, himself a follower of Caravaggio. Trained by her father, Artemisia soon outstripped him in technical proficiency and imagination. Since women were not

Figure 20.10 Artemisia Gentileschi, *Judith Slaying Holofernes*, ca. 1614–1620. Oil on canvas, 6 ft. 6⅓ in. × 5 ft. 4 in. Uffizi Gallery, Florence.

permitted to draw from live male models, they rarely painted large-scale canvases with biblical and mythological themes, which required monumental nude figures; instead, their efforts were confined to the genres of portrait painting and still life (see chapter 22). Gentileschi's paintings, however, challenged this tradition. Her canvas *Judith Slaying Holofernes* (Figure **20.10**), which compares in size and impact with Caravaggio's *Crucifixion of Saint Peter* (see Figure 20.9), illustrates the decapitation of an Assyrian general and enemy of Israel at the hands of a clever Hebrew widow. A tale found in the Apocrypha (the unofficial books of the Bible), the slaying of the tyrannical Holofernes was a favorite Renaissance allegory of liberty and religious defiance. Gentileschi invested this painting with the dramatic techniques of Caravaggio: realistically conceived figures, stark contrasts of light and dark, and a composition that brings the viewer painfully close to the event; but she invested her subject with fierce intensity—the pinwheel arrangement of human limbs forces the eye to focus on the gruesome action of the swordblade as it severs head from neck in a shower of blood.

Gentileschi's favorite subjects were biblical heroines—she painted the Judith story some seven times. The violence she brought to these particular subjects may have been influenced by her profound sense of victimization: At the age of eighteen, she was raped by her drawing teacher and (during the sensational trial of her assailant) subjected to torture as a test of the truth of her testimony.

Figure 20.11 Gianlorenzo Bernini, Fountain of the Four Rivers, 1648–1651. Travertine and marble. Piazza Navona, Rome. Scala, Florence.

Figure 20.12 Anonymous, *Cornaro Chapel*, ca. 1644. Oil on canvas, 5 ft. 6¼ in. × 3 ft. 11¼ in. Staatliches Museum, Schwerin, Germany. Photo: E. Walford, Hamburg.

Baroque Sculpture in Italy

Gianlorenzo Bernini (1598–1680), Caravaggio's contemporary, brought the theatrical spirit of baroque painting to Italian architecture and sculpture. A man of remarkable technical virtuosity, Bernini was the chief architect of seventeenth-century Rome, as well as one of its leading sculptors. Under Bernini's direction, Rome became the "city of fountains." Richly adorned with dolphins, mermaids, and tritons, the fountain—its waters dancing and sparkling in the shifting wind and light—was a favorite ornamental device of the baroque era (Figure **20.11**).

Bernini's most important contribution to baroque religious sculpture was his multimedia masterpiece *The Ecstasy of Saint Teresa* (see Figure 20.2), executed between 1645 and 1652 for the Cornaro Chapel of Santa Maria della Vittoria in Rome (Figure **20.12**). The piece illustrates Bernini's dazzling skill in bringing to life Saint Teresa's autobiographical description of divine seduction (see Reading 4.2). Bernini depicts the swooning saint with head sunk back and eyes half closed. A smiling angel, resembling a teenage cupid, gently lifts Teresa's bodice to insert the flaming arrow of divine love. Bold illusionism heightens the sensuous effect: The angel's marble draperies seem to flutter and

Figure 20.13 Saint Peter's Basilica and the Vatican, Rome. Apse and dome by Michelangelo, 1547–1564; dome completed by Giacomo della Porta, 1588–1592; nave and facade by Carlo Maderno, 1601–1626; colonnades by Gianlorenzo Bernini, 1656–1663. Height of facade 147 ft., width 374 ft., height of dome 452 ft. Alinari/Art Resource, New York.

billow with tense energy, while the slack and heavy gown of Teresa echoes the emotion of ecstatic surrender. The vision takes place on a marble cloud which floats in heavenly space, while the uncertain juxtaposition of the saint and the cloud on which she reclines suggests the experience of levitation described in her vision. Sweetness and eroticism are the central features of this extraordinary image.

But Bernini's conception goes beyond the sculpture of the two figures to achieve a dramatic unity of figure and setting. In bringing theatrical intensity to Teresa's mystical experience, Bernini engaged the tools of architecture, sculpture, and painting: He situated Teresa beneath a colonnaded marble canopy from which radiate gilded wood rays (representing supernatural light). Real light entering through the glazed yellow panes of a concealed window above the chapel bathes the saint in a golden glow—an effect comparable to the spotlighting in a Caravaggio painting. At the ceiling of the chapel a host of angels both painted and sculpted in **stucco** (a light, pliable plaster) appears to descend from the heavens. Agate and dark green marble walls provide a somber setting for the gleaming white and gold central image. On either side of the chapel, the members of the Cornaro family (conceived in marble) behold Teresa's ecstasy from behind prayer desks that resemble theater boxes. These life-sized figures extend the supernatural space of the chapel and reinforce the viewer's role as witness to an actual event. It is no coincidence that Bernini's tour de force appeared contemporaneously with the birth of opera in Italy, for both share the baroque affection for dramatic expression on a monumental scale.

Baroque Architecture in Italy

The city of Rome carries the stamp of Bernini's flamboyant style. Commissioned to complete the *piazza*, the broad public space in front of Saint Peter's Basilica, Bernini designed a trapezoidal space that opens out to a larger oval—the two shapes comprise, perhaps symbolically, a keyhole. Bernini's courtyard is bounded by a spectacular colonnade that incorporates 284 Doric columns (each 39 feet high) as well as 96 statues of saints (each 15 feet tall). In a manner consistent with the ecumenical breadth of Jesuit evangelism, the gigantic pincerlike arms of the colonnade reach out to embrace an area that can accommodate over 250,000 people (Figure **20.13**)—a vast proscenium on which devotional activities of the Church of Rome are staged to this day. The proportions of Bernini's colonnade are symbolic of the baroque preference for the grandiose, a preference equally apparent in the artist's spectacular setting for the Throne of Saint Peter and in the immense bronze canopy (*baldacchino*) he raised over the high altar of the cathedral (Figure **20.14**).

Figure 20.14 (opposite) Gianlorenzo Bernini, *Baldacchino*, ca. 1624–1633. Bronze with gilding, height 93 ft. 6 in. Saint Peter's, Rome. Scala/Art Resource, New York.

Figure 20.15 Giacomo da Vignola, interior of Il Gesù, Rome, 1568–1573. Length approx. 240 ft. Foto Marburg.

Figure 20.16 Giacomo da Vignola and Giacomo della Porta, facade of Il Gesù, Rome, ca. 1575–1584. Height 105 ft., width 115 ft. The Conway Library, Courtauld Institute of Art, London.

Italian churches of the seventeenth century were designed to reflect the mystical and evangelical ideals of the Catholic Reformation. Il Gesù (the Church of Jesus) in Rome was the mother church of the Jesuit order and the model for hundreds of Counter-Reformation churches built throughout Europe and Latin America. Designed by Giacomo da Vignola (1507–1573), Il Gesù bears the typical features of the baroque church interior: a broad Latin cross nave with domed crossing and deeply recessed chapels (Figure **20.15**). Lacking side aisles, the 60-foot-wide nave allowed a large congregation to assemble close enough to the high altar and the pulpit to see the ceremony and hear the sermon. The wide nave also provided ample space for elaborate religious processions. Il Gesù's interior, with its magnificent altarpiece dedicated to Ignatius Loyola, exemplifies the baroque inclination to synthesize various media, such as painted stucco, bronze, and precious stones, in the interest of achieving sumptuous and ornate effects.

The exterior of Il Gesù, completed by Giacomo della Porta, is equally dramatic (Figure **20.16**). Its design—especially the elegant buttressing scrolls—looks back to Alberti's two-storied facade of Santa Maria Novella (Figure **20.17**). But in contrast to the linear sobriety of his Florentine model, della Porta's facade, with its deeply carved decorative elements, has a dynamic sculptural presence. For dramatic effect, the architect added structurally functionless engaged columns topped with Corinthian capitals. An ornate

Figure 20.17 Leon Battista Alberti, facade of Santa Maria Novella, Florence, completed 1470. Width approx. 117 ft. Scala, Florence.

Figure 20.18 Francesco Borromini, façade of San Carlo alle Quattro Fontane, Rome, 1667. Length 52 ft., width 34 ft., width of facade 38 ft. Alinari/Art Resource, New York.

cartouche (oval tablet) and a double cornice accentuate the central doorway, inviting the worshiper to enter. While the Renaissance facade was conceived in two dimensions, according to an essentially geometric linear pattern, the baroque churchfront is conceived in three. Like a Caravaggio painting, Il Gesù exploits dramatic contrasts of light and dark and of shallow and deep space.

The most daring of the Italian baroque architects was Francesco Borromini (1599–1667). Borromini designed the small monastic church of San Carlo alle Quattro Fontane (Saint Charles at the Four Fountains; Figure **20.18**) to fit a narrow site at the intersection of two Roman streets. Rejecting the rules of classical design, he combined convex and concave units to produce a sense of fluid and undulating movement. The facade consists of an assortment of deeply cut decorative elements: monumental Corinthian columns, a scrolled gable over the doorway, and life-sized angels that support a cartouche at the roofline. Borromini's aversion to the circle and the square—the "perfect" shapes of Renaissance architecture—extends to the interior of San Carlo, which is oval in plan. The dome, also oval, is lit by hidden windows that flood the interior with light. Carved with geometric motifs that diminish in size toward the apex, the shallow cupola appears to recede deep into space (Figure **20.19**). Such inventive illusionism, accented by dynamic spatial contrasts, characterized the Roman baroque style of church architecture at its best.

Figure 20.19 (left) Francesco Borromini, interior of dome, San Carlo alle Quattro Fontane, Rome, ca. 1638. Width approx. 52 ft. Alinari/Art Resource, New York.

Figure 20.20 (opposite) Andrea Pozzo, *Apotheosis of Saint Ignatius*, 1691. Fresco. Nave ceiling, Sant'Ignazio, Rome. Scala, Florence.

But the theatricality of the baroque style went further still: By painting religious scenes on the walls and ceilings of churches and chapels, baroque artists turned houses of God into theaters for sacred drama. Such is the case with the Church of Sant'Ignazio in Rome, the barrel-vaulted ceiling of which bears a breathtaking *trompe l'oeil* vision of Saint Ignatius' apotheosis—his elevation to divine status (Figure **20.20**; see also Part Opener, p. 2). A master of the techniques of linear perspective and dramatic foreshortening, the Jesuit architect and sculptor Andrea Pozzo (1642–1709) made the walls above Sant'Ignazio's clerestory appear to open up, so that the viewer gazes "through" the roof into the heavens that receive the levitating body of the saint. Pozzo's cosmic rendering—one of the first of numerous illusionistic ceilings found in seventeenth- and eighteenth-century European churches and palaces—may be taken to reflect a new perception of physical space inspired, in part, by European geographic exploration and discovery. Indeed, Pozzo underlines the global ambitions of Roman Catholic evangelism by adding at the four corners of the ceiling the allegorical figures of Asia, Africa, Europe, and America. The vast, illusionistic spatial fields of Italian baroque frescoes also may be seen as a response to the new astronomy of the Scientific Revolution, which presented a view of the universe as spatially infinite and dynamic rather than finite and static (see chapter 22). Whatever its inspiration, the spatial illusionism of baroque painting and architecture gave apocalyptic grandeur to Counter-Reformation ideals.

Baroque Music

In an effort to rid sacred music of secular influence, the Council of Trent condemned complex polyphony and the borrowing of popular tunes, both of which had become popular in religious music since the late Middle Ages. Above all, the reformers stressed the intelligibility of the sacred text: The message of the words was primary. The Italian composer Giovanni di Palestrina (1525–1594) took these recommendations as strict guidelines: His over one hundred polyphonic masses and 450 motets feature clarity of text, skillful counterpoint, and regular rhythms. The *a cappella* lines of Palestrina's Pope Marcellus Mass flow with the smooth grace of a mannerist painting. Called "the music of mystic serenity," Palestrina's compositions embody the conservative and contemplative side of the Catholic Reformation rather than its inventive, dramatic aspect. In the religious compositions of Palestrina's Spanish contemporary Tomás Luis de Victoria, there is a brooding but fervent mystical intensity. Like El Greco, his colleague at the court of Philip II, Victoria brought passion and drama to religious themes. And, recognizing that the Council of Trent had forbidden Palestrina to compose secular music, Victoria wrote not one note of secular song.

The Genius of Gabrieli

At the turn of the sixteenth century, the opulent city of Venice was the center of European religious musical activity. Giovanni Gabrieli (1555–1612), principal organist at Saint Mark's Cathedral in Venice and one of the greatest composers of his time, ushered in a new and dramatic style of choral and instrumental music. Gabrieli composed expansive **polychoral** religious pieces featuring up to five choruses. Abandoning the *a cappella* style favored in Rome, he included solo and ensemble groups of instruments—especially the trombones and cornets commonly used in Venice's ritual street processions. Gabrieli was the first composer to indicate a specific instrument for each voice part in the musical composition, earning him the name "the father of orchestration." Like baroque painters and sculptors, who sought sharp contrasts of light and shadow and dramatic spatial effects, Gabrieli created coloristic contrasts in sound. He was among the first composers to write into his scores the words *piano* (soft) and *forte* (loud) to govern the **dynamics** (the degree of loudness or softness) of the piece.

Gabrieli was also the first musician to make use of a divided choir employed in *concertato*, that is, in opposing or contrasting bodies of sound. At Saint Mark's, an organ was located on each side of the chancel, and four choirs were stationed on balconies high above the nave. The antiphonal play of chorus, instruments, and solo voices produced exhilarating sonorities (evident in the excerpt from Gabrieli's motet, *In Ecclesiis*♪) that met and mingled in the magical space above the heads of the congregation. In some of Gabrieli's compositions, echo effects produced by alternating voices and the use of unseen (offstage) voices achieve a degree of musical illusionism comparable to the visual illusionism of mannerist and baroque art. Like the extremes of light and dark in the paintings of El Greco and Caravaggio, Gabrieli's alternating bodies of sound (chorus versus chorus, solo voice versus chorus, chorus versus instruments) and contrasting musical dynamics (loud and soft) and pitches (high and low) produce strong harmonic textures and rich, dramatic effects. The *concertato* technique was the essence of early seventeenth-century baroque music and, in Gabrieli's hands, it was nothing less than majestic.

Gabrieli explored a type of musical organization that would come to dominate baroque music: *tonality* based on the melodic, harmonic, and rhythmic vocabulary of the major–minor key system. **Tonality** refers to the arrangement of a musical composition around a central note, called the "tonic" or "home tone" (usually designated as the "key" of a given composition). A keynote or tonic can be built on any of the twelve tones of the **chromatic scale** (the twelve tones—seven white and five black keys—of the piano keyboard). In baroque music—as in most music written to this day—all of the tones in the composition relate to the home tone. Tonality provided baroque composers with a way of achieving dramatic focus in a piece of music—much in the way that light served baroque painters to achieve dramatic focus in their compositions. By the mid-seventeenth century, the even progress of Renaissance polyphony, like the even lighting of Renaissance painting, had given way to the dynamic use of individual voices and the inventive combination of choral and instrumental textures.

Monteverdi and the Birth of Opera

The master of baroque vocal expression and the greatest Italian composer of the seventeenth century was Claudio Monteverdi (1567–1643). Monteverdi served the court of Mantua until he became chapel master of Saint Mark's in Venice in 1621, a post he held for the rest of his life. During his long career, he wrote various kinds of religious music, as well as ballets, madrigals, and operas. Like Gabrieli, Monteverdi discarded the intimate dimensions of Renaissance chamber music and cultivated an expansive, dramatic style. His compositions reflect a typically baroque effort to imbue music

♪See Music Listening Selections at end of chapter.

with a vocal expressiveness that reflected the emotional charge of poetry. "The [written] text," declared Monteverdi, "should be the master of the music, not the servant." Monteverdi linked "affections" or specific emotional states with appropriate sounds: anger, for instance, with the high voice register, moderation with the middle voice register, and humility with the low voice register. With Monteverdi, the union of music and speech sought in the word painting techniques of Josquin (see chapter 17) blossomed into full-blown opera: that form of theater that combined all aspects of baroque artistic expression—music, drama, dance, and the visual arts.

Born in Italy, opera emerged out of Renaissance efforts to revive the music-drama of ancient Greek theater. While humanist composers had no idea what Greek music sounded like, they sought to imitate the ancient unity of music and poetry. The earliest performances of Western opera resembled the Renaissance masque, a form of musical entertainment that included dance and poetry, along with rich costumes and scenery. Baroque operas were more musically complex, however, and more dramatically cohesive than most Renaissance masques. The first opera house was built in Venice in 1637, and by 1700 Italy was home to seventeen more such houses, a measure of the vast popularity of the new genre. By the end of the seventeenth century, Italian courts and public theaters boasted all of the essential features of the modern theater: the picture-frame stage, the horseshoe-shaped auditorium, and tiers of galleries or boxes (Figure 20.21). Interestingly enough, some of these opera houses, resplendent with life-sized sculptures and illusionistic frescoes, are aesthetically indistinguishable from Italian baroque church and chapel interiors (see Figures 20.12 and 20.15).

Monteverdi's *Orfeo*,♮ composed in 1607 for the duke of Mantua, was Monteverdi's first opera and one of the first full-length operas in music history. The libretto (literally, "little book") or text of the opera was written by Alessandro Striggio and based on a classical theme—the descent of Orpheus, the Greek poet-musician, to Hades. *Orfeo* required an orchestra of more than three dozen instruments, including 10 viols, 3 trombones, and 4 trumpets. The instrumentalists performed the **overture**, an orchestral introduction to the opera. They also accompanied vocal music that consisted of **arias** (elaborate solo songs or duets) alternating with **recitatives** (passages spoken or recited to sparse chordal accompaniment). The aria tended to develop a character's feelings or state of mind, while the recitative served to narrate the action of the story or to heighten its dramatic effect.

Monteverdi believed that opera should convey the full range of human passions. To that end, he contrived inventive contrasts between singer and accompaniment, recitative and aria, soloist and chorus. He also employed abrupt changes of key to emphasize shifts in mood and action. And he introduced such novel and expressive instrumental effects as *pizzicato*, the technique of plucking rather than bowing a stringed instrument. A multimedia synthesis of music, drama, and visual display, Italian opera, whether secular or religious in theme, became the ideal expression of the baroque sensibility and the object of imitation throughout Western Europe.

SUMMARY

In the wake of the Protestant Reformation, the Roman Catholic Church launched a reform movement that took late sixteenth-century Europe by storm. Loyola's *Spiritual Meditations* and the autobiographical writings of Saint Teresa of Avila set the tone for a new, more mystical Catholicism. In the spirit of Saint Teresa's ecstatic visions, such Catholic poets as Richard Crashaw wrote rhapsodic lyrics that fused sensual and spiritual yearnings. The arts of the seventeenth century reflect the religious intensity of the Catholic Reformation, even as they mirror the insecurities of the religiously divided and politically turbulent West.

Figure 20.21 P. D. Olivier, *The Teatro Regio, Turin*. Painting of the opening night, December 26, 1740. Five tiers of boxes are fitted into the sides of the proscenium, one even perched over the semicircular pediment. Note the orchestra, without a conductor; the girls distributing refreshments; and the armed guard protecting against disorder. Courtesy of the Museo Civico, Turin.

♮See Music Listening Selections at end of chapter.

The baroque style, which came to dominate Western Europe between 1600 and 1750, was born in Italy. The mannerist paintings of Parmigianino, Tintoretto, and El Greco anticipated the baroque style by their figural distortions, irrational space, bizarre colors, and general disregard for the "rules" of Renaissance painting. Italian baroque art, as typified by Caravaggio's paintings and Bernini's sculpture, featured dynamic contrasts of light and dark, an expanded sense of space, and the operatic staging of subject matter. Counter-Reformation churches, embellished with visionary paintings and sculptures, were ornate theaters for the performance of Catholic ritual. Bernini's *Ecstasy of Saint Teresa* and Pozzo's ceiling for the Church of Saint Ignatius in Rome achieved new heights of illusionistic theatricality. Addressing the passions rather than the intellect, baroque art broadcast the visionary message of Catholic reform to a vast audience that extended from Europe to the Americas.

Rome and Venice were fountainheads for Italian baroque art and music. Palestrina's polyphonic masses and motets emphasized clarity of text and calm sublimity, while Gabrieli's lofty polychoral compositions, performed at Saint Mark's Cathedral in Venice, featured dynamic contrasts between and among voices and musical instruments. The daring contrasts, rich color, and sheer volume of Gabrieli's music find their parallel in the canvases of Caravaggio.

The most important development in seventeenth-century European music was the birth of opera. Borrowing themes from classical mythology and history, Claudio Monteverdi integrated text and music to create the new and noble art of music-drama. In its synthesis of all forms of performance—music, literature, and the visual arts—Italian opera became the supreme expression of the theatrical exuberance and spiritual vitality of the baroque style.

GLOSSARY

aria an elaborate solo song or duet, usually with instrumental accompaniment, performed as part of an opera or other dramatic musical composition

cartouche an oval tablet or medallion, usually containing an inscription or heraldic device

chromatic scale a series of twelve tones represented by the seven white and five black keys of the piano keyboard; see also Glossary, chapter 6, "scale"

concertato (Italian, *concerto* = "opposing" or "competing") an early baroque style in which voices or instruments of different rather than similar natures are used in an opposing or contrasting manner

dynamics the degree of loudness or softness in music

foreshortening a perspective device by which figures or objects appear to recede or project into space

overture an instrumental introduction to a longer musical piece, such as an opera

piazza (Italian) a broad, open public space

pizzicato (Italian) the technique of plucking (with the fingers) rather than bowing a stringed instrument

polychoral music written for two or more choruses, performed both in turn and together

recitative a textual passage recited to sparse chordal accompaniment; a rhythmically free vocal style popular in seventeenth-century opera

stucco a light, pliable plaster made of gypsum, sand, water, and ground marble

tonality the use of a central note, called the *tonic*, around which all other tonal material of a composition is organized, and to which the music returns for a sense of rest and finality

SUGGESTIONS FOR READING

Bantel, Linda, and M. B. Burke. *Spain and New Spain: Mexican Colonial Arts in their European Context.* Corpus Christi, Tex.: Art Museum of South Texas, 1992.

Bazin, Germain. *The Baroque: Principles, Styles, Modes, Themes.* New York: Norton, 1978.

Bianconi, Lorenzo. *Music in the Seventeenth Century,* translated by David Bryant. New York: Cambridge University Press, 1987.

Burke, Peter. *Popular Culture in Early Modern Europe.* New York: New York University Press, 1971.

Dickens, A. G. *The Counter-Reformation.* London: Thames and Hudson, 1968.

Lavin, Irving. *Bernini and the Unity of the Visual Arts.* New York: Oxford University Press, 1980.

Hammond, Frederick. *Music and Spectacle in Baroque Rome.* New Haven: Yale University Press, 1994.

Martin, John Rupert. *Baroque.* New York: Harper, 1977.

Norberg-Schulz, Christian. *Baroque Architecture.* New York: Rizzoli, 1986.

Petersson, Robert T. *The Art of Ecstasy: Teresa, Bernini and Crashaw.* New York: Atheneum, 1970.

Wallace, Robert. *The World of Bernini, 1598–1680.* Library of Art Series. New York: Time-Life Books, 1970.

Wittkower, Rudolf. *Art and Architecture in Italy: 1600–1750.* New York: Viking, 1959.

———, and Irma B. Jaffe, eds. *Baroque Art: The Jesuit Contribution.* New York: Fordham University Press, 1972.

MUSIC LISTENING SELECTIONS

Cassette II Selection 1 Gabrieli, Motet, "In Ecclesiis," 1615, excerpt.

Cassette II Selection 2 Monteverdi, *Orfeo*, Aria: "Vi recorda, o boschi ombrosi," 1607.

21

The Baroque in the Protestant North

Throughout Italy, Spain, and other parts of the West, the baroque style mirrored the spirit of the Catholic Reformation; but in Northern Europe, where Protestant loyalties remained strong, another phase of the style emerged. The differences between the two are easily observed in the arts: In Italy, church interiors were ornate and theatrical; but in England, the Netherlands, and Northern Germany, where Protestants as a matter of faith were committed to private devotion rather than public ritual, churches were stripped of ornamentation, and the mood was more somber and intimate. Protestant devotionalism shared with Catholic mysticism an anti-intellectual bias, but Protestantism shunned all forms of theatrical display. In Northern Europe, where a largely Protestant population valued personal piety and private devotion, the Bible exercised an especially significant influence on the arts. Pietism, a seventeenth-century religious movement that originated in Germany, encouraged Bible study as the principal means of cultivating the "inner light" of religious truth.

If the Bible was a shaping influence on the arts of the Protestant North, so too was the patronage of a rising middle class. Having benefited financially from worldwide commerce, middle-class merchants demanded an art that reflected their keen interests in secular life. And while princely patronage in the North did not slacken during the seventeenth century, the landmark examples of Northern European art pay tribute to the vitality of this wealthy commercial class.

The Rise of the English Commonwealth

In England, Queen Elizabeth I (1558–1603) was succeeded by the first Stuart monarch James I (1566–1625). A Scot, and a committed proponent of absolute monarchy, James ruled England by personal decree. His son, Charles I (1600–1649; Figure **21.1**), followed his example, alienating large segments of the English population, including the growing number of Puritans (English Calvinists who demanded church reform and greater strictness in religious observance). Allying with antiroyalist factions, mostly of the middle class, the Puritans constituted a powerful political group. With the support of the Puritans, leaders in Parliament raised an army to oppose King Charles, ultimately defeating the royalist forces in a civil war that lasted from 1642 to 1648 and executing the king on charges of treason. The government that followed this civil war, led by the Puritan general Oliver Cromwell (1599–1658), was known as the "Commonwealth." Bearing the hallmarks of a republic, the new government issued a written constitution that proposed the formation of a national legislature elected by universal manhood suffrage. The Commonwealth, however, was unable to survive without military support. When Cromwell died, Stuart monarchs were invited to return to the throne; but by then Parliament's place in English government was firmly established, along with its authority to limit the power of English monarchs.

In the 1680s, when King James II (1633–1701) attempted to fill a new Parliament with his Catholic supporters, the opposition rebelled again. They expelled the king and offered the crown of England to William of Orange, ruler of the Netherlands, and his wife Mary, the Protestant daughter of James II. During the "Glorious Revolution" of 1688, Parliament enacted a Bill of Rights prohibiting the king from suspending parliamentary laws or interfering with the ordinary course of justice. The Bill of Rights also enforced religious toleration and other civil liberties. Most importantly, however, the "bloodless revolution" reestablished constitutional monarchy in England and struck a major victory for popular sovereignty.

Figure 21.1 Anthony van Dyck, *Charles I on Horseback*, ca. 1638.
Oil on canvas, 12 ft. × 9 ft. 7 in. National Gallery, London.

The King James Bible

These dramatic political events, so closely tied to religious issues, occurred in the years following one of the most influential cultural events of the seventeenth century: the new English translation of the Bible. If, indeed, tradition is formed by the perpetuation of systems of ideas, then, surely, English tradition and Western European culture in general owe a major debt to the 1611 publication of the King James version of the Bible. Drawing on a number of earlier English translations of Scripture made during the sixteenth century, a committee of fifty-four scholars recruited by James I of England produced an "authorized" English-language edition of the Old and New Testaments. This edition of Scripture emerged during the very decades in which Shakespeare was writing his last major dramas (see chapter 18)—a time when the English language reached its peak in eloquence. Along with the writings of Shakespeare, the King James Bible had a shaping influence on the English language and on all of English literature.

The new translation of Scripture preserved the spiritual fervor of the Old Testament Hebrew and the narrative vigor of the New Testament Greek. Like Shakespeare's poetry, the language of the King James Bible is majestic and compelling. Some appreciation of these qualities may be gleaned from comparing the two following translations. The first, a sixteenth-century translation based on Saint Jerome's Latin Vulgate edition and published in the city of Douay in France in 1609, lacks the concise language, the poetic imagery, and the lyrical rhythms of the King James version (the second example), which, though deeply indebted to a number of sixteenth-century English translations, also drew directly on the original Hebrew texts.

READING 4.4

From the Douay Bible, 1609
The Twenty-Third Psalm

Our Lord ruleth me, and nothing shall be wanting to me; in place of pasture there he hath placed me.

Upon the water of refection he hath brought me up; he hath converted my soul.

He hath conducted me upon the paths of justice, for his name.

For although I shall walk in the midst of the shadow of death, I will not fear evils; because thou art with me.

Thy rod and thy staff, they have comforted me.

Thou hast prepared in my sight a table against them that trouble me.

Thou hast fatted my head with oil, and my chalice inebriating, how goodly is it!

And thy mercy shall follow me all the days of my life.

And that I may dwell in the house of our Lord in longitude of days.

From the King James Bible, 1611
The Twenty-Third Psalm

The Lord is my shepherd; I shall not want.

He maketh me to lie down in green pastures: he leadeth me beside the still waters.

He restoreth my soul: he leadeth me in the paths of righteousness for his name's sake.

Yea, though I walk through the valley of the shadow of death, I will fear no evil: for thou art with me; thy rod and thy staff they comfort me.

Thou preparest a table before me in the presence of mine enemies: thou anointest my head with oil; my cup runneth over.

Surely goodness and mercy shall follow me all the days of my life: and I will dwell in the house of the Lord for ever.

◆

English Literature of the Seventeenth Century

John Donne

One of the most eloquent voices of religious devotionalism in the Protestant North was that of the poet John Donne (1571–1631). Born and raised as a Roman Catholic, Donne studied at Oxford and Cambridge. He traveled widely before converting to Anglicanism and becoming a priest of the Church of England. A formidable preacher as well as a man of great intellectual prowess, Donne wrote eloquent sermons that challenged the parishioners at Saint Paul's Cathedral in London (Figure **21.2**), where he acted as dean. At Saint Paul's, Donne developed the sermon as a vehicle for philosophic meditation. In *Meditation 17* (an excerpt from which follows), Donne pictures humankind—in typically baroque terms—as part of a vast, cosmic plan. His image of human beings as "chapters" in the larger "book" of God's design is an example of Donne's affection for unusual, extended metaphors.

READING 4.5

From Donne's *Meditation 17*

All mankind is of one author, and is one volume; when   1
one man dies, one chapter is not torn out of the book,
but translated into a better language; and every chapter
must be so translated. God employs several translators;
some pieces are translated by age, some by sickness,
some by war, some by justice; but God's hand is in every
translation, and his hand shall bind up all our scattered
leaves again for that library where every book shall lie
open to one another. As therefore the bell that rings to a
sermon calls not upon the preacher only but upon the   10
congregation to come, so this bell calls us all. . . . No

man is an island entire of itself; every man is a piece of the continent, a part of the main. If a clod be washed away by the sea, Europe is the less, as well as if a promontory were, as well as if a manor of thy friend's or of thine own were. Any man's death diminishes me, because I am involved in mankind, and therefore never send to know for whom the bell tolls; it tolls for thee.

◆

The tolling bell that figures so powerfully in the last lines of Donne's *Meditation* makes reference to an age-old tradition (perpetuated at Saint Paul's) of ringing the church bells to announce the death of a parishioner. Donne's poetry was as unconventional as his prose: Both abound in "conceits," that is, elaborate metaphors that compare two apparently dissimilar objects or emotions, often with the intention of shocking or surprising. In that the conceits of Donne (and other seventeenth-century writers) borrowed words and images from the new science (see chapter 22), critics called these devices and the poetry they embellished "metaphysical." Metaphysical poetry reflects the baroque affection for

Figure 21.2 Christopher Wren, west facade of Saint Paul's Cathedral, London, 1675–1710. Width approx. 90 ft. Photo: A. F. Kersting, London.

dramatic contrast, for frequent and unexpected shifts of viewpoint, and for the dramatic synthesis of discordant images. These features are apparent in some of Donne's finest works, including the group of religious poems known as the *Holy Sonnets*. In the first of the following two sonnets, Donne challenges Death in conceiving itself as powerful and influential. Instead of regarding Death, according to convention, as a "mighty and dreadful" ruler, Donne demeans Death as a slave who keeps bad company ("poison, war, and sickness"); he concludes with the artful device of Death itself "dying." Donne's defiance of Death stands in contrast to the submissive tone of medieval preachers (see chapter 12), but his view of physical death as "a short sleep" from which "we wake eternally" is confidently Christian.

In the second sonnet, Donne compares himself to a fortress that has been seized by the enemies of the Lord. Donne describes Reason as the ruler ("Your viceroy in me") who has failed to defend the fortress. He now pleads with God to "ravish" and "imprison" him. The poem abounds in intriguing paradoxes that link sinfulness with deliverance, conquest with liberation, and imprisonment with freedom. Donne's unexpected juxtapositions and paradoxical images are typical of English metaphysical poetry, but his rejection of conventional poetic language in favor of a conversational tone (much celebrated by modern poets) represents a revolutionary development in European literature.

READING 4.6

From Donne's *Holy Sonnets*

Death be not proud, though some have called thee	1
Mighty and dreadful, for thou art not so;	
For those whom thou think'st thou dost overthrow	
Die not, poor Death, nor yet canst thou kill me.	
From rest and sleep, which but thy pictures be,	5
Much pleasure, then from thee much more must flow,	
And soonest our best men with thee do go,	
Rest of their bones and souls' delivery.	
Thou art slave to fate, chance, kings, and desperate men,	
And dost with poison, war, and sickness dwell,	10
And poppy, or charms can make us sleep as well,	
And better than thy stroke; why swell'st thou then?	
One short sleep past, we wake eternally,	
And Death shall be no more; Death, thou shalt die.	

. . . .

Batter my heart, three-personed God; for You	15
As yet but knock, breath, shine, and seek to mend;	
That I may rise, and stand, o'erthrow me, and bend	
Your force, to break, blow, burn, and make me new.	
I, like an usurped town to another due,	
Labour to admit You, but oh! to no end;	20

Reason, Your viceroy in me, me should defend,
But is captived and proves weak or untrue.
Yet dearly I love You, and would be loved fain,[1]
But am betrothed unto Your enemy.
Divorce me, untie, or break that knot again,   25
Take me to You, imprison me, for I
Except You enthrall me, never shall be free;
Nor ever chaste, except You ravish me.

————————◆————————

The Genius of John Milton

John Milton (1608–1674) was a devout Puritan and a defender of the Cromwellian Commonwealth that collapsed in 1658. His career as a humanist and poet began at Cambridge University and continued throughout his eleven-year tenure as secretary to the English Council of State. Though shy and retiring, Milton became a political activist and a persistent defender of religious, political, and intellectual freedom. He challenged British society with expository prose essays on a number of controversial subjects. In one pamphlet, he defended divorce between couples who were spiritually and temperamentally incompatible—a subject possibly inspired by his first wife's unexpected decision to abandon him briefly just after their marriage. In other prose works, Milton opposed Parliament's effort to control free speech and freedom of the press. "Who kills a man kills a reasonable creature," wrote Milton, "but he who destroys a good book, kills reason itself."

Milton's verse compositions include lyric poems and elegies, but the greatest of his contributions are his two epic poems: *Paradise Lost* and *Paradise Regained*. Milton wrote both of these monumental poems during the last decades of his life, when he was totally blind—a condition he erroneously attributed to long nights of reading. Legend has it that he dictated the poems to his two young daughters. In *Paradise Lost* Milton created a cosmic (and earth-centered) vision of Heaven, Hell, and Paradise comparable to that drawn by Dante (see chapter 12) but more philosophic in its concern with the issues of knowledge, sin, and free will. Considered the greatest of modern epics, *Paradise Lost* is impressive in its vast intellectual sweep, its wide-ranging allusions to history and literature, and its effort to address matters of time, space, and causality.

Milton was already fifty years old when he resolved to compose a modern epic that rivaled the majesty of the classic works of Homer and Virgil. At the outset, he considered various themes, one of which was the story of King Arthur. But he settled instead on a Christian theme that allowed him to examine an issue particularly dear to his Protestant sensibilities: the meaning of evil in a universe created by a benevolent God. The twelve books of *Paradise Lost* retell the story of the fall of Adam and Eve, beginning with the activities of the rebellious archangel Satan and culminating in the expulsion of the First Parents from Paradise. The poem concludes with the angel Michael's explanation to Adam of how fallen Man, through Christ, will recover immortality. This august theme, rooted in biblical history, permitted Milton to explore questions of human knowledge, freedom, and morality and, ultimately, to "justify the ways of God to Man."

Central in this cosmic drama is the figure of Satan, who is painted larger than life. Milton vividly recounts the demon's passage from Hell to Earth and the fall of the rebel angels—a lengthy account that was probably inspired by the English Civil War. The titanic Satan is a metaphor for the Puritan conception of evil in the world. Less vividly drawn, Adam is an expression of Protestant pessimism—a figure who, for all his majesty, is incapable of holding on to Paradise. *Paradise Lost* may be considered a Christian parable of the human condition. In its cosmic scope and verbal exuberance, it is also a mirror of the baroque imagination.

Paradise Lost rivals the achievements of Shakespeare. Like Shakespeare, Milton used blank verse: unrhymed lines of ten syllables each with accents on every second syllable. This form allowed Milton to carry the thread of a single thought past the end of the line and thereby group ideas in rich verse paragraphs. The language of *Paradise Lost* is intentionally lofty; it is designed to convey epic breadth and to narrate (as Milton promised) "things unattempted yet in prose or rhyme." The following excerpts convey some sense of the power and majesty of Milton's verse. In the first twenty-six lines of Book I, Milton announces the subject of the poem: the loss of humankind's spiritual innocence. The second excerpt, also from Book I, relates the manner in which Satan tears himself from Hell's burning lake and proudly assumes his place as ruler of the fallen legions. In the third excerpt (from Book IX), Adam resolves to perish with his beloved partner, Eve, by imitating her in eating the Forbidden Fruit. Finally, in the passage from Book XII, Adam hears the angel Michael's prophetic description of humankind's destiny and prepares to leave Paradise.

---

[1]Willingly.

READING 4.7

From Milton's *Paradise Lost*
(Books I, IX, XII)

Of man's first disobedience, and the fruit   1
Of that forbidden tree, whose mortal taste
Brought death into the world, and all our woe,
With loss of Eden, till one greater Man[1]
Restore us, and regain the blissful seat,
Sing Heav'nly Muse, that on the secret top
Of Oreb, or of Sinai,[2] didst inspire
That shepherd, who first taught the chosen seed,
In the beginning how the heav'ns and earth
Rose out of chaos: or if Sion hill   10
Delight thee more, and Siloa's brook[3] that flowed
Fast by the oracle of God; I thence
Invoke thy aid to my advent'rous song,
That with no middle flight intends to soar
Above th' Aonian mount,[4] while it pursues
Things unattempted yet in prose or rhyme.
And chiefly thou O Spirit, that dost prefer
Before all temples th' upright heart and pure,
Instruct me, for thou know'st; thou from the first
Wast present, and with mighty wings outspread   20
Dove-like sat'st brooding on the vast abyss
And mad'st it pregnant: what in me is dark
Illumine, what is low raise and support;
That to the highth of this great argument
I may assert Eternal Providence,
And justify the ways of God to men.

. . . .

Forthwith upright he rears from off the pool
His mighty stature; on each hand the flames
Driv'n backward slope their pointing spires, and rolled
In billows, leave i' th' midst a horrid vale.   30
Then with expanded wings he steers his flight
Aloft, incumbent on the dusty air
That felt unusual weight, till on dry land
He lights, if it were land that ever burned
With solid, as the lake with liquid fire,
And such appeared in hue; as when the force
Of subterranean wind transports a hill
Torn from Pelorus,[5] or the shattered side
Of thund'ring Etna, whose combustible
And fuelled entrails thence conceiving fire,   40
Sublimed with mineral fury, aid the winds,
And leave a singèd bottom all involved
With stench and smoke: such resting found the sole
Of unblest feet. Him followed his next mate,

Both glorying to have escaped the Stygian[6] flood
As gods, and by their own recovered strength,
Not by the sufferance of supernal power.
    "Is this the region, this the soil, the clime,"
Said then the lost Archangel, "this the seat
That we must change for heav'n, this mournful gloom   50
For that celestial light? Be it so, since he
Who now is sovran[7] can dispose and bid
What shall be right: farthest from him is best
Whom reason hath equaled, force hath made supreme
Above his equals. Farewell, happy fields,
Where joy for ever dwells: hail horrors, hail,
Infernal world, and thou, profoundest hell
Receive thy new possessor: one who brings
A mind not to be changed by place or time.
The mind is its own place, and in itself   60
Can make a heav'n of hell, a hell of heav'n.
What matter where, if I be still the same,
And what I should be, all but less than he
Whom thunder hath made greater? Here at least
We shall be free; th' Almighty hath not built
Here for his envy, will not drive us hence:
Here may we reign secure, and in my choice
To reign is worth ambition though in hell:
Better to reign in hell, than serve in heav'n."

. . . .

On th' other side, Adam, soon as he heard   70
The fatal trespass done by Eve, amazed,[8]
Astonied[9] stood and blank, while horror chill
Ran through his veins, and all his joints relaxed;
From his slack hand the garland wreathed for Eve
Down dropped, and all the faded roses shed:
Speechless he stood and pale, till thus at length
First to himself he inward silence broke.
    "O fairest of creation, last and best
Of all God's works, creature in whom excelled
Whatever can to sight or thought be formed,   80
Holy, divine, good, amiable, or sweet!
How art thou lost, how on a sudden lost,
Defaced, deflow'red, and now to death devote?[10]
Rather how hast thou yielded to transgress
The strict forbiddance, how to violate
The sacred fruit forbidd'n! some cursèd fraud
Of enemy hath beguiled thee, yet unknown,
And me with thee hath ruined, for with thee
Certain my resolution is to die;
How can I live without thee, how forgo   90
Thy sweet converse and love so dearly joined,
To live again in these wild woods forlorn?
Should God create another Eve, and I

---

[1]Christ.
[2]As was the case with epic poets of old, Milton here invokes a divine source of inspiration. Milton's muse, however, is an abstraction of Judeo-Christian wisdom, identified with the muse that inspired Moses at Mount Horeb (Deut. 4.10) or on Mount Sinai (Exod. 19.20).
[3]A spring near Mount Zion in Jerusalem where, in the Hebrew Bible, God spoke to his people.
[4]In Greece, the Muses were thought to live on Mount Helicon, also known as the "Aonian mountain."
[5]A promontory near the volcanic Mount Etna in Sicily.

[6]Referring to the River Styx, in Greek mythology the principal river of the Underworld.
[7]Sovereign.
[8]Confused, terror-stricken.
[9]Stunned.
[10]Devoted, doomed.

Another rib afford, yet loss of thee
Would never from my heart; no no, I feel
The link of nature draw me: flesh of flesh,
Bone of my bone thou art, and from thy state
Mine never shall be parted, bliss or woe."
   So having said, as one from sad dismay
Recomforted,[11] and after thoughts disturbed   100
Submitting to what seemed remédiless,
Thus in calm mood his words to Eve he turned.
   "Bold deed thou hast presumed, advent'rous Eve,
And peril great provoked, who thus hast dared
Had it been only coveting to eye
That sacred fruit, sacred to abstinence,
Much more to taste it under ban to touch.
But past who can recall, or done undo?
Not God omnipotent, nor fate; yet so
Perhaps thou shalt not die, perhaps the fact[12]   110
Is not so heinous now, foretasted fruit,
Profaned first by the serpent, by him first
Made common and unhallowed ere our taste;
Nor yet on him found deadly, he yet lives,
Lives, as thou saidst, and gains to live as man
Higher degree of life, inducement strong
To us, as likely tasting to attain
Proportional ascent, which cannot be
But to be gods, or angels demi-gods.
Nor can I think that God, Creator wise,   120
Though threat'ning, will in earnest so destroy
Us his prime creatures, dignified so high,
Set over all his works, which in our fall,
For us created, needs with us must fail,
Dependent made; so God shall uncreate,
Be frustrate, do, undo, and labor lose,
Not well conceived of God, who though his power
Creation could repeat, yet would be loath
Us to abolish, lest the Adversary
Triumph and say; 'Fickle their state whom God   130
Most favors, who can please him long? Me first
He ruined, now mankind; whom will he next?'
Matter of scorn, not to be given the Foe.
However I with thee have fixed my lot,
Certain to undergo like doom; if death
Consort with thee, death is to me as life;
So forcible within my heart I feel
The bond of nature draw me to my own.
My own in thee, for what thou art is mine;
Our state cannot be severed, we are one,   140
One flesh: to lose thee were to lose myself."
     . . . .

[. . . to the Angel] Adam last replied.
"How soon hath thy prediction, seer blest,
Measured this transient world, the race of time,

Till time stand fixed: beyond is all abyss,
Eternity, whose end no eye can reach.
Greatly instructed I shall hence depart,
Greatly in peace of thought, and have my fill
Of knowledge, what this vessel can contain;
Beyond which was my folly to aspire.   150
Henceforth I learn, that to obey is best,
And love with fear the only God, to walk
As in his presence, ever to observe
His providence, and on him sole depend,
Merciful over all his works, with good
Still overcoming evil, and by small
Accomplishing great things, by things deemed weak
Subverting worldly strong, and worldly wise
By simply meek; that suffering for truth's sake
Is fortitude to highest victory,   160
And to the faithful death the gate of life;
Taught this by his example whom I now
Acknowledge my Redeemer ever blest."
   To whom thus also th' angel last replied:
"This having learnt, thou hast attained the sum
Of wisdom; hope no higher, though all the stars
Thou knew'st by name, and all th' ethereal powers,
All secrets of the deep, all nature's works,
Or works of God in heav'n, air, earth, or sea,
And all the riches of this world enjoy'dst,   170
And all the rule, one empire; only add
Deeds to thy knowledge answerable, add faith,
Add virtue, patience, temperance, add love,
By name to come called charity, the soul
Of all the rest: then wilt thou not be loath
To leave this Paradise, but shalt possess
A paradise within thee, happier far.
Let us descend now therefore from this top
Of speculation; for the hour precise
Exacts our parting hence; and see the guards,   180
By me encamped on yonder hill, expect
Their motion,[13] at whose front a flaming sword,
In signal of remove,[14] waves fiercely round;
We may no longer stay: go, waken Eve;
Her also I with gentle dreams have calmed
Portending good, and all her spirits composed
To meek submission: thou at season fit
Let her with thee partake what thou hast heard,
Chiefly what may concern her faith to know,
The great deliverance by her seed to come   190
(For by the Woman's Seed) on all mankind.
That ye may live, which will be many days,
Both in one faith unanimous though sad,
With cause for evils past, yet much more cheered
With meditation on the happy end."

————————◆————————

---

[11]Comforted, refreshed.
[12]Crime, deed.

[13]Await their marching orders.
[14]Departure.

The London of Christopher Wren

London at the time of Donne and Milton was a city of vast extremes. England's commercial activities in India and the Americas made London a center for stock exchanges, insurance firms, and joint-stock companies. Amongst the wealthy Londoners, a great number of people remained poor. While one-fourth of London's inhabitants (among a population of a quarter of a million people) could neither read nor write, intellectuals advanced scientific learning. For some time Londoners enjoyed some of the finest libraries and theaters in Western Europe, but, under the Puritan-dominated Parliament of the 1640s, stage plays were suppressed, and many old theaters, including Shakespeare's Globe, were torn down. The restoration of the monarchy in 1660 brought with it a revived interest in drama and in the construction of indoor theaters (as opposed to the open-air theaters of Shakespeare's time).

In 1666, a devastating fire tore through London and destroyed three-fourths of the city, including thirteen thousand homes, eighty-seven parish churches, and the cathedral church of Saint Paul's, where John Donne had served as dean some decades earlier. Following the fire, there was an upsurge of large-scale building activity and a general effort to modernize London. The architect Christoper Wren (1632–1723) played a leading role in this effort. A child prodigy in mathematics, an experimental scientist, and professor of astronomy at London and Oxford, Wren was one of the founding fathers of the Royal Society of London for Improving Natural Knowledge. Following the Great Fire, Wren prepared designs for the reconstruction of London. Although his plans for new city streets (based on Rome) were rejected, he was commissioned to rebuild more than fifty churches, including Saint Paul's—the first church in Christendom to be completed in the lifetime of its architect. Wren's early designs for Saint Paul's featured the Greek cross plan that Michelangelo had proposed for Saint Peter's in Rome (see chapter 17). However, the clergy of Saint Paul's preferred a Latin cross structure. The final church was a compromise that combined classical, Gothic, Renaissance, and baroque architectural features. Saint Paul's dramatic two-story facade, with its ornate twin clock towers and its strong surface contrasts of light and dark (see Figure 21.2), looks back to Borromini (see Figure 20.18), but its massive scale and overall design—a large dome set upon a Latin cross basilica—are reminiscent of Saint Peter's (see Figure 20.13). As at Saint Peter's, Wren's dome, which physically resembles Bramante's

Figure 21.3 Cross-section of Saint Paul's showing Wren's three domes.

Tempietto (see chapter 17), is equal in its diameter to the combined width of the nave and side aisles. And the dimensions of Saint Paul's are colossal: 366 feet from ground level to the top of the lantern cross (Saint Peter's reaches 405 feet).

Wren envisioned a dome that was both impressive from the outside and easily visible from the inside. He came up with an inventive and complex device: Two domes, one exterior (made of timber covered with lead) and the other interior (made of light brick), are supported by a third, cone-shaped, middle dome, which is hidden between the other two (Figure **21.3**). The monumental silhouette of Wren's exterior dome, some 102 feet in diameter, remains an impressive presence on the London skyline. From within the church, there is the equally impressive illusionism of the *trompe l'oeil* heavens painted on the inner surface of the central cupola. Like Milton's *Paradise Lost*, Wren's Saint Paul's is a majestic synthesis of classical and Christian traditions, while its huge size, dramatic exterior, and light-filled interior are baroque in conception and effect.

Rembrandt and Protestant Devotionalism

In the Netherlands, developments in painting rivaled those in English architecture. Among the great artists of the Protestant North, Rembrandt van Rijn (1606–1669) stands out as a man of towering stature and talent. His contribution to the humanistic tradition is better understood in the context of his time and place.

Since 1560, when Spain had invaded the Dutch Lowlands, the seventeen provinces of the Netherlands had been engaged in a bitter struggle against the Catholic forces of the Spanish king Philip II. In 1579, after years of bloodshed, the Dutch forced Philip's armies to withdraw. In 1581, the seven hearty provinces of the North Netherlands declared their independence. By the end of the century the predominantly Calvinist Dutch Republic (also called "Holland") was a self-

Figure 21.4 Rembrandt van Rijn, *The Return of the Prodigal Son*, ca. 1662–1668. Oil on canvas, 8 ft. 8 in. × 6 ft. 8 in. Hermitage Museum, Saint Petersburg. Bridgeman Art Library, London.

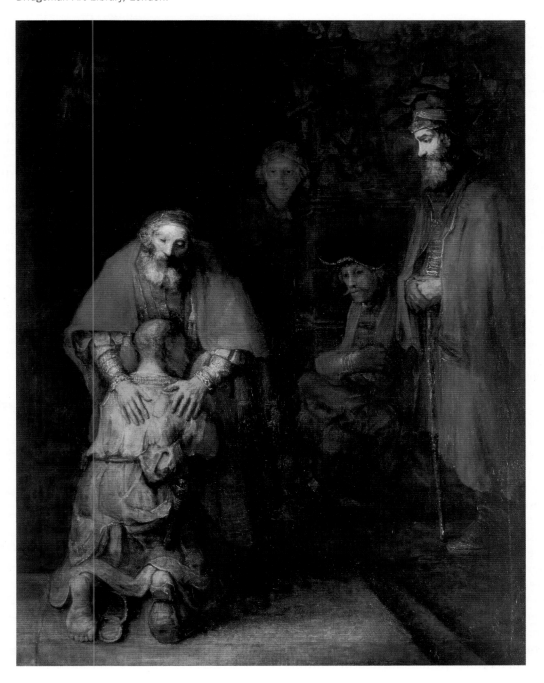

governing state and one of the most commercially active territories in Western Europe. Dutch shipbuilders produced some of the finest trading vessels on the high seas, while skilled Dutch seamen brought those vessels to all parts of the world. In Amsterdam, as in hundreds of other Dutch towns, merchants and craftspeople shared the responsibilities of local government, profiting handsomely from the smooth-running, primarily maritime economy.

The autonomous towns of the North Netherlands, many of which supported fine universities, fostered freedom of thought and a high rate of literacy. Hardworking, thrifty, and independent minded, the seventeenth-century Dutch enjoyed a degree of independence and material prosperity unmatched elsewhere in the world. Their proletarian tastes, along with a profound appreciation for the physical comforts of home and hearth, inspired their calls for such secular subjects as portraits, still lifes, landscapes, and scenes of domestic life (see chapter 22). While the arts in Italy reflected the Mediterranean love for outdoor display, in the North, where a harsher climate prevailed, artistic expression centered on the domestic interior. And, in the North, where the remains of ancient Greece and Rome were fewer, the classical heritage figured less visibly in the arts.

Since Calvinism strongly discouraged the use of religious icons, sculpture was uncommon in the Protestant North. But paintings, especially those with scriptural subjects, were favored sources of seventeenth-century moral knowledge and instruction. The Old Testament was especially popular among the Dutch, who viewed themselves God's "chosen" people, elected to triumph over Spain. In this milieu emerged Amsterdam's leading painter, Rembrandt van Rijn. The Leyden-born Rembrandt rose to fame as a painter of biblical subjects that were uncommon in Catholic art. His moving representation of *The Return of the Prodigal Son* (Figure **21.4**), for instance, shows the moment when the wayward son in Jesus' parable returns home in rags and, humbly kneeling before his father, receives forgiveness (Luke 15.11–32). The figures of father and son, bathed in golden light, form an off-center triangle balanced by the sharply lit vertical figure to the right. The composition is thus "open" and asymmetrical, rather than "closed" and symmetrical in the manner of High Renaissance art (see chapter 17). As if to symbolize spiritual revelation itself, Rembrandt "pulls" figures out of the shadowy depths of the background. His rich contrasts between bright **impasto** areas (produced by building up thick layers of paint) and dark, brooding passages work to increase the dramatic impact of the composition. Rembrandt learned much about theatrical staging from Caravaggio, but, in his simpler, more restrained compositions, Rembrandt reaches further

below surface appearances to explore the psychological depths of his subjects.

Rembrandt's unidealized treatment of sacred subject matter belonged to a long tradition of Northern European religious devotionalism (see chapter 15), but his sympathetic depiction of the poor and the persecuted was uniquely Protestant. His Anabaptist upbringing, with its fundamentalist approach to Scripture and its solemn attention to the role of individual conscience in daily life, surely contributed to Rembrandt's preference for portraying biblical subjects in literal, human terms. The people of the streets provided him with a cast of characters, and his Bible narratives abound with the faces of Spanish and Jewish refugees, whom he regularly sketched in the ghettos of Amsterdam.

Rembrandt's technical virtuosity as a draftsman made him more famous in his own time as a printmaker than as a painter. Like the woodcuts and engravings of his Northern Renaissance predecessors Dürer and Holbein (see chapter 18), Rembrandt's **etchings** met the demands of middle-class patrons who sought private devotional images that—by comparison with paintings—were inexpensive. A consummate printmaker, Rembrandt used the **burin** (a steel cutting tool) to

Figure 21.5 Etching is an intaglio printing process. A metal plate is coated with resin (*a*) then images are scratched through the coating with a burin, or graver (*b*). Acid is applied, which "eats" or etches the metal exposed by the scratches (*c*). The resin is then removed and ink is rubbed into the etched lines on the metal plate (*d*). After the plate is wiped clean, it is pressed onto paper and the ink-filled lines are deposited on the paper surface. Other intaglio processes include engraving and aquatint. From Richard Phipps and Richard Wink, *Invitation to the Gallery.* Copyright © 1987 Wm. C. Brown Publishers, Dubuque, Iowa. All rights reserved. Reprinted by permission.

(a)

(b)

(c)

(d)

Figure 21.6 (above) Rembrandt van Rijn, *Christ Preaching* ("The Hundred-Guilder Print"), ca. 1648–1650. Etching, 11 x 15½ in. Rijksmuseum, Amsterdam.

develop dramatic contrasts of rich darks and emphatic lights (Figure **21.5**). *Christ Preaching* (Figure **21.6**)—also known as "The Hundred-Guilder Print," because it sold for one hundred Dutch guilders in a seventeenth-century auction—illustrates parts of the Gospel of Matthew. In the etching, Rembrandt depicts Jesus addressing the members of the Jewish community: the sick and the lame (foreground), "the little children" (middle left), the ill and infirm (right), and an assembly of Pharisees (far left). With an extraordinary economy of line—no more than a few deft strokes of the pen—the artist brings to life the woes of the poor, the down-trodden, and the aged (Figure **21.7**). So colloquial is Rembrandt's handling of the biblical story that it seems an event that might have taken place in Rembrandt's time and place, or in ours.

Figure **21.7** Rembrandt van Rijn, detail of *Christ Preaching* ("The Hundred-Guilder Print"), 1648–1650. Etching. The Metropolitan Museum of Art, New York. Bequest of Mrs. H. O. Havemeyer, 1929. The H. O. Havemeyer Collection (29.107.35).

The Music of the Protestant North
Handel and the English Oratorio

In the same way that the Protestant North produced memorable works of religious literature and art, it also generated great works of music. The careers of two extraordinary German composers, George Frederick Handel (1685–1756) and Johann Sebastian Bach (1685–1750), represent the culmination of the baroque style in Northern European music.

Born in the Lutheran trading city of Halle, Germany, George Frederick Handel was determined to pursue his childhood musical talents. When his father, who intended for him a career in law, refused to provide him with a musical instrument, he smuggled a small clavichord into the attic. After proving himself at the keyboard and as a successful violinist and composer in the courts of Hamburg, Rome, Paris, Naples, and Venice, he migrated to London in 1710 and became an English citizen in 1726. Like many of his contemporaries, Handel began his career as a student of Italian opera. He composed forty-six operas in Italian and four in his native German. He also produced a prodigious number of instrumental works. But it was for his development of the **oratorio** that he earned fame among the English, who called him "England's greatest composer."

An oratorio is the musical setting of a long text that is performed in concert by a narrator, soloists, chorus, and orchestra (Figure 21.8). Like operas, oratorios are large in scale and dramatic in intent but, unlike opera, they are performed without scenery, costumes, or dramatic action. Soloists and chorus assume the roles of the main characters in the narrative. The word "oratorio" refers to a church chapel, and most oratorios were religious in content; however, they were never intended for church services. Rather, they were performed in public concert halls. With the oratorio came the shift from music written and performed for church or court

Figure 21.8 Performance of an oratorio; Handel (far right) is conducting. Woodcut. Fotomas Index, London.

to music composed for concert halls (or opera houses) and enjoyed by the general public. Appropriately, in the late seventeenth century, public concerts (and entrance fees) made their first appearance in the social history of music.

In his lifetime, Handel composed more than thirty oratorios. Like Rembrandt and Milton (whose verses he borrowed for the oratorio *Samson*), Handel brought Scripture to life. The most famous of Handel's oratorios is *Messiah*, which was written in the English of the King James Bible. Composed, remarkably enough, in twenty-four days, it was performed for the first time in Dublin in 1742. It received instant acclaim. One of the most moving pieces of choral music ever written, *Messiah* celebrates the birth, death, and resurrection of Jesus. Unlike most of Handel's oratorios, *Messiah* is not a biblical dramatization but rather a collection of verses from the Old and New Testaments. The first part of the piece recounts Old Testament prophecies of a Savior, the second relates the suffering and death of Jesus, and the third rejoices in the redemption of humankind through Christ's resurrection.

Messiah is typical of the baroque sensibility: Indeed, the epic proportions of its score and libretto call to mind Milton's *Paradise Lost*. It is also baroque in its style, which features vigorous contrasts of tempo and dynamics and dramatic interaction between participating ensembles—solo voices, chorus, and instruments. A master of theatrical effects, Handel employed word painting and other affective devices throughout the piece. For example, the music for the last words of the sentence, "All we, like sheep, have gone astray," consists of deliberately divergent melodic lines. The best-loved choral work in the English language, *Messiah* has outlasted its age. Indeed, in many Christian communities, it has become traditional to perform Handel's *Messiah* during both the Christmas and Easter seasons. The jubilant "Hallelujah Chorus"♮ (which ends the second of the three parts of the oratorio) still brings audiences to their feet, as it did King George II of England, who introduced this tradition by rising from his seat when he first heard it performed in London in 1743.

Handel's *Messiah* features polyphonic textures at the start of many of the choruses, such as the "For unto us, a Child is born." Nevertheless, like Handel's other oratorios, much of *Messiah* is essentially **homophonic**; that is, its musical organization depends on the use of a dominant melody supported by chordal accompaniment. The homophonic organization of melody and chords differed dramatically from the uninterrupted polyphonic interweaving of voices that characterized most music prior to the seventeenth century. The

Figure 21.9 Elias Gottlob Haussman, *Johann Sebastian Bach*, 1746. Oil on canvas. William H. Scheide Library, Princeton University.

chords in a homophonic composition serve to support—or, in the visual sense, to "spotlight"—a primary melody. In the seventeenth century, there evolved a form of musical shorthand that allowed musicians to fill in the harmony for a principal melody. The **figured bass**, as this shorthand was called, consisted of a line of music with numbers written below it to indicate the harmony accompanying the primary melody. The use of the figured bass (also called the "continuo," since it played throughout the duration of the piece) was one of the main features of baroque music.

Bach and Religious Music

Johann Sebastian Bach (Figure **21.9**) was born in the small town of Eisenach, very near the castle in which Martin Luther—hiding from the wrath of the Roman papacy—had first translated the Bible into German. Unlike the cosmopolitan Handel, Bach never strayed more than a couple of hundred miles from his birthplace. Nor did he depart from his Protestant roots: Luther's teachings and Lutheran hymn tunes were Bach's major sources of religious inspiration, and the organ—the principal instrument of Protestant church music—was one of his favorite instruments. The Germans were the masters of the organ at this period, and

♮See Music Listening Selections at end of chapter.

Figure 21.10 Joseph Gabler, organ in the Benedictine Abbey Church, Ochsenhausen, Germany, 1729–1733. © 1984, Office du Livre, S.A.

Bach was acknowledged to be the finest of organ virtuosi. He even served as a consultant in the construction of baroque organs, whose ornately embellished casings made them the glory of many Protestant churches (Figure **21.10**). As organ master and choir director of the Lutheran Church of Saint Thomas in Leipzig, Bach assumed the responsibility of composing music for each of the Sunday services and for holy days. A pious Lutheran, who, in the course of two marriages, fathered twenty children (five of whom became notable musicians), Bach humbly dedicated his compositions "to the glory of God."

Bach's religious vocal music included such forms as the oratorio, the Mass, and the **cantata.** The cantata is a multimovement work with a text in verse sung by chorus and soloists and accompanied by a musical instrument or instruments. Like the oratorio, the cantata may be sacred or secular in subject matter and lyric or dramatic in style. Bach composed cantatas as musical commentaries on the daily scriptural lessons of the Lutheran church service. Extraordinary in their florid counterpoint, Bach's 195 surviving cantatas were usually inspired by the simple melodies of Lutheran chorales. Cantata No. 80♯ is based on Luther's

---
♯See Music Listening Selections at end of chapter.

"A Mighty Fortress is Our God," the most important hymn of the Lutheran church (see chapter 18). Bach used Protestant chorales, with their regular rhythms and rugged melodies, not only for his cantatas but as the basis for many of his instrumental compositions (see chapter 22), including the 170 organ **preludes** that he composed to precede and set the mood for congregational singing.

At the apex of Bach's achievement in vocal music is the *Passion According to Saint Matthew*, an oratorio written for the Good Friday service at the Church of Saint Thomas in Leipzig. This majestic piece of religious music consists of the sung texts of chapters 26 and 27 of Matthew's Gospel, which describe Christ's Passion: the events between the Last Supper and the Resurrection. The biblical verses alternate with narrative commentary from a text written by a local German poet. Bach's combination of Bible and moral commentary dramatize Scripture with eloquence and expressive power.

The *Passion According to Saint Matthew* is written for a double chorus whose members take the parts of the disciples, the Pharisees, and other characters in the biblical account. The chorus alternates with soloists (representing Matthew, Jesus, Judas, and others) who sing the arias and recitatives. Two orchestras accompany the voices. The three-and-a-half-hour-long piece consists of two parts, the first originally to be sung before the Vespers sermon and the second after it. In Bach's time, the church congregation participated in the performance of the choral portions, thus adding to the sheer volume of sound produced by choirs and orchestras. Performed today in the church or in the concert hall, Bach's oratorio still conveys the devotional spirit of the Protestant North. In its imaginative use of Scripture, as well as in its vivid tonal color and dramatic force, the *Passion According to Saint Matthew* compares with the best of Rembrandt's Bible narratives, Handel's *Messiah*, and Milton's *Paradise Lost*.

SUMMARY

In seventeenth-century Northern Europe, a unique set of circumstances shaped the progress of the baroque style. These circumstances featured the dominance of Protestantism, with its strong scriptural and devotional emphasis, rising commercialism, and—especially in England and Holland—passionate antiauthoritarian efforts to sustain personal rights and political liberties. The study of sacred Scripture was central to the ideals of Pietism and Protestant belief. Consequently, Northern baroque artistic expression turned inward to the personal and subjective, rather than outward to spectacular forms of religious display.

In the literary domain, the King James translation of the Bible brought the English language to new heights of eloquence. The Anglican John Donne and the Puritan John Milton produced poetry that reflected Protestant perspectives of morality, evil, and death. Donne's metaphysical poetry featured ingenious conceits and paradoxes. Milton's *Paradise Lost*, the last great epic poem in Western literature, recast the heritage of the Hebrew Bible according to Puritan views of sin and salvation. The poem's cosmic scope, colossal proportions, and majestic language exemplify the baroque spirit in the Protestant North.

The religious works of the Dutch master Rembrandt van Rijn present a visual parallel to these literary landmarks. Rembrandt illustrated the contents of Holy Scripture in paintings, drawings, and etchings that were at once realistic, theatrical, and psychologically profound. With bold compositions and an inventive use of light, he described sacred events as though they had occurred in his own time and place.

The genius of Rembrandt was matched in music by the German masters Johann Sebastian Bach and George Frederick Handel. Handel dramatized scriptural narrative by means of the oratorio, a new musical form that typified the baroque taste for rich color and dramatic effect. Handel's *Messiah*, an early landmark in homophonic composition, remains one of the most stirring examples of baroque music. Handel's Lutheran contemporary, Johann Sebastian Bach, dedicated much of his life to composing music that honored God. His cantatas and his preludes employ melodies borrowed largely from Lutheran hymns. In the *Passion According to Saint Matthew*, Bach brought polyphonic choral music to new heights of dramatic grandeur. Like Milton's *Paradise Lost* and the paintings of Rembrandt, Bach's music invested Protestant Christianity with a sublime and deeply personal sense of human tragedy. In all, the contributions of Milton, Rembrandt, Handel, and Bach constitute the crowning achievements of the baroque style in the Protestant North.

GLOSSARY

burin a steel tool used for engraving and incising

cantata (Italian, *cantare* = "to sing") a multimovement composition for voices and instrumental accompaniment; smaller in scale than the *oratorio*

etching a kind of engraving in which a metal plate is covered with resin, then incised with a *burin*; acid is applied to "eat" away the exposed lines, which are inked before the plate is wiped clean and printed; see Figure 21.5

figured bass in baroque music, the line of music with numbers written below (or above) it to indicate the required harmonies, usually improvised in the form of keyboard chords accompanying the melody; also called "continuo"

homophony a musical texture consisting of a dominant melody supported by chordal accompaniment that is far less important than the melody; compare monophony (see Glossary, chapter 6) and polyphony (see Glossary, chapter 13)

impasto a style in painting in which the paint is applied thickly or heavily

oratorio (Latin, *oratorium* = "church chapel") a musical setting of a long text, either religious or secular, for soloists, chorus, narrator, and orchestra; usually performed without scenery, costumes, or dramatic action

prelude a piece of instrumental music that introduces either a church service or another piece of music; see also Glossary, chapter 29

SUGGESTIONS FOR READING

Arnold, Denis. *Bach.* New York: Oxford University Press, 1984.
Bukofzer, Manfred. *Music in the Baroque Era.* New York: Norton, 1947.
Clark, Kenneth. *An Introduction to Rembrandt.* New York: Harper, 1978.
Kahr, Madlyn M. *Dutch Painting in the Seventeenth Century.* New York: Harper, 1978.
Palisca, C. V. *Baroque Music*, 3rd ed. Englewood Cliffs, N.J.: Prentice-Hall, 1991.
Price, J. L. *Culture and Society in the Dutch Republic during the Seventeenth Century.* New York: Scribners, 1974.
Schama, Simon. *An Embarrassment of Riches: An Interpretation of Dutch Art.* New York: Knopf, 1987.
Schwendowius, Barbara, and Wolfgang Dömling, eds. *Johann Sebastian Bach: Life, Times, Influence.* Basel: Bärenreiter Kassel, 1977.
Wallace, Robert. *The World of Rembrandt 1606–1669.* Library of Art Series. New York: Time-Life Books, 1968.

MUSIC LISTENING SELECTIONS

Cassette II Selection 3 Handel, *Messiah*, "Hallelujah Chorus," 1742.
Cassette II Selection 4 Bach, Cantata No. 80, "Ein feste Burg ist unser Gott" ("A Mighty Fortress is Our God"), Chorale, 1724.

22
The Scientific Revolution and the New Learning

While the seventeenth century was a period of religious turbulence and heightened spirituality, it was also an age of scientific discovery and development. The Scientific Revolution that occurred in Europe between approximately 1600 and 1750 was not entirely sudden, nor were its foundations exclusively European. It owed much to a long history of science and technology that reached back to ancient Egypt, China, and Islam, to the construction of pyramids and cathedrals, the formulation of Euclidean geometry, and the invention of the windmill, the magnetic compass, and the printing press. As Renaissance artist-scientists diligently investigated the visible world, the will to control nature by means of practical knowledge gained impetus in the West. Following the pioneering efforts of Leonardo da Vinci, the Flemish physician Andreas Vesalius (1514–1574) dissected cadavers to make an accurate record of the human anatomy. The Swiss alchemist Philippus Ambrosius Paracelsus (1493–1541) compounded medical remedies from minerals rather than from the older, botanical substances. And the Polish humanist, physician, and astronomer Nicolas Copernicus (1473–1543) opposed the traditional **geocentric** (earth-centered) explanation of the cosmos with the **heliocentric** (sun-centered) theory according to which the earth and all the other planets circle around the sun.

The Scientific Revolution

Those who launched the Scientific Revolution differed from their Asian and European predecessors in effectively combining the tools of mathematics and experimentation. They invented new instruments with which to measure more precisely natural phenomena, to test scientific hypotheses, and to predict the operations of nature (Figure 22.1). They also differed from their predecessors in asserting that *scientia* (the Latin word for "knowledge") existed separate and apart from divine power and authority. If medieval intellectuals viewed the universe as the extension of an absolute and eternal God, modern scientists regarded it as a mechanism that operated according to its own laws. Modern scientists took nature out of the hands of poets and priests and put it inside the laboratory.

Kepler and Galileo

Even before the second century C.E., when the Greek geographer Ptolemy published his theory of a geometric universe, learned individuals regarded the earth as fixed in space and spherical in shape. They envisioned the earth at the center of a series of endlessly turning crystalline spheres, one for each of the celestial bodies: the Moon, Mercury, Venus, the Sun, Mars, Jupiter, and Saturn—a cosmology enshrined in Dante's *Divine Comedy* (see chapter 12). According to Aristotle, movement in nature was the work of a *prime mover* or, in the later, Christian view, of some supernatural force. During the one hundred years following the publication of Copernicus' treatise *On the Revolution of the Heavenly Spheres* in 1543, these earlier theories came under scrutiny. Early in the seventeenth century, the German mathematician Johannes Kepler (1571–1630) made detailed records of the planets' movements which substantiated the heliocentric theory. Challenging the conventional assumption that the planetary orbits had

1608 the telescope is invented in Holland; in Italy, Galileo improves the design to provide three-power magnification

1610 Johannes Kepler perfects the compound microscope

1619 William Harvey accurately describes the circulation of the blood

Figure 22.1 Jan Vermeer, *The Geographer*, ca. 1668. Oil on canvas, 20⅞ × 18¼ in. Städelsches Kunstinstitut, Frankfurt. Courtesy Blauel/Gramm—ARTOTHEK, Peissenberg.

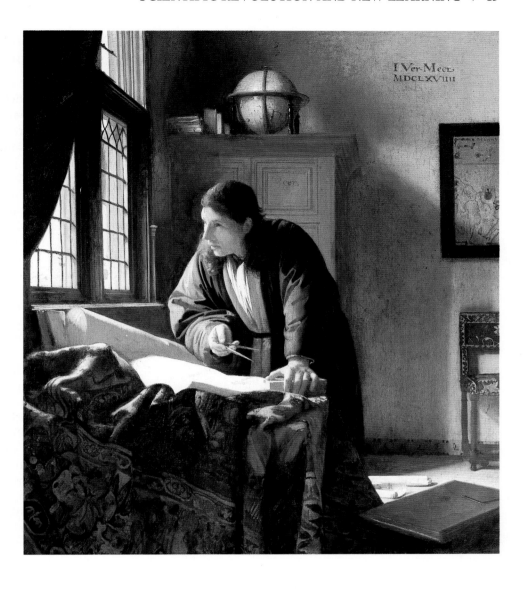

to be perfectly circular, Kepler also showed that the five known planets moved around the sun in elliptical paths. He argued that the magnetic force emitted by the sun determined the movements of the planets and their distances from the sun. Kepler's new physics, which advanced the idea of a universe in motion, contradicted the Aristotelian notion of a fixed and unchanging cosmos. It also stood in opposition to the Bible—where, for example, the Hebrew hero Joshua is described as making the sun stand still, a miraculous event that could have occurred only if the sun normally moved around the earth. Although Catholics and Protestants were at odds on many theological matters, in defending the inviolable truth of Scripture against the claims of the new science, they were one.

In Italy, Kepler's contemporary Galileo Galilei (1564–1642) was experimenting with matters of terrestrial motion. His assertions concerning motion and gravity stood contrary to long-held opinions based on Aristotle. Whether or not Galileo actually dropped different-sized weights from the top of the leaning Tower of Pisa—as legend has it—in an effort to determine rates of speed relative to mass, the Florentine astronomer formulated the *law of falling bodies*, which proclaimed that the earth's gravity attracts all objects—regardless of shape, size, or density—at the same rate of acceleration. In 1608, shortly after the publication of this theorem, a Dutch lensmaker invented an instrument that magnified objects seen at a great distance. Perfected by Galileo, the telescope literally revealed new worlds. Through its lens, one could see the craters of the moon, the rings of Saturn, and the moons of Jupiter, which, Galileo observed, operated exactly like earth's moon. The telescope turned the heliocentric theory into fact.

Galileo's discoveries immediately aroused opposition from Catholics and Protestants committed to maintaining orthodox Christian beliefs, especially as set forth in Scripture. Not only did the theory of a heliocentric universe contradict God's word and challenge the Christian concept of a stable and finite universe, it also deprived human beings of their central place in that universe. The heliocentric theory made humanity seem incidental to God's plan and the heavens seem material and "corruptible." Such an idea did not go unchallenged. The first institutional attack on "the new science" had occurred in 1600, when the Catholic Inquisition tried, condemned, and publicly executed the Italian astronomer Giordano Bruno, who had asserted that the universe was infinite and without center. Bruno had also suggested that other solar systems might exist in space. Sixteen years after Bruno was burned at the stake, Copernicus' writings were put on the Catholic Index of Forbidden Books. Galileo added to the controversy by making his own findings public; and more so because he wrote in the everyday Italian rather than in Latin, the traditional language of Western authority.

More inflammatory still in the eyes of the Church was the publication of Galileo's *Dialogue Concerning the Two Principal Systems of the World* (1632), a fictional conversation between a Copernican and the defenders of the old order, one of whom resembled the pope. Earlier in his career, when it had become evident that his gravitational theories contradicted Aristotle, Galileo had been forced to give up his position as mathematics professor at the University of Pisa. Now he was brought before the Inquisition and, after a long and unpleasant trial, Church officials, threatening torture, forced the aging astronomer to "admit his errors." Legend has it that after publicly denying that the earth moved around the sun, he muttered under his breath, "Eppur si muove" ("But it *does* move!"). Though condemned to indefinite imprisonment, Galileo was permitted to reside—under "house arrest"—in a villa outside of Florence.

Despite unrelenting Church opposition, scientists pressed on to devise new instruments for measurement and new procedures for experimentation and analysis. The slide rule, the magnet, the microscope, the mercury barometer, and the air pump were among the many products of the European quest to calculate, investigate, predict, and ultimately master nature. Seventeenth-century Western scientists investigated the workings of the human eye and explored the genesis and propagation of light, thus advancing the science of optics beyond the frontiers of Islamic and Renaissance scholarship. They accurately described the action of gases and the circulation of the blood. And they devised the branches of higher mathematics known as coordinate geometry, trigonometry, and infinitesimal calculus, by means of which modern scientists might analyze the phenomena of space and motion.

The New Learning
Bacon and the Empirical Method

One of the most characteristic features of the Scientific Revolution was its glorification of the empirical method, a manner of inquiry that depended on direct observation and experimentation. Natural phenomena, argued seventeenth-century scientists, provided evidence from which one might draw general conclusions or axioms, according to a process known as **inductive reasoning**. The leading spokesman for the new learning was the English scientist and politician Francis Bacon (1561–1626). In 1620, Bacon published his *Novum Organum* ("New Method"), an impassioned plea for objectivity and clear thinking and the strongest defense of the empirical method ever written. "Man, being the servant and interpreter of Nature," wrote Bacon, "can do and understand so much and so much only as he has observed in fact or in thought of the course of Nature: beyond this he neither knows anything nor can do anything."

Bacon argued that human beings must be aided by science and scientific study guided by precise methods. He promoted an objective system of experimentation, tabulation, and record keeping that became the touchstone of modern scientific inquiry. In an era dominated by fervent spirituality, he demanded a separation of religion and science. "In every age," observed Bacon, "Natural Philosophy has had a troublesome adversary . . . namely, superstition, and the blind and immoderate zeal of religion." Unlike earlier humanists, Bacon turned his back on Aristotle and classical science. A prophet of the new learning, he sought to eliminate errors in reasoning derived from blind adherence to traditional sources of authority and religious belief. He condemned all obstacles to the progress of science and championed the idea that knowledge was the most powerful tool for material achievement. In advancing his strategy for the acquisition of knowledge, Bacon warned against four "false notions," or Idols, which, as the following excerpts from his *Novum Organum* illustrate, he condemned as hindrances to clear and objective thinking.

READING 4.8

From Bacon's *Novum Organum*

36

One method of delivery alone remains to us; which is simply this: we must lead men to the particulars themselves, and their series and order; while men on their side must force themselves for a while to lay their notions by and begin to familiarize themselves with facts.

The idols and false notions which are now in possession of the human understanding, and have taken deep root therein, not only so beset men's minds that truth can hardly find entrance, but even after entrance obtained, they will again in the very instauration[1] of the sciences meet and trouble us, unless men being forewarned of danger fortify themselves as far as may be against their assaults.

39

There are four classes of Idols which beset men's minds. To these for distinction's sake I have assigned names,—calling the first class *Idols of the Tribe*; the second, *Idols of the Cave*; the third, *Idols of the Marketplace*; the fourth, *Idols of the Theatre*.

41

The Idols of the Tribe have their foundation in human nature itself, and in the tribe or race of men. For it is a false assertion that the sense of man is the measure of things. On the contrary, all perceptions as well of the sense as of the mind are according to the measure of the individual and not according to the measure of the universe. And the human understanding is like a false mirror, which, receiving rays irregularly, distorts and discolors the nature of things by mingling its own nature with it.

42

The Idols of the Cave are the idols of the individual man. For every one (besides the errors common to human nature in general) has a cave or den of his own, which refracts and discolors the light of nature; owing either to his own proper and peculiar nature; or to his education and conversation with others; or to the reading of books, and the authority of those whom he esteems and admires; or to the differences of impressions, accordingly as they take place in a mind preoccupied and predisposed or in a mind indifferent and settled; or the like. So that the spirit of man (according as it is meted out to different individuals) is in fact a thing variable and full of perturbation, and governed as it were by chance. Whence it was well observed by Heraclitus[2] that men look for sciences in their own lesser worlds, and not in the greater or common world.

43

There are also Idols formed by the intercourse and association of men with each other, which I call Idols of the Marketplace, on account of the commerce and consort of men there. For it is by discourse that men associate; and words are imposed according to the apprehension of the vulgar. And therefore the ill and unfit choice of words wonderfully obstructs the understanding. Nor do the definitions or explanations wherewith in some things learned men are wont to guard and defend themselves, by any means set the matter right. But words plainly force and overrule the understanding, and throw all into confusion, and lead men away into numberless empty controversies and idle fancies.

44

Lastly, there are Idols which have immigrated into men's minds from the various dogmas of philosophies, and also from wrong laws of demonstration. These I call Idols of the Theatre; because in my judgment all the received systems are but so many stage-plays, representing worlds of their own creation after an unreal and scenic fashion. Nor is it only of the systems now in vogue, or only of the ancient sects and philosophies, that I speak; for many more plays of the same

kind may yet be composed and in like artificial manner set forth; seeing that errors the most widely different have nevertheless causes for the most part alike. Neither again do I mean this only of entire systems, but also of many principles and axioms in science, which by tradition, credulity, and negligence have come to be received.

———————◆———————

Bacon observes that every culture and every age has "worshiped" the Idols. In describing the fallacies that have their foundations in human nature (*Idols of the Tribe*), he points to the fact that human understanding is self-reflective; it functions like a "false mirror," distorting universal truth. Privately held fallacies (*Idols of the Cave*), on the other hand, derive from individual educations and backgrounds. An individual may assert, for instance, that one or another religion is "the true faith," that certain racial or ethnic groups are superior to others, or that women should be judged by a different set of standards than those applied to men. The errors resulting from human association and communication, the *Idols of the Marketplace*, arise, according to Bacon, from an "ill or unfit choice of words." To offer a modern-day example: The use of the noun "mankind" to designate all human beings and the pronouns "she" and "her" to refer to countries and nation-states may work to cultivate a sexist bias in thinking about human history. Finally, Bacon attacks the *Idols of the Theatre*—false dogmas perpetuated by philosophies and institutions in antiquity and in his own time, as well as those that "may yet be composed." It seems likely that Bacon would have regarded the modern doctrines of "divine right monarchy" (see chapter 24) and "separate but equal education" as examples of this category of Idols.

Bacon's clarion call for intellectual objectivity and experimentation inspired the founding in 1645 of the Royal Society of London for Improving Natural Knowledge. The first of many such European and American societies for scientific advancement, the Royal Society has attracted, over the centuries, thousands of members. Their achievements have confirmed one nineteenth-century historian's assessment of Bacon as "the man that moved the minds that moved the world."

While Bacon wrote his scientific treatises in Latin, he used English for essays designed to instruct the average reader. In *The Advancement of Learning* (1605), a sketch of his key ideas concerning methods for acquiring and classifying knowledge, and in the essay *Of Studies*, Bacon demonstrated the masterful use of prose as a tool for theorizing. Written in the poetic prose of the early seventeenth century, *Of Studies* describes the ways in which books serve the individual and society at large. In the excerpt that follows, Bacon eloquently defends reading as a source of pleasure, but, equally important, as a source of practical knowledge and power.

---

[1]Reorganization or renewal.
[2]A Greek philosopher of ca. 500 B.C.E., who taught that all of nature was in a state of flux.

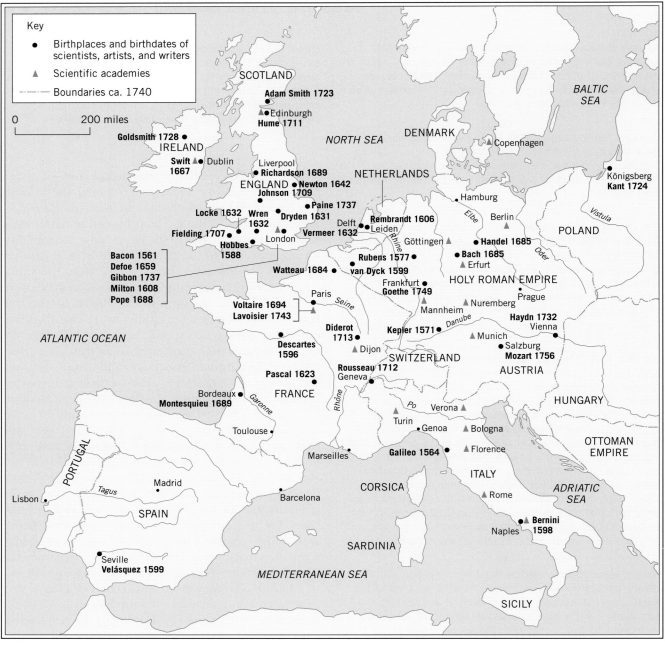

Map 22.1 The Intellectual Revolution of the Seventeenth and Eighteenth Centuries in Western Europe.

READING 4.9

From Bacon's *Of Studies*

Studies serve for delight, for ornament, and for ability. Their chief use for delight is in privateness and retiring; for ornament, is in discourse; and for ability, is in the judgment and disposition of business. For expert men can execute, and perhaps judge of particulars, one by one; but the general counsels and the plots and marshalling of affairs come best from those that are learned. To spend too much time in studies is sloth; to use them too much for ornament is affectation; to make judgment wholly by their rules is the humor of a scholar. They perfect nature, and are perfected by experience: for natural abilities are like natural plants, that need pruning by study; . . . Read

not to contradict and confute; nor to believe and take for granted; nor to find talk and discourse, but to weigh and consider. Some books are to be tasted, others to be swallowed, and some few to be chewed and digested; that is, some books are to be read only in parts; others to be read, but not curiously; and some few to be read wholly, and with diligence and attention. . . . Reading maketh a full man; conference a ready man; and writing an exact man. And therefore, if a man write little, he had need have a great memory; if he confer little, he had need have a present wit; and if he read little, he had need have much cunning, to seem to know that he does not. Histories make men wise; poets witty; mathematics subtile; natural philosophy deep; moral [philosophy] grave; logic and rhetoric able to contend. . . .

1

10

20

◆

Descartes and the Birth of Modern Philosophy

Born in France, René Descartes (1596–1650; Figure **22.2**) is regarded as the founder of modern Western philosophy and the father of analytic geometry. His writings revived the ancient Greek quest to discover how one knows what one knows, and his methods made the discipline of philosophy wholly independent of theology.

Whereas Bacon gave priority to knowledge gained through the senses, Descartes, the supreme rationalist, valued abstract reasoning and mathematical speculation. Descartes did not deny the importance of the senses in the search for truth, but he observed that our senses might deceive us. As an alternative to inductive reasoning, he championed a procedure for investigation called **deductive reasoning**. The reverse of the inductive method, the deductive process began with clearly established general premises and moved toward the establishment of particular truths. Among the rules Descartes set forth were the following: Never accept anything as true that you do not clearly know to be true; dissect a problem into as many parts as possible; reason from simple to complex knowledge; and finally, draw complete and exhaustive conclusions. In the *Discourse on the Method of Rightly Conducting the Reason and Seeking for Truth in the Sciences*, perhaps the most important of all his philosophic works, Descartes began by systematically calling everything into doubt. He then proceeded to identify the first thing that he could not doubt—his existence as a thinking individual. This one clear and distinct idea of himself as a "thinking thing," expressed in the proposition "Cogito, ergo sum" ("I think, therefore I am"), became Descartes' "first principle" and the premise for all of his major arguments.

For Descartes, the clear and unbiased mind was the source of all natural understanding. "Except [for] our own thoughts," he insisted, "there is nothing absolutely in our power." Having established rational consciousness as the only sure point of departure for knowledge, Descartes proceeded to examine the world. He made a clear distinction between physical and psychical phenomena, that is, between matter and mind, and between body and soul. According to this dualistic model, the human body operates much like a computer, with the immaterial mind (the software)

Figure 22.2 Frans Hals, *Portrait of René Descartes*, 1649. Oil on wood. 7½ × 5½ in. Royal Museum of Fine Arts, Copenhagen.

"informing" the physical components of the body (the hardware). The **Cartesian** view of the human mind as a thinking substance distinct from the human body dominated European philosophic thought until the end of the nineteenth century and still has some strong adherents today.

READING 4.10

From Descartes' *Discourse on Method* (Part IV)

. . . . I do not know that I ought to tell you of the first   1
meditations there made by me, for they are so
metaphysical and so unusual that they may perhaps not
be acceptable to everyone. And yet at the same time, in
order that one may judge whether the foundations which I
have laid are sufficiently secure, I find myself constrained
in some measure to refer to them. For a long time I had
remarked that it is sometimes requisite in common life to
follow opinions which one knows to be most uncertain,
exactly as though they were indisputable, as has been said   10
above. But because in this case I wished to give myself
entirely to the search after Truth, I thought that it was
necessary for me to take an apparently opposite course,
and to reject as absolutely false everything as to which I
could imagine the least ground of doubt, in order to see if
afterwards there remained anything in my belief that was
entirely certain. Thus, because our senses sometimes

1626   Francis Bacon uses snow in experiments to
          refrigerate chickens
1637   René Descartes introduces analytic geometry
1656   Christian Huygens develops the first accurate
          pendulum clock
1660   Anton van Leeuwenhoek discovers microscopic
          protozoa

deceive us, I wished to suppose that nothing is just as they cause us to imagine it to be; and because there are men who deceive themselves in their reasoning and fall into paralogisms,[1] even concerning the simplest matters of geometry, and judging that I was as subject to error as was any other, I rejected as false all the reasons formerly accepted by me as demonstrations. And since all the same thoughts and conceptions which we have while awake may also come to us in sleep, without any of them being at that time true, I resolved to assume that everything that ever entered into my mind was no more true than the illusions of my dreams. But immediately afterwards I noticed that whilst I thus wished to think all things false, it was absolutely essential that the "I" who thought this should be somewhat, and remarking that this truth "*I think, therefore I am*" was so certain and so assured that all the most extravagant suppositions brought forward by the sceptics were incapable of shaking it, I came to the conclusion that I could receive it without scruple as the first principle of the Philosophy for which I was seeking.

And then, examining attentively that which I was, I saw that I could conceive that I had no body, and that there was no world nor place where I might be; but yet that I could not for all that conceive that I was not. On the contrary, I saw from the very fact that I thought of doubting the truth of other things, it very evidently and certainly followed that I was; on the other hand if I had only ceased from thinking, even if all the rest of what I had ever imagined had really existed, I should have no reason for thinking that I had existed. From that I knew that I was a substance the whole essence or nature of which is to think, and that for its existence there is no need of any place, nor does it depend on any material thing; so that this "me," that is to say, the soul by which I am what I am, is entirely distinct from body, and is even more easy to know than is the latter; and even if body were not, the soul would not cease to be what it is.

After this I considered generally what in a proposition is requisite in order to be true and certain; for since I had just discovered one which I knew to be such, I thought that I ought also to know in what this certainly consisted. And having remarked that there was nothing at all in the statement "*I think, therefore I am*" which assures me of having thereby made a true assertion, excepting that I see very clearly that to think it is necessary to be, I came to the conclusion that I might assume, as a general rule, that the things which we conceive very clearly and distinctly are all true—remembering, however, that there is some difficulty in ascertaining which are those that we distinctly conceive.

Following upon this, and reflecting on the fact that I doubted, and that consequently my existence was not quite perfect (for I saw clearly that it was a greater perfection to know than to doubt), I resolved to inquire whence I had learnt to think of anything more perfect than I myself was; and I recognised very clearly that this conception must proceed from some nature which was really more perfect. As to the thoughts which I had of many other things outside of me, like the heavens, the earth, light, heat, and a thousand others, I had not so much difficulty in knowing whence they came, because, remarking nothing in them which seemed to render them

superior to me, I could believe that, if they were true, they were dependencies upon my nature, in so far as it possessed some perfection; and if they were not true, that I held them from nought, that is to say, that they were in me because I had something lacking in my nature. But this could not apply to the idea of a Being more perfect than my own, for to hold it from nought would be manifestly impossible; and because it is no less contradictory to say of the more perfect that it is what results from and depends on the less perfect, than to say that there is something which proceeds from nothing, it was equally impossible that I should hold it from myself. In this way it could but follow that it had been placed in me by a Nature which was really more perfect than mine could be, and which even had within itself all the perfections of which I could form any idea—that is to say, to put it in a word, which was God. . . .

◆

Religion and the New Learning

The new learning, a composite of scientific method and rational inquiry, presented its own challenge to traditional religion. From "self-evident" propositions, Descartes arrived at conclusions to which empirical confirmation was irrelevant. His rationalism—like Plato's—involved a process of the mind independent of the senses. Reasoning that the concept of perfection ("something more perfect than myself") had to proceed from "some Nature which in reality was more perfect," Descartes "proved" the existence of God as Absolute Substance. Since something cannot proceed from nothing, argued Descartes, the idea of God held by human beings must come from God. Moreover, the idea of Perfection (God) embraces the idea of existence, for, if something is perfect, it must exist. Raised by Jesuits, Descartes believed in the existence of a Supreme Creator, but he shared with many seventeenth-century intellectuals the view that God was neither Caretaker nor Redeemer. Indeed, Descartes often identified God with "the mathematical order of nature." The idea that God did not interfere with the laws of humanity and nature was central to **deism**, a system of thought advocating a "natural" religion based on human reason rather than revelation. Deists purged religion of superstition, myth, and ritual. They viewed God as a master mechanic who had created the universe, then stepped aside and allowed his World-Machine to run unattended.

Unlike Bacon, Descartes did not envision any conflict between science and religion. He optimistically concluded that "all our ideas or notions contain in them some truth; for otherwise it could not be that God, who is wholly perfect and veracious, should have placed them in us." Like other deists of his time, Descartes held that to follow reason was to follow God.

In Amsterdam, a city whose reputation for freedom of thought attracted Descartes—he lived there between 1628 and 1649—the Jewish philosopher Baruch

---

[1]Fallacious arguments.

Spinoza (1632–1677) addressed the question of the new science versus the old faith. Stripping God of his traditional role as Creator (and consequently finding himself ousted from the local synagogue), Spinoza claimed that God was neither behind, nor beyond, nor separate from nature but, rather, identical with nature. Every physical thing, including human beings, was an expression of God in some variation of mind combined with matter. In a pantheistic spirit reminiscent of Hinduism and Daoism, Spinoza held that the greatest good was the union of the human mind with the whole of nature.

For the French physicist-mathematician Blaise Pascal (1623–1662), on the other hand, science and religion were irreconcilable. Having undergone a mystical experience that converted him to devout Roman Catholicism, he believed that the path to God was through the heart rather than through the head. Although reason might yield a true understanding of nature, it could in no way prove God's existence. We are capable, wrote Pascal, of "certain knowledge and of absolute ignorance." In his collected meditations on human nature, called simply *Pensées* ("Thoughts"), Pascal proposed a wager that challenged the indifference of skeptics: If God does *not* exist, skeptics lose nothing by believing in him, but if God *does* exist, they reap eternal life. The spiritual quest for purpose and value in a vast, impersonal universe moved the precision-minded Pascal—inventor of a machine that anticipated the digital calculator—to confess: "The eternal silence of these infinite spaces frightens me."

Locke and the Culmination of the Empirical Tradition

The writings of the English philosopher and physician John Locke (1632–1704) firmly defended the empirical tradition in seventeenth-century thought and provided a clearly reasoned basis for centuries of philosophic debate. Written seventy years after Bacon's *Novum Organum*, Locke's *Essay Concerning Human Understanding* (1690) confirmed his predecessor's thesis that everything one knows derives from sensory experience. According to Locke, the human mind at birth is a *tabula rasa* ("blank slate") upon which experience—consisting of sensation, followed by reflection—writes the script. No innate moral principles or ideas exist; rather, human knowledge consists of the progressive accumulation of the evidence of the senses.

The implications of Locke's principles of knowledge strongly affected European and (later) American thought and helped to shape an optimistic view of human destiny. For, if experience influenced human knowledge and behavior, argued the empiricists, then, surely, improving the social environment would work to perfect the human condition. Locke's ideas became basic to eighteenth-century liberalism, as well as to all political ideologies that held that human knowledge, if properly applied, would produce happiness for humankind (see chapter 24).

READING 4.11

From Locke's *Essay Concerning Human Understanding*

Idea is the Object of Thinking.—Every man being conscious to himself that he thinks, and that which his mind is applied about whilst thinking, being the ideas that are there, it is past doubt that men have in their minds several ideas, such as are those expressed by the words whiteness, hardness, sweetness, thinking, motion, man, elephant, army, drunkenness, and others. It is in the first place then to be inquired how he comes by them. I know it is a received doctrine that men have native ideas and original characters stamped upon their minds in their very first being. This opinion I have at large examined already; and I suppose what I have [already] said . . . will be much more easily admitted when I have shown whence the understanding may get all the ideas it has, and by what ways and degrees they may come into the mind; for which I shall appeal to every one's own observation and experience.

All Ideas come from Sensation or Reflection.—Let us then suppose the mind to be, as we say, white paper, void of all characters, without any ideas; how comes it to be furnished? Whence comes it by that vast store which the busy and boundless fancy of man has painted on it with an almost endless variety? Whence has it all the materials of reason and knowledge? To this I answer in one word, from experience; in that all our knowledge is founded, and from that it ultimately derives itself. Our observation employed either about external sensible objects, or about the internal operations of our minds, perceived and reflected on by ourselves, is that which supplies our understandings with all the materials of thinking. These two are the fountains of knowledge from whence all the ideas we have or can naturally have do spring.

The Objects of Sensation, one Source of Ideas.—First, our senses, conversant about particular sensible objects, do convey into the mind several distinct perceptions of things, according to those various ways wherein those objects do affect them: and thus we come by those ideas we have, of yellow, white, heat, cold, soft, hard, bitter, sweet, and all those which we call sensible qualities; which when I say the senses convey into the mind, I mean, they from external objects convey into the mind what produces there those perceptions. This great source of most of the ideas we have, depending wholly upon our senses, and derived by them to the understanding, I call Sensation.

The Operations of our Minds, the other Source of them.—Secondly, the other fountain, from which experience furnishes the understanding with ideas, is the perception of the operations of our own mind within us, as it is employed about the ideas it has got; which operations, when the soul comes to reflect on and consider, do furnish the understanding with another set of ideas, which could

1

10

20

30

40

50

Figure 22.3 Jan Davidsz de Heem, *Still Life with View of the Sea*, 1646. Oil on canvas, 23⅜ × 36½ in. Courtesy of the Toledo Museum of Art, Toldeo, Ohio. Purchased with funds from the Libbey Endowment. Gift of Edward Drummond Libbey.

not be had from things without; and such are perception, thinking, doubting, believing, reasoning, knowing, willing, and all the different actings of our own minds; which we being conscious of, and observing in ourselves, do from these receive into our understandings as distinct ideas, as we do from bodies affecting our senses. This source of ideas every man has wholly in himself; and though it be not sense, as having nothing to do with external objects, yet it is very like it, and might properly enough be called internal 60 sense. But as I call the other Sensation, so I call this Reflection, the ideas it affords being such only as the mind gets by reflecting on its own operations within itself. By reflection then, in the following part of this discourse, I would be understood to mean that notice which the mind takes of its own operations, and the manner of them; by reason whereof there come to be ideas of these operations in the understanding. These two, I say, *viz.*, external material things, as the objects of sensation; and the operations of our own minds within, as the objects of 70 reflection; are to me the only originals from whence all our ideas take their beginnings. . . .

All our Ideas are of the one or the other of these.— The understanding seems to me not to have the least glimmering of any ideas which it doth not receive from one of these two. External objects furnish the mind with the ideas of sensible qualities, which are all those different perceptions they produce in us; and the mind furnishes the understanding with ideas of its own operations.

These, when we have taken a full survey of them, and 80 their several modes, combinations, and relations, we shall find to contain all our whole stock of ideas; and that we have nothing in our minds, which did not come in one of these two ways. Let any one examine his own thoughts, and thoroughly search into his understanding; and then let him tell me, whether all the original ideas he has

there, are any other than of the objects of his senses, or of the operations of his mind, considered as objects of his reflection: and how great a mass of knowledge soever he imagines to be lodged there, he will, upon taking a strict 90 view, see that he has not any idea in his mind, but what one of these two have imprinted. . . .

❖

Newton's Scientific Synthesis

The work of the great English astronomer and mathematician Isaac Newton (1642–1727) represents a practical synthesis of seventeenth-century physics and mathematics and the union of the inductive and deductive methods. Newton advanced the new science from its speculative and empirical phases (represented by Copernicus and Galileo, respectively) to the stage of codification. He brought Kepler's laws of celestial mechanics and Galileo's terrestrial law of falling bodies into an all-embracing theory of universal gravitation that described every physical movement in the universe—from the operation of the tides to the effects of a planet upon its moons. In 1687 Newton published his monumental treatise on gravitation and the three laws of motion: the *Philosophiae Naturalis Principia Mathematica* ("Mathematical Principles of Natural Philosophy"). Newton's *Principia,* the fundamentals of which went unchallenged until the late nineteenth century, promoted the idea of a uniform and intelligible universe that operated as systematically as a well-oiled machine. Newton not only desanctified nature; he proved that nature's laws applied equally to terrestrial and celestial

Figure 22.4 Maria van Oosterwyck, *Vanitas Still Life*, 1668. Oil on canvas, 29 × 35 in. Kunsthistorisches Museum, Vienna.

matter. He replaced Aristotle's description of the physical world with simple mathematical equations that would become the basis of modern physics. Essentially, Newton confirmed that by means of mathematical analysis and scientific observation, enlightened individuals might comprehend and control their world more completely than had ever before been possible.

The Impact of the Scientific Revolution on Art

Northern Baroque Painting

If the new science engendered a spirit of objective inquiry in literature, it also had a profound influence on the visual arts. In the cities of seventeenth-century Holland, where Dutch lensmakers had produced the first telescopes and microscopes, there evolved a style of painting that reflected an obsessive attention to the appearance of the natural world. In still lifes, portraits, landscape, and scenes of everyday life—all secular subjects—Dutch masters practiced the "art of describing."* The almost photographic realism of such paintings as

*See Svetlana Alpers, *The Art of Describing: Dutch Art in the Seventeenth Century.* Chicago: University of Chicago Press, 1983.

Jan Davidsz de Heem's *Still Life with View of the Sea* (Figure **22.3**) is typical of the new "Baconian" attention to the natural world: Plump oysters and crabs, a succulent ham, ripe melons and peaches, a gleaming tankard are all rendered with keen precision and detail. A distant view of the sea and a storm-tossed vessel in the background of the painting are less than subtle reminders that Dutch maritime activity financed the bounties of the dinner table.

While de Heem's fruits and meats celebrate the robust pleasures of life, the objects in Maria van Oosterwyck's realistic *Still Life* of 1668—a skull, insects (the moth and the fly), a tiny mouse nibbling at some grain—make cloaked reference to the transience of earthly pleasures (Figure **22.4**). Van Oosterwyck's *Still Life* belongs to a large group of European *vanitas* paintings, the contents of which suggest the corruptibility of

1666	Isaac Newton uses a prism to analyze the color spectrum	
1671	Gottfried Wilhelm Leibniz invents a calculating machine that multiplies and divides	
1684	Leibniz publishes his first paper on differential calculus	
1687	Newton publishes his *Principia Mathematica*	

worldly goods and the inevitability of death. Such paintings look back upon a long tradition, shared by such Netherlanders as Jan van Eyck (see chapter 17) and Hieronymus Bosch (see chapter 18), that favored hidden or secondary meanings in realistically depicted imagery. Van Oosterwyck brings the naturalist's passion for detail to every item in the painting: the radiant flowers (which include a magnificent Dutch tulip), the microscopically precise fly, the worn book, the rotting skull, the meticulously detailed globe, and the minute self-portrait (reflected in the carafe on the left).

In addition to still-life subjects, genre paintings packed with images of everyday life were in high demand in seventeenth-century Holland. The domestic scenes painted by Pieter de Hooch (1629–1684) show Dutch art to be societal—an art concerned with conviviality and companionship. In one painting, de Hooch uses a spacious courtyard filled with cool, bright light as the setting for such ordinary pleasures as pipe smoking and beer drinking (Figure **22.5**; see also Frontispiece, p. ii). He captures a mood of domestic intimacy in his loving attention to humble fact: the crumbling brick wall, the gleaming tankard, the homely matron, and the pudgy child. The strict verticals and horizontals of the composition—established with Cartesian clarity and precision—create a sense of tranquillity and order.

Music making, one of the major domestic entertainments of the seventeenth century, is the subject of many Northern baroque paintings, including de Hooch's *Portrait of a Family Making Music* (Figure **22.6**). Holland was a center for the manufacture of musical instruments, and the Dutch household, pictured here with a variety of stringed and wind instruments, fondly engage in amateur musical performance. The popularity of music in Holland followed closely upon the proliferation of amateur music societies. Music making also figures in the delightful painting called *The Suitor's Visit* by Gerard ter Borch (1617–1681). The narrative is staged like a scene from a play: A well-dressed gentleman, who has just entered the parlor of a well-to-do middle-class family, bows before a young woman whose coy apprehension suggests that she is the object of courtship (Figure **22.7**). The father and the family dog take note of the tense moment, while a younger woman, absorbed in playing the lute, ignores the interruption. Ter Borch was famous for his virtuosity in painting silk and satin fabrics that subtly gleam from within the shadowy depths of domestic interiors. Equally impressive, however, was his ability to dignify an inconsequential social event with profound human meaning.

Figure 22.6 (above) Pieter de Hooch, *Portrait of a Family Making Music*, 1663. Oil on canvas, 38⅞ × 45¹⁵⁄₁₆ in. © The Cleveland Museum of Art 1998. Gift of the Hanna Fund (1951.355).

Figure 22.7 Gerard ter Borch, *The Suitor's Visit*, ca. 1658. Oil on canvas, 31½ × 29⅝ in. © 1998 Board of Trustees, National Gallery of Art, Washington, D.C. Andrew W. Mellon Collection.

Figure 22.8 A *camera obscura*; the image formed by the lens and reflected by the mirror on the ground glass is traced by the artist. Photo courtesy Beaumont Newhall.

Figure 22.9 Jan Vermeer, *View of Delft*, 1658. Oil on canvas, 3 ft. 2¾ in. × 3 ft. 10 in. Mauritshuis, The Hague. Scala/Art Resource, New York.

Vermeer and Dutch Painting

Seventeenth-century Dutch artists developed the naturalistic landscape (the very word derives from the Dutch *landschap*) as a major artistic subject. In landscape painting as in genre subjects, Dutch artists described nature with a close attention to detail and a sensitivity to atmosphere that rivaled the landscapes of their Northern European predecessors, Dürer and Brueghel (see chapter 18). Holland's leading artists were familiar with the optical experiments of Dutch scientists: The Delft artist Jan Vermeer (1632–1675) is thought to have conceived his paintings with the use of the *camera obscura* (Figure **22.8**), an optical device that anticipated the modern pinhole camera (though it lacked the means of capturing the image on film). Vermeer's *View of Delft*, a topographical study of the artist's native city, reveals a typically Dutch affection for the visible world and its all-embracing light (Figure **22.9**). Vermeer lowers the horizon line of the painting to give increased

Figure 22.10 Jan Vermeer, *Woman Holding a Balance*, ca. 1664. Oil on canvas, 16¾ × 15 in. © 1998 Board of Trustees, National Gallery of Art, Washington, D.C. The Widener Collection, 1962.

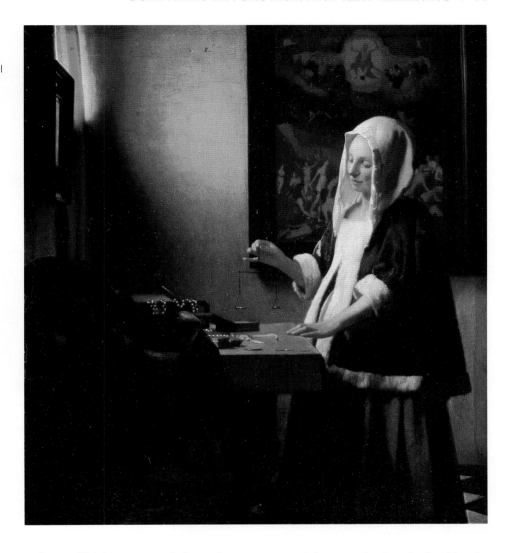

attention to the sky—a reflection perhaps of his interest in the new astronomy. Unlike the great landscape painters of China (see chapter 14), who employed multiple vanishing points to create vistas that unfold only gradually, Vermeer fixes a single point of view at a single moment in time. Nevertheless, the broad horizon in the Vermeer painting seems to reach beyond the limits of the frame to embrace a world that exceeds the mundane boundaries of seventeenth-century Delft. Dwarfed by their setting, two groups of tiny figures (artfully placed in the left foreground) behold the city-scape from within the painting as we do from without.

The exemplar of an age of observation, Vermeer brought to his compositions a keen sensitivity to light. Small beads of light, an effect produced by the *camera obscura*, twinkle on the surface of his canvases. In *The Geographer*, a warm golden light highlights the scientist's face and hands, while it creates a unifying atmosphere for the scholarly tools and instruments of his studio-laboratory (see Figure 22.1). In *Woman Holding a Balance* (Figure 22.10), light transforms a mundane subject—the weighing of gold—into an allegory that suggests the

balance between material prosperity (symbolized by the jewels on the table) and spiritual destiny (represented by the painting of the Last Judgment that hangs on the wall). With cool intellectualism, Vermeer balances the negative space of the background against the positive figure of the pregnant woman. He weighs light against dark as he sets realistic details against broadly generalized shapes. These formal devices, conceived with painstaking technical precision, reinforce the allegorical theme of balance. Whether or not Vermeer intended the painting as an allegory, the affective power of Figure 22.10 lies in its intimacy and in the meditative mood created by light, which, entering from a nearby window, subtly illuminates the face and body of the young woman. (Vermeer's Netherlandish ancestor, Jan van Eyck, had captured a similar mood in the Arnolfini marriage portrait executed two centuries earlier—see chapter 17). Women, usually self-contained and self-possessed, and always without children, were one of Vermeer's favorite subjects. He pictured them in comfortable domestic interiors, playing musical instruments, reading letters, and enjoying the company of men.

Dutch Portraiture

The vogue of portraiture in Northern baroque art reflected the self-conscious materialism of a rising middle class. Like the portraits of wealthy Renaissance aristocrats (see chapter 17), the painted likenesses of seventeenth-century Dutch burghers fulfilled the desire to immortalize one's worldly self. But in contrast to Italian portraits, the painted images of middle-class Dutch men and women are usually unidealized and often even unflattering. They capture a truth to nature reminiscent of late Roman portraiture (see chapter 7) but surpass even these in their self-scrutiny and probing, self-reflective character.

Two contemporaries, Frans Hals (1581–1666) and Rembrandt van Rijn (the latter introduced in chapter 21), dominated the genre of portraiture in seventeenth-century Dutch painting. Hals was the leading painter of Haarlem and one of the great realists of the Western portrait tradition. His talent lay in capturing the fleeting expressions that characterized the personality and physical presence of his sitters. Hals rendered the jaunty self-confidence of a Dutch officer (Figure **22.11**) with the same fidelity to nature that he used to convey the dour solemnity of the scholar-philosopher Descartes (see

Figure 22.11 Frans Hals, *Portrait of a Member of the Haarlem Civic Guard*, ca. 1636–1638. Oil on canvas, 33¾ × 27 in. © 1998 Board of Trustees, National Gallery of Art, Washington, D.C. Andrew W. Mellon Collection, 1937.

Figure 22.12 Judith Leyster, *Self-Portrait*, ca. 1630. Oil on canvas, 29⅜ × 25⅞ in. © 1998 Board of Trustees, National Gallery of Art, Washington, D.C. Gift of Mr. and Mrs. Robert Woods Bliss.

Figure 22.2). A master of the brush, Hals brought his forms to life by means of quick, loose, staccato brushstrokes and impasto highlights. Immediacy, spontaneity, and impulsive movement—features typical of baroque art—are captured in Hals' vigorous portraits.

These qualities also appear in the work of Judith Leyster (1609–1660), an artist from the Netherlands province of Utrecht, whose canvases until this century were usually attributed to her teacher, Frans Hals. Leyster's *Self-Portrait* achieves a sense of informality through the casual manner in which the artist turns away from her canvas as if to greet the viewer (Figure **22.12**). The laughing violinist that is the subject of the painting within the painting provides an exuberant counterpoint to Leyster's robust visage. Leyster's portrait is a personal comment on the role of the artist as muse and artisan.

Hals' and Leyster's portraits are astute records of surface appearance and the social milieu. By comparison, Rembrandt's portraits are studies of the inner life of his sitters. A keen observer of human individuality and a master technician, Rembrandt became the leading portrait painter in the city of Amsterdam. The commissions he received at the beginning of his career exceeded his ability to fill them. But after a meteoric rise to fame, he saw his fortunes decline. Accumulated debts led to poverty, bankruptcy, and psychological

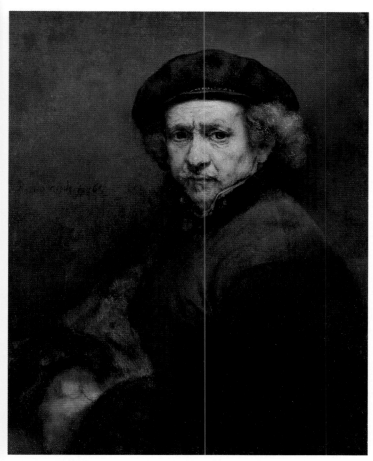

Figure 22.13 Rembrandt van Rijn, *Self-Portrait*, 1659.
Oil on canvas, 33¼ × 26 in. © 1998 Board of Trustees, National
Gallery of Art, Washington, D.C. Andrew W. Mellon Collection.
Photo: Richard Carafelli.

depression—the last compounded by the loss of his
beloved wife in 1642. The history of Rembrandt's career
is mirrored in his self-portraits, over sixty of which survive; these are a kind of visual diary, a lifetime record of
the artist's passionate enterprise in self-scrutiny. His *Self-
Portrait* of 1659, with its slackened facial muscles and
furrowed brow, directly engages the viewer with the
image of a noble and yet vulnerable personality (Figure
22.13). Portraiture of this kind, which has no equivalent
in any non-Western culture, may be considered among
the outstanding examples of probing individualism.

Among the most lucrative of Rembrandt's commissions was the group portrait, a uniquely Dutch genre
which commemorated the achievements of wealthy
families, guild members, and militia officers. Some of
these paintings, which measure more than 12 by 14
feet, reflect the baroque taste for colossal proportion
and theatrical setting. But Rembrandt skillfully fused
dramatic effect with sober, unidealized characterization.
These features are especially obvious in *The Anatomy
Lesson of Dr. Nicolaes Tulp* (1632), the painting that established Rembrandt's reputation as a master portraitist
(Figure **22.14**). Rembrandt eliminated the posed look of
the conventional group portrait by staging the scene as
a dissection in progress. Here, as in his religious compositions (compare Figure 21.4), he manipulates light for
dramatic purposes: He spotlights the dissected corpse in
the foreground and balances the darker area on the
right, dominated by the figure of the doctor, with a triangle formed by the illuminated heads of the students
(whose names appear on the piece of paper held by the
central figure). The faces of Tulp's students carry the
force of individual personalities and capture the spirit of
inquisitiveness peculiar to the Age of Science.

Figure 22.14 Rembrandt van Rijn, *The
Anatomy Lesson of Dr. Nicolaes Tulp*, 1632.
Oil on canvas, 5 ft. 3⅜ in. × 7 ft. 1¼ in.
Mauritshuis, The Hague.
Scala/Art Resource, New York.

Baroque Instrumental Music

Until the sixteenth century, almost all music was written for the voice rather than for musical instruments. Even during the Renaissance, instrumental music was, for the most part, the result of substituting an instrument for a voice in music written for singing or dancing. The seventeenth century marked the rise of music that lacked extramusical meaning. Like a mathematical equation or a geometric formula, the instrumental music of the early modern era carried no explicit narrative content—it was neither a vehicle of religious expression nor a means of supporting a secular vocalized text. Such music was written without consideration for the associational content traditionally provided by a set of sung lyrics. The idea of music as an aesthetic exercise, composed for its own sake rather than to serve a religious or communal purpose, was a notable feature of the seventeenth century and one that has distinguished modern Western European music from the musical traditions of Asia and Africa.

Not surprisingly, the rise of instrumental music was accompanied by improvements in instruments and

Figure 22.15 Johannes Couchet (maker), Flemish Harpsichord-double-banked; compass, four octaves, and a fifth F to C (each keyboard), ca. 1650. Case decorated with carving and gilt gesso work. The Metropolitan Museum of Art, New York. The Crosby Brown Collection of Musical Instruments, 1889 (89.4.2363).

refinements in tuning. Indeed, instrumental music came to dominate musical composition at the very moment that Western musicians were perfecting such stringed instruments as the violin, viola, and cello (see Figure 22.6) and such keyboard instruments as the organ and harpsichord (Figure **22.15**). By the early eighteenth century, musicians were adopting the system of tuning known as **equal temperament**, whereby the octave was divided into twelve half-steps of equal size. Equal temperament made the chromatic scale uniform among instruments. J. S. Bach's *Well-Tempered Keyboard* (1722) was an attempt to popularize this system to a skeptical musical public. The new attention paid to improving instruments and systematizing key mirrored the efforts of scientists and philosophers to bring precision and uniformity to the tools and methods for scientific inquiry.

In the seventeenth century, Northern Italy was the world center for the manufacture of violins. The Amati, Guarneri, and Stradivari families of Cremona, Italy, established the techniques of making quality violins that were sought in all of the great courts of Europe. Transmitted from father to son, the construction techniques used to produce these instruments were guarded so secretly that modern violinmakers have never successfully imitated them. Elsewhere, around 1650, earlier instruments were standardized and refined. The ancient double-reed wind instrument known as the shawm, for instance, developed into the modern oboe. While amateur music making was widespread, professional performance also took a great leap forward, as a new breed of virtuosi inspired the writing of treatises on performance techniques.

Three main types of composition—the sonata, the suite, and the concerto—dominated seventeenth-century instrumental music. All three reflect the baroque taste for dramatic contrasts in tempo and texture. The **sonata** (from the Italian word for "sounded," that is, music played and not sung) is a piece written for a few instruments—often no more than one or two. It usually consisted of three **movements** of contrasting tempo—fast/slow/fast—each based on a song or dance form of the time. The **suite**, written for any combination of instruments, is a sequence or series of movements derived from various European court or folk dances—for example, the sarabande, the pavane, the minuet, and the gigue, or jig. Henry Purcell (1659–1695) in England, François Couperin (1668–1733) in France (see chapter 26), and Johann Sebastian Bach (1685–1750) in Germany all contributed to the development of the suite as a musical genre. Finally, the **concerto** (from the same root as *concertato*, which describes opposing or contrasting bodies of sound; see chapter 20) is a composition consisting of two groups of instruments, one small and the other large, playing in "dialogue." The typical baroque concerto, the **concerto grosso** ("large concerto") featured several movements, whose number and kind varied considerably.

The leading Italian instrumental composer of the baroque era was Antonio Vivaldi (1678–1741), a Roman Catholic priest and the son of a prominent violinist at Saint Mark's Cathedral in Venice. Vivaldi wrote some 450 concertos. He systematized the concerto grosso into a three-movement form (fast/slow/fast) and increased the distinctions between solo and ensemble groups in each movement. Of the many exciting compositions Vivaldi wrote for solo violin and ensemble, the most glorious is *The Four Seasons*,♪ a group of four violin concertos, each of which musically describes a single season. Vivaldi intended that this piece be "programmatic," that is, that it carry meaning outside of the music itself. As if to ensure that the music duplicate the descriptive power of the traditional vocal lines, he added poems at appropriate passages in the score for the instruction of the performers. At the section called "Spring," for instance, Vivaldi's verses describe "flowing streams" and "singing birds." While the music offers listeners the challenge of detecting such extramusical references to nature, the brilliance of this instrumental masterpiece lies not in its programmatic innovations but, rather, in its vibrant rhythms, its lyrical solos, and its exuberant "dialogues" between violin and small orchestra.

Rivaling Vivaldi's *Four Seasons* in their spiraling melodies and expansive rhythms are Bach's Brandenburg Concertos, which Bach completed in 1721 on commission from Christian Ludwig, the Margrave of Brandenburg. Though there is no record that the six concertos were ever performed during Bach's lifetime, they were probably intended for performance by the Brandenburg court orchestra. The Brandenburg Concertos employ as soloists most of the principal instruments of the baroque orchestra: violin, oboe, recorder, trumpet, and harpsichord. Totally unconcerned with extramusical meaning, Bach applied himself to developing rich contrasts of tone and texture between the two "contending" groups of instruments—note especially the massive sound of the entire ensemble versus the lighter sounds of the small sections in the first movement of the fourth concerto.♪ Here, tightly drawn webs of counterpoint are spun between upper and lower instrumental parts, while musical lines, driven by an unflagging rhythm and energy, unfold majestically.

Only one year before he died, in 1749, Bach undertook one of the most monumental works of his career, a compelling example of baroque musical composition that came to be called *The Art of Fugue*.♪ A **fugue**

(literally "flight") is a polyphonic composition in which a single musical theme (or subject) is restated in sequential phrases. As in the more familiar canon known as a "round"—for instance, "Three Blind Mice"—a melody in one voice part is imitated in other voice parts, so that melody and repetitions overlap. The musical subject can be arranged to appear backward or inverted (or both), augmented (the time value of the notes doubled, so that the melody moves twice as slowly), or diminished (note values halved, so that the melody moves twice as fast). In the hands of a great composer, this form of imitative counterpoint might become a majestic tapestry of sound. Such is the case with Bach's *Art of Fugue*, in the last portion of which he went so far as to sign his name with a musical motif made up of the letters of his name—B flat, A, C, and B natural (pronounced as an H in German). Even the listener who cannot read music or analyze the intricacies of Bach's inventions is struck by the concentrated brilliance of a Bach fugue. No less than Newton's codification of the laws of nature, *The Art of Fugue* was a triumphant expression of the Age of Science.

SUMMARY

During the seventeenth century, European scientists advanced a new picture of the cosmos. They showed that the earth, like the other planets, follows an elliptical and therefore irregular path around the sun, which stands at the center of the solar system. Clearly, the planet earth and its human inhabitants could no longer be regarded as the hub of a motionless universe. The progress of the Scientific Revolution moved from the stage of methodical speculation (represented by Copernicus and Kepler) to that of empirical confirmation (provided by Galileo's telescope) and, ultimately with Newton's *Principia*, to codification. Between 1600 and 1750, many new scientific instruments were invented, and the sciences of physics and astronomy, along with the language of higher mathematics, were firmly established.

While the new science demystified nature, the new learning provided a methodology for more accurately describing and predicting the operations of nature. Francis Bacon championed induction and the empirical method, which gave priority to knowledge gained through the senses. John Locke, the most influential philosopher of the age, defended the empirical tradition by claiming that all ideas came from sensation and reflection. René Descartes opposed such views; he gave priority to deductive reasoning and mathematical analysis. Despite their differences, seventeenth-century intellectuals shared the deist notions of God as a master mechanic and the universe as a great machine that operated independent of divine intervention.

♪See Music Listening Selections at end of chapter.

The Scientific Revolution and the new learning ushered in a phase of the baroque style marked by an empirical attention to detail, a fascination with light and space, and an increased demand for such subjects as still life, landscape, portraiture, and genre painting. The many examples of each produced in this era testify to the secular preoccupations of middle-class patrons. In seventeenth-century art, cosmic landscapes such as Vermeer's *View of Delft* are balanced by the genre paintings of de Hooch and ter Borch, which explore the intimate pleasures of house and home, and by the portraits of Hals, Leyster, and Rembrandt, which give clear evidence of the robust confidence of the age.

Modern science also touched the art of music. During the seventeenth century, the violin and the organ were perfected, and keyboard instruments (and musical performance in general) benefited from the development of a uniform system of tuning. Treatises on the art of instrumental performance became increasingly popular. The seventeenth century saw the rise of wholly instrumental music and of such instrumental forms as the sonata, the suite, and the concerto. Vivaldi and Bach perfected the concerto grosso, a multimovement form characterized by vivid contrasts between small and large instrumental groups. Bach exploited the art of the fugue in musical compositions whose complexity and intricacy remain unrivaled. These instrumental forms captured the exuberance of the baroque spirit, just as they summed up the dynamic intellectualism of the age.

GLOSSARY

Cartesian of or relating to René Descartes or his philosophy

concerto (Italian, "opposing" or "competing") an instrumental composition consisting of one or more solo instruments and a larger group of instruments playing in "dialogue"

concerto grosso a "large concerto," the typical kind of baroque concerto, consisting of several movements

deductive reasoning a method of inquiry that begins with clearly established general premises and moves toward the establishment of particular truths

deism a movement or system of thought advocating natural religion based on human reason rather than revelation; deists describe God as Creator, but deny that God interferes with the laws of the universe

equal temperament a system of tuning that originated in the seventeenth century, whereby the octave is divided into twelve half-steps of equal size; since intervals have the same value in all keys, music may be played in any key, and a musician may change from one key to another with complete freedom.

fugue ("flight") a polyphonic composition in which a theme (or subject) is imitated, restated, and developed by successively entering voice parts

geocentric earth-centered

heliocentric sun-centered

inductive reasoning a method of inquiry that begins with direct observation and experimentation and moves toward the establishment of general conclusions or axioms

movement a major section in a long instrumental composition

sonata an instrumental composition consisting of three movements of contrasting tempo, usually fast/slow/fast; see also Glossary, chapter 26

suite an instrumental composition consisting of a sequence or series of movements derived from court or folk dances

vanitas (Latin, "vanity") a type of still life consisting of objects that symbolize the brevity of life and the transience of earthly pleasures and achievements

SUGGESTIONS FOR READING

Alpers, Svetlana. *The Art of Describing: Dutch Art in the Seventeenth Century*. Chicago: University of Chicago Press, 1983.

——*Rembrandt's Enterprise: The Studio and the Market*. Chicago: University of Chicago Press, 1990.

Chapman, H. P. *Rembrandt's Self-Portraits: A Study in Seventeenth-Century Identity*. Princeton, N.J.: Princeton University Press, 1990.

Donington, Robert. *Baroque Music: Style and Performance*. New York: Norton, 1982.

Hall, A. Rupert. *The Revolution in Science: 1500–1750*. New York: Longman, 1983.

Havens, George R. *The Age of Ideas*. New York: Holt, 1955.

Jacob, Margaret C. *The Cultural Meaning of the Scientific Revolution*. New York: Knopf, 1988.

Montias, John M. *Vermeer and His Milieu*. Princeton, N.J.: Princeton University Press, 1991.

Nussbaum, Frederick L. *The Triumph of Science and Reason*. New York: Harper, 1953.

Rossi, Paolo. *Francis Bacon: From Magic to Science*. Chicago: University of Chicago Press, 1968.

Shapin, Steven. *The Scientific Revolution*. Chicago: University of Chicago Press, 1996.

Stechow, Wolfgang. *Dutch Landscape Painting of the Seventeenth Century*. London: Phaidon, 1966.

Wheelock, Arthur K., Jr. *Vermeer and the Art of Painting*. New Haven: Yale University Press, 1995.

MUSIC LISTENING SELECTIONS

Cassette II Selection 5 Vivaldi, *The Four Seasons*, "Spring," Concerto in E Major, Op. 8, No. 1; first movement, 1725.

Cassette II Selection 6 Bach, Brandenburg Concerto No. 4 in G Major, first movement, 1721.

Cassette II Selection 7 Bach, *The Art of Fugue*, Canon in the 12th, 1749–1750.

23
Absolute Power and the Aristocratic Style

The early modern era in the West is sometimes called the Age of Absolutism. Absolutism, a political theory asserting that unlimited power be vested in one or more rulers, confirmed longstanding theocratic tradition. During the seventeenth and well into the eighteenth century, divine right kings—rulers who were believed to hold their power directly from God—exercised unlimited power within their individual nation-states.

But the term "Age of Absolutism" is equally appropriate to the period as it unfolded in the lands beyond Europe, for in China, India, and elsewhere, divine right monarchs also held unlimited control over their own vast states or empires (Map **23.1**).

Absolute rulers maintained their authority by controlling a centralized bureaucracy and a standing army, and by pursuing economic policies designed to

Map 23.1 Empires in the Late Sixteenth and Early Seventeenth Centuries.

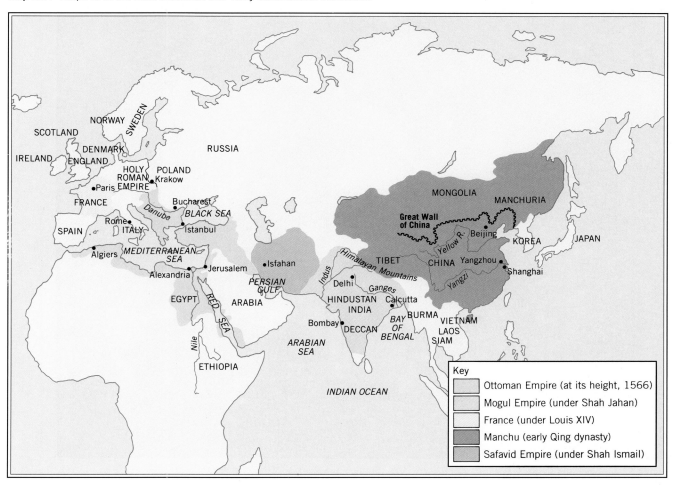

Key
- Ottoman Empire (at its height, 1566)
- Mogul Empire (under Shah Jahan)
- France (under Louis XIV)
- Manchu (early Qing dynasty)
- Safavid Empire (under Shah Ismail)

Figure 23.1 Hyacinthe Rigaud, *Portrait of Louis XIV*, 1701. Oil on canvas, 9 ft. 1 in. × 6 ft. 4⅜ in. Louvre, Paris. Giraudon, Paris.

19. Handy: St. Louis Blues—Bessie Smith, vocal; Louis Armstrong, cornet; Fred Longshaw, reed organ[*]
20. Hardin: Hotter Than That—Louis Armstrong[*]
21. Ellington: Ko-Ko—Charlie Parker, Dizzy Gillespie[h]
22. Ligeti: Atmospheres—excerpt—New York Philharmonic; Leonard Bernstein, conductor[*]
23. Babbitt: Ensembles for Synthesizer—excerpt[*]
24. McClean: Etunytude—Fairlight Computer Musical Instrument[i]
25. Glass: "Knee 1," from *Einstein on the Beach*—Lucinda Childs, speaker; Cheryl Sutton, speaker; Philip Glass, organ,[*] ℗ 1979 Sony Music Entertainment Inc.

Courtesy Lines

[*] Courtesy of Sony Music Entertainment Inc.
a. Courtesy of EMI Records Ltd.
b. Courtesy of Omega Records
c. Courtesy of Serenus Records
d. Courtesy of Nimbus Records Ltd.

e. Courtesy of Telarc Records
f. Courtesy of Moss Music Group
g. Courtesy of New World Records
h. Courtesy of Nippon Columbia Co. Ltd.
i. Courtesy of Smithsonian Folkways Records

The Humanistic Tradition
Volume II

Gloria Fiero

Cassette Number PT 22300, Side A

1. Gabrieli: Motet: *In Ecclesiis*—excerpt—Gregg Smith Singers; Texas Boys' Choir; Edward Tarr Brass Ensemble; E. Power Biggs, organ; Vittorio Negri, conductor
2. Monteverdi: "Vi recorda, o boschi ombrosi," from *Orfeo*, Act. 2—Nigel Rogers, tenor; London Baroque; Charles Medlam, director.[a] ● 1984 Original Sound Recording made by EMI Records Ltd.
3. Handel: "Hallelujah" Chorus from *Messiah*—Mormon Tabernacle Choir; Richard P. Condie, director; Philadelphia Orchestra; Eugene Ormandy, conductor
4. Bach: Cantata No. 80, final chorus, "Ein Feste Burg ist unser Gott"—Amor Artis Chorale; English Chamber Orchestra; Johannes Somary, conductor[b]
5. Vivaldi: "Spring" Concerto, first movement, from *The Four Seasons*—St. Paul Chamber Orchestra; Pinchas Zukerman, violinist and conductor. ● 1981 Sony Music Entertainment Inc.
6. Bach: Brandenburg Concerto No. 4 in G Major, first movement—excerpt—Philharmonia Virtuosi; Richard Kapp, conductor.[c] ● 1984 Sony Music Entertainment Inc.
7. Bach: The Art of Fugue: Canon in the 12th—Gustav Leonhardt, harpsichord[b]
8. Couperin: "Le Croc en Jambe," from *Ordre 22*—Sylvia Marlowe, harpsichord[d]
9. Haydn: Symphony No. 94 in G Major, "Surprise," second movement—excerpt—Hanover Band; Roy Goodman, conductor.[d] ● 1987 Nimbus Records Ltd.
10. Mozart: Serenade in G Major, K. 525, "Eine Kleine Nachtmusik," first movement—excerpt—Prague Chamber Orchestra; Charles Mackerras, conductor.[c] ● 1985 Telarc
11. Beethoven: Symphony No. 3 in E-flat Major, first movement—excerpt—New York Philharmonic; Leonard Bernstein, conductor[c]
12. Schubert: Gretchen am Spinnrade—Kiri Te Kanawa, soprano; Richard Amner, piano.[*] ● 1980 Sony Music Entertainment Inc.

Cassette Number PT 22300, Side B

13. Berlioz: Symphonie Fantastique, Op. 14, fourth movement, "March to the Scaffold"—excerpt—The Berlin Philharmonic; Daniel Barenboim, conductor.[*] ● 1985 Sony Music Entertainment Inc.
14. Chopin: Etude in G-flat Major, Op. 10, No. 5—Abbey Simon, piano[f]
15. Debussy: Prelude a l'apres midi d'un faune—excerpt—New Philharmonia Orchestra; Pierre Boulez, conductor
16. Schoenberg: *Pierrot Lunaire*, Op. 21, Part 3, No. 15, "Heimweh"—Yvonne Minton, sprechstimme; Pinchas Zukerman, violin; Lynn Harrell, cello; Michel Debost, piccolo; Anthony Pay, clarinet; Daniel Barenboim, piano; Pierre Boulez, conductor.[*] ● 1978 Sony Music Entertainment Inc.
17. Stravinsky: "Sacrificial Dance," from *The Rite of Spring*—Columbia Symphony Orchestra; Igor Stravinsky, conductor
18. Cage: Sonata V—Robert Miller, prepared piano[g]

List of Cassette Recordings

to Accompany

The Humanistic Tradition

Volume II
(Books 4-6)

Gloria Fiero

ISBN 0-697-14856-4

© 1992 Sony Music Entertainment Inc./© 1992 Sony Music Entertainment Inc./Sony Music Special Products Manufactured by Columbia Records/666 Fifth Ave., P.O. Box 4450, New York NY 10101-4450/"Columbia" Reg. US Patent & TM Office/Marca Registrada/

PT 22300

1657 the first fountain pens are manufactured in Paris
1688 the French army introduces bayonets attached to muskets
1698 champagne is invented in France

maximize the wealth of the state. In Western Europe, the mightiest of such potentates was King Louis XIV of France. During the nearly three-quarters of a century that Louis occupied the French throne (1643–1715), he dictated the political, economic, and cultural policies of the country. Under his guidance, France assumed a position of political and military leadership in Western Europe. As cultural arbiter, Louis helped to bring about a phase of the baroque called the *classical baroque*. This style pervaded the arts of seventeenth-century France and became one of the hallmarks of French absolutism. It also impressed its stamp on the rest of Europe and, somewhat later, on an emergent American culture.

Outside of Europe, absolute rulers also held sway: Suleiman the Magnificent (grand vizier of the Ottoman Empire), the Safavids of Persia in Southwest Asia, the Moguls in India, the Ming and Qing emperors in China, and the Tokugawa rulers in Japan. Within each of these territories, as within the European nation-states, the arts flourished as an expression of the majesty of the ruler and of the wealth and strength of his domain.

The Aristocratic Style in France

Louis XIV and French Absolutism

Like the pharaohs of ancient Egypt and in the tradition of his medieval ancestors, Louis XIV (1638–1715) governed France as the direct representative of God on earth (Figure **23.1**). Neither the Church, nor the nobility, nor the will of his subjects limited his power. During his seventy-two years on the throne, the Estates General, France's representative assembly, was never once called into session. As absolute monarch, Louis brought France to a position of political and military preeminence among the European nation-states. He challenged the power of the feudal nobility and placed the Church under the authority of the state, thus centralizing all authority in his own hands. By exempting the nobility and upper middle class from taxation and offering them important positions at court, he turned potential opponents into supporters. Even if Louis never uttered the famous words attributed to him, "I am the state," he surely operated according to that precept. Indeed, as an expression of his unrivaled authority, he took as his official insignia the image of the classical sun god Apollo and referred to himself as *le roi soleil* ("the Sun King").

As ruler of France, Louis was one of the world's most influential figures. Under his leadership, the center of artistic patronage and productivity shifted from Italy to France. French culture in all of its forms—from art and architecture to fashions and fine cuisine—came to dominate European tastes, a condition that prevailed until well into the early twentieth century. Although Louis was not an intellectual, he was both shrewd and ambitious. He chose first-rate advisers to execute his policies and financed those policies with money from taxes that fell primarily upon the backs of French peasants. Vast amounts of money were spent to make France the undisputed military leader of Western Europe. But Louis, who instinctively recognized the propaganda value of the arts, also used the French treasury to glorify himself and his office. His extravagances left France in woeful financial condition, a circumstance that contributed to the outbreak of the revolution at the end of the eighteenth century. Incapable of foreseeing these circumstances, Louis cultivated the arts as an adjunct to majesty.

Versailles: Symbol of Royal Absolutism

Architecture played a vital role in the vocabulary of royal power. The French royal family traditionally resided in Paris, at the palace known as the Louvre. But Louis, who detested Paris, moved his capital to a spot from which he might more directly control the nobility and keep them dependent upon him for honors and financial favors. Early in his career he commissioned a massive renovation of his father's hunting lodge at the village of Versailles, some 12 miles from Paris. It took thirty-six thousand workers and nearly twenty years to build Versailles, but, in 1682, the French court finally established itself in the apartments of this magnificent unfortified *château* (castle). More than a royal residence, Versailles was—in its size and splendor—the symbol of Louis' absolute supremacy over the landed aristocracy, the provincial governments, the urban councils, and the Estates General.

The wooded site that constituted the village of Versailles, almost half the size of Paris, was connected to the old capital by a grand boulevard that (following the path of the sun) ran from the king's bedroom—where most state business was transacted—to the Avenue de Paris. Even a cursory examination of the plan of Versailles, laid out by the French architect Louis Le Vau (1612–1670), reveals esteem for the rules of symmetry, clarity, and geometric regularity (Figure **23.2**). These principles, in combination with a taste for spatial grandeur, dramatic contrast, and theatrical display, were the distinguishing features of the classical baroque style.

Shaped like a winged horseshoe, the almost 2,000-foot-long royal residence—best viewed in its entirety

Figure 23.2 Louis Le Vau, plan of Versailles. Musée de Versailles.

Figure 23.3 Anonymous seventeenth-century painting of Versailles. © The Bettmann Archive, New York.

Figure 23.4 Louis Le Vau and Jules Hardouin-Mansart, facade of Versailles, viewed from the north flower bed. 1669–1685. Length of facade approx. 2,000 ft. Musée de Versailles. Lauros-Giraudon, Paris.

Figure 23.5 Claude Perrault, Louis Le Vau, and Charles Le Brun, east facade of the Louvre, Paris, 1667–1670. Photo: James Austin, Cambridge, U.K.

Figure 23.6 Ornamental Lake and Fountain of Latone, Versailles. Musée de Versailles. Photo: Gloria Fiero.

from the air—was the focus of an immense complex of parks, lakes, and forest (Figure **23.3**). The central building of the palace was designed by Le Vau, while the two additional wings were added by Jules Hardouin-Mansart (1646–1708). Three levels of vertically aligned windows march across the palace facade like soldiers in a formal procession (Figure **23.4**). Porches bearing free-standing Corinthian columns accent the second level, and ornamental statues at the roofline help to relieve the monotonous horizontality of the structure. In its total effect, the palace is dignified and commanding, a grand synthesis of classical and Palladian elements. Its calm nobility provides a striking contrast to the robust theatricality of most Italian baroque structures (see Figures 20.16 and 20.18).

The grandeur and majesty of Versailles made it the model for hundreds of palace-estates and city planning projects in both Europe and America for the following two centuries. Le Vau's facade became the prototype for the remodeled royal palace in Paris, the Louvre. Designed by Claude Perrault (1613–1688), the east facade of the Louvre echoes the basic classical baroque features of Louis' residence at Versailles: a strong rectilinear organization, paired Corinthian columns, and a gabled entrance that provides dramatic focus (Figure **23.5**).

The palace at Versailles housed Louis' family, his royal mistresses (one of whom bore him nine children), and hundreds of members of the French nobility whose presence was politically useful to Louis. Life at the court of the Sun King was both formal and public—a small army of servants, courtiers, ministers, and pet animals constantly surrounded Louis. All forms of behavior were fixed by protocol. Rank at court determined where one sat at the dinner table and whether one or both panels of Versailles' "French doors" were to be opened upon entering.

Flanking the palace were barracks for honor guards, lodgings for over fifteen hundred servants, kennels, greenhouses, and an orangery with over two thousand orange trees. Over 7 miles of gardens were designed by André Le Nôtre with the same compelling sense of order that Le Vau brought to the architecture. The great park featured an array of hedges clipped into geometric shapes, sparkling fountains (that favorite of all baroque mechanical devices), artificial lakes, grottoes, a zoo, theaters, and outdoor "rooms" for private gatherings and clandestine meetings. When in bloom, the gardens—some planted with over four million tulip bulbs, which Louis imported annually from Holland—were a spectacular sight. They framed and embellished the long walkways that radiate from the central building. On the garden side of the palace, artificial pools reflected sculptures whose subject matter glorified

Figure 23.7 Jean Le Pautre, *Marble Court, Versailles*. Engraving showing a performance of Lully's *Alceste*, 1674. The Metropolitan Museum of Art, New York. Harris Brisbane Dick Fund, 1930 (30–22.32[53]).

Figure 23.8 Apartment of the Queen/Salon of the Nobles, Versailles. Length 31 ft.; width 32 ft.; height 24 ft. 8 in. Musée de Versailles. Giraudon/Art Resource, New York.

the majesty of the king (Figure **23.6**). Itself a kind of outdoor theater, the royal palace provided the ideal backdrop for the ballets, operas, and plays that were regular features of court life (Figure **23.7**).

If the exterior of Versailles symbolized the grandeur of the king, the interior was a monument to princely self-indulgence (Figure **23.8**). Though now shorn of many of their original furnishings, Versailles' sumptuous *salons* (drawing rooms) still testify to Louis' success at cultivating French trades in such luxury items as crafted silver, clocks, lace, brocades, porcelain, and fine glass. During the seventeenth century, the silk industry reached its peak, French carpets competed with those of Turkey and Persia, the art of **marquetry** (inlaid wood) rivaled that of Italy, and the tapestries produced at the Gobelins factory in Paris outclassed those woven in Flanders. Versailles' *salons* were adorned with illusionistic frescoes, gilded stucco moldings, crystal chandeliers, and huge, ornate mirrors. The rooms housed some of the most lavish *objets d'art* (art objects) in Western history, all of which, it is sobering to recall, were enjoyed at a time when the peasant majority of the French population lived in one-room, thatch-roofed houses filled with coarse wooden furniture. Equally sobering is the fact that despite its splendor, the palace lacked any kind of indoor plumbing. Servants carried out the slops, but the unpleasant odor of human waste was difficult to mask, even with the finest French perfumes.

Each of Versailles' rooms illustrates a specific theme: The Salon de Venus was decorated by Charles Le Brun (1619–1690) with ceiling paintings portraying the influence of love on various kings in history. In the Salon de la Guerre (Drawing Room of War) an idealized, equestrian Louis, carved in low-relief marble, is shown receiving the victor's crown (Figure **23.9**)—though, in actual fact, Louis himself rarely took part in combat. The most splendid room at Versailles, however, is the 240-foot-long Galerie des Glaces (Hall of Mirrors), which once connected the royal apartments with the chapel (Figure **23.10**). Embellished with glorious frescoes, marble pilasters, and gilded bronze capitals, and furnished with ornate candelabra and bejeweled trees (the latter have since disappeared), the hall features a wall of seventeen mirrored arcades that face an equal number of high-arched windows opening on to the garden. Framing this opulent royal passageway, mirrors and

Figure 23.9 Jules Hardouin-Mansart, Salon de la Guerre (Drawing Room of War), Versailles. Length and width 33 ft. 8 in; height 37 ft. 9 in. Musée de Versailles. Lauros-Giraudon, Paris.

Figure 23.10 Jules Hardouin-Mansart and Charles Le Brun, Galerie des Glaces (Hall of Mirrors), Versailles, ca. 1680. Length 240 ft. Musée de Versailles. Giraudon/Art Resource, New York.

windows set up a brilliant counterpoint of image and reflection. Mirrors were to Versailles what fountains were to Rome: vehicles for the theatrical display of changing light in unbounded space.

Louis as Patron of the Arts

At the center of his court, Louis was the arbiter of fashion and manners. Within his dining *salons*, linen napkins came into use, forks replaced fingers for eating, and elaborate dishes were served to suit the royal palate. Graced with an eye for beauty and a passion for aggrandizement, Louis increased the number of paintings in the French royal collection from the two hundred he inherited upon his accession to the throne to the two thousand he left at his death. These paintings formed the basis of the permanent collection at the Louvre, now a world-renowned art museum.

On a grander scale Louis dictated the standards for all forms of artistic production. Following in the tradition of his father, Louis XIII, who had instituted the French Royal Academy of Language and Literature in 1635, he created and subsidized government-sponsored institutions in the arts, appointing his personal favorites to oversee each. In 1648, Louis founded the Academy of Painting and Sculpture; in 1661 he established the Academy of Dance; in 1666, the Academy of Sciences; in 1669, the Academy of Music; and in 1671, the Academy of Architecture. The creation of the academies was a symptom of royal efforts to fix standards, but Louis had something more personal in mind: He is said to have told a group of academicians, "Gentlemen, I entrust to you the most precious thing on earth— my fame." His trust was well placed, for the academies brought glory to the king and set standards that would govern the arts for at least two centuries. These

Figure 23.11 Gianlorenzo Bernini, *Louis XIV*, 1665. Marble, height 33⅛ in. Musée de Versailles. Photo: © R.M.N., Paris.

Figure 23.12 François Girardon, *Apollo Attended by the Nymphs*, ca. 1666–1672. Marble, life-sized. Musée de Versailles. Giraudon, Paris.

standards were enshrined in "rules" inspired by the legacy of ancient Greece and Rome, thus *neoclassicism*—the revival of classical style and subject matter—became the accepted style of academic art.

In the early days of his reign, when Italy was the leader in artistic style, Louis invited Italian artists to execute royal commissions. Among these artists was the master architect-sculptor Gianlorenzo Bernini (see chapter 20). Bernini had submitted designs for a remodeled Louvre, and although his plans were rejected ultimately in favor of Perrault's, his vigorous style survives in such works as the life-sized marble portrait bust of Louis completed in 1665 (Figure **23.11**). Originally designed to stand on a gilded enamel globe inscribed with a message celebrating the king's lofty position, this sculpture—with its billowing draperies, elaborate coiffure, and idealized features—glorifies the ruler in typically baroque fashion. Bernini's theatrical exuberance contrasts sharply with the sober neoclassicism of the French academician François Girardon (1628–1715). Girardon drew on Hellenistic models for the ideally proportioned statues that he arranged in graceful tableaux for the gardens of Versailles. In one such tableau, Girardon's neoclassical nymphs are seen entertaining the sun god Apollo—an obvious reference to Louis as *roi soleil* (Figure **23.12**).

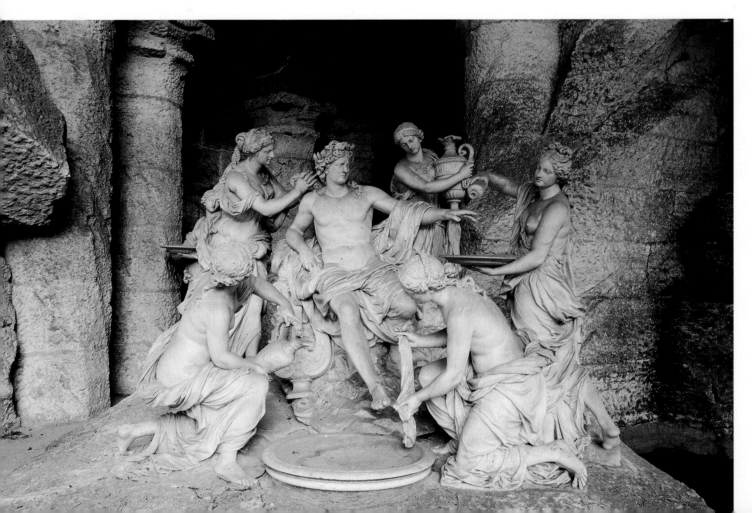

Poussin and the Academic Style in Painting

Girardon's compositions owed much to the paintings of the leading exponent of French academic art, Nicolas Poussin (1594–1665). Poussin spent most of his life in Rome, absorbing the rich heritage of the classical and Renaissance past. He revered Raphael, master of the High Renaissance, as the leading proponent of the classical style, and, like many neoclassicists, he shared Raphael's esteem for lofty subjects drawn from Greco-Roman mythology and Christian legend. In an influential treatise on painting, Poussin formalized the rules that would govern academic art for centuries. These principles, drawn largely from the aesthetic theories of seventeenth-century Italian painters, would come to characterize the Grand Manner in Western art: Artists should choose only serious and elevated subjects drawn from classical or Christian history, and reject crude, bizarre, and ordinary subject matter. As to the manner of representation, artists should make the physical action suit the mood of the narrative, avoiding, at all cost, the gross aspects of ordinary existence and any type of exaggeration. They should present their subjects clearly and evenly in harmonious compositions that were free of irrelevant and sordid details. Restraint, moderation, and decorum—that is, propriety and good taste —should govern all aspects of pictorial representation.

Poussin faithfully practiced the rules of the academic or Grand Manner style. His *Arcadian Shepherds*, completed in 1639, transports us to the idyllic region in ancient Greece known as Arcadia, a place where men and women were said to live in perfect harmony with nature (Figure **23.13**). Three shepherds have come upon an ancient tomb, a symbol of death, which—as the allegorical Muse of History (right) confirms—reigns even in this most perfect of places. Poussin's painting, a pastoral elegy and a *memento mori*, instructs us that death is universal. Cool, bright colors and even lighting enhance the elegiac mood, while sharp contours and the sure use of line provide absolute clarity of design. But the real power of the painting lies in its rigorous composition. Poussin arrived at this composition by arranging and rearranging miniature wax models of his figures within a small rectangular box. He then posed these figures—statuesque, heroically proportioned, and idealized—so that their every gesture served to narrate

Figure 23.13 Nicolas Poussin, *Arcadian Shepherds*, 1638–1639. Oil on canvas, 33½ × 47⅝ in. Louvre, Paris. Scala/Art Resource, New York.

Figure 23.14 Claude Lorrain (Claude Gellée), *The Marriage of Isaac and Rebekah (The Mill)*, 1642. Oil on canvas, 4 ft. 11 in. × 6 ft. 5 in. National Gallery, London.

the story. Indeed, all of the elements in the painting, from the Muse's feet (which parallel the horizontal picture plane) to the trees in the landscape and at the right edge of the tomb (which parallel the vertical picture plane) contribute to the geometric order of the pictorial structure.

Despite the grand theatricality of Poussin's paintings, order dominates over spontaneity. Both in form and in content, Poussin's canvases are intellectual; that is, they appeal to the mind rather than to the senses. In contrast to Italian baroque painters such as Caravaggio, whose works he detested, Poussin soberly advanced the aesthetics of neoclassicism.

Poussin and his contemporary, Claude Gellée (1600–1682), known as Claude Lorrain, were responsible for creating the genre known as the "ideal landscape," a landscape painted in the high-minded, idealized style usually found in traditional moral subjects. For such paintings, academic artists made careful renderings of the countryside around Rome. They then deliberately assembled and combined the contents of their sketches according to the classical ideals of balance and clarity. Lorrain's landscapes, characterized by haunting qualities of light, were tranquil settings for lofty mythological or biblical subjects (Figure **23.14**). Unlike the Dutch landscape painters, who rendered nature with forthright realism (see Figure 22.9), academic artists imposed a preconceived, rationalized order upon the natural world.

The Aristocratic Portrait

The Age of the Baroque was the great period of aristocratic portraiture. Commissioned by the hundreds by Louis XIV and the members of his court, aristocratic portraits differ dramatically from the portraits of such artists as Hals, Leyster, and Rembrandt. Whereas Dutch artists investigated the personalities of their sitters, bringing to their portraits a combination of psychological intimacy and forthrightness, French artists were concerned primarily with outward appearance. The classic example of French aristocratic portraiture is the image of Louis XIV shown at the beginning of this chapter (see Figure 23.1), painted in 1701 by Hyacinthe Rigaud (1659–1743). Rigaud shows the aging monarch in his coronation garments, with the royal paraphernalia: the scepter, the crown (on the cushion at the left), and the sword of state. He is adorned with ermine-lined coronation robes, silk stockings, lace cravat, high-heeled shoes, and a well-manicured wig—all but the first were fashionable hallmarks of upper-class wealth. Louis' mannered pose, which harks back to classical models, reflects self-conscious pride in status. Rigaud employed special devices to enhance the themes of authority and regality: Satin curtains theatrically dignify the king and a lone column compositionally and metaphorically underscores his rectitude. Such devices would become standard conventions in European and American portraits of the eighteenth century (see Figure 26.25).

The Aristocratic Style in Europe
Velásquez, Rubens, and van Dyck

In Spain, Diego Velásquez (1599–1660), court painter to King Philip IV, became that country's most prestigious artist. Velásquez excelled at modeling forms so that they conveyed the powerful presence of real objects in atmospheric space. For the Spanish court, Velásquez painted a variety of classical and Christian subjects, but his greatest enterprise was the informal group portrait known as *Las Meninas* (*The Maids of Honor*; Figure **23.15**). In this painting, Velásquez depicted himself at his easel, alongside the members of the royal court: the *infanta* (the five-year-old daughter of the king), her maids of honor, her dwarf, a mastiff hound, and the royal escorts. In the background is a mirror that reflects the images of the king and queen of Spain—presumably the subjects of the large canvas Velásquez shows himself painting in the left foreground. Superficially, this is a group portrait of the kind we have already encountered in the art of

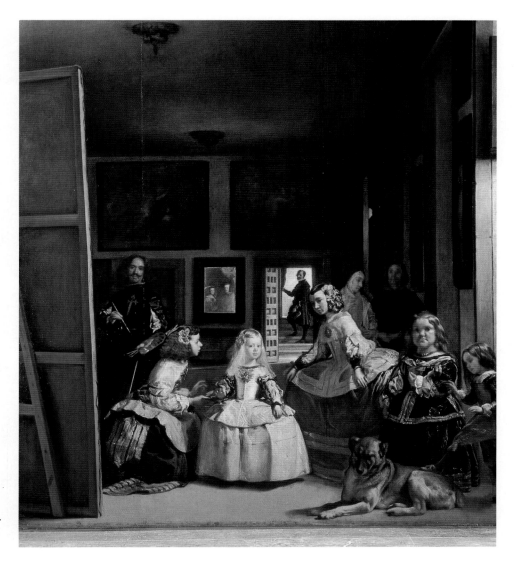

Figure 23.15 Diego Velásquez, *Las Meninas* (*The Maids of Honor*), 1656. Oil on canvas, 10 ft. 5 in. × 9 ft. Prado, Madrid. Ampliaciones y Reproducciones Mas (Arxiu Mas), Madrid.

Rembrandt (see Figure 22.14), but it is far more complex in composition and in content—its "meaning" has been the subject of extensive debate among art historians. Indisputably, however, *Las Meninas* comments intriguingly on the relationship between the perceived and the perceiver. Almost all of the characters in the painting, including the painter himself, are shown gazing at the royal couple, who must be standing outside of the picture space in the very spot occupied by the viewer. With baroque inventiveness, Velásquez expands the spatial field to include the beholder; at the same time he cunningly suggests a variety of vantage points. The painting becomes a visual "conceit" that provokes a dialogue between viewer and viewed and between patron and artist.

A contemporary of Velásquez, the internationally renowned Flemish painter Peter Paul Rubens (1577–1640) established his reputation in the courts of Europe. Fluent in six languages, he traveled widely as a diplomat and art dealer for royal patrons in Italy, England, and France. He also headed a large studio workshop that trained scores of assistants to help fill his many commissions—a total lifetime production of some 1,800 paintings. For the Luxembourg Palace of Paris, Rubens and his studio executed twenty-one monumental canvases that glorified Marie de' Medici, Louis XIV's grandmother, and her late husband, King Henry IV of France. Like Poussin, Rubens studied in Italy and was familiar with both classical and High Renaissance art. Rubens deeply admired the flamboyant colorists Titian and Tintoretto, and he developed a style that, by comparison with Poussin's, was painterly in technique and dynamic in composition.

One of Rubens' most memorable canvases, the *Rape of the Daughters of Leucippus* (Figure 23.16), depicts the abduction of two mortal women by the Roman gods Castor and Pollux. Rubens' portrayal of the classical story brims with vigor and imagination: Pressing against the picture plane are the fleshy bodies of the nude maidens, their limbs arranged in the pattern of a slowly

Figure 23.16 Peter Paul Rubens, *Rape of the Daughters of Leucippus*, ca. 1618. Oil on canvas, 7 ft. 3 in. × 6 ft. 10 in. Alte Pinakothek, Munich.

revolving pinwheel. The masterful paintstrokes exploit sensuous contrasts of luminous pink flesh, burnished armor, gleaming satins, and dense horsehide. Probably commissioned to commemorate the double marriage of Louis XIII of France to a Spanish princess and Philip IV of Spain to a French princess (and, thus, to celebrate the diplomatic alliance of France and Spain), the subtext of the painting is a message of (male) power over (female) privilege—and, by extension, of political absolutism. Images of subjugation by force, whether in the form of lion hunts (as in ancient Assyrian reliefs; see chapter 3) or in paintings and sculptures depicting mythological stories of rape, were metaphors for the sovereign authority of the ruler over his subjects, hence a veiled expression of political absolutism.

In England, the most accomplished seventeenth-century portraitist was the Flemish master Anthony van Dyck (1599–1641). Born in Antwerp, van Dyck had been an assistant to Rubens and may have worked with him on the *Rape of the Daughters of Leucippus*. Unwilling to compete with Rubens, van Dyck moved to Genoa and then to London, where he became the court painter to King Charles I of England. Van Dyck's many commissioned portraits of European aristocrats are striking for their polished elegance and idealized grandeur, features that are especially evident in his equestrian portrait of King Charles I (see Figure 21.1). In this painting, which revives the traditional motif of ruler-on-horseback (see chapters 7, 11, and 17), van Dyck shows the king, who was actually short and undistinguished looking, as handsome and regal. The combination of fluid composition and naturalistic detail, and the shimmering vitality of the brushwork make this one of the most memorable examples of aristocratic baroque portraiture.

Figure 23.17 King Louis XIV as the sun in the 1653 *Ballet de la Nuit*. Bibliothèque Nationale, Paris.

Music and Dance at the Court of Louis XIV

The court at Versailles was the setting for an extraordinary outpouring of music, theater, and dance. To provide musical entertainments for state dinners, balls, and operatic performances, Louis established a permanent orchestra, the first in European history. Its director, the Italian-born (but French-educated) Jean-Baptiste Lully (1632–1687), also headed the French Academy of Music. Often called the father of French opera, Lully oversaw all phases of musical performance, from writing scores and conducting the orchestra to training the chorus and staging operatic productions. Many of Lully's operas were based on themes from classical mythology. Their semidivine heroes, prototypes of Louis himself, flattered his image as ruler.

Lully's operas shared the pomp and splendor of Le Brun's frescoes, the strict clarity of Poussin's paintings,

and the formal correctness of classical drama. Though Lully's compositions were generally lacking in spontaneity and warmth of feeling, they were faithful to the neoclassical unity of words and music. Lully modified the music of the recitative to follow precisely and with great clarity the inflections of the spoken word. He also introduced to opera the "French overture," an instrumental form that featured contrasts between a slow first part in homophonic texture and a fast, contrapuntal second part. Under Lully's leadership, French opera also developed its most characteristic feature: the inclusion of formal dance.

At the court of Louis XIV, dancing and fencing were the touchstones of aristocratic grace. All members of the upper class were expected to perform the basic court dances, including the very popular *minuet*, and the courtier who could not dance was judged rude and inept. Like his father, Louis XIII, who had commissioned and participated in extravagantly expensive ballets, Louis XIV was a superb dancer. Dressed as the sun, he danced the lead in the 1653 performance of the *Ballet de la Nuit* (Figure **23.17**). Of lasting significance was Louis' contribution to the birth of professional dance and the transformation of court dance into an independent art form. During the late seventeenth century, French ballet masters of the Royal Academy of Dance established rules for the five positions that have become the basis for classical dance. Clarity, balance, and proportion, along with studied technique—elements characteristic of classicism in general—became the ideals of the classical ballet.

By 1685 female dancers were permitted to join the previously all-male French dance ensembles in staged performances. And in 1700 Raoul Auget Feuillet published a system of abstract symbols for recording specific dance steps and movements, thus facilitating **choreography**. Ballet, itself a metaphor for the strict etiquette and ceremony of court life, enriched all aspects of the French theater. However, since classical ballet demanded a rigorous attention to proper form, it soon became too specialized for any but professionals to perform, and so there developed the gap between performer and audience that exists to this day in the art of dance.

Neoclassicism and French Literature

As with other forms of artistic expression in seventeenth-century France, in literature neoclassical precepts of form and content held sway. French writers addressed questions of human dignity and morality in a language that was clear, polished, and precise. Their prose is marked by refinement, good taste, and the concentrated presentation of ideas.

One literary genre that typified the neoclassical spirit was the **maxim**. A maxim is a short, concise, and often witty saying, usually drawn from experience and offering some practical advice. Witty sayings that distilled wisdom into a few words were popular in many cultures, including those of the Hebrews, the Greeks, and the Africans. But in seventeenth-century France, the cautionary or moralizing aphorism was exalted as the ideal means of teaching good sense and decorum. Terse and lean, the maxim exalted precision of language and thought. France's greatest maxim writer was François de La Rochefoucauld (1613–1680), a nobleman who had participated in a revolt against Louis XIV early in his reign. Withdrawing from court society, La Rochefoucauld wrote with a cynicism that

reflected his conviction that self-interest, hypocrisy, and greed motivated the behavior of most human beings—including and especially the aristocrats of his day. As the following maxims illustrate, however, La Rochefoucauld's insights into human behavior apply equally well to individuals of all social classes and to any age.

READING 4.12
From La Rochefoucauld's *Maxims*

Truth does less good in the world than its appearances do harm.

Love of justice in most men is only a fear of encountering injustice.

We often do good that we may do harm with impunity.

As it is the mark of great minds to convey much in few words, so small minds are skilled at talking at length and saying little.

Virtue would not go nearly so far if vanity did not keep her company.

We confess to small faults to create the impression that we have no great ones.

To be rational is not to use reason by chance, but to recognize it, distinguish it, appreciate it.

————◆————

Like La Rochefoucauld's maxims, but on a larger scale, French drama, too, reflected the neoclassical effort to restrain passionate feeling by means of cool objectivity and common sense. The leading French tragedian of the seventeenth century, Jean Racine (1639–1699), wrote plays that treated high-minded themes in an elevated language. Racine added to Aristotle's unities of action and time (see chapter 6) a strict unity of place, thus manifesting his abiding commitment to intellectual control. In the play *Phèdre* (1677), itself based on Greek models, Racine explored the conflict between human passions (Phaedra's "unnatural" infatuation with her stepson) and human reason (Phaedra's sense of duty as the wife of Theseus, king of Athens). As in all of Racine's tragedies of passion, *Phèdre* illustrates the disastrous consequences of emotional indulgence—a weakness especially peculiar to Racine's female characters. Indeed, while Racine created some of the most dramatic female roles in neoclassical theater, he usually pictured women as weak, irrational, and cruel.

Molière's Human Comedy

Jean-Baptiste Poquelin (1622–1673), whose stage name was Molière, was France's leading comic dramatist. His comic genius is demonstrated through a technique that emphasizes some aspect of human behavior which, through exaggeration, is held up to ridicule. His standard of measurement for such behavior is reason and moderation, the norms of classicism. Thus by contrasting an incident of hypocrisy, pomposity, or other human foible with a balanced view, he illustrates that excesses of human passion and vanity enfeeble human dignity.

Molière, the son of a wealthy upholsterer, abandoned a career in law in favor of acting and play writing. He learned much from the *commedia dell'arte*, a form of improvised Italian street theater that depended on buffoonery, slapstick humor, and pantomime. Molière's plays involve simple story lines that bring to life the comic foibles of such stock characters as the miser, the hypochondriac, the hypocrite, the misanthrope, and the would-be gentleman. The last of these, a character whose attempts to assume the trappings of upper-class respectability turn him into a dupe, is the subject of one of Molière's last plays, *Le Bourgeois Gentilhomme* ("The Tradesman Turned Gentleman"; 1670). *Le Bourgeois Gentilhomme* was designed as a *comédie-ballet*, a dramatic performance that incorporated interludes of song and dance (in a manner similar to modern musical comedy). Lully provided the music, choreographed the ballet, and directed the entire production, which, like many other of Molière's plays, was well received by the king and his court.

But even beyond Versailles, Molière's hilarious comedy had wide appeal. French aristocrats, convinced that they were above imitation, embraced the play. So did upper-middle-class patrons who, while claiming an increasingly prominent place in the social order, refused to see themselves as "tradesmen turned gentlemen." Women found themselves endowed in Molière's play with confidence and guile, while servants discovered themselves invested with admirable common sense. The comedy, for all its farce, reflected the emerging class structure of early modern European society, with its firmly drawn lines between the sexes. In a single stroke, *Le Bourgeois Gentilhomme* captured the spirit of the seventeenth century—its class tensions and social contradictions, along with its ambitions and high expectations. Yet, for all its value as a mirror of a particular time and place, *Le Bourgeois Gentilhomme* is universal and timeless. The portions of the first and second act of the play included here offer a representative sampling of Molière's rollicking exposition of human nature.

READING 4.13

From Molière's *Le Bourgeois Gentilhomme*

Characters

Mr. Jourdain	His Scholar
Mrs. Jourdain, *his wife*	A Dancing-Master
Lucile, *his daughter*	A Fencing-Master
Cléonte, *suitor of Lucile*	A Philosophy-Master
Dorimene, *a marquise*	A Master-Tailor
Dorante, *a count, in love with Dorimene*	A Journeyman-Tailor
Nicole, *servant to Mr. Jourdain*	Two Lackeys
Covielle, *valet to Cléonte*	Musicians, Dancers, Cooks, Journeymen Tailors, and
A Music-Master	other characters to dance in the interludes

The scene is at Paris

Act I

Overture, played by a full orchestra; in the middle of the stage the Music-Master's Scholar, seated at a table, is composing the air for a serenade which Mr. Jourdain has ordered.

Scene I

Music-Master, Dancing-Master, Three Singers, Two Violinists, Four Dancers

MUSIC-MASTER (*To the singers*): Here, step inside, and wait until he comes. 1

DANCING-MASTER (*To the dancers*): And you too, this way.

MUSIC-MASTER (*To his scholar*): Is it finished?

SCHOLAR: Yes.

MUSIC-MASTER: Let's see . . . That's good.

DANCING-MASTER: Is it something new?

MUSIC-MASTER: Yes, 'tis the air for a serenade which I have had him compose, while waiting for our gentleman to wake up. 10

DANCING-MASTER: May I see it?

MUSIC-MASTER: You shall hear it, with the words, when he comes. He won't be long.

DANCING-MASTER: You and I have no lack of occupation now.

MUSIC-MASTER: That's true. We have found a man here who is just what we both needed. He's a nice little source of income for us, this Mr. Jourdain, with his visions of nobility and gallantry that he has got into his noddle. And 'twould be a fine thing for your dancing and my music if everybody were like him. 20

DANCING-MASTER: No, no, not quite; I could wish, for his sake, that he had some true understanding of the good things we bring him.

MUSIC-MASTER: 'Tis true he understands them ill, but he pays for them well; and that is what the arts need most nowadays.

DANCING-MASTER: For my part, I'll own, I must be fed somewhat on fame. I am sensitive to applause, and I feel that in all the fine arts 'tis a grievous torture to show one's talents before fools, and to endure the barbarous judgments of a dunce upon our compositions. There's great pleasure, I tell you, in working for people who are capable of feeling the refinements of art, who know how to give a flattering reception to the beauties of your work, 30 and recompense your toil by titillating praise. Yes, the most agreeable reward possible for what we do, is to see it understood, to see it caressed by applause that honors us. Nothing else, methinks, can pay us so well for all our labors; and enlightened praise gives exquisite delight.   40

MUSIC-MASTER: I grant you that, and I relish it as you do. There is surely nothing more gratifying than such praise as you speak of; but man cannot live on applause. Mere praise won't buy you an estate; it takes something more solid. And the best way to praise, is to praise with open hands. Our fellow, to be sure, is a man of little wit, who discourses at random about anything and everything, and never applauds but at the wrong time. But his money sets right the errors of his mind; there is judgment in his purse; his praises pass current; and this ignorant   50 shopkeeper is worth more to us, as you very well see, than the enlightened lord who introduced us to his house.

DANCING-MASTER: There is some truth in what you say; but methinks you set too much store by money; and self-interest is something so base that no gentleman should ever show a leaning towards it.

MUSIC-MASTER: Yet I haven't seen you refuse the money our fellow offers you.

DANCING-MASTER: Certainly not; but neither do I find therein all my happiness; and I could still wish that with   60 his wealth he had good taste to boot.

MUSIC-MASTER: I could wish so too; and 'tis to that end that we are both working, as best we may. But in any case, he gives us the means to make ourselves known in the world; he shall pay for others, and others shall praise for him.

DANCING-MASTER: Here he comes.

[Act I, Scene II: Mr. Jourdain converses with his music- and dancing-masters, who dispute as to which is the more important art: music or dance. A dialogue in music, written by the music-master, follows, then a ballet choreographed by the dancing-master.

Act II, Scene I: Mr. Jourdain dances the minuet for the dancing-master, and then learns how to make a "proper" bow.]

Act II, Scene II
Mr. Jourdain, Music-Master, Dancing-Master, Lackey

LACKEY: Sir, here is your fencing-master.   1

MR. JOURDAIN: Tell him to come in and give me my lesson here. (*To the music-master and dancing-master*) I want you to see me perform.

Scene III
Mr. Jourdain, Fencing-Master, Music-Master, Dancing-Master, a Lackey *with two foils*

FENCING-MASTER (*Taking the two foils from the lackey and giving one of them to Mr. Jourdain*): Now, sir, your salute. The body erect. The weight slightly on the left thigh. The legs not so far apart. The feet in line. The wrist in line with the thigh. The point of your sword in line with your shoulder. The arm not quite so far extended. The left hand on a level with the eye. The left shoulder farther back.   10 Head up. A bold look. Advance. The body steady. Engage my sword in quart[1] and finish the thrust. One, two. Recover. Again, your feet firm. One, two. Retreat. When

you thrust, sir, your sword must move first, and your body be held well back, and sideways. One, two. Now, engage my sword in tierce,[2] and finish the thrust. Advance. Your body steady. Advance. Now, from that position. One, two. Recover. Again. One, two. Retreat. On guard, sir, on guard (*the fencing-master gives him several thrusts*), on guard.

MR. JOURDAIN: Well?   20

MUSIC-MASTER: You do wonders.

FENCING-MASTER: I've told you already: the whole secret of arms consists in two things only: hitting and not being hit. And as I proved to you the other day by demonstrative logic, it is impossible that you should be hit if you know how to turn aside your adversary's sword from the line of your body; and that depends merely on a slight movement of the wrist, inwards or outwards.

MR. JOURDAIN: So, then, without any courage, one may be sure of killing his man and not being killed?   30

FENCING-MASTER: Certainly. Didn't you see the demonstration of it?

MR. JOURDAIN: Yes.

FENCING-MASTER: And by this you may see how highly our profession should be esteemed in the State; and how far the science of arms excels all other sciences that are of no use, like dancing, music . . .

DANCING-MASTER: Softly, Mr. Swordsman; don't speak disrespectfully of dancing.

MUSIC-MASTER: Learn, pray, to appreciate better the   40 excellences of music.

FENCING-MASTER: You are absurd fellows, to think of comparing your sciences with mine.

MUSIC-MASTER: Just see the man of consequence!

DANCING-MASTER: The ridiculous animal, with his padded stomacher![3]

FENCING-MASTER: My little dancing-master, I will make you dance to a tune of my own, and you, little songster, I will make you sing out lustily.

DANCING-MASTER: Mr. Ironmonger, I'll teach you your own   50 trade.

MR. JOURDAIN (*To the dancing-master*): Are you mad, to pick a quarrel with him, when he knows tierce and quart and can kill a man by demonstrative logic?

DANCING-MASTER: A fig for his demonstrative logic, and his tierce and his quart.

MR. JOURDAIN (*To the dancing-master*): Softly, I tell you.

FENCING-MASTER (*To the dancing-master*): What, little Master Impudence!

MR. JOURDAIN: Hey! my dear fencing-master.   60

DANCING-MASTER (*To the fencing-master*): What, you great cart-horse!

MR. JOURDAIN: Hey, my dear dancing-master.

FENCING-MASTER: If I once fall upon you . . .

MR. JOURDAIN (*To the fencing-master*): Gently.

DANCING-MASTER: If I once lay hands on you . . .

MR. JOURDAIN (*To the dancing-master*): So, so.

FENCING-MASTER: I will give you such a dressing . . .

MR. JOURDAIN (*To the fencing-master*): I beg you.

DANCING-MASTER: I will give you such a drubbing . . .   70

MR. JOURDAIN (*To the dancing-master*): I beseech you . . .

MUSIC-MASTER: Let us teach him manners a little.

MR. JOURDAIN: Good Heavens! do stop.

[1] A defensive posture in the art of fencing.
[2] Another fencing posture.
[3] Protection used in fencing.

Scene IV

Professor of Philosphy, Mr. Jourdain, Music-Master, Dancing-Master, Fencing-Master, Lackey

MR. JOURDAIN: Oho! Mr. Philosopher, you've arrived in the nick of time with your philosophy. Do come and set these people here at peace.

THE PHILOSOPHER: How now? What is the matter, gentlemen?

MR. JOURDAIN: They have put themselves in a passion about the precedence of their professions, and even 80 insulted each other and almost come to blows.

THE PHILOSOPHER: O fie, gentlemen! Should a man so lose his self-control? Have you not read the learned treatise which Seneca composed, *Of Anger*?[4] Is there anything more base or shameful than this passion, which of a man makes a savage beast? Should not reason be mistress of all our emotions?

DANCING-MASTER: How, how, sir! Here he comes and insults us both, by condemning dancing, which I practise, and music, which is his profession. 90

THE PHILOSOPHER: A wise man is above all the insults that can be offered him; and the chief answer which we should make to all offences, is calmness and patience.

FENCING-MASTER: They both have the insolence to think of comparing their professions with mine!

THE PHILOSOPHER: Should that move you? 'Tis not for vainglory and precedence that men should contend; what really distinguishes us from each other is wisdom and virtue.

DANCING-MASTER: I maintain to his face that dancing is a 100 science which cannot be too highly honored.

MUSIC-MASTER: And I, that music is a science which all ages have reverenced.

FENCING-MASTER: And I maintain, against both of them, that the science of fencing is the finest and most indispensable of all sciences.

THE PHILOSOPHER: But what then becomes of philosophy? I think you are all three mighty impertinent to speak with such arrogance before me, and impudently to give the name of science to things which ought not even to 110 be honored with the name of art, and which may best be classed together as pitiful trades, whether of prize-fighters, ballad-mongers, or mountebanks.[5]

FENCING-MASTER: Go to, dog of a philosopher.

MUSIC-MASTER: Go to, beggarly pedagogue.

DANCING-MASTER: Go to, past master pedant.

THE PHILOSOPHER: What, you rascally knaves! . . .
(He falls upon them, and they all three belabor him with blows.)

MR. JOURDAIN: Mr. Philosopher!

THE PHILOSOPHER: Villains! varlets! insolent vermin!

MR. JOURDAIN: Mr. Philosopher! 120

FENCING-MASTER: Plague take the beast!

MR. JOURDAIN: Gentlemen!

THE PHILOSOPHER: Brazen-faced ruffians!

MR. JOURDAIN: Mr. Philosopher!

DANCING-MASTER: Deuce take the old pack-mule!

MR. JOURDAIN: Gentlemen!

THE PHILOSOPHER: Scoundrels!

MR. JOURDAIN: Mr. Philosopher!

MUSIC-MASTER: Devil take the impertinent puppy!

MR. JOURDAIN: Gentlemen! 130

THE PHILOSOPHER: Thieves! vagabonds! rogues! impostors!

MR. JOURDAIN: Mr. Philosopher! Gentlemen! Mr. Philosopher! Gentlemen! Mr. Philosopher!
(Exit fighting.)

Scene V

Mr. Jourdain, Lackey

MR. JOURDAIN: Oh! fight as much as you please; I can't help it, and I won't go spoil my gown trying to part you. I should be mad to thrust myself among them and get some blow that might do me a mischief.

Scene VI

The Philosopher, Mr. Jourdain, Lackey

THE PHILOSOPHER *(Straightening his collar)*: Now for our lesson.

MR. JOURDAIN: Oh! sir, I am sorry for the blows you got. 140

THE PHILOSOPHER: That's nothing. A philosopher knows how to take things aright; and I shall compose a satire against them in Juvenal's manner,[6] which will cut them up properly. But let that pass. What do you want to learn?

MR. JOURDAIN: Everything I can; for I have the greatest desire conceivable to be learned; it throws me in a rage to think that my father and mother did not make me study all the sciences when I was young.

THE PHILOSOPHER: That is a reasonable sentiment; *nam, sine doctrina, vita est quasi mortis imago.* You 150 understand that, for of course you know Latin.

MR. JOURDAIN: Yes; but play that I don't know it; and explain what it means.

THE PHILOSOPHER: It means that, *without learning, life is almost an image of death.*

MR. JOURDAIN: That same Latin's in the right.

THE PHILOSOPHER: Have you not some foundations, some rudiments of knowledge?

MR. JOURDAIN: Oh! yes, I can read and write.

THE PHILOSOPHER: Where will you please to have us 160 begin? Shall I teach you logic?

MR. JOURDAIN: What may that same logic be?

THE PHILOSOPHER: 'Tis the science that teaches the three operations of the mind.

MR. JOURDAIN: And who are they, these three operations of the mind?

THE PHILOSOPHER: The first, the second, and the third. The first is to conceive aright, by means of the universals; the second, to judge aright, by means of the categories; and the third, to draw deductions aright, by means of the 170 figures: *Barbara, Celarent, Darii, Ferio, Baralipton.*[7]

MR. JOURDAIN: There's a pack of crabbed words. This logic doesn't suit me at all. Let's learn something else that's prettier.

THE PHILOSOPHER: Will you learn ethics?

MR. JOURDAIN: Ethics?

THE PHILOSOPHER: Yes.

---

[4]A treatise by the first-century Roman stoic, Lucius Annaeus Seneca (see chapter 7).
[5]Charlatans or quacks.

[6]A Roman satirist of the early second century (see chapter 7).
[7]Part of a series of Latin names used by medieval logicians to help remember the valid forms of syllogisms.

MR. JOURDAIN: What is your ethics about?

THE PHILOSOPHER: It treats of happiness, teaches men to moderate their passions, and . . .   180

MR. JOURDAIN: No; no more of that. I am choleric as the whole pack of devils, ethics or no ethics; no, sir, I'll be angry to my heart's content, whenever I have a mind to it.

THE PHILOSOPHER: Is it physics you want to learn?

MR. JOURDAIN: And what has this physics to say for itself?

THE PHILOSOPHER: Physics is the science which explains the principles of natural phenomena, and the properties of bodies; which treats of the nature of the elements, metals, minerals, stones, plants, and animals, and teaches us the causes of all such things as meteors, the   190 rainbow, St. Elmo's fire,[8] comets, lightning, thunder, thunderbolts, rain, snow, hail, winds, and whirlwinds.

MR. JOURDAIN: There's too much jingle-jangle in that, too much hurly-burly.

THE PHILOSOPHER: Then what to do you want me to teach you?

MR. JOURDAIN: Teach me spelling.

THE PHILOSOPHER: With all my heart.

MR. JOURDAIN: And afterward, you shall teach me the almanac, so as to know when there's a moon, and when   200 there isn't.

THE PHILOSOPHER: Very well. To follow up your line of thought logically, and treat this matter in true philosophic fashion, we must begin, according to the proper order of things, by an exact knowledge of the nature of the letters, and the different method of pronouncing each one. And on that head I must tell you that the letters are divided into vowels, so called—*vowels*—because they express the sounds of the *voice* alone; and consonants, so called—*con-sonants*—because they *sound* with the vowels, and   210 only mark the different articulations of the voice. There are five vowels, or voices: A, E, I, O, U.

MR. JOURDAIN: I understand all that.

THE PHILOSOPHER: The vowel A is formed by opening the mouth wide: A.

MR. JOURDAIN: A, A. Yes.

THE PHILOSOPHER: The vowel E is formed by lifting the lower jaw nearer to the upper: A, E.

MR. JOURDAIN: A, E; A, E. On my word, 'tis so. Ah! how fine!   220

THE PHILOSOPHER: And the vowel I, by bringing the jaws still nearer together, and stretching the corners of the mouth toward the ears: A, E, I.

MR. JOURDAIN: A, E, I, I, I, I. That is true. Science forever!

THE PHILOSOPHER: The vowel O is formed by opening the jaws, and drawing in the lips at the corners: O.

MR. JOURDAIN: O, O. Nothing could be more correct: A, E, I, O, I, O. 'Tis admirable! I, O; I, O.

THE PHILOSOPHER: The opening of the mouth looks exactly like a little circle, representing an O.   230

MR. JOURDAIN: O, O, O. You are right. O. Ah! What a fine thing it is to know something!

THE PHILOSOPHER: The vowel U is formed by bringing the teeth together without letting them quite touch, and thrusting out the lips, at the same time bringing them together without quite shutting them: U.

MR. JOURDAIN: U, U. Nothing could be truer: U.

THE PHILOSOPHER: Your lips are extended as if you were pouting; therefore if you wish to make a face at anyone, and mock at him, you have only to say U.   240

MR. JOURDAIN: U, U. 'Tis true. Ah! would I had studied sooner, to know all that!

THE PHILOSOPHER: To-morrow, we will consider the other letters, namely the consonants.

MR. JOURDAIN: Are there just as curious things about them as about these?

THE PHILOSOPHER: Certainly. The consonant D, for instance, is pronounced by clapping the tip of the tongue just above the upper teeth: D.

MR. JOURDAIN: D, D. Yes! Oh! what fine things! what fine   250 things!

THE PHILOSOPHER: The F, by resting the upper teeth on the lower lip: F.

MR. JOURDAIN: F, F. 'Tis the very truth. Oh! father and mother of me, what a grudge I owe you!

THE PHILOSOPHER: And the R by lifting the tip of the tongue to the roof of the mouth; so that being grazed by the air, which comes out sharply, it yields to it, yet keeps returning to the same point, and so makes a sort of trilling: R, Ra.

MR. JOURDAIN: R, R, Ra, R, R, R, R, R, Ra. That is fine.   260 Oh! what a learned man you are, and how much time I've lost! R, R, R, Ra.

THE PHILOSOPHER: I will explain all these curious things to you thoroughly.

MR. JOURDAIN: Do, I beg you. But now, I must tell you a great secret. I am in love with a person of very high rank, and I wish you would help me to write her something in a little love note which I'll drop at her feet.

THE PHILOSOPHER: Excellent!

MR. JOURDAIN: 'Twill be very gallant, will it not?   270

THE PHILOSOPHER: Surely. Do you want to write to her in verse?

MR. JOURDAIN: No, no; none of your verse.

THE PHILOSOPHER: You want mere prose?

MR. JOURDAIN: No, I will have neither prose nor verse.

THE PHILOSOPHER: It must needs be one or the other.

MR. JOURDAIN: Why?

THE PHILOSOPHER: For this reason, that there is nothing but prose or verse to express oneself by.

MR. JOURDAIN: There is nothing but prose or verse?   280

THE PHILOSOPHER: No, sir. All that is not prose is verse, and all that is not verse is prose.

MR. JOURDAIN: But when we talk, what is that, say?

THE PHILOSOPHER: Prose.

MR. JOURDAIN: What! When I say: "Nicole, bring me my slippers and give me my nightcap," that's prose?

THE PHILOSOPHER: Yes, sir.

MR. JOURDAIN: Oh my word, I've been speaking prose these forty years, and never knew it; I am infinitely obliged to you for having informed me of this. Now I want to write to her   290 in a note: *Fair Marquise,*[9] *your fair eyes make me die of love;* but I want it to be put in gallant fashion, and neatly turned.

THE PHILOSOPHER: Say that the fires of her eyes reduce your heart to ashes; that night and day you suffer for her all the tortures of a . . .

MR. JOURDAIN: No, no, no, I want none of all that. I will have nothing but what I told you: *Fair Marquise, your fair*

---

[8]Electrical discharges seen by sailors before and after storms at sea and named after the patron saint of sailors.

[9]The wife of a nobleman ranking below a duke and above an earl or count.

eyes make me die of love.

THE PHILOSOPHER: You must enlarge upon the matter a little.   300

MR. JOURDAIN: No, I tell you. I'll have none but those very words in the note, but put in a fashionable way, arranged as they should be. Pray tell me over the different ways they can be put, so that I may see.

THE PHILOSOPHER: You can first of all put them as you said: *Fair Marquise, your fair eyes make me die of love.* Or else: *Of love to die me make, fair Marquise, your fair eyes.* Or else: *Your fair eyes of love me make, fair Marquise, to die.* Or else: *To die your fair eyes, fair Marquise, of love me make.* Or else: *Me make your fair*   310 *eyes die, fair Marquise, of love.*

MR. JOURDAIN: But which of all these ways is the best?

THE PHILOSOPHER: The way you said it: *Fair Marquise, your fair eyes make me die of love.*

MR. JOURDAIN: And yet I never studied, and I did it at the first try. I thank you with all my heart, and beg you to come again to-morrow early.

THE PHILOSOPHER: I shall not fail to.

Scene VII
Mr. Jourdain, Lackey

MR. JOURDAIN (*To the lackey*): What! Haven't my clothes come yet?   320

LACKEY: No, sir.

MR. JOURDAIN: That cursed tailor makes me wait a long while, on a day when I'm so busy. I am furious. May the quartan ague[10] wring this villain of a tailor unmercifully! To the devil with the tailor! Plague choke the tailor! If I had him here now, that wretch of a tailor, that dog of a tailor, that scoundrel of a tailor, I'd . . .

Scene VIII
Mr. Jourdain, A Master-Tailor; A Journeyman-Tailor, *carrying Mr. Jourdain's suit*; Lackey

MR. JOURDAIN: Ah! so there you are! I was just going to get angry with you.

MASTER-TAILOR: I could not come sooner. I had twenty   330 men at work on your clothes.

MR. JOURDAIN: You sent me some silk stockings so tight that I had dreadful work getting them on, and there are two stitches broke in them already.

MASTER-TAILOR: If anything, they will grow only too loose.

MR. JOURDAIN: Yes, if I keep on breaking out stitches. And you made me some shoes that pinch horribly.

MASTER-TAILOR: Not at all, sir.

MR. JOURDAIN: What! Not at all?

MASTER-TAILOR: No, they do not pinch you.   340

MR. JOURDAIN: I tell you they do pinch me.

MASTER-TAILOR: You imagine it.

MR. JOURDAIN: I imagine it because I feel it. A fine way of talking!

MASTER-TAILOR: There, this is one of the very handsomest and best matched of court costumes. 'Tis a masterpiece to have invented a suit that is dignified, yet not of black; and I'd give the most cultured tailors six trials and defy them to equal it.

MR. JOURDAIN: What's this? You have put the flowers   350 upside down.

MASTER-TAILOR: You didn't tell me you wanted them right end up.

MR. JOURDAIN: Was there any need to tell you that?

MASTER-TAILOR: Why, of course. All persons of quality wear them this way.

MR. JOURDAIN: Persons of quality wear the flowers upside down?

MASTER-TAILOR: Yes, sir.

MR. JOURDAIN: Oh! that's all right then.   360

MASTER-TAILOR: If you wish, I will put them right end up.

MR. JOURDAIN: No, no.

MASTER-TAILOR: You have only to say the word.

MR. JOURDAIN: No, I tell you; you did rightly. Do you think the clothes will fit me?

MASTER-TAILOR: A pretty question! I defy any painter, with his brush, to make you a closer fit. I have in my shop a fellow that is the greatest genius in the world for setting up a pair of German breeches; and another who is the hero of our age for the cut of a doublet.[11]   370

MR. JOURDAIN: Are the wig and the feathers just as they should be?

MASTER-TAILOR: Everything is just right.

MR. JOURDAIN (*Looking at the tailor's suit*): Ah! ah! Mr. Tailor here is some of the cloth from my last suit you made me. I know it perfectly.

MASTER-TAILOR: The cloth seemed to me so fine that I thought well to cut a suit for myself out of it.

MR. JOURDAIN: Yes; but you ought not to have cabbaged[12] it out of mine.   380

MASTER-TAILOR: Will you put on your suit?

MR. JOURDAIN: Yes; let me have it.

MASTER-TAILOR: Wait. That is not the way to do things. I have brought my men with me to dress you to music; clothes such as these must be put on with ceremony. Ho! enter, you fellows.

Scene IX
Mr. Jourdain, Master-Tailor, Journeyman-Tailor; Dancers, *in the costume of journeymen-tailors*; Lackey

MASTER-TAILOR (*To his journeymen*): Put on the gentleman's suit, in the style you use for persons of quality.

First Ballet
Enter four journeymen-tailors, two of whom pull off Mr. Jourdain's breeches that he has on for his exercise, and   390 the other two his jacket; then they put on his new suit; and Mr. Jourdain walks about among them, showing off his suit, to see if it is all right. All this to the accompaniment of full orchestra.

JOURNEYMAN-TAILOR: Noble Sir, please give the tailor's men something to drink.

MR. JOURDAIN: What did you call me?

JOURNEYMAN-TAILOR: Noble Sir.

MR. JOURDAIN: Noble Sir! That is what it is to dress as a person of quality! You may go clothed as a tradesman all   400 your days, and nobody will call you Noble Sir. (*Giving him money*) There, that's for Noble Sir.

---

[10]An intermittent fever.

[11]A man's close-fitting jacket.
[12]Stolen or filched.

JOURNEYMAN-TAILOR: My Lord, we are greatly obliged to you.

MR. JOURDAIN: My Lord! Oh! oh! My Lord! Wait, friend; My Lord deserves something, 'tis no mean word, My Lord! There, there's what His Lordship gives you.

JOURNEYMAN-TAILOR: My Lord, we will all go and drink Your Grace's health.

MR. JOURDAIN: Your Grace! Oh! oh! oh! wait; don't go.   410 Your Grace, to me! (Aside) Faith, if he goes as far as Your Highness he'll empty my purse. (Aloud) There, there's for Your Grace.

JOURNEYMAN-TAILOR: My Lord, we thank you most humbly for your generosity.

MR. JOURDAIN: He did well to stop. I was just going to give it all to him.

Absolute Power and the Aristocratic Style Beyond Europe

Fueled by curiosity and commercial ambition, cross-cultural contacts between Europe and Asia flourished during the early modern era. In the 1700s, ambassadors of the Shah (the word means "king") of Persia and of other Asian potentates were splendidly received at Versailles, while, at the same time, Christian missionaries and official representatives of the European monarchs found their way to Hindu, Buddhist, and Muslim lands. France had long maintained diplomatic ties with the

Figure 23.18 Ceremonial canteen, Ottoman Empire, second half of sixteenth century. Gold decorated with jade plaques and gems. Topkapi Sarayi Museum, Istanbul.

Figure 23.19 Safavid carpet, Persia, seventeenth century. Silk and wool, 24 ft. 11 in. × 10 ft. 8 in. Austrian Museum for Applied Art, Vienna.

Ottoman Turks, the Muslim successors of the Seljuk Turks in Southwest Asia, North Africa, and parts of southeastern Europe (see Map 23.1). So powerful were the Ottoman forces and so vast were their territories that one of Louis' ancestors, Francis I, had attempted to tip the balance of power in Western Europe by forming, in 1536, an "unholy" alliance with the great Muslim leader Suleiman (1494–1566).

Under Suleiman's rule the Ottoman Empire became a model of Muslim absolutism. Unlimited power in matters political and religious lay in Suleiman's hands. Known in Turkish history as the "Lawgiver," Suleiman oversaw the establishment of a

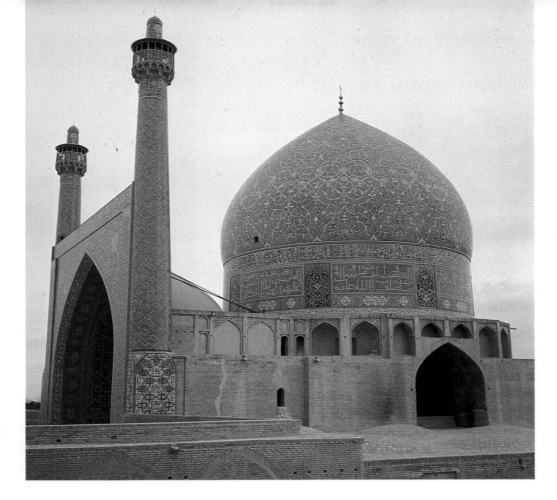

Figure 23.20 Imperial Mosque, Isfahan, Iran, 1637. Surface decorated with colored glazed tiles, height of dome 177 ft. © E. Böhm, Mainz.

legal code that fixed specific penalties for routine crimes and introduced the concept of balanced financial budgets. State revenues some eighty times those of France permitted Suleiman to undertake an extensive program of architectural and urban improvement in Mecca, Constantinople, and Jerusalem. A goldsmith and a poet of some esteem, Suleiman initiated a golden age of literature and art. Pomp and luxury characterized Suleiman's court, and the arts that flourished under his patronage shared with those of seventeenth-century France a taste for the ornate and a high degree of technical skill (Figure **23.18**). Suleiman, whom Europeans called "the magnificent," personally oversaw the activities of official court poets, painters, architects, and musicians. He established a model for imperial patronage that ensured the triumph of the aristocratic style not only in Turkish lands but in all parts of his multiethnic empire.

Neither absolutism nor its manifestation in the arts were the invention of Suleiman, any more than they were the creation of Louis XIV. Suleiman's ancestors, as well as his successors and their rivals, were equally autocratic. During the seventeenth century, as the Ottoman Empire fell into decline, Muslims of the Safavid dynasty rose to power in Persia under the astute leadership of Shah Abbas (1557–1629). Shah Abbas united a multiethnic population to make theocratic Persia (present-day Iran) the political, economic, and cultural leader of Asia. By the year 1600, Persian silk rivaled that of China at European markets. Carpet weaving became a national industry which employed over twenty-five thousand people in the capital city of Isfahan alone. Persian tapestries, intricately woven in silk and wool (Figure **23.19**), and finely ornamented ceramics were avidly sought across the world, and Persian manuscripts embellished with brightly printed illustrations came to be imitated throughout Asia. The arts were as much an adjunct to the majesty of Shah Abbas as they had been to Suleiman and would be to Louis XIV.

In the field of architecture, the outstanding monument to Safavid wealth and power was the Imperial Mosque, commissioned by Shah Abbas for the city of Isfahan (Figure **23.20**). Completed in 1637, this magnificent structure, flanked by two minarets, encloses a square main hall covered by a splendid dome which rises to 177 feet. The surfaces of the mosque, both inside and out, are covered with colored glazed tiles (compare the Ishtar Gate from Babylon, 604–562 B.C.E., illustrated in chapter 2) ornamented with delicate blue and yellow blossoms. French aristocrats in the service of Louis XIV brought back to France enthusiastic reports of the Imperial Mosque—a fact that has led scholars to detect the influence of Persian art on some of Louis' more lavish enterprises at Versailles.

The Aristocratic Style in India

Muslims had ruled parts of India for almost a thousand years, but it was not until the sixteenth century that a Muslim dynasty, known as the Moguls (the name derives from "Mongol"), actually succeeded in uniting all of India (see Map 23.1). Distant cousins of the Safavid princes, the Moguls created an Indian empire and ruled India as absolute monarchs from 1526 to 1707. They imported Persian culture and language into India in much the same way that Louis XIV brought Italian culture into France. The creators of a cultural style that blended Muslim, Hindu, Turkish, Persian, Arabic, and African traditions, the Moguls encouraged the development of an aristocratic style, which—like that of the Sun King—served as an adjunct to majesty.

The founder of the Mogul empire, Akbar (1542–1605), came to the throne at the age of thirteen and laid the foundations for a luxurious court style that his son and grandson would perpetuate. India's most dynamic ruler since Emperor Asoka of the third century B.C.E., Akbar ruled over a court consisting of thousands of courtiers, servants, wives, and concubines. He exercised political control over feudal noblemen and court officials who, unlike their French counterparts, received paid salaries. Amidst the primarily Hindu population, Akbar tirelessly pursued a policy of religious toleration, a position that complemented his own quest for a synthesis of faiths that would surpass the teaching of any one religion. To this end, he brought to his court learned representatives of Christianity, Judaism, Hinduism, and other religions to debate with Muslim theologians. He also made every effort to rid India of such outmoded traditions as the immolation of wives on their husbands' funeral pyres. Despite Akbar's reforms, however, the lower classes and especially the peasants were taxed heavily (as were the French peasants under Louis) to finance the luxuries of the upper-class elite.

In the seventeenth century, the Moguls governed the wealthiest state in the world, a state whose

Figure 23.21 *Heavenly Joys Come to Earth for Akbar*, painted miniature in Mogul manuscript of 1588. Opaque watercolor on paper, 5½ × 3 in. The Harvard University Art Museum. Gift of John Goelet.

1717	inoculation against smallpox is introduced in Europe (from Ottoman Turkey)
1736	expansion of the Indian shipbuilding industry in Bombay
1780	a European version of Chinese silk-reeling machines is introduced in Bengal
1781	Turkish methods for producing high-quality cloth are copied in England
1790	India uses military rockets based on Ottoman technology in warfare

revenues were ten times greater than those of France. Akbar commissioned magnificent works of music, poetry, painting, and architecture—the tangible expressions of princely affluence and taste. As was the case in Louis' court, most of these exquisite objects were designed for domestic, not liturgical, use. A state studio of over one hundred artists working under Persian masters created a library of over twenty-four thousand illuminated manuscripts, the contents of which ranged from love poetry to Hindu epics and religious tales. Mogul paintings reveal the brilliant union of delicate line, vivid color, and strong surface patterns—features that also appear in Asian carpets. A miniature illustrating the "heavenly joys" of Akbar shows the ruler holding a gold goblet. He sits on a cushioned throne beneath an elegant canopy, while female dancers and musicians entertain him with flutes, sitars, castanets, and cymbals (Figure **23.21**). Bright colors and the absence of Western perspective give the scene a strong decorative quality.

The Patronage of Jahangir and Shah Jahan

Under the rule of Akbar's son, Jahangir (ruled 1605–1627), aristocratic court portraiture came into fashion in India. The new genre reflects the influence of European painting, which had been eagerly embraced by the Moguls, and suggests the gradual relaxation of Muslim prohibition against the representation of the human figure. Relatively small in comparison with the aristocratic portraits executed by Rigaud or van Dyck (see Figures 21.1, 23.1), the painted likeness of Jahangir (the name means "world seizer") reflects, nevertheless, the will to glorify royalty in a realistic and psychologically probing style (Figure **23.22**). The artist Bichitr (fl. 1625), whose self-portrait appears in the lower left corner, shows the Shah enthroned atop an elaborate hourglass throne, a reference to the brevity of life, and possibly an allusion to Jahangir's declining health. Jahangir welcomes a sufi (a Muslim mystic), who stands in the company of a Turkish dignitary and the European King James I of England. Four Western-style angels frame the scene: The upper two seem to lament the impermanence of worldly power (as suggested in the inscription above them), while the bottom two inscribe the base of the hourglass with the prayer, "O Shah, may the span of your life be a thousand years." Just as Louis XIV assumed the guise of the Sun King, so Jahangir—as notorious for his overconsumption of wine and opium as Louis was for fine food and sex—is apotheosized by a huge halo consisting of the sun and the moon.

Well before the seventeenth century, Mogul rulers had initiated the tradition of building huge ceremonial and administrative complexes, veritable cities in

Figure 23.22 *Jahangir Preferring a Sufi Shaikh to Kings*, from the *Leningrad Album of Bichitr*, seventeenth century. Color and gold, 10 × 7⅛ in. Courtesy of the Freer Gallery of Art, Smithsonian Institution, Washington, D.C. (42.15A).

Figure 23.23 Anonymous Delhi artist, *The Red Fort*, ca. 1820. The building dates from the Shah Jahan period, after 1638. Courtesy of the British Library, London.

Figure 23.24 Foliated arcades and perforated monolithic screens in the Red Fort (Shahjahanabad), Delhi, Shah Jahan period, after 1638.

themselves. Such complexes symbolized Muslim wealth and authority in India. Akbar had personally overseen the construction of a palace complex near Agra, which, comparable with Versailles, featured an elaborate residence surrounded by courtyards and mosques, as well as by formal gardens and fountains watered by means of artificial conduits. The garden, a this-worldly counterpart of the Garden of Paradise described in the Quran (see chapter 10) and a welcome refuge from India's intense heat, was a characteristic feature of the Mogul palace complex.

Inspired by the elaborate ceremonial centers built by his father and his grandfather, Shah Jahan (1627–1666) commissioned the most sumptuous of all Mogul palaces, the Shahjahanabad (present-day Old Delhi). The red sandstone walls of the Shahjahanabad (nicknamed the "Red Fort") enclosed a palatial residence of white marble, flanked by magnificent gardens, public and private audience halls, courtyards, pavilions, baths, and the largest mosque in India (Figure 23.23). The Red Fort's 3:4 rectangular plan was bisected by an axis that led through successive courts to the public audience hall, a pattern that anticipated the rigid symmetry of Versailles (compare Figure 23.2).

The hot Indian climate inclined Mogul architects to open up interior space by means of foliated arcades (see chapter 10) and latticed screens through which breezes might blow uninterrupted. These graceful architectural features distinguish the Shah's palace at the Red Fort (Figure 23.24). The most ornate of all Mogul interiors, Shah Jahan's audience hall consists of white marble arcades and ceilings decorated with geometric and floral patterns popular in Mogul embroidery, a craft traditionally dominated by women. The rich designs consist of inlaid precious and semiprecious stones (*pietra dura*), a type of mosaic work that the Moguls had borrowed from Italy (Figure 23.25). At the center of the hall, the Shah once sat on the prized (but no longer existing) Peacock Throne, fashioned in solid gold and studded with emeralds, rubies, diamonds, and pearls. Above the throne (which served as the imperial throne of India until it was plundered by Persian warriors in 1732) was a canopy on which stood two gold peacocks, and above the canopy, around the ceiling of the hall, were inscribed the words, "If there is a paradise on the face of the earth, It is this, oh! it is this, oh! it is this."

Surpassing the splendor of the palace at Delhi (badly damaged by the British army during the nineteenth century) is Shah Jahan's most magnificent gift to world architecture: the Taj Mahal (Figure 23.26). Shah

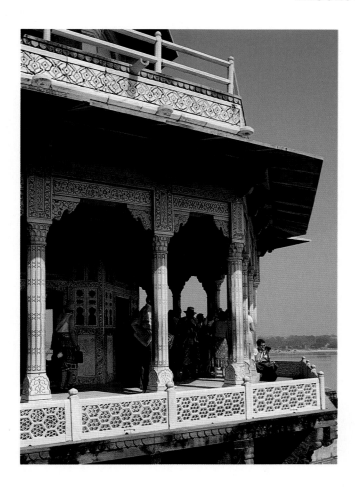

Jahan built the Taj Mahal as a mausoleum to honor the memory of his favorite wife, Mumtaz Mahal (the name means "light of the world"). When Mumtaz died giving birth to their fourteenth child, her husband, legend has it, was inconsolable. He directed his architects to construct alongside the Jumna River a glorious tomb, a twin to one he planned for himself on the adjoining riverbank. Fabricated in cream-colored marble, the Taj rises majestically above a tree-lined pool which mirrors its elegant silhouette so that the mausoleum seems to be floating in air. Although the individual elements of the building—minarets, bulbous domes, and octagonal base—recall Byzantine and Persian prototypes (see chapter 9 and Figure 23.20), the total effect is unique: Shadowy voids and bright solids play against one another on the surface of the exterior, while delicate patterns of light and dark are repeated in the latticed marble screens and exquisitely carved walls of the interior. The garden complex, divided into quadrants by waterways and broad footpaths, is an earthly recreation of the Muslim garden of paradise. The Taj Mahal is the product of some twenty thousand West Asian builders and craftsmen working under the direction of a Persian architect. It is a brilliant fusion of the best aspects of Byzantine, Muslim, and Hindu traditions and, hence, an emblem of Islamic cohesion. But it is also an extravagant expression of conjugal devotion and, to generations of Western visitors, an eloquent symbol of romantic love.

Figure 23.25 (above)
Pietra dura inlay in the Mussamman Burj, Red Fort, Agra Mogul, Shah Jahan period, ca. 1637. Spectrum Color Library, London.

Figure 23.26 Taj Mahal, Agra, India, 1623–1643. Scala, Florence.

The Aristocratic Style in China: The Ming and Manchu Dynasties

From the earliest days of Chinese history, Chinese emperors—the "Sons of Heaven"—ruled on earth by divine authority, or, as the Chinese called it, "the Mandate of Heaven" (see chapter 3). In theory, all of China's emperors were absolute rulers. Nevertheless, over the centuries, their power was frequently contested by feudal lords, military generals, and government officials. In 1368, native Chinese rebels drove out the last of the Mongol rulers (see chapter 14) and established the Ming dynasty, which ruled China until 1644. The Ming dynasty governed the largest and most sophisticated empire on earth, an empire of some 120 million people. In the highly centralized Chinese state, Ming emperors oversaw a bureaucracy that included offices of finance, laws, military affairs, and public works. They rebuilt the Great Wall (see chapter 7) and revived the ancient Chinese tradition of the examination system, which had been suspended by the Mongols. By the seventeenth century, however, the Ming had become autocrats who, like the foreigners they had displaced, took all power into their own hands. They transformed the civil service into a non-hereditary bureaucracy that did not dare to threaten the emperor's authority. The rigid court protocol that developed around the imperial rulers of the late Ming dynasty symbolized this shift toward autocracy. Officials, for instance, knelt in the presence of the emperor, who, as the Son of Heaven, sat on an elevated throne in the center of the imperial precinct.

Beset by court corruption and popular revolts, the Ming fell prey to the invading hordes of Tartars (descendants of Mongols, Turks, and other tribes) known as the Manchu. Under the rule of the Manchu, who established the Qing dynasty (1644–1911), the

Figure 23.27 Forbidden City (now the Palace Museum) from the Southwest, Beijing, China, mostly Ming dynasty.

conditions of imperial autocracy intensified. As a symbol of submission, every Chinese male was required to adopt the Manchu hairstyle, by which one shaved the front of the head and wore a pigtail at the back. Qing rulers retained the administrative traditions of their predecessors, but government posts were often sold rather than earned by merit. When the Qing dynasty reached its zenith—during the very last years that Louis XIV ruled France—it governed the largest, most populous, and one of the most unified states in the world (see Map 23.1). Despite internal peace, however, uprisings were common. They reflected the discontent of peasant masses beset by high taxes and rents and periodic famines. Like the lower classes of France and India, Chinese villagers and urban workers supported the luxuries of royal princes, government officials, and large landholders, who (as in France and India) were themselves exempt from taxation. The early Manchu rulers imitated their predecessors as royal sponsors of art and architecture. Like Louis XIV and Shah Jahan, the Chinese emperor and his huge retinue resided in an impressive ceremonial city (Figure 23.27). This metropolis, the symbol of entrenched absolutism and the majesty of the ruler, was known as the Forbidden City—so-called because of its inaccessibility to ordinary Chinese citizens.

Figure 23.28 (above) Plan of the imperial palace, Forbidden City, Beijing, China.

 1 Gate of Divine Pride
 2 Pavilion of Imperial Peace
 3 Imperial Garden
 4 Palace of Earthly Tranquillity
 5 Hall of Union
 6 Palace of Heavenly Purity
 7 Gate of Heavenly Purity
 8 Hall of the Preservation of Harmony
 9 Hall of Perfect Harmony
10 Hall of Supreme Harmony
11 Gate of Supreme Harmony
12 Meridian Gate
13 Kitchens
14 Gardens
15 Former Imperial Printing House
16 Flower Gate
17 Palace of the Culture of the Mind
18 Hall of the Worship of the Ancestors
19 Pavilion of Arrows
20 Imperial Library
21 Palace of Culture
22 Palace of Peace and Longevity
23 Nine Dragon Screen

Figure 23.29 Three-tiered stone terrace and Hall of Supreme Harmony, Forbidden City, Beijing, China, Ming dynasty. Hall approx. 200 ft. × 100 ft. Len Sirman Press, Geneva.

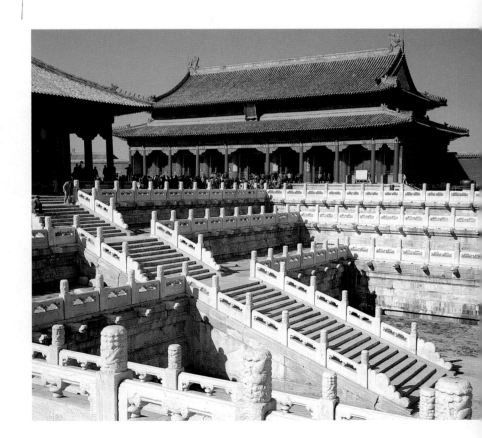

The Forbidden City

Comparable in size and conception to Versailles in the West and to the Mogul palaces of India, the Forbidden City—a walled complex of palaces, tombs, and gardens located in Beijing—was the most elaborate imperial monument of the Ming and Qing eras. Construction on the imperial palace began under sixteenth-century Ming emperors and was continued by the Manchus. For almost five hundred years, this vast ceremonial complex—which, like Versailles, is now a park and museum—was the administrative center of China and the home of Chinese emperors, their families, and the members of their courts.

Inside the walls of the Forbidden City are grand avenues, broad courtyards, government offices, mansions of princes and dignitaries, artificial lakes, lush gardens, spacious temples, theaters, a library, and a printing house (Figure **23.28**). Entering from the south, one passes under the majestic, five-towered entranceway through a succession of courtyards and gates reminiscent of the intriguing boxes within boxes at which Chinese artisans excel. At the heart of the rectangular complex, one proceeds up the three-tiered stone terrace (Figure **23.29**), into the Hall of Supreme Harmony (approximately 200 by 100 feet), where the Sons of Heaven once sat (see Figure 23.27), and beyond, to the imperial living quarters at the rear of the complex. Fragrant gardens, watered by fountains and artificial pools, once graced the private quarters of the royal officials who lived here. During the seventeenth century, courtyard gardening itself developed into a fine art. Often flanked by a covered walkway from which it could be viewed, the garden was an arrangement of seemingly random (but actually carefully placed) rocks, plants, and trees—a miniature version of the natural world. Like the Chinese landscape scroll, the Chinese garden was designed to be enjoyed progressively, as an object of gentle contemplation. Such gardens, with their winding, narrow paths, delicate ferns, and quivering bamboos, have become a hallmark of East Asian culture.

The Forbidden City was the nucleus of imperial power and the symbol of Chinese absolutism. Laid out with a gridiron regularity that rivaled Mogul and French palatial complexes, the arrangement of buildings, courtyards, gates, and terraces was nevertheless uniquely Chinese. This ceremonial arrangement reflects an adherence to ancient Confucian principles of correctness and to the Chinese taste for self-enclosure. Buildings are lined up along the traditional north/south axis and their relative sizes and functions determined by the rigors of Chinese court procedure, a strict protocol based on rank, age, and gender. During the Ming Era, for instance, imperial legislation prescribed nine rooms for the emperor, seven for a prince, five for a court official, and three for an ordinary citizen. Most of the buildings of the Forbidden City are no more than a single story high, their walls serving only as screens that divide interior space. What the Chinese sacrificed in monumentality, however, they recovered in ornamental splendor and in the creation of an architecture that sought harmony with (rather than dominance over) nature. Chinese architects deliberately preserved such traditional features as the rectangular hall with fully exposed wooden rafters and the pitched roof with projecting eaves and gleaming yellow tiles—the latter symbolic of the mantle of heaven. In the Forbidden City, as in all Chinese culture prior to the twentieth century, tradition enhanced the majesty of the ruler.

Imperial Patronage of the Arts

The Ming and Manchu emperors were great patrons of the arts. They encouraged the traditional schools of landscape painting and oversaw the production of such luxury items as inlaid bronze vessels, carved ivories and jades, lacquer ware, embroidered silk, and painted ceramics. Chinese porcelains had been much sought-after since the seventh century; by the seventeenth century they were world famous, so much so that in the West the word "Ming" became synonymous with porcelain. (More generally, the word "china" has come to signify fine ceramics and tableware.)

Qing artists used bright colors more freely than in earlier times. Vessels with solid color glazes of ox-blood red and peach-blossom pink (Figure **23.30**) alternated

Figure 23.30 Flower vase, Qing dynasty. Chinese pottery, "peach-bloom" glaze, height 7¾ in. Courtesy of the Freer Gallery of Art, Smithsonian Institution, Washington, D.C. (42.20).

Figure 23.31 *Famille verte*, Qing dynasty, early eighteenth-century. Foliated porcelain bowl, diameter 6½ in. Ashmolean Museum, Oxford, Department of Eastern Art.

with colorful landscapes filled with songbirds, flowering trees, human figures, and mythical animals. One Qing bowl ornamented with a rich five-color palette shows a group of elegantly attired men, women, and servants in a luxurious interior (Figure **23.31**). As this delightful scene suggests, neither in the porcelains nor in the paintings of this period did the Chinese develop any interest in the kinds of heroic and moralizing themes that dominated baroque art in the West. This difference notwithstanding, imperial tastes dictated the style of aristocratic art in China every bit as much as the royal academies of France influenced seventeenth-century French style. By 1680, there were over thirty official palace workshops serving the imperial court. Out of these workshops poured increasingly flamboyant works

Figure 23.32 Incense burner in the shape of a *li* (tripod), Ming dynasty, fifteenth or possibly early sixteenth century. *Cloisonné* enamel. Courtesy of the Freer Gallery of Art, Smithsonian Institution, Washington, D.C. (F61.12).

Figure 23.33 Section of a screen panel, Ming dynasty, 1368–1644. Tapestry weave with silk and gold thread, 78 × 26 in. © The Cleveland Museum of Art 1998. Gift of Mr. & Mrs. J. H. Wade (CMA 1916.1334).

of art: exotic jewelry, painted enamels, *cloisonné* vessels (Figure **23.32**), intricate jade carvings, and lavishly embroidered silk and gold tapestries (Figure **23.33**). Many of these objects found their way into Europe, where they inspired *chinoiserie*, a style reflecting the influence of Chinese art. Cultural exchange between East and West, however, was mutual: Delegations of Jesuits, who arrived in China in 1601, introduced the rules of linear perspective to Chinese art, even as they transmitted to Europe (often by means of prints and engravings) a knowledge of Chinese techniques and materials. And French prints in turn prompted early Manchu rulers to build a Chinese version of Versailles, complete with fountains, at the imperial summer palace northwest of Beijing.

Chinese Literature and the Theater Arts

Ming and Manchu rulers worked hard to preserve the rich literary heritage of China. Under Ming patronage, a group of two thousand scholars began the enormous task of collecting and copying the most famous of China's literary and historical works. The Manchu contemporary of Louis XIV, Emperor Kangxi (1662–1722), hired fifteen thousand calligraphers and 360 editors to compile a vast assortment of dictionaries, encyclopedias, and anthologies of the Chinese classics. Increasing numbers of literate middle-class men and women in China's growing cities demanded printed books for everyday use. These included almanacs, guides to letter writing, short stories, collections of proverbs and maxims, chronicles, ballads, and romances. Novels, a literary genre that had emerged as early as the twelfth century in China and even earlier in Japan (see chapter 14), remained extremely popular during the Ming and Qing eras. The typical Chinese novel recounted historical events and often made fun of religious and secular authorities. In the mid-eighteenth century, Cao Xueqin produced China's greatest novel, *The Dream of the Red Chamber* (also known as *The Story of the Stone*). This four-thousand-page work, which was to become the most popular example of Chinese fiction, is a love story involving two noble Beijing families. Filled with realistic detail as well as fantastic dream sequences, the novel provides a fascinating picture of upper-class Qing society.

Plots drawn from popular novels such as *The Dream of the Red Chamber* provided the themes for staged performances, which always included mime, dance, and vocal and instrumental music. This type of theatrical performance—which Westerners would call "opera"—was the only form of drama that existed in China prior to the twentieth century (when, imitating Western drama, Chinese writers began to produce exclusively spoken plays). In the Chinese theater, performers were exclusively male, and male actors would play the parts of such stock characters as the coquette or the virtuous maid. Since troupes of players moved from city to city, elaborate costumes and stage scenery might be minimal. In place of costumes and scenery, a system of conventions arose in the performance of Chinese plays to indicate setting or circumstance: A chair might represent a mountain, a whip might signify that the actor was on horseback, and a black cloth might be used to indicate that a character was invisible. Colors symbolized conventional character types: Red represented loyalty and dignity, white symbolized villainy or treachery, and so on. During the Ming Era, when sumptuous costumes and masklike makeup became popular, such earlier stage symbols and conventions were still preserved. Indeed, to this day, Chinese theater retains traditional, highly stylized features.

Despite the differences in their origins, Chinese and European opera developed at roughly the same time—the seventeenth century. And, by the late eighteenth century (when the first permanent Chinese opera company appeared in the capital city of Beijing), both appealed to an increasingly wealthy social class. Both employed many artificial conventions and both employed male performers for female roles. Chinese music, however, sounded distinctly different from Western music. Rich in melodic and rhythmic nuances, Chinese opera[†] shunned the dramatic contrasts in texture and timbre that have characterized Western opera (and Western music in general since the Renaissance). Elaborately staged (and usually many hours long), Chines opera might be said to have greater popular appeal than European opera. While European operas usually borrowed themes from Greco-Roman mythology and biblical history—themes often employed to glorify a royal patron or flatter upper-class tastes—Chinese operas mainly drew on a traditional repertory of love stories, social events, and the adventures of folk heroes. Such operas often featured stock characters resembling those of Molière's plays, and, like Molière's plays, they had wide and lasting popularity.

The Aristocratic Style in Japan

By the seventeenth century, feudal Japan (see chapter 11) had taken the direction of a unified and centralized state led by members of the Tokugawa dynasty (1600–1868). In contrast to China, whose aristocracy consisted of a scholarly elite recruited through civil service examinations, Japan had an aristocracy that consisted of a warrior elite (the *samurai*) recruited in battle.

[†]See Music Listening Selection I 12, an excerpt from a Chinese opera described in chapter 14.

Figure 23.34 Ogata Korin, *Irises at Yatuhashi*, from the *Tale of Ise* (*Ise Monogatari*), Edo Period. One of a pair of six-panelled screens, ink and color and gilded paper, with black lacquered frames, each screen 4 ft. 11½ in. × 11 ft. 3¼ in. Nezu Institute of Fine Arts, Tokyo.

In the style of Louis XIV, the Tokugawa *shogun* (general-in-chief) demanded that his feudal lords attend his court in Edo (modern-day Tokyo), from which center he enforced court etiquette as faithfully as he solidified political and economic control. Unique to Japan was its policy of isolation from the West. In the 1630s Tokugawa rulers initiated a policy of national seclusion. Determined to maintain internal stability and peace, they expelled foreigners and forbade citizens to travel abroad, thus sealing off Japan from the outside world.

While a large segment of Japan's peasantry led barely subsistent lives, the pleasure-loving court at Edo (a city of one million people by the year 1700) and the rising commercial classes of the towns enjoyed one of the most creative periods in Japanese history. In the Tokugawa court, the traditional Japanese decorative style came to a peak: Evident in multipanel screens (used to divide the Japanese interior), hand-painted scrolls, ceramics, and lacquer boxes (often associated with the tea ceremony), it treated natural motifs with restrained elegance and simplicity. This aristocratic aesthetic tradition is best expressed in brightly painted, multifold screens usually adorned with stylized flowers, birds, or landscape motifs. The large six-fold screen by Ogata Korin (ca. 1657–1716), pictured in Figure **23.34**, reflects the Japanese love of bold, decorative shapes organized by means of a subtle balance of figures and ground (positive and negative space) that evokes an astonishing purity of design. Such screens reveal a unique blend of elegant simplicity and luxury (the ground of the screen is gold leaf) which distinguishes the Japanese court style at its best.

Another expression of Japanese taste for elegant simplicity was the ritual tea ceremony—a unique combination of art and theater that typified Japanese aestheticism. Introduced into Japan from China during the ninth century, tea served as an aid to Buddhist meditation. The tea ceremony developed in sixteenth-century Japan in conjunction with Zen Buddhism, a variety of Buddhism that stresses the attainment of spiritual enlightenment through intuitive illumination (see chapter 8). With the cultivation of better types of tea plants in Japan, the Way of Tea (as the philosophy of tea-drinking was called) became widely practiced in Japanese society and gradually came to symbolize the elite conservatism of the Japanese aristocracy. A mainstay of Zen monastic life, tea and the etiquette of tea-drinking influenced a revival of Zen painting among eighteenth-century artist-monks. One of the greatest of these masters was Hakuin Ekaku (1685–1768), whose magnificent ink scrolls are noted for their vigorous yet subtle brush drawing. In *Two Blind Men Crossing a Log Bridge* (Figure **23.35**), Hakuin illustrates his vision of the precarious nature of the human journey to spiritual enlightenment: Two monks, one with his sandals hanging on his staff so as to grasp the log's surface more directly, make their way unsteadily across the narrow bridge, which, like each Japanese character, is executed with a single, confident calligraphic brushstroke. Hakuin adds the accompanying poem:

Both inner life and the floating world outside us
Are like the blind man's round log bridge—
An enlightened mind is the best guide.

Although both the ink scrolls and Korin's screens share the Japanese preference for a stripped style of the utmost simplicity, the spontaneous brushwork of the Zen masters contrasts sharply with the stylized elegance of the screen painters.

Figure 23.35 Hakuin Ekaku, *Two Blind Men Crossing a Log Bridge*, Edo Period. Hanging scroll, ink on paper, 11¹⁄₁₆ × 33 in. New Orleans Museum of Art. Kurt and Millie Gitter Collection.

Parallel with the flowering of the aristocratic style in Tokugawa Japan was the rise of popular culture and popular art. Between the mid-seventeenth and mid-eighteenth centuries, three of Japan's best-known modes of artistic expression emerged: *kabuki* theater, the woodblock print, and the light verse form known as the *haiku*. Kabuki theater evolved out of the popular dances and skits presented by troupes of female performers. Although women's kabuki was banned after 1629, male actors continued to work this popular form of urban entertainment (Figure **23.36**). Kabuki drama—whose domestic, historical, and contemporary themes called for elaborate scenery and magnificent costumes—featured tales of romance marked by violent passions and "love suicides." It provided an alternative to the classical drama of Japan, the Nō play, whose stylized action, traditional literary subjects, choral interludes, and masked players resembled Greek drama.

Often mirroring the expressive moods of kabuki, seventeenth- and eighteenth-century woodblock prints, with their actors (see chapter 31), courtesans, and leisure-time entertainments, capture the "floating world" (*ukiyo*)—the world of fugitive urban pleasures and delights, often marked by bawdy entertainment. Executed in black and white, or colored by hand or with inked blocks, such prints are evidence of Japanese virtuosity in calligraphic design. As with Korin's screens, these prints display a rare unity of simplicity, elegance, and control. Similar qualities characterize Tokugawa lyric poetry, the most notable of which is the *haiku*. The effectiveness of the *haiku*—a seventeen-syllable poem arranged in three lines of 5/7/5 syllables—depends on the pairing of contrasting images. Its resonance is the product of an emotion or mood evoked, rather than a condition or event described. The *haiku* is unique not merely in its structure, but in the balance between what

Figure 23.36 Toshusai Sharaku, *Bust Portrait of the Actor Segawa Tomisaburo as Yadorigi, the Wife of Ogishi Kurando*, 1794–1795. Woodblock print, 14½ × 9¼ in. Photograph © 1997, The Art Institute of Chicago, All Rights Reserved. Clarence Buckingham Collection, 1928.1056.

is said and what is left unsaid. Witness one of the best-known *haikus* of Japan's most famous *haiku* poet, Matsuo Bashō (1644–1694): "On a withered branch/a crow has settled—/autumn nightfall."

SUMMARY

The aristocratic style in the arts of the seventeenth century reflects the influence of absolutism in the political history of the West, as well as in Central and East Asia. In Europe, the most notable figure of the Age of Absolutism was Louis XIV. Under Louis' leadership, the arts worked to serve the majesty of the crown. At Versailles, the classical baroque style—an amalgam of Greco-Roman subject matter, classical principles of design (often derived from Renaissance models), and baroque theatricality—became the vehicle of French royal authority. Luxury, grandeur, and technical refinement became the hallmarks of elitism.

Louis XIV was instrumental in founding most of the royal academies of France, whose members established neoclassical guidelines for painting, sculpture, music, literature, and dance. Poussin's canvases, Girardon's sculptures, La Rochefoucauld's maxims, Lully's operas, Racine's tragedies, and Molière's comedies all assert the neoclassical view that the mind must prevail over the passions. Under Louis' leadership, the ballet emerged as an independent art form and one that epitomized neoclassical order and grace. Outside of France, Velásquez and van Dyck painted elegant portraits that flattered aristocratic patrons, while Rubens produced dramatic allegories of royal authority.

In Southwest Asia, the Ottoman Emperor Suleiman established a pattern of princely patronage that was imitated by Muslim rulers for at least two centuries. The Persian Shah Abbas and the Mogul rulers of India—Akbar, Jahangir, and Shah Jahan—were great patrons of the arts and commissioned some of the most magnificent monuments in architectural history. Like Versailles in France, the Imperial Mosque at Isfahan, the Red Fort at Old Delhi, and the Taj Mahal—though serving different functions—epitomize the wealth, authority, and artistic vision of a privileged minority. So too, the imperial complex at the Forbidden City in Beijing stands as a symbol of the absolute authority of China's rulers. Finally, in the sheltered society of Tokugawa Japan, the decorative tradition in the arts reached new heights of sophistication and refinement.

Though the aristocratic style has a rich history whose origins may be traced back to the pharaohs of Egypt, that style held a particularly important place in the seventeenth century, when it served to legitimatize and glorify the power of the ruling elite throughout Europe and Asia. Flamboyant and lavish, the aristocratic style touched all forms of intellectual and artistic expression, including drama, opera, architecture, and dance. And although the artists of Asia tapped a heritage that was essentially different from that of Europeans, the East produced works of art that in every way rivaled those of the West.

GLOSSARY

chinoiserie European imitation of Chinese art, architecture, and decorative motifs; also any objects that reflect such imitation

choreography the art of composing, arranging, and/or notating dance movements

comédie-ballet (French) a dramatic performance that features interludes of song and dance

haiku a light verse form consisting of seventeen syllables (three lines of five, seven, and five)

marquetry a decorative technique in which patterns are created on a wooden surface by means of inlaid wood, shell, or ivory

maxim a short, concise, and often witty saying

objet d'art (French) art object

pietra dura (Italian, "hard stone") an ornamental technique involving inlaid precious and semiprecious stones

salon (French, "drawing room") an elegant apartment or drawing room

SUGGESTIONS FOR READING

Asher, Catherine B. *Architecture of Mughal India*. New York: Cambridge University Press, 1992.

Davies, Philip. *The Splendors of the Raj*. New York: Viking Penguin, 1985.

Desai, Vishakha N. *Life at Court: Art for India's Rulers 16th–19th Centuries*. Boston: Boston Museum of Fine Arts, 1985.

Gascoigne, Bamber. *The Great Moghuls*. New York: Harper and Row, 1971.

Hatton, Ragnhild M., ed. *Louis XIV and Absolutism*. Columbus: Ohio University Press, 1976.

Howarth, W. D. *Molière: A Playwright and his Audience*. Cambridge: Cambridge University Press, 1982.

Lablaude, Pierre A. *The Gardens of Versailles*. New York: Scala, 1996.

Lach, Donald F. and E. J. Van Kley. *Asia in the Making of Europe*. Vol. 3: *A Century of Advance*. Chicago: University of Chicago Press, 1992.

Michell, George. *The Royal Palaces of India*. London: Thames and Hudson, 1994.

Mitford, Nancy. *The Sun King: Louis XIV at Versailles*. New York: Harper and Row, 1966.

Walker, Hallam. *Molière*. Boston: Twayne, 1990.

Wright, Christopher. *The French Painters of the Seventeenth Century*. New York: New York Graphic Society, 1986.

Yu Zhuoyun, ed. *Palaces of the Forbidden City*, translated by Ng Mau-Sang and others. New York: Viking, 1984.

PART

II

THE AGE OF THE ENLIGHTENMENT

The Age of the Enlightenment, as the eighteenth century is often called, was a time of buoyant optimism. Educated Europeans envisioned themselves as the most civilized people in history: Having survived a millennium of darkness, they now ushered in a new era of light—the light of reason. Reason, they optimistically predicted, would dispel the mists of human ignorance, superstition, and prejudice. Eighteenth-century intellectuals were the heirs to Newtonian science. They viewed the universe as a great machine that operated according to unchanging "natural" laws. Just as Newton had systematized the laws of the physical universe, so these rationalists tried to regulate the laws of human behavior. Such practical powers, they argued, were not only attainable, but they were essential to the progress and betterment of humankind. The ideals of rationalism, humanitarianism, and social progress fueled the Enlightenment—the major cultural and intellectual movement of the eighteenth century. And although this movement did not directly touch the lives of millions of peasants and villagers, it profoundly influenced the course of modern history.

During the eighteenth century, learning freed itself from the Church, and literacy became widespread. Among middle-class Europeans, ninety to one hundred percent of the males and almost seventy-five percent of the females could read and write. This new, more literate middle class competed with a waning aristocracy for social and political prestige. The public interest in

literature and the arts spurred the rise of the newspaper, the novel, and the symphony. Satire became a popular vehicle for dramatizing the contradictions between the polite society of the upper classes and the poverty and illiteracy of the lower classes. In educated circles, debate raged over the powers of rulers versus those of the ruled. And in France and North America, visionary treatises defended the unalienable rights of citizens and fanned the flames of revolt.

The chapters that follow examine the Enlightenment as the central theme of the eighteenth century and as a shaping force in the evolution of the humanistic tradition. Chapter 24, "The Promise of Reason," deals with the Enlightenment concepts of natural law and the social contract as manifested in the writings of Thomas Hobbes, John Locke, Thomas Jefferson, and Adam Smith. The crusade for human progress is illustrated in the birth of the encyclopedia and the writings of Antoine Nicolas de Condorcet, while the middle-class interest in the particulars of everyday life is seen in the rise of the novel. In chapter 25, entitled "The Limits of Reason," we hear the voices of intellectuals whose faith in reason was tempered by cynicism, pessimism, and skepticism. Voltaire's brilliant satire, *Candide*, Swift's *Modest Proposal*, the controversial treatises of Jean Jacques Rousseau, and the caustic prints of William Hogarth are included in this chapter, as are representative examples of satiric prose from eighteenth-century China. Chapter 26, "Eighteenth-Century Art, Music, and Society," compares the rococo and neoclassical styles in art and architecture and analyzes the rise of classical music. The paintings of Boucher, Fragonard, and David and the music of Haydn and Mozart are discussed here, especially as they mirror the shifting tastes and values of eighteenth-century society.

(opposite) Jacques-Louis David, detail of *The Death of Socrates*, 1787. Oil on canvas, full image 4 ft. 3 in. × 6 ft. 5¼ in. The Metropolitan Museum of Art, New York. Catharine Lorillard Wolfe Collection. Wolfe Fund, 1931 (31.45).

24

The Promise of Reason

In the year 1680, a comet blazed across the skies over Western Europe. The English astronomer Edmund Halley (1656–1742) observed the celestial body, calculated its orbit, and predicted its future appearances. Stripped of its former role as a portent of catastrophe or a harbinger of natural calamity, Halley's comet now became merely another natural phenomenon, the behavior of which invited scientific investigation. This new, objective attitude toward nature and the accompanying confidence in the liberating role of reason were hallmarks of the Enlightenment—the period between 1687 (the date of Newton's *Principia*) and 1789 (the beginning of the French Revolution). Indeed, the eighteenth century marks the divide between the essentially medieval view of the world as controlled by an omnipotent God and governed by the principles of faith, and the modern, secular view of the world as dominated by humankind and governed by the principles of reason. It also marks the beginning of an optimistic faith in the human ability to create a kind of happiness on earth that in former ages had been thought to exist only in heaven.

One of the principal preoccupations of Enlightenment thinkers was the comprehension of human nature in scientific terms—without reference to divine authority. "Theology," wrote one Enlightenment skeptic, "is only ignorance of natural causes." Just as Halley explained the operations of the celestial bodies as a logical part of nature's mechanics, so eighteenth-century intellectuals explained human nature in terms of *natural law*. The unwritten and divinely sanctioned law of nature, or natural law, included certain "natural rights": the right to life, liberty, property, and just treatment by the ruling order. Moreover, Enlightenment thinkers argued that a true understanding of the human condition was the first step toward progress, that is, toward the gradual betterment of human life. It is no wonder, then, that the eighteenth century saw the

formation of the social sciences: anthropology, sociology, economics, and political science. These new disciplines, devoted to the study of humankind, optimistically confirmed that the promise of reason was the realization of an enlightened social order.

The Political Theories of Hobbes and Locke

An enlightened social order required a redefinition of the role of government and the rights of citizens. Not since the Golden Age of Athens had the relationship between the ruler and the ruled received so much intellectual attention as in the early modern era, the age of the rising European nation-state. During the sixteenth century, the political theorist Machiavelli had argued that the survival of the state was more important than the well-being of its citizens. Later in that century, the French lawyer Jean Bodin (1530–1596) had used biblical precepts and longstanding tradition to defend theories of divine right monarchy. In the seventeenth century, the Dutch statesman Hugo Grotius (1583–1645) proposed an all-embracing system of international law based on reason, which he identified with nature. Grotius' idea of a political contract based in natural law profoundly influenced the thinking of two of England's finest philosophers, Thomas Hobbes (1588–1679) and John Locke, the latter of whom we met in chapter 22 as a champion of the empirical method.

Hobbes and Locke took up the urgent question of human rights versus the sovereignty of the ruler. Shaken by the conflict between royalist and antiroyalist factions that had fueled the English Civil War (see chapter 21), both thinkers rejected the principle of divine right monarchy. Instead, they advanced the idea that government must be based in a **social contract**. For Hobbes, the social contract was a covenant among individuals who willingly surrendered a portion of their freedom to a governing authority or ruler, in whose hands should rest ultimate authority. Some forty years later, Locke agreed with Hobbes that government must be formed by a contract that laid the basis for social order and individual happiness. But he believed that power must remain with the ruled.

The divergent positions of Hobbes and Locke proceeded from their contrasting perceptions of human nature. Whereas Locke described human beings as naturally equal, free, and capable (through reason) of defining the common good, Hobbes viewed human beings as selfish, greedy, and warlike. Without the state, he argued, human life was "solitary, poor, nasty, brutish, and short." Bound by an irrevocable and irreversible social contract, government under one individual or a ruling assembly was, according to Hobbes, society's only hope for peace and security. The collective safety of society lay in its willingness to submit to a higher authority, which Hobbes dubbed the "Leviathan," after the mythological marine monster described in the Bible. Hobbes aired these views in a treatise called the *Leviathan*, which he published in 1651—only two years after England's antiroyalist forces had beheaded the English monarch Charles I.

READING 4.14
From Hobbes'*Leviathan*

Part 1   Chapter 13: Of the Natural Condition of Mankind as Concerning their Felicity and Misery

Nature has made men so equal in the faculties of the body and mind as that, though there be found one man sometimes manifestly stronger in body or of quicker mind than another, yet, when all is reckoned together, the difference between man and man is not so considerable as that one man can thereupon claim to himself any benefit to which another may not pretend as well as he. For as to the strength of body, the weakest has strength to kill the strongest, either by secret machination or by confederacy with others that are in the same danger with himself. . . .   10

From this equality of ability arises equality of hope in the attaining of our ends. And therefore if any two men desire the same thing, which nevertheless they cannot both enjoy, they become enemies; and in the way to their end, which is principally their own conservation, and sometimes their delectation only, endeavor to destroy or subdue one another. And from hence it comes to pass that where an invader has no more to fear than another man's single power, if one plant, sow, build, or possess a convenient seat, others may probably be expected to   20 come prepared with forces united to dispossess and deprive him, not only of the fruit of his labor, but also of his life or liberty. And the invader again is in the like danger of another. . . .

So that in the nature of man we find three principal causes of quarrel: first, competition; secondly, diffidence;[1] thirdly, glory.

The first makes men invade for gain, the second for safety, and the third for reputation. The first use violence to make themselves masters of other men's persons,   30 wives, children, and cattle; the second, to defend them; the third, for trifles, as a word, a smile, a different opinion, and any other sign of undervalue, either direct in their persons or by reflection in their kindred, their friends, their nation, their profession, or their name.

Hereby it is manifest that, during the time men live without a common power to keep them all in awe, they are in that condition which is called war, and such a war as is of every man against every man. For WAR consists not in battle only, or the act of fighting, but in a tract of time   40 wherein the will to contend by battle is sufficiently known; and therefore the notion of *time* is to be considered in the nature of war as it is in the nature of weather. For as the nature of foul weather lies not in a shower or two of rain but in an inclination thereto of many days together, so the nature of war consists not in actual fighting but in the known disposition thereto, during all the time there is no assurance to the contrary. All other time is PEACE.

Whatsoever, therefore, is consequent to a time of war where every man is enemy to every man, the same is   50 consequent to the time wherein men live without other security than what their own strength and their own invention shall furnish them withal. In such condition there is no place for industry, because the fruit thereof is uncertain; and consequently no culture of the earth; no navigation nor use of the commodities that may be imported by sea; no commodious building; no instruments of moving and removing such things as require much force; no knowledge of the face of the earth; no account of time; no arts; no letters; no society; and, which is worst   60 of all, continual fear and danger of violent death; and the life of man solitary, poor, nasty, brutish, and short. . . .

Part II   Chapter 17: Of the Causes, Generation, and Definition of a Commonwealth

The final cause, end, or design of men, who naturally love liberty and dominion over others, in the introduction of that restraint upon themselves in which we see them live in commonwealths, is the foresight of their own preservation, and of a more contented life thereby—that is to say, of getting themselves out from that miserable condition of war which is necessarily consequent . . . to the natural passions of man when there is no visible   70 power to keep them in awe and tie them by fear of punishment to the performance of their covenants and observations of [the] laws of nature. . . .

For the laws of nature—as *justice, equity, modesty, mercy*, and, in sum, *doing to others as we would be done to*—of themselves, without the terror of some power to cause them to be observed, are contrary to our natural passions, that carry us to partiality, pride, revenge, and the like. And covenants without the sword are but words, and of no strength to secure a man at all. Therefore,   80 notwithstanding the laws of nature . . . , if there be no power erected, or not great enough for our security, every man will—and may lawfully—rely on his own strength and art for caution against all other men. . . .

The only way to erect such a common power as may be able to defend them from the invasion of foreigners and the

---
[1]Lack of confidence

injuries of one another, and thereby to secure them in such sort as that by their own industry and by the fruits of the earth they may nourish themselves and live contentedly, is to confer all their power and strength upon one man, or upon one assembly of men that may reduce all their wills, by plurality of voices, unto one will; which is as much as to say, to appoint one man or assembly of men to bear their person, and everyone to own and acknowledge to himself to be author of whatsoever he that so bears their person shall act or cause to be acted in those things which concern the common peace and safety, and therein to submit their wills every one to his will, and their judgments to his judgment. This is more than consent or concord; it is a real unity of them all in one and the same person, made by covenant of every man with every man, in which manner as if every man should say to every man, *I authorize and give up my right of governing myself to this man, or to this assembly of men, on this condition, that you give up your right to him and authorize all his actions in like manner.* This done, the multitude so united in one person is called a COMMONWEALTH, in Latin CIVITAS. This is the generation of that great LEVIATHAN (or rather, to speak more reverently, of that *mortal god*) to which we owe, under the *immortal God*, our peace and defense. For by this authority, given him by every particular man in the commonwealth, he has the use of so much power and strength conferred on him that, by terror thereof, he is enabled to form the wills of them all to peace at home and mutual aid against their enemies abroad. And in him consists the essence of the commonwealth, which, to define it, is *one person, of whose acts a great multitude, by mutual covenants one with another, have made themselves every one the author, to the end he may use the strength and means of them all as he shall think expedient for their peace and common defense.* And he that carries this person is called SOVEREIGN and said to have *sovereign power*: and everyone besides, his SUBJECT.

The attaining to this sovereign power is by two ways. One, by natural force. . . . The other is when men agree among themselves to submit to some man or assembly of men voluntarily, on confidence to be protected by him against all others. This latter may be called a political commonwealth, or commonwealth by *institution*, and the former a commonwealth by *acquisition*. . . .

Part II   Chapter 30: Of the Office of the Sovereign Representative

The office of the sovereign, be it a monarch or an assembly, consists in the end for which he was trusted with the sovereign power, namely, the procuration of the *safety of the people*; to which he is obliged by the law of nature, and to render an account thereof to God, the author of that law, and to none but him. But by safety here is not meant a bare preservation but also all other contentments of life which every man by lawful industry, without danger or hurt to the commonwealth, shall acquire to himself.

And this is intended should be done, not by care applied to individuals further than their protection from injuries when they shall complain, but by a general providence contained in public instruction, both of doctrine and example, and in the making and executing of good laws, to which individual persons may apply their own cases.

And because, if the essential rights of sovereignty . . . be taken away, the commonwealth is thereby dissolved and every man returns into the condition and calamity of a war with every other man, which is the greatest evil that can happen in this life, it is the office of the sovereign to maintain those rights entire, and consequently against his duty, first, to transfer to another or to lay from himself any of them. For he that deserts the means deserts the ends. . . .

————————◆————————

Locke's Government of the People

Locke (Figure **24.1**) disagreed with Hobbes' view of humankind as self-serving and aggressive. He held that since human beings were born without any preexisting qualities, their natural state was one of perfect freedom. Whether people became brutish or otherwise depended solely upon their experiences and their environment. People have, by their very nature as human beings, said Locke, the right to life, liberty, and estate (or "property"). Government must arbitrate between the exercise of one person's liberty and that of the next. The social contract thus preserves the natural rights of the governed. And, although individuals may willingly consent to give up some of their liberty in return for the ruler's protection, they may never relinquish their ultimate authority. If a ruler is tyrannical or oppressive, the people have not only the right but the obligation to rebel and seek a new ruler. Locke's defense of political rebellion in the face of tyranny served as justification for the "Glorious Revolution" of 1688, as well as inspiration for the revolutions that took place in America and in France toward the end of the eighteenth century.

If for Hobbes the state was sovereign, for Locke sovereignty rested with the people, and government existed only to protect the natural rights of its citizens. In his *First Treatise on Government* (1690), Locke argued that individuals might attain their maximum development only in a society free from the unnatural restrictions imposed by absolute rulers. In his second treatise, called *Of Civil Government* (an excerpt from which follows), Locke expounded on the idea that government must rest upon the consent of the governed. While Locke's views were basic to the development of modern liberal thought, Hobbes' views provided the justification for all forms of tyranny, including the enlightened despotism of such eighteenth-century rulers as Frederick of Prussia and Catherine II of Russia, who claimed that their authority was founded in the general consent of the people. Nevertheless, the notion of government as the product of a social contract between the ruler and the ruled has become one of the dominating ideas of modern Western—and more recently of Eastern European and Asian—political life.

READING 4.15
From Locke's *Of Civil Government*

Book II Chapter II: Of the State of Nature

To understand political power right and derive it from its
original, we must consider what state all men are
naturally in, and that is a state of perfect freedom to
order their actions and dispose of their possessions and
persons as they think fit, within the bounds of the law of
nature without asking leave or depending upon the will
of any other man.

A state also of equality, wherein all the power and
jurisdiction is reciprocal, no one having more than
another; there being nothing more evident than that
creatures of the same species and rank, promiscuously
born to all the same advantages of nature and the use of
the same faculties, should also be equal one amongst
another without subordination or subjection; unless the
Lord and Master of them all should, by any manifest
declaration of his will, set one above another and confer
on him, by an evident and clear appointment, an
undoubted right to dominion and sovereignty. . . .

Chapter V: Of Property

God, who hath given the world to men in common, hath
also given them reason to make use of it to the best
advantage of life and convenience. The earth and all that
is therein is given to men for the support and comfort of
their being. And though all the fruits it naturally
produces and beasts it feeds belong to mankind in
common . . . , there must of necessity be a means to
appropriate them some way or other before they can be
of any use, or at all beneficial to any particular man. . . .

Though the earth and all inferior creatures be common
to all men, yet every man has a property in his own
person: this nobody has any right to but himself. The
labor of his body, and the work of his hands we may say,
are properly his. Whatsoever then he removes out of the
state that nature has provided and left it in, he has
mixed his labor with and joined to it something that is
his own, and thereby makes it his property. . . .

Chapter VIII: The Beginning of Political Societies

Men being, as has been said, by nature all free, equal,
and independent, no one can be put out of this estate
and subjected to the political power of another without
his own consent. The only way whereby any one divests
himself of his natural liberty and puts on the bonds of
civil society is by agreeing with other men to join and
unite into a community for their comfortable, safe, and
peaceable living one amongst another, in a secure
enjoyment of their properties, and a greater security
against any that are not of it. This any number of men
may do, because it injures not the freedom of the rest;
they are left as they were in the liberty of the state of
nature. When any number of men have so consented to
make one community or government, they are thereby
presently incorporated and make one body politic,
wherein the majority have a right to act and conclude
the rest.

Figure 24.1 John Greenhill, *Portrait of John Locke*,
ca. 1672–1676. Oil on canvas, 22⅛ × 18½ in.
By courtesy of the National Portrait Gallery, London.

For when any number of men have, by the consent of
every individual, made a community, they have thereby
made that community one body, with a power to act as
one body, which is only by the will and determination of
the majority: . . . And therefore we see that in assemblies
empowered to act by positive laws, where no number is
set by that positive law which empowers them, the act of
the majority passes for the act of the whole and of course
determines; as having, by the law of nature and reason,
the power of the whole.

And thus every man, by consenting with others to make
one body politic under one government, puts himself
under an obligation to every one of that society to submit
to the determination of the majority and to be concluded
by it; or else this original compact whereby he with others
incorporate into one society, would signify nothing and be
no compact if he be left free and under no other ties than
he was in before in the state of nature. . . .

Chapter IX: Of the Ends of Political Society and Government

If man in the state of nature be so free as has been said;
if he be absolute lord of his own person and possessions,
equal to the greatest, and subject to nobody, why will he
part with his freedom, why will he give up this empire and
subject himself to the dominion and control of any other
power? To which it is obvious to answer that though in the
state of nature he has such a right, yet the enjoyment of it
is very uncertain and constantly exposed to the invasion
of others; for all being kings as much as he, every man his
equal and the greater part no strict observers of equity and

justice, the enjoyment of the property he has in this state is very unsafe, very unsecure. This makes him willing to quit a condition, which, however free, is full of fears and continual dangers: and it is not without reason that he seeks out and is willing to join in society with others who are already united or have a mind to unite for the mutual preservation of their lives, liberties, and estates, which I call by the general name property.

The great and chief end, therefore, of men's uniting into commonwealths, and putting themselves under   90
government, is the preservation of their property. . . .

Chapter XVIII: Of Tyranny

As usurpation is the exercise of power, which another hath a right to, so tyranny is the exercise of power beyond right, which nobody can have a right to. And this is making use of the power any one has in his hands, not for the good of those who are under it, but for his own private, separate advantage—when the governor, however entitled, makes not the law, but his will, the rule; and his commands and actions are not directed to the preservation of the properties of his people, but [to] the   100
satisfaction of his own ambition, revenge, covetousness, or any other irregular passion. . . .

Wherever law ends, tyranny begins, if the law be transgressed to another's harm; and whosoever in authority exceeds the power given him by the law, and makes use of the force he has under his command, . . . ceases in that to be a [magistrate]; and, acting without authority, may be opposed as any other man who by force invades the right of another. . . .

"May the commands then of a prince be opposed?   110
may he be resisted as often as any one shall find himself aggrieved, and but imagine he has not right done him? This will unhinge and overturn all politics, and, instead of government and order, leave nothing but anarchy and confusion."

To this I answer that force is to be opposed to nothing but to unjust and unlawful force; whoever makes any opposition in any other case, draws on himself a just condemnation both from God and man. . . .

◆

The Influence of Locke on Montesquieu and Jefferson

Locke's political treatises were read widely. So too, his defense of religious toleration (issued even as Louis XIV forced all Calvinists to leave France), his plea for equality of education among men and women, and his arguments for the use of modern languages in place of Latin won the attention of many intellectuals. Published during the last decade of the seventeenth century, Locke's treatises became the wellspring of the Enlightenment in both Europe and America.

In France, the keen-minded aristocrat Charles Louis de Secondat Montesquieu (1689–1755) championed Locke's views on political freedom and expanded on his theories. Intrigued by the ways in which nature seemed to govern social behavior, the Baron de

Montesquieu investigated the effects of climate and custom on human conduct, thus pioneering the field of sociology. In his elegantly written thousand-page treatise *The Spirit of the Laws* (1748), Montesquieu defended liberty as the free exercise of the will and condemned slavery as fundamentally "unnatural and evil." A proponent of constitutional monarchy, he advanced the idea of a separation of powers among the executive, legislative, and judicial agencies of government, advising that each monitor the activities of the others in order to ensure a balanced system of government. He warned that when legislative and executive powers were united in the same person (or body of magistrates), or when judicial power was inseparable from legislative and executive powers, human liberty might be gravely threatened. Montesquieu's system of checks and balances was later enshrined in the Constitution of the United States of America (1787).

Across the Atlantic, the most eloquent expression of Locke's ideas appeared in the preamble to the statement declaring the independence of the North American colonies from the rule of the British king George III. Written by the leading American apostle of the Enlightenment, Thomas Jefferson (1743–1826; see Figure 26.22), and adopted by the Continental Congress on July 4, 1776, the American Declaration of Independence echoes Locke's ideology of revolt as well as his view that governments derive their just powers from the consent of the governed. Following Locke and Montesquieu, Jefferson justified the establishment of a social contract between ruler and ruled as the principal means of fulfilling natural law—the "unalienable right" to life, liberty, and the pursuit of happiness. While Jefferson did not include "property" among the unalienable rights, he was, as well, fully committed to the individual's natural right to property.

READING 4.16

From Jefferson's Declaration of Independence

When, in the course of human events, it becomes   1
necessary for one people to dissolve the political bands which have connected them with another, and to assume among the powers of the earth, the separate and equal station to which the laws of nature and of nature's God entitle them, a decent respect to the opinions of mankind requires that they should declare the causes which impel them to separation.

We hold these truths to be self-evident: That all men are created equal; that they are endowed by their Creator   10
with certain unalienable rights; that among these are life, liberty and the pursuit of happiness; that to secure these rights governments are instituted among men, deriving their just powers from the consent of the governed; that whenever any form of government becomes destructive of these ends, it is the right of the people to alter or to

abolish it, and to institute new government, laying its foundation on such principles and organizing its powers in such form, as to them shall seem most likely to effect their safety and happiness. . . . 20

◆

The Declaration of Independence made clear the belief of America's "founding fathers" in equality among men. Equality between the sexes was, however, another matter: Although both Locke and Jefferson acknowledged that women held the same natural rights as men, they did not consider women—or slaves, or children, for that matter—capable of exercising such rights. Recognizing this bias, Abigail Adams (d. 1818) wrote to her husband, John, who was serving as a delegate to the Second Continental Congress (1777), as follows:

> I . . . hear that you have declared an independency, and, by the way, in the new code of laws which I suppose it will be necessary for you to make, I desire you would remember the ladies and be more generous and favorable to them than were your ancestors. Do not put such unlimited power into the hands of husbands. Remember all men would be tyrants if they could. If particular care and attention are not paid to the ladies we are determined to foment a rebellion, and will not hold ourselves bound to obey any laws in which we have no voice or representation.*

Despite the future First Lady's spirited admonitions, however, American women did not secure the legal right to vote or to hold political office until well into the twentieth century.

If the Declaration of Independence constituted a clear expression of Enlightenment theory in justifying revolution against tyrannical rule, the Constitution of the new United States of America represented the practical outcome of the Revolution: the creation of a viable new nation with its government based ultimately on Enlightenment principles. The U.S. Constitution, framed in 1787 and ratified by popular vote in 1788–1789, articulated the mechanics of self-rule. First, it created a form of government new to the modern world: a system of representative government embodying the principal of "Republicanism," that is, government by the elected representatives of the people. Second, following the precepts of Montesquieu, the framers of the Constitution divided the new government into three branches—legislative, executive, and judicial—each to

be "checked and balanced" by the others to prevent the possible tyranny of any one branch. Third, the new republic was granted sufficient power to govern primarily through the authority granted the president to execute national laws and constitutional provisions. Withal, the U.S. Constitution would prove effective for over two centuries, and would serve as the model for the constitutions of all the new-born republics to be created throughout the world, even until today.

Adam Smith and the Birth of Economic Theory

While Enlightenment thinkers were primarily concerned with matters of political equality, they also addressed questions related to the economy of the modern European state. The Scottish philosopher Adam Smith (1723–1790) applied the idea of natural law to the domains of human labor, productivity, and the exchange of goods. In his epoch-making synthesis of ethics and economics, *An Inquiry into the Nature and Causes of the Wealth of Nations*, published in 1776, Smith set forth the "laws" of labor, production, and trade with an exhaustiveness reminiscent of Newton's *Principia Mathematica* (see chapter 22). Smith contended that labor, a condition natural to humankind (as Locke had observed), was the foundation for prosperity. A nation's wealth is not its land or its money, said Smith, but its labor force. In the "natural" economic order, individual self-interest guides the progress of economic life, and certain natural forces, such as the "law of supply and demand," motivate a market economy. Since government interference would infringe on this order, reasoned Smith, such interference is undesirable. He thus opposed all artificial restraints on economic progress and all forms of government regulation and control. The modern concepts of free enterprise and *laissez-faire* (literally, "leave alone") economics spring from Smith's incisive formulations. In the following excerpt, Smith examines the origin of the division of labor among human beings and defends the natural and unimpeded operation of trade and competition among nations.

READING 4.17

From Smith's *An Inquiry into the Nature and Causes of the Wealth of Nations*

Book I   Chapter II: The Principle which Occasions the Division of Labor

[The] division of labor, from which so many advantages are   1
derived, is not originally the effect of any human wisdom, which foresees and intends that general opulence to which it gives occasion. It is the necessary, though very slow and gradual, consequence of a certain propensity in human

---

*Letter of March 31, 1776, in *Familiar Letters of John Adams and His Wife Abigail Adams During the Revolution*, ed. Charles Francis Adams (New York: Hurd and Houghton, 1876. Reprint: Freeport, N.Y.: Books for Library Press, 1970), p. 148.

nature which has in view no such extensive utility; the propensity to truck, barter, and exchange one thing for another.

. . . [This propensity] is common to all men, and to be found in no other race of animals, which seem to know   10
neither this nor any other species of contracts. Two greyhounds, in running down the same hare, have sometimes the appearance of acting in some sort of concert. Each turns her towards his companion, or endeavors to intercept her when his companion turns her towards himself. This, however, is not the effect of any contract, but of the accidental concurrence of their passions in the same object at that particular time. Nobody ever saw a dog make a fair and deliberate exchange of one bone for another with another dog. . . .   20
In almost every other race of animals each individual, when it is grown up to maturity, is entirely independent, and in its natural state has occasion for the assistance of no other living creature. But man has almost constant occasion for the help of his brethren, and it is in vain for him to expect it from their benevolence only. He will be more likely to prevail if he can interest their self-love in his favor, and show them that it is for their own advantage to do for him what he requires of them. Whoever offers to another a bargain of any kind,   30
proposes to do this. Give me that which I want, and you shall have this which you want, is the meaning of every such offer; and it is in this manner that we obtain from one another the far greater part of those good offices which we stand in need of. It is not from the benevolence of the butcher, the brewer, or the baker, that we expect our dinner, but from their regard to their own interest. We address ourselves, not to their humanity, but to their self-love; and never talk to them of our own necessities, but of their advantages. . . .   40

As it is by treaty, by barter, and by purchase, that we obtain from one another the greater part of those mutual good offices which we stand in need of, so it is this same trucking disposition which originally gives occasion to the division of labor. In a tribe of hunters or shepherds a particular person makes bows and arrows, for example, with more readiness and dexterity than any other. He frequently exchanges them for cattle or for venison with his companions; and he finds at last that he can in this manner get more cattle and venison, than if he himself   50
went to the field to catch them. From a regard to his own interest, therefore, the making of bows and arrows grows to be his chief business. . . .

Book IV   Chapter III, Part II: Of the Unreasonableness of Restraints [on Trade]

Nations have been taught that their interest consisted in beggaring all their neighbors. Each nation has been made to look with an invidious eye upon the prosperity of all the nations with which it trades, and to consider their gain as its own loss. Commerce, which ought naturally to be, among nations as among individuals, a bond of union and friendship, has become the most fertile source of   60
discord and animosity. The capricious ambition of kings and ministers has not, during the present and the preceding century, been more fatal to the repose of Europe, than the impertinent jealousy of merchants and

manufacturers. The violence and injustice of the rulers of mankind is an ancient evil, for which, I am afraid, the nature of human affairs can scarce admit of a remedy. But the mean rapacity, the monopolizing spirit of merchants and manufacturers, who neither are, nor ought to be, the rulers of mankind, though it cannot   70
perhaps be corrected, may very easily be prevented from disturbing the tranquility of anybody but themselves.

That it was the spirit of monopoly which originally both invented and propagated this doctrine, cannot be doubted; and they who first taught it were by no means such fools as they who believed it. In every country it always is and must be the interest of the great body of the people to buy whatever they want of those who sell it cheapest. The proposition is so very manifest, that it seems ridiculous to take any pains to prove it; nor could   80
it ever have been called in question had not the interested sophistry of merchants and manufacturers confounded the common sense of mankind. Their interest is, in this respect, directly opposed to that of the great body of the people. . . .

The wealth of a neighboring nation, though dangerous in war and politics, is certainly advantageous in trade. In a state of hostility it may enable our enemies to maintain fleets and armies superior to our own; but in a state of peace and commerce it must likewise enable them to   90
exchange with us to a greater value and to afford a better market, either for the immediate produce of our own industry or for whatever is purchased with that produce. As a rich man is likely to be a better customer to the industrious people in his neighborhood, than a poor, so is likewise a rich nation. . . .

———————◆———————

The Philosophes

When Louis XIV died in 1715, the French nobility fled the Palace of Versailles and settled in townhouses in Paris, often decorated in the latest fashion. Socially ambitious noblewomen, many of whom championed a freer and more public role for their gender, organized gatherings in the *salons*, where nobility and middle-class thinkers met to exchange views on morality, politics, and religion and to voice opinions on everything ranging from diet to the latest fashions in theater and dress (Figure **24.2**). Inevitably, new ideas began to circulate in these meetings, and Paris became the hub of intellectual activity.

A small circle of well-educated individuals came to be known as *philosophes* (the French word for "philosophers"). Intellectuals rather than philosophers in the strictest sense of the word, the *philosophes* dominated the intellectual activity of the Enlightenment. Like the humanists of fifteenth-century Florence, their interests were mainly secular and social. Unlike their Renaissance counterparts, however, the *philosophes* scorned all forms of authority—they believed that they had surpassed the ancients, and they looked beyond the

Figure 24.2 François Dequevauviller after N. Lavréince, *Assembly in a Salon*, 1745–1807. Engraving, 15¹³⁄₁₆ × 19⅝ in. The Metropolitan Museum of Art, New York. Harris Brisbane Dick Fund, 1935 (35.100.17).

present state of knowledge to the establishment of a superior moral and social order.

Most *philosophes* held to the deist view of God as Creator and providential force behind nature and natural law, rather than as personal Redeemer. They believed in the immortality of the soul, not out of commitment to any religious doctrine, but because they saw human beings as fundamentally different from other living creatures. They viewed the Bible as mythology rather than as revealed truth, and scorned Church hierarchy and ritual. Their antipathy to irrationality, superstition, and religious dogma (as reflected, for instance, in the Catholic doctrine of original sin) alienated them from the Church and set them at odds with the established authorities—a position memorably expressed in the acerbic pronouncement that "men will not be free until the last king is strangled with the entrails of the last priest." The quest for a nonauthoritarian, secular morality led the *philosophes* to challenge all existing forms of intolerance, inequality, and injustice. The banner cry of the *philosophes*, "Ecrasez l'infame" ("Wipe out all evils"), sparked a commitment to social reforms that led to the French Revolution (see chapter 25).

Diderot and the *Encyclopédie*

The basic ideals of the Enlightenment were summed up in a monumental literary endeavor to which many of the *philosophes* contributed: the thirty-five-volume *Encyclopédie* (including eleven volumes of engraved plates), published between 1751 and 1772 and edited by Denis Diderot (1713–1784; Figure 24.3). Modeled on the two-volume Chambers' Encyclopedia printed in England in 1751, Diderot's *Encyclopédie*—also known as *The Analytical Dictionary of the Sciences, Arts, and Crafts*—was the largest compendium of contemporary social, philosophic, artistic, scientific, and technological knowledge ever produced in the West. A collection of "all the knowledge scattered over the face of the earth," as Diderot explained, it manifested the zealous desire of the *philosophes* to dispel human ignorance and transform society. It was also, in part, a response to rising literacy and to the widespread public interest in the facts of everyday life. Not all members of society welcomed the enterprise, however: King Louis XV, who claimed that the *Encyclopédie* was doing "irreparable damage to morality and religion," twice banned its printing; some

Figure 24.3 Jean-Antoine Houdon, *Diderot*, 1773. Marble, height 20⁷⁄₁₆ in. The Metropolitan Museum of Art, New York. Gift of Mr. and Mrs. Charles Wrightsman, 1974 (1974.291).

volumes were published and distributed secretly.

Diderot's *Encyclopédie* was the most ambitious and influential literary undertaking of the eighteenth century. Some two hundred individuals contributed seventy-two thousand entries on subjects ranging from political theory, cultural history, and art criticism to the technology of theater machinery, the making of silk stockings, and the varieties of wigs (Figure **24.4**). Articles on Islam, India, and China indicate a more than idle curiosity about civilizations that remained to most Westerners remote and exotic. Diderot enlisted as contributors to the *Encyclopédie* the most progressive minds of the Enlightenment: François-Marie Arouet (1694–1778), known as Voltaire, wrote on "matters of nature and art"; the French philosopher and educator Jean Jacques Rousseau (1712–1778; see chapter 25) provided articles on music; François Quesnay wrote on political economy; Montesquieu (whose articles were published posthumously) examined the different types of governments; Jean Le Rond d'Alembert (1717–1783) treated the subject of higher education; and Diderot himself prepared numerous entries on art and politics.

Although women contributed moral and financial support to the *Encyclopédie*, none was invited to participate in its production. Moreover, not one of the thirty-one entries on women makes reference to the contributions of exceptional eighteenth-century women such as Gabrielle-Emilie Le Tonnelier de Breteuil, the Marquise du Châtelet (1706–1749; Figure **24.5**). An impeccable scholar and a brilliant mathematician, Madame du

Châtelet translated the Latin works of Virgil, Horace, and Ovid into eloquent French; she wrote original poetry and conducted experiments in physics and chemistry. She was also a reckless gambler, a champion of the fashionably low-cut neckline, and the mistress of Voltaire, who lived at her *château* until her death in 1749. Voltaire confessed that he could hardly live without the Marquise, whom he regarded "as a great man." In their assessment of the abilities and the rights of women, the *philosophes* were ambivalent at best, their personal sentiments characterized by Rousseau's self-scorning complaint that one of his greatest misfortunes was "always to be connected with some literary woman." Nevertheless, the *Encyclopédie* remains a monument to secular knowledge and to the Enlightenment faith in the promise of reason—a spirit summed up in Voltaire's proclamation, "Let the facts prevail." The following excerpts come from the entry on natural law written by the French lawyer Antoine-Gaspart Boucher d'Argis and from the long article on black Africans written by Le Romain (first name and dates unknown).

Figure 24.4 *Wigs*, a plate from the *Encyclopédie* illustrating the varieties of men's wigs that were fashionable in Europe in the 1750s. Thomas J. Watson Library, The Metropolitan Museum of Art, New York.

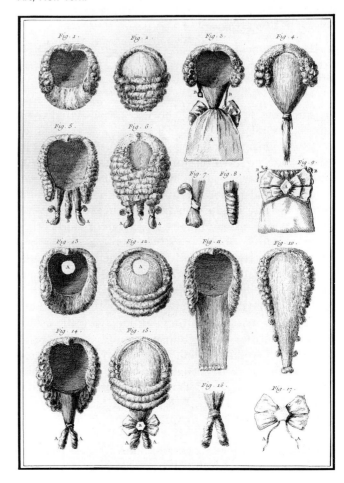

READING 4.18

From the *Encyclopédie*

Law of Nature or Natural Law

In its broadest sense the term is taken to designate [1]
certain principles which nature alone inspires and which
all animals as well as all men have in common. On this
law are based the union of male and female, the
begetting of children as well as their education, love of
liberty, self-preservation, concern for self-defense.

It is improper to call the behavior of animals natural
law, for, not being endowed with reason, they can know
neither law nor justice.

More commonly we understand by natural law certain [10]
laws of justice and equity which only natural reason has
established among men, or better, which God has
engraved in our hearts.

The fundamental principles of law and all justice are:
to live honestly, not to give offense to anyone, and to
render unto each whatever is his. From these general
principles derive a great many particular rules which
nature alone, that is, reason and equity, suggest
to mankind.

Since this natural law is based on such fundamental [20]
principles, it is perpetual and unchangeable: no
agreement can debase it, no law can alter it or exempt
anyone from the obligation it imposes. . . .

The principles of natural law, therefore, form part of
the law of nations, particularly the primitive law of
nations; they also form part of public and of private law:
for the principles of natural law, which we have stated,
are the purest source of the foundation of most of private
and public law. . . .

The authority of natural laws stems from the fact that [30]
they owe their existence to God. Men submit to them
because to observe them leads to the happiness of men
and society. This is a truth demonstrated by reason. It is
equally true that virtue by itself is a principle of inner
satisfaction whereas vice is a principle of unrest and
trouble. It is equally certain that virtue produces great
external advantage, while vice produces great ills. . . .

Negroes[1]

For the last few centuries the Europeans have carried on
a trade in Negroes whom they obtain from Guinea and
other coasts of Africa and whom they use to maintain the [40]
colonies established in various parts of America and in
the West Indies. To justify this loathsome commerce,
which is contrary to natural law, it is argued that
ordinarily these slaves find the salvation of their souls in
the loss of their liberty, and that the Christian teaching
they receive, together with their indispensable role in the
cultivation of sugar cane, tobacco, indigo, etc., softens
the apparent inhumanity of a commerce where men buy
and sell their fellow men as they would animals used in
the cultivation of the land. [50]

[1]A term originally used by the Spanish and Portuguese to identify black
Africans.

Figure 24.5 Nicolas de Largillière, *Gabrielle-Emilie Le Tonnelier
de Breteuil, Marquise du Châtelet*, ca. 1740. Oil on canvas,
4 ft. 3½ in. × 3 ft. 4¼ in. Columbus Museum of Art, Columbus,
Ohio. Bequest of Frederick W. Schumacher.

Trade in Negroes is carried on by all the nations which
have settlements in the West Indies, and especially by
the French, the English, the Portuguese, the Dutch, the
Swedes, and the Danes. The Spaniards, in spite of the
fact that they possess the greatest part of the Americas,
have no direct way of acquiring slaves but have
concluded treaties with other nations to furnish them
with Negroes. . . .

As soon as the trade is completed no time must be lost
in setting sail. Experience has shown that as long as [60]
these unfortunates are still within sight of their
homeland, they are overcome by sorrow and gripped by
despair. The former is the cause of many illnesses from
which a large number perish during the crossing; the
latter inclines them to suicide, which they effect either
by refusing nourishment or by shutting off their
breathing. This they do in a way they know of turning
and twisting their tongues which unfailingly suffocates
them. Others again shatter their head against the sides
of the ship or throw themselves into the sea if the [70]
occasion presents itself. . . .

Punishment of the Negroes, policing, and regulations concerning these matters:

If the Negro commits a slight offense the overseer may
on his own responsibilty punish him with a few strokes of
the whip. If, however, it is a serious matter, the master

has the culprit clapped in irons and then decides the number of strokes with which he will be punished. If all men were equally just, these necessary punishments would be kept within limits, but it often happens that certain masters abuse the authority which they claim over their slaves and chastise these unfortunates too 80 harshly. Yet the masters themselves may be responsible for the situation which led to the offense. To put an end to the cruelties of these barbarous men who would be capable of leaving their slaves without the basic necessities of life while driving them to forced labor, the officers of His Majesty, who are resident in the colonies, have the responsibility of enforcing the edict of the king, which is called the Black Code. In the French islands of America this code regulates the governing and the administration of justice and of the 90 police, as well as the discipline of the slaves and the slave-trade. . . .

———————————◆———————————

The Encyclopedic Cast of Mind

The *Encyclopédie* had an enormous impact on eighteenth-century culture. Although few individuals actually read or understood all of it, it fostered an encyclopedic cast of mind. Indeed, the emphasis on the accumulation, codification, and systematic preservation of knowledge linked the eighteenth century to the Scientific Revolution and to that other Enlightenment "bible," Newton's *Principia*.

Eighteenth-century scientists made notable advances in the fields of chemistry, electricity, biology, and the medical sciences. They produced the mercury thermometer and the stethoscope and introduced the science of immunology to the West—some seven centuries after the Chinese had invented the first inoculations against smallpox. Antoine Lavoisier (1743–1794) published the *Elementary Treatise of Chemistry* (1789) and launched chemistry as an exact science. The Swede Carolus Linnaeus (1707–1778) produced a systematic method for classifying plants, and the French naturalist Georges Louis Leclerc, Comte de Buffon (1707–1788), made landmark advances in zoology.

Valuable efforts to accumulate and classify knowledge took place in the arts as well: The English critic and poet Samuel Johnson (1709–1784) published the first dictionary of the English language and Rousseau produced the first Western dictionary of music. In the social sciences, Voltaire's seven-volume general history (published in 1756), which included a monumental account of the age of Louis XIV, provided a model for a new universal and rationalist kind of history-writing. Voltaire was among the first to recognize Europe's debt to Arab science and Asian thought. He rejected all explanations of the past as the workings of divine Providence and was generally critical of the role played by

	1702	the world's first daily newspaper is published in England
	1704	the first alphabetical encyclopedia in English is printed
	1714	a London engineer patents the first known typewriter
	1765	Diderot's *Encyclopédie* is issued in seventeen volumes

the Catholic Church in Western history. But it fell to the English historian Edward Gibbon (1737–1794) to provide the rationale that attacked Christianity for the collapse of Rome. *The Decline and Fall of the Roman Empire* (1776) was the product of Gibbon's unique interpretation of the sociological forces at work within ancient cultures.

Eighteenth-century China lay beyond the immediate influence of the European Enlightenment; nevertheless, in the East an encyclopedic impulse similar to that prevailing in the West came to a climax at this time. Qing rulers followed their Ming predecessors in directing groups of scholars to assemble exhaustive collections of information, some filling as many as thirty-six thousand manuscript volumes. These "encyclopedias" were actually anthologies of the writings of former Chinese artists and scholars, rather than comprehensive collections of contemporary knowledge. Nevertheless, as in France, some of China's rulers deemed the indiscriminate accumulation of information itself dangerous, and at least one eighteenth-century Qing emperor authorized the official burning of thousands of books.

The Crusade for Progress

Among European intellectuals, the belief in the reforming powers of reason became the basis for a progressive view of human history. The German mathematician and philosopher Gottfried Wilhelm Leibniz (1646–1716) systematically defended the view that human beings live in perfect harmony with God and nature. Leibniz linked optimism to the logic of probability: His *principle of sufficient reason* held, simply, that there must be a reason or purpose for everything in nature. In response to the question, Why does evil exist in a world created by a good God? Leibniz answered that all events conformed to the preestablished harmony of the universe. Even evil, according to Leibniz, was necessary in a world that was "better than any other possible world"—a position that came to be called "philosophic optimism."

For the *philosophes*, the key to social reform lay in a true understanding of human nature, which, they argued, might best be acquired by examining human history. They interpreted the transition from Paleolithic hunting and gathering to the birth of civilization as clear evidence of the steady march toward social improvement. Faith in that steady march motivated the Enlightenment crusade for progress. The Italian lawyer and social reformer Cesare de Beccaria (1738–1794) enlisted in this crusade when he wrote his treatise *On Crimes and Punishments,* in which he suggested that torturing criminals did not work to deter crime. Rather, argued Beccaria, society should seek methods by which to rehabilitate those who commit crimes. Although Beccaria's book generated no immediate changes, it went through six editions in eighteen months and ultimately contributed to movements for prison reform in Europe and the United States. The questions that Beccaria raised concerning the value of punishment are still being debated today.

The most passionate warrior in the Enlightenment crusade for progress was the French aristocrat Antoine Nicolas de Condorcet (1743–1794). Condorcet was a mathematician, a social theorist, and a political moderate amidst revolutionary extremists. His *Sketch for a Historical Picture of the Progress of the Human Mind,* written during the early days of the French Revolution, was the preface to a longer work he never completed, for he committed suicide shortly after being imprisoned as an "enemy" of the Revolution. Condorcet believed that human nature could be perfected through reason and the sciences. All errors in politics and morals, he argued, were based in philosophic and scientific errors. "There is not a religious system nor a supernatural extravagance," wrote Condorcet, "that is not founded on ignorance of the laws of nature." Fiercely optimistic about the future of humankind, Condorcet was one of the first modern champions of sexual equality. He called for the "complete annihilation of the prejudices that have brought about an inequality of rights between the sexes, an inequality fatal even to the party in whose favor it works." Such inequality, he protested, "has its origin solely in an abuse of strength, and all the later sophistical attempts that have been made to excuse it are vain."

In his *Sketch,* the visionary Condorcet traced the "progress" of humankind through ten stages, from ignorance and tyranny to the threshold of enlightenment and equality. The utopian tenth stage, subtitled "The Future Progress of the Human Mind" (an excerpt of which follows), sets forth ideas that were well ahead of their time, such as a guaranteed livelihood for the aged, a universal system of education, fewer work hours, and the refinement of a technology for the accumulation of knowledge. (How computers would have delighted this prophet of the Information Age!) The educational goals that Condorcet outlines toward the end of the excerpt still carry the force of sound judgment.

READING 4.19

From Condorcet's *Sketch for a Historical Picture of the Progress of the Human Mind*

If man can, with almost complete assurance, predict phenomena when he knows their laws, and if, even when he does not, he can still, with great expectation of success, forecast the future on the basis of his experience of the past, why, then, should it be regarded as a fantastic undertaking to sketch, with some pretense to truth, the future destiny of man on the basis of his history? The sole foundation for belief in the natural sciences is this idea that the general laws directing the phenomena of the universe, known or unknown, are necessary and constant. Why should this principle be any less true for the development of the intellectual and moral faculties of man than for the other operations of nature? Since beliefs founded on past experience of like conditions provide the only rule of conduct for the wisest of men, why should the philosopher be forbidden to base his conjectures on these same foundations, so long as he does not attribute to them a certainty superior to that warranted by the number, the constancy, and the accuracy of his observations? . . .

The time will therefore come when the sun will shine only on free men who know no other master but their reason; when tyrants and slaves, priests and their stupid or hypocritical instruments will exist only in works of history and on the stage; and when we shall think of them only to pity their victims and their dupes; to maintain ourselves in a state of vigilance by thinking on their excesses; and to learn how to recognize and so to destroy, by force of reason, the first seeds of tyranny and superstition, should they ever dare to reappear among us.

In looking at the history of societies we shall have had occasion to observe that there is often a great difference between the rights that the law allows its citizens and the rights that they actually enjoy, and, again, between the equality established by political codes and that which in fact exists among individuals. . . .

These differences have three main causes: inequality in wealth, inequality in status between the man whose means of subsistence are hereditary and the man whose means are dependent on the length of his life, or, rather, on that part of his life in which he is capable of work; and, finally, inequality in education.

We therefore need to show that these three sorts of real inequality must constantly diminish without however disappearing altogether: for they are the result of natural and necessary causes which it would be foolish and dangerous to wish to eradicate. . . .

[As to education] we can teach the citizen everything that he needs to know in order to be able to manage his household, administer his affairs, and employ his labor and his faculties in freedom; to know his rights and to be able to exercise them; to be acquainted with his duties and fulfill them satisfactorily; to judge his own and other men's actions according to his own lights and to be a stranger to none of the high and delicate feelings which honor human nature; not to be in a state of blind dependence upon those to whom he must entrust his affairs or the exercise of his rights; to be in a proper condition to choose and supervise them; to be no longer 60 the dupe of those popular errors which torment man with superstitious fears and chimerical hopes; to defend himself against prejudice by the strength of his reason alone; and, finally, to escape the deceits of charlatans who would lay snares for his fortune, his health, his freedom of thought, and his conscience under the pretext of granting him health, wealth, and salvation. . . .

The real advantages that should result from this progress, of which we can entertain a hope that is almost a certainty, can have no other term than that of the 70 absolute perfection of the human race; since, as the various kinds of equality come to work in its favor by producing ampler sources of supply, more extensive education, more complete liberty, so equality will be more real and will embrace everything which is really of importance for the happiness of human beings. . . .

———————◆———————

The Journalistic Essay and the Birth of the Modern Novel

As Condorcet's treatise attests, social criticism assumed an important place in Enlightenment literature. Such criticism now also manifested itself in a new literary genre known as the journalistic essay. Designed to address the middle-class reading public, prose essays and editorials were the stuff of magazines and daily newspapers. The first daily emerged in London during the eighteenth century, although a weekly had been published since 1642. With the rise of newspapers and periodicals, the "poetic" prose of the seventeenth century—characterized by long sentences and magisterial phrases (see Bacon's *Of Studies*, Reading 4.9)—gave way to a more informal prose style, one that reflected the conversational chatter of the *salons* and the *cafés*. Journalistic essays brought "philosophy out of the closets and libraries, schools and colleges, to dwell in clubs and assemblies, at tea-tables and in coffee houses," explained Joseph Addison (1672–1719), the leading British prose stylist of his day. In collaboration with his lifelong friend, Richard Steele (1672–1729), Addison published two London periodicals, the *Tatler* and the *Spectator*, which featured penetrating commentaries on

current events and social behavior. The *Spectator* had a circulation of some twenty-five thousand readers. Anticipating modern news magazines, eighteenth-century broadsheets and periodicals offered the literate public timely reports and diverse opinions on all aspects of popular culture. They provided entertainment as they also helped to shape popular opinion.

The most important new form of eighteenth-century literary entertainment, however, was the novel. The novel first appeared in world literature in China and Japan (see chapters 14 and 23). The most famous of the early Japanese novels, *The Tale of Genji*, was written by an unknown eleventh-century author known as Lady Shikibu Murasaki. In China, where the history of the novel reached back to the twelfth century, prose tales of travel, love, and adventure were popular sources for operas and plays. Neither Japanese nor Chinese prose fiction had any direct influence on Western writers. Nevertheless, the vernacular novel became a major form of social entertainment in both East Asia and the West during the eighteenth century. In both East and West, the rise of the novel occurred at a moment of increasing urbanization. Its popularity reflected the demands of a larger reading public, although, in China, literacy was still confined to the educated elite—only ten percent of Chinese women, for instance, could read and write.

The modern novel made its appearance in England at the beginning of the eighteenth century with the publication of the popular adventure story *Robinson Crusoe* (1719), by Daniel Defoe (1660–1731). Defoe's novel, based on actual experience, was sharply realistic and thus quite different from the fantasy-laden prose of his sixteenth-century predecessors, Cervantes and Rabelais (see chapter 18). The novels of Defoe and his somewhat later contemporaries Samuel Richardson (1689–1761) and Henry Fielding (1707–1754) featured graphic accounts of the personalities and daily lives of the lower and middle classes. With an exuberance reminiscent of Chaucer, these prose narratives brought to life tales of criminals, pirates, and prostitutes. Not surprisingly, such novels appealed to the tastes of the same individuals who enjoyed the spicy realism and journalistic prose of contemporary broadsheets.

Pope: Poet of the Age of Reason

If any single poet typified the spirit of the Enlightenment, it was surely Alexander Pope (1688–1744), the greatest English poet of the eighteenth century. Pope, a semi-invalid from the age of twelve, was a great admirer of Newton and a champion of the scientific method. He was also a staunch neoclassicist who devotedly revived the wit and polish of the Golden-Age Roman poets Virgil and Horace. Largely self-taught (in his time

1714	the mercury thermometer and the Fahrenheit scale are invented in Germany
1726	the first measurement of blood pressure is taken in England
1751	the first mental hospital opens in London
1774	Franz Mesmer (Austrian) uses hypnotism to aid in curing disease

Roman Catholics were barred from attending English universities), Pope defended the value of education in Greek and Latin, and his own love of the classics inspired him to produce new translations of Homer's *Iliad* and *Odyssey*. "A *little learning* is a dangerous thing," warned Pope in pleading for a broader and more thorough survey of the past.

Pope's poems are as controlled and refined as a Poussin painting or a Bach fugue. His epigrammatic verses, written in **heroic couplets**, ring with concentrated brilliance. Pope's choice of the heroic couplet for most of his numerous satires, as well as for his translations of Homer, reflects his commitment to the qualities of balance and order; and his mastery of the polished two-rhymed line bears out his claim that "True ease in writing comes from art, not chance,/As those move easiest who have learned to dance."

Pope's most famous poem was his *Essay on Man*. Like Milton's *Paradise Lost*, but on a smaller scale, the *Essay* tried to explain humankind's place in the universal scheme. But whereas Milton had explained evil in terms of human will, Pope—a Catholic turned deist—asserted that evil was simply part of God's design for the universe, a universe that Pope described as "A mighty maze! but not without a plan." According to Pope (and to Leibniz, whom he admired), whatever occurs in nature has been "programmed" by God and is part of God's benign and rational order. Pope lacked the reforming zeal of the *philosophes*, but he caught the optimism of the Enlightenment in a single statement: "Whatever is, is right." In the *Essay on Man*, Pope warns that we must not presume to understand the whole of nature. Nor should we aspire to a higher place in the great "chain of being." Rather, he counsels the reader, "Know then thyself, presume not God to scan;/The proper study of Mankind is Man."

READING 4.20

From Pope's *Essay on Man*

Epistle I

. . . .

IX What if the foot, ordain'd the dust to tread,   1
Or hand, to toil, aspir'd to be the head?
What if the head, the eye, or ear repin'd[1]
To serve mere engines to the ruling Mind?
Just as absurd for any part to claim
To be another, in his gen'ral frame:
Just as absurd, to mourn the tasks or pains.
The great directing Mind of All ordains.

All are but parts of one stupendous whole,
Whose body Nature is, and God the soul;   10

That, chang'd thro' all, and yet in all the same;
Great in the earth, as in th' ethereal frame;
Warms in the sun, refreshes in the breeze,
Glows in the stars, and blossoms in the trees,
Lives thro' all life, extends thro' all extent,
Spreads undivided, operates unspent;
Breathes in our soul, informs our mortal part,
As full, as perfect, in a hair as heart:
As full, as perfect, in vile Man that mourns,
As the rapt Seraph[2] that adores and burns: 20
To him no high, no low, no great, no small;
He fills, he bounds, connects, and equals all.

X Cease then, nor Order Imperfection name:
Our proper bliss depends on what we blame.
Know thy own point: This kind, this due degree
Of blindness, weakness, Heav'n bestows on thee.
Submit—In this, or any other sphere,
Secure to be as blest as thou canst bear:
Safe in the hand of one disposing Pow'r,
Or in the natal, or the mortal hour.   30
All Nature is but Art,[3] unknown to thee;
All Chance, Direction, which thou canst not see;
All Discord, Harmony not understood;
All partial Evil, universal Good:
And, spite of Pride, in erring Reason's spite,
One truth is clear, WHATEVER IS, IS RIGHT.

Epistle II

I Know then thyself, presume not God to scan;[4]
The proper study of Mankind is Man.
Plac'd on this isthmus of a middle state,[5]
A Being darkly wise, and rudely great: 40
With too much knowledge for the Sceptic side,
With too much weakness for the Stoic's pride,
He hangs between; in doubt to act, or rest;
In doubt to deem himself a God, or Beast;
In doubt his Mind or Body to prefer,
Born but to die, and reas'ning but to err;
Alike in ignorance, his reason such.
Whether he thinks too little, or too much:
Chaos of Thought and Passion, all confus'd;
Still by himelf abus'd, or disabus'd;   50
Created half to rise, and half to fall;[6]
Great lord of all things, yet a prey to all;
Sole judge of Truth, in endless Error hurl'd:[7]
The glory, jest, and riddle of the world!

. . . .

———————————◆———————————

---

[1] Complained.

[2] A member of the highest order of angels.
[3] Compare Hobbes: "Nature is the art whereby God governs the world."
[4] Investigate.
[5] Between the angels (above) and the animal kingdom (below). Compare Pico della Mirandola's view of human beings as creatures who partake of both earthly and celestial qualities and can therefore ascend or descend the great "chain of being" (chapter 16).
[6] See note 5.
[7] Cast back and forth.

SUMMARY

The Age of the European Enlightenment marks the beginning of the Western notion of social progress and human perfectibility. In political thought, Thomas Hobbes and John Locke advanced the idea of government based on a social contract between ruler and ruled. While Hobbes envisioned this contract as a bond between individuals who surrendered some portion of their freedom to a sovereign authority, Locke saw government as an agent of the people—bound to exercise the will of the majority. According to Locke, government must operate according to the consent of the governed.

Locke's writings provided the intellectual foundation for the Enlightenment faith in reason as the sure guide to social progress. Jefferson, Montesquieu, and Adam Smith adapted Locke's views on natural law to political and economic life. The idea that human beings, free from the bonds of ignorance and superstition and operating according to the principles of reason, might achieve the good life here on earth inspired the philosophic optimism of Leibniz in Germany and the progressive theories of Beccaria in Italy and Condorcet in France.

The prime symbol of the Enlightenment zeal for knowledge was the *Encyclopédie*, produced by Diderot with the assistance of the *philosophes*. A similar zeal for the ordering of socially useful information inspired the writing of dictionaries, biographies, and histories. The journalistic essay and the early modern novel entertained the new reading public, just as they offered an intimate examination of everyday, secular life. And in poetry, the elegant verbal tapestries of Alexander Pope optimistically pictured human beings as the enlightened inhabitants of an orderly and harmonious universe.

The promise of reason and the gospel of progress—two fundamental ideas of the Enlightenment—have shaped the course of modern Western culture. Imported to America during the eighteenth century, they became the informing ideals of a new order of society. They served a "cult of utility," which promoted the idea that rational thought and its application in science and technology would advance and improve the quality of life for all members of society. More recently, the promise of reason and the gospel of progress have worked to challenge tyranny and injustice in many other parts of the world, including Africa and Asia—a sign of the durability of Enlightenment thought within the humanistic tradition.

GLOSSARY

heroic couplet a pair of rhymed iambic pentameter lines that reach completion in structure and in sense at the end of the second line

laissez-faire (French, "leave alone") a general policy of noninterference in the economy, defended by such classical economists as Adam Smith

philosophes (French, "philosophers") the intellectuals of the European Enlightenment

social contract an agreement made between citizens leading to the establishment of the state

SUGGESTIONS FOR READING

Becker, Carl L. *The Heavenly City of the Eighteenth-Century Philosophers.* New Haven: Yale University Press, 1932.

Furbank, P. N. *Diderot: A Critical Biography.* New York: Knopf, 1993.

Gay, Peter. *The Enlightenment: An Interpretation.* 2 vols. New York: Norton, 1977.

Hampson, Norman. *A Cultural History of the Enlightenment.* New York: Pantheon Books, 1968.

Havens, George R. *The Age of Ideas.* New York: Henry Holt, 1955.

Krieger, Leonard. *Kings and Philosophies 1689–1789.* Vol. 3 of *The Norton History of Modern Europe.* New York: Norton, 1970.

Outram, Dovinda. *The Enlightenment.* New York: Cambridge University Press, 1995.

Richard, Carl J. *The Founders and the Classics: Greece, Rome, and the American Enlightenment.* Cambridge, Mass.: Harvard University Press, 1994.

Vyverberg, Henry. *Human Nature, Cultural Diversity, and the French Enlightenment.* New York: Oxford University Press, 1989.

Watt, Ian. *The Rise of the Novel: Studies in Defoe, Richardson, and Fielding.* Berkeley, Calif.: University of California Press, 1957.

25
The Limits of Reason

Even that most enthusiastic optimist, Alexander Pope, acknowledged in his *Essay on Man* that human beings were "Born to die and reas'ning but to err"—that is, that people were finite and fallible. Pope and other eighteenth-century champions of reason were, in fact, ambivalent: While generally committed to the belief in human perfectibility and the rational potential of humankind, they observed that people often acted in ways that were wholly irrational. Reason was all too frequently ignored or abandoned altogether. Moreover, the critical exercise of reason, when taken to an extreme, often deteriorated into bitter skepticism and cynicism.

Perhaps the greatest obstacle to the belief in the promise of reason lay, however, in the hard realities of everyday life. In eighteenth-century Europe, where Enlightenment intellectuals were exalting the ideals of human progress, there was clear evidence of human ignorance, depravity, and despair. Upon visiting the much-acclaimed city of Paris, Jean Jacques Rousseau lamented its "dirty, stinking streets, filthy black houses, an air of slovenliness" and alleys filled with beggars. Indeed, outside the elegant drawing rooms of Paris and London lay clear signs of poverty, violence, and degradation. Science and technology spawned a new barbarism in the form of machines that were as potentially destructive as they were beneficial. In England, the invention of the "flying shuttle" (1733), the "spinning jenny" (1765), and the power loom (1785)—machines for the manufacture of textile goods—encouraged the rise of the factory system and sparked the Industrial Revolution. James Watt's steam engine (1775) provided a new power source for textiles and other industries. But such technological achievements, allied with unregulated capitalism, gave rise to dangerous working conditions and the exploitation of labor. In many of London's factories, children tended the new machines for twelve- to fourteen-hour shifts, following which they were boarded in shabby barracks. And in the mines of Cornwall and Durham, women and children were paid a pittance to labor like animals, pulling carts laden with coal. Some miners worked such long hours that they never saw the light of day.

The Transatlantic Slave Trade

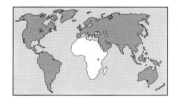

In human terms, however, the most glaring evidence of the failure of the Enlightenment to achieve immediate social reforms was the perpetuation of the slave trade, which, despite the condemnation of many of the *philosophes*, flourished until the mid-nineteenth century. Begun by the Portuguese in the fifteenth century (see chapter 19), the transatlantic slave trade, by which millions of Africans were bought and shipped against their will to colonies in the "New World," reached its peak in the eighteenth century. As England—lured by the lucrative sugar trade—became the leading player in the transatlantic traffic, some six to seven million slaves were transported to work on sugar plantations in the West Indies and elsewhere in the Americas. To feed this market, Africans, including African children, were frequently kidnapped by unscrupulous natives who profited handsomely by selling their captives to white slave traders. The fate of the African slave who survived the perilous "Middle Passage" between Africa and the Americas—it is estimated that roughly one-third perished in transit—was a life of unspeakable suffering (Figure 25.1).

A first-hand account of this inhumane system is central to the autobiographical narrative of Olaudah Equiano (1745–1797), who was born in the West African kingdom of Benin and kidnapped and enslaved at the age of eleven. Both as a slave and after his release from slavery in 1766, Equiano traveled widely; during his stay in England (as one of only thirty thousand blacks in mid-eighteenth-century England), he mastered the English language and became an outspoken abolitionist (Figure 25.2). The following excerpt from Equiano's autobiographic narrative recounts with dramatic simplicity the traumatic experience of an eleven-year-old child who was rudely sold into bondage.

Figure 25.1 Johann Moritz Rugendas, *The Hold of a Slave Ship*, 1827, from J. M. Rugendas, *Voyage pittoresque dans le Brésil*, Paris, 1827–1835. Lithograph, 6 × 10 in.

READING 4.21
From Equiano's *Travels*

That part of Africa known by the name of Guinea to which   1
the trade for slaves is carried on extends along the coast
above 3,400 miles, from the Senegal to Angola, and
includes a variety of kingdoms. Of these the most
considerable is the kingdom of Benin, both as to extent
and wealth, the richness and cultivation of the soil, the
power of its king, and the number and warlike disposition
of the inhabitants. . . . This kingdom is divided into many
provinces or districts, in one of the most remote and
fertile of which, called Eboe, I was born in the year   10
1745, situated in a charming fruitful vale, named
Essaka. The distance of this province from the capital of
Benin and the sea coast must be very considerable, for I
had never heard of white men or Europeans, nor of the
sea, and our subjection to the king of Benin was little
more than nominal; for every transaction of the
government, as far as my slender observation extended,
was conducted by the chiefs or elders of the place. . . .

My father, besides many slaves, had a numerous family
of which seven lived to grow up, including myself and a   20
sister who was the only daughter. As I was the youngest of
the sons I became, of course, the greatest favourite with
my mother and was always with her; and she used to take
particular pains to form my mind. I was trained up from
my earliest years in the art of war, my daily exercise was
shooting and throwing javelins, and my mother adorned

me with emblems[1] after the manner of our greatest
warriors. In this way I grew up till I was turned the age of
11, when an end was put to my happiness in the
following manner. Generally when the grown people in the   30
neighbourhood were gone far in the fields to labour, the
children assembled together in some of the neighbours'
premises to play, and commonly some of us used to get
up a tree to look out for any assailant or kidnapper that
might come upon us, for they sometimes took those
opportunities of our parents' absence to attack and carry
off as many as they could seize. One day, as I was
watching at the top of a tree in our yard, I saw one of
those people come into the yard of our next neighbour
but one to kidnap, there being many stout young people   40
in it. Immediately on this I gave the alarm of the rogue
and he was surrounded by the stoutest of them, who
entangled him with cords so that he could not escape till
some of the grown people came and secured him. But
alas! ere long it was my fate to be thus attacked and to
be carried off when none of the grown people were nigh.
One day, when all our people were gone out to their works
as usual and only I and my dear sister were left to mind
the house, two men and a woman got over our walls, and
in a moment seized us both, and without giving us time   50
to cry out or make resistance they stopped our mouths
and ran off with us into the nearest wood. Here they tied
our hands and continued to carry us as far as they could

---

[1]Body decorations, such as scarification.

till night came on, when we reached a small house where the robbers halted for refreshment and spent the night. We were then unbound but were unable to take any food, and being quite overpowered by fatigue and grief, our only relief was some sleep, which allayed our misfortune for a short time. The next morning we left the house and continued travelling all the day. For a long time we had 60 kept to the woods, but at last we came into a road which I believed I knew. I had now some hopes of being delivered, for we had advanced but a little way before I discovered some people at a distance, on which I began to cry out for their assistance: but my cries had no other effect than to make them tie me faster and stop my mouth, and then they put me into a large sack. They also stopped my sister's mouth and tied her hands, and in this manner we proceeded till we were out of the sight of these people. . . . It was in vain that we besought them 70 not to part us; she was torn from me and immediately carried away, while I was left in a state of distraction not to be described. I cried and grieved continually, and for several days I did not eat anything but what they forced into my mouth. At length, after many days' travelling, during which I had often changed masters, I got into the hands of a chieftain in a very pleasant country. . . .

[Equiano describes his tenure with African masters; he is sold a number of times (during a period of six to seven months) before he is taken to the sea coast.]

The first object which saluted my eyes when I arrived on the coast was the sea, and a slave ship which was then riding at anchor and waiting for its cargo. These 80 filled me with astonishment, which was soon converted into terror when I was carried on board. I was immediately handled and tossed up to see if I were sound by some of the crew, and I was now persuaded that I had gotten into a world of bad spirits and that they were going to kill me. Their complexions too differing so much from ours, their long hair and the language they spoke (which was very different from any I had ever heard) united to confirm me in this belief. Indeed such were the horrors of my views and fears at the moment that, if ten thousand 90 worlds had been my own, I would have freely parted with them all to have exchanged my condition with that of the meanest slave in my own country. When I looked round the ship too and saw a large furnace or copper boiling and a multitude of black people of every description chained together, every one of their countenances expressing dejection and sorrow, I no longer doubted of my fate; and quite overpowered with horror and anguish, I fell motionless on the deck and fainted. When I recovered a little I found some black people about me, who I 100 believed were some of those who had brought me on board and had been receiving their pay; they talked to me in order to cheer me, but all in vain. I asked them if we were not to be eaten by those white men with horrible looks, red faces, and loose hair. They told me I was not, and one of the crew brought me a small portion of spirituous liquor in a wine glass, but being afraid of him I would not take it out of his hand. One of the blacks therefore took it from him and gave it to me, and I took a little down my palate, which instead of reviving me, as 110 they thought it would, threw me into the greatest

Figure 25.2 *Olaudah Equiano*, 1789.

consternation at the strange feeling it produced, having never tasted any such liquor before. Soon after this the blacks who brought me on board went off, and left me abandoned to despair.

I now saw myself deprived of all chance of returning to my native country or even the least glimpse of hope of gaining the shore, which I now considered as friendly; and I even wished for my former slavery in preference to my present situation, which was filled with horrors of 120 every kind, still heightened by my ignorance of what I was to undergo. I was not long suffered to indulge my grief; I was soon put down under the decks, and there I received such a salutation in my nostrils as I had never experienced in my life: so that with the loathsomeness of the stench and crying together, I became so sick and low that I was not able to eat, nor had I the least desire to taste anything. I now wished for the last friend, death, to relieve me; but soon, to my grief, two of the white men offered me eatables, and on my refusing to eat, one of 130 them held me fast by the hands and laid me across I think the windlass,[2] and tied my feet while the other flogged me severely. I had never experienced anything of this kind before, and although, not being used to the water, I naturally feared that element the first time I saw it, yet nevertheless could I have got over the nettings I would have jumped over the side, but I could not; and besides, the crew used to watch us very closely who were not chained down to the decks, lest we should leap into

---

[2]The device that works the ship's anchor.

the water: and I have seen some of these poor African prisoners most severely cut for attempting to do so, and hourly whipped for not eating. This indeed was often the case with myself. In a little time after, amongst the poor chained men I found some of my own nation,[3] which in a small degree gave ease to my mind. I inquired of these what was to be done with us; they gave me to understand we were to be carried to these white people's country to work for them. I then was a little revived, and thought if it were no worse than working, my situation was not so desperate: but still I feared I should be put to death, the white people looked and acted, as I thought, in so savage a manner; for I had never seen among my people such instances of brutal cruelty, and this not only shewn towards us blacks but also to some of the whites themselves. One white man in particular I saw, when we were permitted to be on deck, flogged so unmercifully with a large rope near the foremast that he died in consequence of it; and they tossed him over the side as they would have done a brute. This made me fear these people the more, and I expected nothing less than to be treated in the same manner. I could not help expressing my fears and apprehensions to some of my countrymen: I asked them if these people had no country but lived in this hollow place (the ship): they told me they did not, but came from a distant one. "Then," said I, "how comes it in all our country we never heard of them?" They told me because they lived so very far off. I then asked where were their women? had they any like themselves? I was told they had: "and why," said I, "do we not see them?" They answered, because they were left behind. . . . The stench of the hold while we were on the coast was so intolerably loathsome that it was dangerous to remain there for any time, and some of us had been permitted to stay on the deck for the fresh air; but now that the whole ship's cargo were confined together it became absolutely pestilential. The closeness of the place and the heat of the climate, added to the number in the ship, which was so crowded that each had scarcely room to turn himself, almost suffocated us. This produced copious perspirations, so that the air soon became unfit for respiration from a variety of loathsome smells, and brought on a sickness among the slaves, of which many died, thus falling victims to the improvident avarice, as I may call it, of their purchasers. This wretched situation was again aggravated by the galling of the chains, now become insupportable, and the filth of the necessary tubs, into which the children often fell and were almost suffocated. The shrieks of the women and the groans of the dying rendered the whole a scene of horror almost inconceivable. Happily perhaps for myself I was soon reduced so low here that it was thought necessary to keep me almost always on deck, and from my extreme youth I was not put in fetters. In this situation I expected every hour to share the fate of my companions, some of whom were almost daily brought upon deck at the point of death, which I began to hope would soon put an end to my miseries. Often did I think many of the inhabitants of the deep much more happy than myself. I envied them the freedom they enjoyed, and as often wished I could change my condition for theirs. Every circumstance I met with served only to render my state more painful, and heighten my apprehensions and my opinion of the cruelty of the whites. One day they had taken a number of fishes, and when they had killed and satisfied themselves with as many as they thought fit, to our astonishment who were on the deck, rather than give any of them to us to eat as we expected, they tossed the remaining fish into the sea again, although we begged and prayed for some as well as we could, but in vain; and some of my countrymen, being pressed by hunger, took an opportunity when they thought no one saw them of trying to get a little privately; but they were discovered, and the attempt procured them some very severe floggings. One day, when we had a smooth sea and moderate wind, two of my wearied countrymen who were chained together (I was near them at the time), preferring death to such a life of misery, somehow made through the nettings and jumped into the sea: immediately another quite dejected fellow, who on account of his illness was suffered to be out of irons, also followed their example; and I believe many more would very soon have done the same if they had not been prevented by the ship's crew, who were instantly alarmed. Those of us that were the most active were in a moment put down under the deck, and there was such a noise and confusion amongst the people of the ship as I never heard before, to stop her and get the boat out to go after the slaves. However two of the wretches were drowned, but they got the other and afterwards flogged him unmercifully for thus attempting to prefer death to slavery. In this manner we continued to undergo more hardships than I can now relate, hardships which are inseparable from this accursed trade. . . . At last we came in sight of the island of Barbados, at which the whites on board gave a great shout and made many signs of joy to us. We did not know what to think of this, but as the vessel drew nearer we plainly saw the harbour and other ships of different kinds and sizes, and we soon anchored amongst them off Bridgetown. Many merchants and planters now came on board, though it was in the evening. They put us in separate parcels[4] and examined us attentively. They also made us jump,[5] and pointed to the land, signifying we were to go there. We thought by this we should be eaten by these ugly men, as they appeared to us; and when soon after we were all put down under the deck again, there was much dread and trembling among us, and nothing but bitter cries to be heard all the night from these apprehensions, insomuch that at last the white people got some old slaves from the land to pacify us. They told us we were not to be eaten but to work, and were soon to go on land where we should see many of our countrypeople. This report eased us much; and sure enough soon after we were landed there came to us Africans of all languages. We were conducted immediately to the merchant's yard, where we were all pent up together like so many sheep in a fold without regard to sex or age. . . . We were not many days in the merchant's custody before we were sold after their usual manner, which is this: On a signal given, (as the beat of a drum) the buyers rush at once into the yard where the

---

[3]Ethnic group.

[4]Groups.
[5]In order to determine whether they were healthy.

slaves are confined, and make choice of that parcel they 260
like best. The noise and clamour with which this is
attended and the eagerness visible in the countenances
of the buyers serve not a little to increase the
apprehensions of the terrified Africans, who may well be
supposed to consider them as the ministers of that
destruction to which they think themselves devoted. In
this manner, without scruple, are relations and friends
separated, most of them never to see each other again. I
remember in the vessel in which I was brought over, in
the men's apartment there were several brothers who, in 270
the sale, were sold in different lots; and it was very
moving on this occasion to see and hear their cries at
parting. O, ye nominal Christians! might not an African
ask you, Learned you this from your God who says unto
you, Do unto all men as you would men should do unto
you? Is it not enough that we are torn from our country
and friends to toil for your luxury and lust of gain? Must
every tender feeling be likewise sacrificed to your avarice?
Are the dearest friends and relations, now rendered more
dear by their separation from their kindred, still to be 280
parted from each other and thus prevented from cheering
the gloom of slavery with the small comfort of being
together and mingling their sufferings and sorrows? Why
are parents to lose their children, brothers their sisters, or
husbands their wives? Surely this is a new refinement in
cruelty which, while it has no advantage to atone for it,
thus aggravates distress and adds fresh horrors even to
the wretchedness of slavery. . . .

———————◆———————

Satire: Weapon of the Enlightenment

The discrepancies between the sordid realities of
eighteenth-century life and the progressive ideas of
the Enlightenment provoked indignant protests, and
none so potent as those couched in literary satire. The
eighteenth century was history's greatest age of satire.
The favorite weapon of many Enlightenment intellectuals, satire fused wit and irony to underscore human
folly and error. The genre that had served Juvenal in
imperial Rome (see chapter 7) and Erasmus in the age
of the Reformation (see chapter 18) now became the
favorite tool of social reformers, who drew attention to
the vast contradictions between morals and manners,
intentions and actions, and, more generally, between
Enlightenment aspirations and contemporary injustice.

The Satires of Jonathan Swift

The premier British sat-
irist of the eighteenth
century was Jonathan
Swift (1667–1745). Unlike
the *philosophes*, this Dublin-
born Anglican priest took

a pessimistic view of human nature. He once confided (in
a letter to the poet Alexander Pope) that he hated the
human race, whose misuse of reason produced, in his
view, an irredeemably corrupt society. Such negativism
accompanied Swift's self-acclaimed "savage indigna-
tion." Yet, Swift was not a man of despair, for no
despairing personality could have produced such a profoundly moralizing body of literature. In 1726, Swift
published his most famous work, *Gulliver's Travels*. At the
simplest level, *Gulliver's Travels* is a story of travel and
adventure that (somewhat like Equiano's true-to-life
travels) describes the fortunes of a hero in imaginary
lands peopled with midgets, giants, and other fabulous
creatures. At a second, symbolic level, however, it is a
social statement on the vagaries of human behavior. In
one chapter, Gulliver visits the Lilliputians, "little people"
whose moral pettiness and inhumanity seem to characterize humankind at its worst; in another, he meets noble
horses whose rational behavior contrasts with the bes-
tiality of their human-looking slaves, the Yahoos. An
immediate popular sensation, *Gulliver's Travels* has
become a landmark in fantasy literature and social satire.

Swift also wrote many pamphlets and letters
protesting social and political ills. Among the most
famous is an essay publicizing the wretched condition of
the Irish peasants, who were exploited unmercifully by
the English government. In his satirical treatise *A Modest
Proposal* (1729), Swift observed that many Irish peasants
were too poor to feed their families; he proposed with
deadpan frankness that Irish children should be bred
and butchered for the English dining table, thus pro-
viding income for the poor and alleviating the miseries
of all. While *Gulliver's Travels* attacks conditions that are
universal and timeless, *A Modest Proposal* mocks a specific crisis of Swift's own time.

READING 4.22

From Swift's *A Modest Proposal*

**for Preventing the Children of Poor People in Ireland from Being a Burden
to Their Parents or Country, and for Making Them Beneficial to the Public**

It is a melancholy object to those who walk through this 1
great town,[1] or travel in the country, when they see the
streets, the roads, and cabin-doors, crowded with
beggars of the female sex, followed by three, four, or six
children, all in rags, and importuning every passenger for
an alms.[2] These mothers, instead of being able to work
for their honest livelihood, are forced to employ all their
time in strolling to beg sustenance for their helpless
infants: who, as they grow up, either turn thieves for
want of work, or leave their dear native country to fight 10
. . . in Spain, or sell themselves to the Barbadoes.[3]

---
[1]Dublin.
[2]Charity.
[3]As slaves in the West Indies.

I think it is agreed by all parties, that this prodigious number of children in the arms, or on the backs, or at the heels of their mothers, and frequently of their fathers, is, in the present deplorable state of the kingdom, a very great additional grievance; and, therefore, whoever could find out a fair, cheap, and easy method of making these children sound, useful members of the commonwealth, would deserve so well of the public, as to have his statue set up for a preserver of the nation.　20

But my intention is very far from being confined to provide only for the children of professed beggars; it is of a much greater extent, and shall take in the whole number of infants at a certain age, who are born of parents in effect as little able to support them, as those who demand our charity in the streets.

As to my own part, having turned my thoughts for many years upon this important subject, and maturely weighed the several schemes of our projectors,[4] I have always found them grossly mistaken in their computation. It is　30 true, a child, just born, may be supported by its mother's milk for a solar year, with little other nourishment; at most, not above the value of two shillings, which the mother may certainly get, or the value in scraps, by her lawful occupation of begging; and it is exactly at one year old that I propose to provide for them in such a manner, as, instead of being a charge upon their parents, or the parish, or wanting food and raiment[5] for the rest of their lives, they shall, on the contrary, contribute to the feeding, and partly to the clothing, of many thousands.　40

There is likewise another great advantage in my scheme, that it will prevent those voluntary abortions, and that horrid practice of women murdering their bastard children, alas, too frequent among us! sacrificing the poor innocent babes, I doubt more to avoid the expense than the shame, which would move tears and pity in the most savage and inhuman breast.

The number of souls in this kingdom being usually reckoned one million and a half, of these I calculate there may be about two hundred thousand couple whose wives　50 are breeders; from which number I subtract thirty thousand couple, who are able to maintain their own children (although I apprehend there cannot be so many, under the present distresses of the kingdom); but this being granted, there will remain a hundred and seventy thousand breeders. I again subtract fifty thousand, for those women who miscarry, or whose children die by accident or disease within the year. There only remain a hundred and twenty thousand children of poor parents annually born. The question therefore is, How this　60 number shall be reared and provided for? which, as I have already said, under the present situation of affairs, is utterly impossible by all the methods hitherto proposed. For we can neither employ them in handicraft or agriculture; we neither build houses (I mean in the country), nor cultivate land: they can very seldom pick up a livelihood by stealing, till they arrive at six years old, except where they are of towardly[6] parts; although I confess they learn the rudiments[7] much earlier. . . .

I am assured by our merchants, that a boy or a girl　70

before twelve years old is no saleable commodity; and even when they come to this age they will not yield above three pounds or three pounds and half-a-crown at most, on the exchange; which cannot turn to account either to the parents or kingdom, the charge of nutriment and rags having been at least four times that value.

I shall now, therefore, humbly propose my own thoughts, which I hope will not be liable to the least objection.

I have been assured by a very knowing American of my acquaintance in London, that a young healthy child, well　80 nursed, is, at a year old, a most delicious, nourishing, and wholesome food, whether stewed, roasted, baked, or boiled; and I make no doubt that it will equally serve in a fricassee or a ragout.

I do therefore humbly offer it to public consideration, that of the hundred and twenty thousand children already computed, twenty thousand may be reserved for breed, whereof only one-fourth part to be males; which is more than we allow to sheep, black-cattle, or swine; and my reason is, that these children are seldom the fruits of　90 marriage, a circumstance not much regarded by our savages, therefore one male will be sufficient for four females. That the remaining hundred thousand may, at a year old, be offered in sale to the persons of quality and fortune through the kingdom; always advising the mother to let them suck[8] plentifully in the last month, so as to render them plump and fat for a good table. A child will make two dishes at an entertainment for friends; and when the family dines alone, the fore or hind quarter will make a reasonable dish, and, seasoned with a little　100 pepper or salt, will be very good boiled on the fourth day, especially in winter.

I have reckoned, upon a medium,[9] that a child just born will weigh twelve pounds, and in a solar year, if tolerably nursed, will increase to twenty-eight pounds.

I grant this food will be somewhat dear, and therefore very proper for landlords, who, as they have already devoured most of the parents, seem to have the best title to the children.

Infants' flesh will be in season throughout the year, but　110 more plentifully in March, and a little before and after: for we are told by a grave author,[10] an eminent French physician, that fish being a prolific diet, there are more children born in Roman Catholic countries about nine months after Lent, than at any other season; therefore, reckoning a year after Lent, the markets will be more glutted than usual, because the number of Popish infants is at least three to one in this kingdom; and therefore it will have one other collateral advantage, by lessening the number of Papists[11] among us.　120

I have already computed the charge of nursing a beggar's child (in which list I reckon all cottagers, labourers, and four-fifths of the farmers) to be about two shillings per annum, rags included; and I believe no gentleman would repine to give ten shillings for the carcass of a good fat child, which, as I have said, will make four dishes of excellent nutritive meat, when he has only some particular friend, or his own family, to dine with him. Thus the squire will learn to be a good landlord,

---

[4]Speculators.
[5]Clothing.
[6]Handsome.
[7]Fundamentals; first principles.

[8]To nurse at the breast.
[9]On an average.
[10]François Rabelais (see chapter 18).
[11]Roman Catholics, especially those who ardently support the pope.

and grow popular among his tenants; the mother will have eight shillings net profit, and be fit for work till she produces another child. 130

Those who are more thrifty (as I must confess the times require) may flay the carcass; the skin of which, artificially dressed, will make admirable gloves for ladies, and summer-boots for fine gentlemen. As to our city of Dublin, shambles[12] may be appointed for this purpose in the most convenient parts of it, and butchers we may be assured will not be wanting; although I rather recommend buying the children alive, then dressing them hot from the knife, as we do roasting pigs. 140

A very worthy person, a true lover of his country, and whose virtues I highly esteem, was lately pleased, in discoursing on this matter, to offer a refinement upon my scheme. He said that many gentlemen of this kingdom, having of late destroyed their deer, he conceived that the want of venison might be well supplied by the bodies of young lads and maidens, not exceeding fourteen years of age, nor under twelve; so great a number of both sexes in every country being now ready to starve for want of work and service; and these to be disposed of by their parents, if alive, or otherwise by their nearest relations. But, with due deference to so excellent a friend, and so deserving a patriot, I cannot be altogether in his sentiments; for as to the males, my American acquaintance assured me, from frequent experience, that their flesh was generally tough and lean, like that of our schoolboys, by continual exercise, and their taste disagreeable; and to fatten them would not answer the charge. Then as to the females, it would, I think, with humble submission, be a loss to the public, because they soon would become breeders themselves: and besides, it is not improbable that some scrupulous people might be apt to censure such a practice (although indeed very unjustly), as a little bordering upon cruelty; which, I confess, has always been with me the strongest objection against any project, how well soever intended. . . . 150 160

I think the advantages by the proposal which I have made are obvious and many, as well as of the highest importance. 170

For first, as I have already observed, it would greatly lessen the number of Papists, with whom we are yearly over-run, being the principal breeders of the nation, as well as our most dangerous enemies; and who stay at home on purpose to deliver the kingdom to the Pretender, hoping to take their advantage by the absence of so many good Protestants, who have chosen rather to leave their country, than stay at home and pay tithes against their conscience to an Episcopal curate.

Secondly, The poorer tenants will have something valuable of their own, which by law may be made liable to distress, and help to pay their landlord's rent; their corn and cattle being already seized, and money a thing unknown. 180

Thirdly, Whereas the maintenance of a hundred thousand children, from two years old and upward, cannot be computed at less than ten shillings a piece per annum, the nation's stock will be thereby increased fifty thousand pounds per annum, beside the profit of a new dish introduced to the tables of all gentlemen of fortune in the kingdom, who have any refinement in taste. And the money will circulate among ourselves, the goods being entirely of our own growth and manufacture. 190

Fourthly, The constant breeders, beside the gain of eight shillings sterling per annum by the sale of their children, will be rid of the charge of maintaining them after the first year.

Fifthly, This food would likewise bring great custom to taverns; where the vintners will certainly be so prudent as to procure the best receipts for dressing it to perfection, and, consequently, have their houses frequented by all the fine gentlemen, who justly value themselves upon their knowledge in good eating: and a skilful cook, who understands how to oblige his guests, will contrive to make it as expensive as they please. 200

Sixthly, This would be a great inducement to marriage, which all wise nations have either encouraged by rewards, or enforced by laws and penalties. It would increase the care and tenderness of mothers toward their children, when they were sure of a settlement for life to the poor babes, provided in some sort by the public, to their annual profit or expense. We should see an honest emulation among the married women, which of them could bring the fattest child to the market. Men would become as fond of their wives during the time of their pregnancy, as they are now of their mares in foal, their cows in calf, their sows when they are ready to farrow; nor offer to beat or kick them (as is too frequent a practice) for fear of a miscarriage. 210

Many other advantages might be enumerated. For instance, the addition of some thousand carcasses in our exportation of barrelled beef; the propagation of swine's flesh, and improvement in the art of making good bacon, so much wanted among us by the great destruction of pigs, too frequent at our table; which are no way comparable in taste or magnificence to a well-grown, fat, yearling child, which, roasted whole, will make a considerable figure at a lord mayor's feast, or any other public entertainment. But this, and many others, I omit, being studious of brevity. . . . 220

———————◆———————

Voltaire and *Candide*

Swift's satires were an inspiration to that most scintillating of French *philosophes* and leading intellectual of French society, François-Marie Arouet (1694–1778), who used the pen name Voltaire (Figure **25.3**). Born into a rising Parisian middle-class family and educated by Jesuits, Voltaire rose to fame as poet, playwright, critic, and as the central figure of the French *salons*. His historical and expository works attacked bigotry as manmade evil and injustice as institutional evil. On two separate occasions, his controversial verse-satires led to his imprisonment in the Bastille (the French state prison). His period of exile in England instilled in him high regard for constitutional government, the principles of toleration, and the concepts of equality found in the writings of John Locke—all of which ideas he championed in his writings.

---

[12]Slaughterhouses.

Figure 25.3 Jean-Antoine Houdon, *Voltaire in Old Age*, 1781. Marble, height 20 in. Musée de Versailles. © The Bettmann Archive, New York.

More than any of the *philosophes*, Voltaire extolled the traditions of non-Western cultures, faiths, and moralities: Having read the works of Confucius in Jesuit translations, he esteemed the ancient teacher as a philosopher-sage. Voltaire was also the first modern intellectual to assess the role of Russia in world society. In his *Essay on Manners*, a universal history that examines the customs of nations around the world, Voltaire gave thoughtful attention to the history of the Russian state. His fascination with Russia as a curious blend of Asian and European traditions became the basis for a lifelong pursuit of things Russian, including a long correspondence with Catherine the Great, who ruled as Empress of Russia from 1762 to 1796.

Like most of the *philosophes*, Voltaire condemned organized religion and all forms of religious fanaticism. A declared deist, he compared human beings to mice, who, living in the recesses of an immense ship, had no cognizance of its captain or its destination. Any confidence Voltaire might have had in beneficent Providence was dashed by the terrible Lisbon earthquake and tidal wave of 1755, which took the lives of more than twenty thousand people. For Voltaire, the realities of natural

disaster and human cruelty were not easily reconciled with the belief that a good God created the universe or the idea that humans were by nature good—views basic to Enlightenment optimism. In the satirical tale *Candide* (subtitled *Optimism*), Voltaire addressed the age-old question of how evil could exist in a universe created and governed by the forces of good. More important, he leveled a major blow at the optimistic credo postulated by the German philosopher Gottfried Wilhelm Leibniz (see chapter 24) that this was "the best of all possible worlds." A parody of the adventure romances and travel tales (Equiano and Swift both come to mind) in vogue in Voltaire's time, *Candide* describes the exploits of a naive and unsophisticated young man whose blissful optimism is daunted by a series of terrible (and hilarious) experiences. Initially, the youthful Candide (literally, "candid" or "frank") approaches life with the glib optimism taught to him by Dr. Pangloss ("all tongue"), Voltaire's embodiment of Leibniz. But Candide soon discovers the folly of believing that "all is for the best in this best of all possible worlds." He experiences the horrors of war (the consequences of two equally self-righteous opposing armies), the evils of religious fanaticism (as manifested by the Spanish Inquisition), the disasters of nature (the Lisbon earthquake), and the dire effects of human greed (an affliction especially prevalent among the aristocracy and derived, according to Voltaire, from boredom). Experience becomes the antidote to the comfortable fatalism of Pope's "Whatever is, is right." After a lifetime of sobering misadventures, Candide ends his days settled on a farm (in Turkey) in the company of his long-lost friends. (Not coincidentally, the aging Voltaire penned *Candide* while living on his farm retreat just outside Geneva.) "We must cultivate our garden," he concludes. This metaphor for achieving personal satisfaction in a hostile world relieves the otherwise devastating skepticism that underlies *Candide*. It is Voltaire's answer to blind optimism and the foolish hope that human reason can allay evil.

Voltaire's genius, and the quality that separates his style from that of Goldsmith or Swift, is his penetrating wit. Like the marksman's sword, Voltaire's satire is sharply pointed, precise in its aim, and devastating in its effect. With a sure hand, Voltaire manipulates the principal satirical devices: irony, understatement, and overstatement. Using irony—the contradiction between literal and intended meanings—he mocks serious matters and deflates lofty pretensions; he calls war, for instance, "heroic butchery" and refers to Paquetta's venereal disease as a "present" she received from "a very learned Franciscan." He exploits understatement when he notes, for example, that Pangloss "only lost one eye and one ear" (as the result of syphilis). And he uses overstatement for moral effect: The 350-pound baroness of Westphalia is "greatly respected"; thus corpulence—actually an indication of self-indulgence—becomes a specious sign of dignity and importance.

Voltaire's mock optimism, dispatched by Candide's persistent view that this is "the best of all possible worlds" even as he encounters repeated horrors, underscores the contradiction between the ideal and the real that lies at the heart of all satire. Although *Candide* was censored in many parts of Europe, the book was so popular that it went through forty editions in Voltaire's lifetime. A classic of Western satire, *Candide* has survived numerous adaptations, including a superb twentieth-century version as a comic-operetta with lyrics by the American poet Richard Wilber and music by the American composer Leonard Bernstein.* Approximately one-third of Voltaire's philosophical tale is included in the following excerpt.

READING 4.23

From Voltaire's *Candide*

Chapter 1

How Candide Was Brought Up in a Fine Castle, and How He Was Expelled From Thence

There lived in Westphalia,[1] in the castle of my Lord the Baron of Thunder-ten-tronckh, a young man, on whom nature had bestowed the most agreeable manners. His face was the index to his mind. He had an upright heart, with an easy frankness; which, I believe, was the reason he got the name of *Candide*. He was suspected, by the old servants of the family, to be the son of my Lord the Baron's sister, by a very honest gentleman of the neighborhood, whom the young lady declined to marry, because he could only produce seventy-one armorial quarterings,[2] the rest of his genealogical tree having been destroyed through the injuries of time.

The Baron was one of the most powerful lords in Westphalia; his castle had both a gate and windows; and his great hall was even adorned with tapestry. The dogs of his outer yard composed his hunting pack upon occasion, his grooms were his huntsmen, and the vicar of the parish was his chief almoner. He was called My Lord by everybody, and everyone laughed when he told his stories.

My Lady the Baroness, who weighed about three hundred and fifty pounds, attracted, by that means, very great attention, and did the honors of the house with a dignity that rendered her still more respectable. Her daughter Cunegonde, aged about seventeen years, was of a ruddy complexion, fresh, plump, and well calculated to excite the passions. The Baron's son appeared to be in every respect worthy of his father. The preceptor, Pangloss,[3] was the oracle of the house, and little Candide listened to his lectures with all the simplicity that was suitable to his age and character.

Pangloss taught metaphysico-theologo-cosmoloonigology.[4] He proved most admirably, that there could not be an effect without cause; that, in this best of possible worlds,[5] my Lord the Baron's castle was the most magnificent of castles, and my Lady the best of Baronesses that possibly could be.

"It is demonstrable," said he, "that things cannot be otherwise than they are: for things having been made for some end, they must necessarily be for the best end. Observe well, that the nose has been made for carrying spectacles; therefore we have spectacles. The legs are visibly designed for stockings, and therefore we have stockings. Stones have been formed to be hewn, and make castles; therefore my Lord has a very fine castle; the greatest baron of the province ought to be the best accommodated. Swine were made to be eaten; therefore we eat pork all the year round: consequently, those who have merely asserted that all is good, have said a very foolish thing; they should have said all is the best possible."

Candide listened attentively, and believed implicitly; for he thought Miss Cunegonde extremely handsome, though he never had the courage to tell her so. He concluded, that next to the good fortune of being Baron of Thunder-ten-tronckh, the second degree of happiness was that of being Miss Cunegonde, the third to see her every day, and the fourth to listen to the teachings of Master Pangloss, the greatest philosopher of the province, and consequently of the whole world.

One day Cunegonde having taken a walk in the environs of the castle, in a little wood, which they called a park, espied Doctor Pangloss giving a lesson in experimental philosophy to her mother's chambermaid; a little brown wench, very handsome, and very docile. As Miss Cunegonde had a strong inclination for the sciences, she observed, without making any noise, the reiterated experiments that were going on before her eyes; she saw very clearly the sufficient reason of the Doctor, the effects and the causes; and she returned greatly flurried, quite pensive, and full of desire to be learned; imagining that she might be a sufficient reason for young Candide, who also, might be the same to her.

On her return to the castle, she met Candide, and blushed; Candide also blushed; she wished him good morrow with a faltering voice, and Candide answered her, hardly knowing what he said. The next day, after dinner, as they arose from table, Cunegonde and Candide happened to get behind the screen. Cunegonde dropped her handkerchief, and Candide picked it up; she, not thinking any harm, took hold of his hand; and the young man, not thinking any harm neither, kissed the hand of the young lady, with an eagerness, a sensibility, and grace, very particular; their lips met, their eyes sparkled, their knees trembled, their hands strayed.—The Baron of Thunder-ten-tronckh happening to pass close by the screen, and observing this cause and effect, thrust

*The 1985 New York City Opera House version is available on cassette and CD, New World label: NW–340/41.
[1]A province in Germany.
[2]Genealogical degrees of noble ancestry; since each quartering represents one generation, the family "tree" is over two thousand years old—an obvious impossibility.
[3]The tutor's name is (literally) "all-tongue."

[4]Note the French *nigaud* ("booby") included in the elaborate title of this pompous-sounding discipline.
[5]One of many allusions in *Candide* to the philosophic optimism systematized by Leibniz and popularized by Pope (see chapter 24).

Candide out of the castle, with lusty kicks [to the behind]. Cunegonde fell into a swoon and as soon as she came to herself, was heartily cuffed on the ears by my Lady the Baroness. Thus all was thrown into confusion in 90 the finest and most agreeable castle possible.

Chapter 2

What Became of Candide Among the Bulgarians[6]

Candide being expelled the terrestrial paradise, rambled a long while without knowing where, weeping, and lifting up his eyes to heaven, and sometimes turning them towards the finest of castles, which contained the handsomest of baronesses. He laid himself down, without his supper, in the open fields, between two furrows, while the snow fell in great flakes. Candide, almost frozen to death, crawled next morning to the neighboring village, which was called Waldber-ghoff-trarbk-dikdorff. Having no money, and 100 almost dying with hunger and fatigue, he stopped in a dejected posture before the gate of an inn. Two men, dressed in blue,[7] observing him in such a situation, "Brother," says one of them to the other, "there is a young fellow well built, and of a proper height." They accosted Candide, and invited him very civilly to dinner.

"Gentlemen," replied Candide, with an agreeable modesty, "you do me much honor, but I have no money to pay my share."

"O sir," said one of the blues, "persons of your 110 appearance and merit never pay anything; are you not five feet five inches high?"

"Yes, gentlemen, that is my height," returned he, making a bow.

"Come, sir, sit down at table; we will not only treat you, but we will never let such a man as you want money; men are made to assist one another."

"You are in the right," said Candide; "that is what Pangloss always told me, and I see plainly that everything is for the best." 120

They entreated him to take a few crowns, which he accepted, and would have given them his note; but they refused it, and sat down to table.

"Do not you tenderly love—"

"O yes," replied he, "I tenderly love Miss Cunegonde."

"No," said one of the gentlemen; "we ask you if you do tenderly love the King of the Bulgarians?"

"Not at all," said he, "for I never saw him."

"How! he is the most charming of kings, and you must drink his health." 130

"O, with all my heart, gentlemen," and drinks.

"That is enough," said they to him; "you are now the bulwark, the support, the defender, the hero of the Bulgarians; your fortune is made, and you are certain of glory." Instantly they put him in irons, and carried him to the regiment. They made him turn to the right, to the left, draw the ramrod, return the ramrod, present, fire, step double; and they gave him thirty blows with a cudgel. The next day, he performed his exercises not quite so badly,

and received but twenty blows; the third day the blows 140 were restricted to ten, and he was looked upon by his fellow-soldiers, as a kind of prodigy.

Candide, quite stupefied, could not well conceive how he had become a hero. One fine Spring day he took it into his head to walk out, going straight forward, imagining that the human, as well as the animal species, were entitled to make whatever use they pleased of their limbs. He had not travelled two leagues, when four other heroes, six feet high, came up to him, bound him, and put him into a dungeon. He is asked by a Court-martial, whether 150 he chooses to be whipped six and thirty times through the whole regiment, or receive at once twelve bullets through the forehead? He in vain argued that the will is free, and that he chose neither the one nor the other; he was obliged to make a choice; he therefore resolved, in virtue of God's gift called *freewill*, to run the gauntlet six and thirty times. He underwent this discipline twice. The regiment being composed of two thousand men, he received four thousand lashes, which laid open all his muscles and nerves, from the nape of the neck to the 160 back. As they were proceeding to a third course, Candide, being quite spent, begged as a favor that they would be so kind as to shoot him; he obtained his request; they hoodwinked him, and made him kneel; the King of the Bulgarians passing by, inquired into the crime of the delinquent; and as this prince was a person of great penetration, he discovered from what he heard of Candide, that he was a young metaphysician, entirely ignorant of the things of this world; and he granted him his pardon, with a clemency which will be extolled in all 170 histories, and throughout all ages. An experienced surgeon cured Candide in three weeks, with emollients prescribed by no less a master than Dioscorides.[8] His skin had already began to grow again, and he was able to walk, when the King of the Bulgarians gave battle to the King of the Abares.

Chapter 3

How Candide Made His Escape From the Bulgarians, and What Afterwards Befell Him

Nothing could be so fine, so neat, so brilliant, so well ordered, as the two armies.[9] The trumpets, fifes, hautboys, drums, and cannon, formed an harmony superior to what hell itself could invent. The cannon 180 swept off at first about six thousand men on each side; afterwards, the musketry carried away from the best of worlds, about nine or ten thousand rascals that infected its surface. The bayonet was likewise the sufficient reason of the death of some thousands of men. The whole number might amount to about thirty thousand souls. Candide, who trembled like a philosopher, hid himself as well as he could, during this heroic butchery.

At last, while each of the two kings were causing *Te Deum*—glory to God—to be sung in their respective 190 camps, he resolved to go somewhere else, to reason upon

---

[6]Voltaire's name for the troops of Frederick the Great, King of Prussia, who, like their king, were widely regarded as Sodomites; the association between the name and the French *bougre* ("to bugger") is patent.
[7]The color of the uniforms worn by the soldiers of Frederick the Great.

[8]A famous Greek physician of the first century C.E. whose book on medicine was for centuries a standard text.
[9]A mocking reference to the Seven Years' War (1756–63) fought between the Prussians (Bulgars) and the French-Austrian coalition, to whom Voltaire gives the name Abares—a tribe of semicivilized Scythians.

the effects and causes. He walked over heaps of the dead and dying; he came at first to a neighboring village belonging to the Abares, but found it in ashes; for it had been burnt by the Bulgarians, according to the law of nations. Here were to be seen old men full of wounds, casting their eyes on their murdered wives, who were holding their infants to their bloody breasts. You might see in another place, virgins outraged after they had satisfied the natural desires of some of those heroes, 200 whilst breathing out their last sighs. Others, half-burnt, praying earnestly for instant death. The whole field was covered with brains, and with legs and arms lopped off.

Candide betook himself with all speed to another village. It belonged to the Bulgarians, and had met with the same treatment from the Abarian heroes. Candide, walking still forward over quivering limbs, or through rubbish of houses, got at last out of the theatre of war, having some small quantity of provisions in his knapsack, and never forgetting Miss Cunegonde. His provisions failed him when he arrived 210 in Holland;[10] but having heard that every one was rich in that country, and that they were Christians, he did not doubt but he should be as well treated there as he had been in my Lord the Baron's castle, before he had been expelled thence on account of Miss Cunegonde's sparkling eyes.

He asked alms from several grave looking persons, who all replied, that if he continued that trade, they would confine him in a house of correction, where he should learn to earn his bread.

He applied afterwards to a man, who for a whole hour 220 had been discoursing on the subject of charity, before a large assembly. This orator, looking at him askance, said to him:

"What are you doing here? are you for the good cause?"

"There is no effect without a cause," replied Candide, modestly; "all is necessarily linked, and ordered for the best. A necessity banished me from Miss Cunegonde; a necessity forced me to run the gauntlet; another necessity makes me beg my bread, till I can get into some business by which to earn it. All this could not be otherwise." 230

"My friend," said the orator to him, "do you believe that the Anti-Christ is alive?"

"I never heard whether he is or not," replied Candide; "but whether he is, or is not, I want bread!"

"You do not deserve to eat any," said the other; "get you gone, you rogue; get you gone, you wretch; never in thy life come near me again!"

The orator's wife, having popped her head out of the chamber window, and seeing a man who doubted whether Anti-Christ was alive, poured on his head a full 240 vessel of. . . . Oh heavens! to what excess does religious zeal transport the fair sex!

A man who had not been baptized, a good Anabaptist,[11] named *James*, saw the barbarous and ignominious manner with which they treated one of his brethren, a being with two feet, without feathers, and endowed with a rational soul.[12] He took him home with him, cleaned him,

gave him bread and beer, made him a present of two florins,[13] and offered to teach him the method of working in his manufactories of Persian stuffs, which are 250 fabricated in Holland. Candide, prostrating himself almost to the ground, cried out, "Master Pangloss argued well when he said, that everything is for the best in this world; for I am infinitely more affected with your very great generosity, than by the hard-heartedness of that gentleman with the cloak, and the lady his wife."

Next day, as he was taking a walk, he met a beggar, all covered over with sores, his eyes half dead, the tip of his nose eaten off, his mouth turned to one side of his face, his teeth black, speaking through his throat, tormented 260 with a violent cough, with gums so rotten, that his teeth came near falling out every time he spit.

Chapter 4

How Candide Met His Old Master of Philosophy, Dr. Pangloss, and What Happened to Them

Candide, moved still more with compassion than with horror, gave this frightful mendicant the two florins which he had received of his honest Anabaptist James. The spectre fixed his eyes attentively upon him, dropt some tears, and was going to fall upon his neck. Candide, affrighted, drew back.

"Alas!" said the one wretch to the other, "don't you know your dear Pangloss?" 270

"What do I hear! Is it you, my dear master! you in this dreadful condition! What misfortune has befallen you? Why are you no longer in the most magnificent of castles? What has become of Miss Cunegonde, the nonpareil of the fair sex, the master-piece of nature?"

"I have no more strength," said Pangloss.

Candide immediately carried him to the Anabaptist's stable, where he gave him a little bread to eat. When Pangloss was refreshed a little, "Well," said Candide, "what has become of Cunegonde?" 280

"She is dead," replied the other.

Candide fainted away at this word; but his friend recovered his senses, with a little bad vinegar which he found by chance in the stable.

Candide, opening his eyes, cried out, "Cunegonde is dead! Ah, best of worlds, where art thou now? But of what distemper did she die? Was not the cause, her seeing me driven out of the castle by my Lord, her father, with such hard kicks on the breech?"

"No," said Pangloss, "she was gutted by some 290 Bulgarian soldiers, after having been barbarously ravished.[14] They knocked my Lord the Baron on the head, for attempting to protect her; my Lady the Baroness was cut in pieces; my poor pupil was treated like his sister; and as for the castle, there is not one stone left upon another, nor a barn, nor a sheep, nor a duck, nor a tree. But we have been sufficiently revenged; for the Abarians have done the very same thing to a neighboring barony, which belonged to a Bulgarian Lord."

At this discourse, Candide fainted away a second time; 300 but coming to himself, and having said all that he ought to say, he enquired into the cause and the effect, and

---

[10]Holland, a mecca of religious freedom for over two centuries, had given asylum to the Anabaptists and other radical religious sects.
[11]A Protestant sect (originating in Zürich in 1524) advocating the baptism of adult believers and the practice of simplicity, mutual help, the exercise of individual conscience, and the separation of Church and state.
[12]The minimalist definition of man ascribed to the philosopher Plato and used here to suggest James' sympathy with all humankind.

[13]Gold coins.
[14]Raped.

into the sufficient reason that had reduced Pangloss to so deplorable a condition. "Alas," said the other, "it was love; love, the comforter of the human race, the preserver of the universe, the soul of all sensible beings, tender love." "Alas!" said Candide, "I know this love, the sovereign of hearts, the soul of our soul; yet it never cost me more than a kiss, and twenty kicks. But how could this charming cause produce in you so abominable an effect?" 310

Pangloss made answer as follows: "Oh my dear Candide, you knew Paquetta, the pretty attendant on our noble Baroness; I tasted in her arms the delights of Paradise, which produced those torments of hell with which you see me devoured. She was infected,[15] and perhaps she is dead. Paquetta received this present from a very learned Franciscan, who had it from an old countess, who received it from a captain of horse, who was indebted for it to a marchioness, who got it from one of the companions of Christopher Columbus. For my part, 320 I shall give it to nobody, for I am dying."

"Oh Pangloss!" cried Candide, "what a strange genealogy! Was not the devil at the head of it?" "Not at all," replied the great man; "it was a thing indispensable; a necessary ingredient in the best of worlds; for if Columbus had not caught, in an island of America, this disease, we should have had neither chocolate nor cochineal. It may also be observed, that to this day, upon our continent, this malady is as peculiar to us, as is religious controversy. The Turks, the Indians, the 330 Persians, the Chinese, the Siamese, and the Japanese, know nothing of it yet. But there is sufficient reason why they, in their turn, should become acquainted with it, a few centuries hence. In the mean time, it has made marvellous progress among us, and especially in those great armies composed of honest hirelings, well disciplined, who decide the fate of states; for we may rest assured, that when thirty thousand men in a pitched battle fight against troops equal to them in number, there are about twenty thousand of them on each side who 340 have the pox.

"This is admirable," said Candide; "but you must be cured." "Ah! how can I?" said Pangloss; "I have not a penny, my friend; and throughout the whole extent of this globe, we cannot get any one to bleed us, or give us a glister, without paying for it, or getting some other person to pay for us."

This last speech determined Candide. He went and threw himself at the feet of his charitable Anabaptist James, and gave him so touching a description of the 350 state his friend was reduced to, that the good man did not hesitate to entertain Dr. Pangloss, and he had him cured at his own expense. During the cure, Pangloss lost only an eye and an ear. As he wrote well, and understood arithmetic perfectly, the Anabaptist made him his bookkeeper. At the end of two months, being obliged to go to Lisbon on account of his business, he took the two philosophers along with him, in his ship. Pangloss explained to him how every thing was such as it could not be better; but James was not of this opinion. "Mankind," 360 said he, "must have somewhat corrupted their nature; for

they were not born wolves, and yet they have become wolves; God has given them neither cannon of twenty-four pounds, nor bayonets; and yet they have made cannon and bayonets to destroy one another. I might throw into the account bankrupts; and the law which seizes on the effects of bankrupts only to bilk the creditors." "All this was indispensable," replied the one-eyed doctor, "and private misfortunes constitute the general good; so that the more private misfortunes there are, the whole is the 370 better." While he was thus reasoning, the air grew dark, the winds blew from the four quarters of the world, and the ship was attacked by a dreadful storm, within sight of the harbor of Lisbon.

Chapter 5

Tempest, Shipwreck, Earthquake and What Became of Dr. Pangloss, Candide and James the Anabaptist

One half of the passengers being weakened, and ready to breathe their last, with the inconceivable anguish which the rolling of the ship conveyed through the nerves and all the humors of the body, which were quite disordered, were not capable of being alarmed at the danger they were in. The other half uttered cries and made prayers; 380 the sails were rent, the masts broken, and the ship became leaky. Every one worked that was able, nobody cared for any thing, and no order was kept. The Anabaptist contributed his assistance to work the ship. As he was upon deck, a furious sailor rudely struck him, and laid him sprawling on the planks; but with the blow he gave him, he himself was so violently jolted, that he tumbled overboard with his head foremost, and remained suspended by a piece of broken mast. Honest James ran to his assistance, and helped him on deck again; but in 390 the attempt, he fell into the sea, in the sight of the sailor, who suffered him to perish, without deigning to look upon him. Candide drew near and saw his benefactor, one moment emerging, and the next swallowed up for ever. He was just going to throw himself into the sea after him, when the philosopher Pangloss hindered him, by demonstrating to him, that the road to Lisbon had been made on purpose for this Anabaptist to be drowned in. While he was proving this, *a priori*, the vessel foundered, and all perished except Pangloss, 400 Candide, and the brutal sailor, who drowned the virtuous Anabaptist. The villain luckily swam ashore, whither Pangloss and Candide were carried on a plank.

When they had recovered themselves a little, they walked towards Lisbon. They had some money left, with which they hoped to save themselves from hunger, after having escaped from the storm.

Scarce had they set foot in the city, bewailing the death of their benefactor, when they perceived the earth to tremble under their feet,[16] and saw the sea swell in the 410 harbor, and dash to pieces the ships that were at anchor. The whirling flames and ashes covered the streets and public places, the houses tottered, and their roofs fell to the foundations, and the foundations were scattered; thirty thousand inhabitants of all ages and sexes were

[15]With venereal disease; syphilis, which entered Europe in the late fifteenth century, was one of the most virulent legacies of the Euro-American exchange.

[16]The first Lisbon earthquake and fire took place on November 1, 1755. It destroyed much of the city and took over 20,000 lives.

crushed to death in the ruins. The sailor, whistling and swearing, said "There is some booty to be got here." "What can be the sufficient reason of this phenomenon?" said Pangloss. "This is certainly the last day of the world," cried Candide. The sailor ran quickly into the 420 midst of the ruins, encountered death to find money, found it, laid hold of it, got drunk, and having slept himself sober, purchased the favors of the first willing girl he met with, among the ruins of the demolished houses, and in the midst of the dying and the dead. While he was thus engaged, Pangloss pulled him by the sleeve; "My friend," said he, "this is not right; you trespass against universal reason, you choose your time badly." "Brains and blood!" answered the other; "I am a sailor, and was born at Batavia; . . . you have found the right man, this 430 time, with your universal reason."

Some pieces of stone having wounded Candide, he lay sprawling in the street, and covered with rubbish. "Alas!" said he to Pangloss, "get me a little wine and oil; I am dying." "This trembling of the earth is no new thing," answered Pangloss. "The City of Lima, in America, experienced the same concussions last year; the same cause has the same effects; there is certainly a train of sulphur under the earth, from Lima to Lisbon." "Nothing is more probable," said Candide; "but, for God's sake, a 440 little oil and wine." "How probable?" replied the philosopher; "I maintain that the thing is demonstrable." Candide lost all sense, and Pangloss brought him a little water from a neighboring fountain.

The day following, having found some provisions, in rummaging through the rubbish, they recruited their strength a little. Afterwards, they employed themselves like others, in administering relief to the inhabitants that had escaped from death. Some citizens that had been relieved by them, gave them as good a dinner as could be 450 expected amidst such a disaster. It is true that the repast was mournful, and the guests watered their bread with their tears. But Pangloss consoled them by the assurance that things could not be otherwise; "For," said he, "all this must necessarily be for the best. As this volcano is at Lisbon, it could not be elsewhere; as it is impossible that things should not be what they are, as all is good."

A little man clad in black, who belonged to the Inquisition,[17] and sat at his side, took him up very politely, and said: "It seems, sir, you do not believe in 460 original sin; for if all is for the best, then there has been neither fall nor punishment."

"I most humbly ask your excellency's pardon," answered Pangloss, still more politely; "for the fall of man and the curse necessarily entered into the best of worlds possible." "Then, sir, you do not believe there is liberty," said the inquisitor. "Your Excellency will excuse me," said Pangloss; "liberty can consist with absolute necessity; for it was necessary we should be free; because, in short, the determinate will—" 470

Pangloss was in the middle of his proposition, when the inquisitor made a signal with his head to the tall armed footman in a cloak, who waited upon him, to bring him a glass of port wine.

Chapter 6

How a Fine *Auto-da-Fé*[18] Was Celebrated to Prevent Earthquakes, and How Candide Was Whipped

After the earthquake, which had destroyed three-fourths of Lisbon, the sages of the country could not find any means more effectual to prevent a total destruction, than to give the people a splendid *auto-da-fé*. It had been decided by the university of Coimbra, that the spectacle of some persons burnt to death by a slow fire, with great 480 ceremony, was an infallible antidote for earthquakes.

In consequence of this resolution, they had seized a Biscayan, convicted of having married his godmother,[19] and two Portuguese, who, in eating a pullet, had stripped off the bacon.[20] After dinner, they came and secured Dr. Pangloss, and his disciple Candide; the one for having spoke too freely, and the other for having heard with an air of approbation. They were both conducted to separate apartments, extremely damp, and never incommoded with the sun.[21] Eight days after, they were both clothed 490 with a gown and had their heads adorned with paper crowns.[22] Candide's crown and gown were painted with inverted flames, and with devils that had neither tails nor claws; but Pangloss' devils had claws and tails, and the flames were pointed upwards. Being thus dressed, they marched in procession, and heard a very pathetic speech followed by fine music on a squeaking organ. Candide was whipped on the back in cadence, while they were singing; the Biscayan, and the two men who would not eat lard, were burnt; and Pangloss, though it was 500 contrary to custom, was hanged. The same day, the earth shook anew,[23] with a most dreadful noise.

Candide, affrighted, interdicted, astonished, all bloody, all panting, said to himself: "If this is the best of possible worlds, what then are the rest? Supposing I had not been whipped now, I have been so, among the Bulgarians; but, Oh, my dear Pangloss; thou greatest of philosophers, that it should be my fate to see thee hanged without knowing for what! Oh! my dear Anabaptist! thou best of men, that it should be thy fate to be drowned in the harbor! Oh! 510 Miss Cunegonde! the jewel of ladies, that it should be thy fate to have been outraged and slain!"

He returned, with difficulty, supporting himself, after being lectured, whipped, absolved, and blessed, when an old woman accosted him, and said: "Child, take courage, and follow me."

Chapter 7

How an Old Woman Took Care of Candide, and How He Found the Object He Loved

Candide did not take courage, but he followed the old woman to a ruinated house. She gave him a pot of pomatum[24] to anoint himself, left him something to eat

---

[17]An officer of the Inquisition, a special church court designed to try heretics; the officer was empowered to arrest anyone he suspected of heresy.

[18]The public ceremony (literally, "act of faith") by which those found guilty of heresy were punished.
[19]A swipe at papal efforts to condemn as incestuous marriages in which the parties might be bound by family relation.
[20]Unwittingly revealing that they were secretly Jews—Jewish dietary laws prohibit the eating of pork. Under the pressure of the Spanish and Portuguese Inquisitions, many Iberian Jews had converted to Christianity.
[21]Prison cells.
[22]Yellow penitential garments worn by the confessed heretic.
[23]A second earthquake occurred in Lisbon on December 21, 1755.
[24]Ointment.

and drink, and showed him a very neat little bed, near 520
which was a complete suit of clothes. "Eat, drink, and
sleep," said she to him, "and may God take care of you. I
will be back to-morrow." Candide, astonished at all he
had seen, at all he had suffered, and still more at the
charity of the old woman, offered to kiss her hand. "You
must not kiss my hand," said the old woman, "I will be
back to-morrow. Rub yourself with the pomatum, eat and
take rest."

Candide, notwithstanding so many misfortunes, ate,
and went to sleep. Next morning, the old woman brought 530
him his breakfast, looked at his back, and rubbed it
herself with another ointment; she afterwards brought
him his dinner; and she returned at night, and brought
him his supper. The day following she performed the
same ceremonies. "Who are you," would Candide always
say to her; "Who has inspired you with so much
goodness? What thanks can I render you?" The good
woman made no answer; she returned in the evening, but
brought him no supper. "Come along with me," said she,
"and say not a word." She took him by the arm, and 540
walked with him into the country about a quarter of a
mile; they arrived at a house that stood by itself,
surrounded with gardens and canals. The old woman
knocked at a little door, which being opened, she
conducted Candide by a private stair-case into a gilded
closet, and leaving him on a brocade couch, shut the
door and went her way. Candide thought he was in a
revery, and looked upon all his life as an unlucky dream,
but at the present moment, a very agreeable vision.

The old woman returned very soon, supporting with 550
difficulty a woman trembling, of a majestic port, glittering
with jewels, and covered with a veil. "Take off that veil,"
said the old woman to Candide. The young man
approached and took off the veil with a trembling hand.
What joy! what surprise! he thought he saw Miss
Cunegonde; he saw her indeed! it was she herself. His
strength failed him, he could not utter a word, but fell
down at her feet. Cunegonde fell upon the carpet. The old
woman applied aromatic waters; they recovered their
senses, and spoke to one another. At first, their words 560
were broken, their questions and answers crossed each
other, amidst sighs, tears and cries. The old woman
recommended them to make less noise, and then left
them to themselves. "How! is it you?" said Candide; "are
you still alive? do I find you again in Portugal? You were
not ravished then, as the philosopher Pangloss assured
me?" "Yes, all this was so," said the lovely Cunegonde;
"but death does not always follow from these two
accidents." "But your father and mother! were they not
killed?" "It is but too true," answered Cunegonde, 570
weeping. "And your brother?" "My brother was killed
too." "And why are you in Portugal? and how did you
know that I was here? and by what strange adventure did
you contrive to bring me to this house?" "I will tell you all
that, presently," replied the lady; "but first you must
inform me of all that has happened to you, since the
harmless kiss you gave me, and the rude kicking which
you received for it."

Candide obeyed her with the most profound respect;
and though he was forbidden to speak, though his voice 580
was weak and faltering, and though his back still pained

him, yet he related to her, in the most artless manner,
every thing that had befallen him since the moment of
their separation. Cunegonde lifted up her eyes to heaven;
she shed tears at the death of the good Anabaptist, and
of Pangloss; after which she thus related her adventures
to Candide, who lost not a word, but looked on her, as if
he would devour her with his eyes.

Chapter 8

The History of Cunegonde

"I was in my bed and fast asleep, when it pleased heaven
to send the Bulgarians to our fine castle of Thunder-ten- 590
tronckh; they murdered my father and my brother, and
cut my mother to pieces. A huge Bulgarian, six feet high,
perceiving the horrible sight had deprived me of my
senses, set himself to ravish me. This abuse made me
come to myself; I recovered my senses, I cried, I struggled,
I bit, I scratched, I wanted to tear out the huge Bulgarian's
eyes, not considering that what had happened in my
father's castle, was a common thing in war. The brute gave
me a cut with his knife, the mark of which I still bear
about me." "Ah! I anxiously wish to see it," said the 600
simple Candide. "You shall," answered Cunegonde; "but
let me finish my story." "Do so," replied Candide.

She then resumed the thread of her story, as follows:
"A Bulgarian captain came in, and saw me bleeding; but
the soldier was not at all disconcerted. The Captain flew
into a passion at the little respect the brute showed him,
and killed him upon my body. He then caused me to be
dressed, and carried me as a prisoner of war to his own
quarters. I washed the scanty linen he had, and cooked
his meals. He found me very pretty, I must say it; and I 610
cannot deny but he was well shaped, and that he had a
white, soft skin; but for the rest, he had little sense or
philosophy; one could plainly see that he was not bred
under Dr. Pangloss. At the end of three months, having
lost all his money, and being grown out of conceit with
me, he sold me to a Jew, named *Don Issachar*, who
traded to Holland and Portugal, and had a most violent
passion for women. This Jew laid close siege to my
person, but could not triumph over me; I have resisted
him better than I did the Bulgarian soldier. A woman of 620
honor may be ravished once, but her virtue gathers
strength from such rudeness. The Jew, in order to render
me more tractable, brought me to this country-house that
you see. I always imagined hitherto, that no place on
earth was so fine as the castle of Thunder-ten-tronckh;
but I am now undeceived.

"The grand inquisitor observing me one day ogled me
very strongly, and sent me a note, saying he wanted to
speak with me upon private business. Being conducted to
his palace, I informed him of my birth; upon which he 630
represented to me, how much it was below my family to
belong to an Israelite. A proposal was then made by him
to Don Issachar, to yield me up to my Lord. But Don
Issachar, who is the court-banker, and a man of credit,
would not come into his measures. The inquisitor
threatened him. At last, my Jew, being affrighted,
concluded a bargain, by which the house and myself
should belong to them both in common; the Jew to have
possession Monday, Friday, and Saturday, and the

inquisitor, the other days of the week. This agreement 640
has now continued six months. It has not, however, been
without quarrels; for it has been often disputed whether
Saturday night or Sunday belonged to the old, or to the
new law. For my part, I have hitherto disagreed with them
both; and I believe that this is the reason I am still
beloved by them.

"At length, to avert the scourge of earthquakes and to
intimidate Don Issachar, it pleased his Lordship the
inquisitor to celebrate. He did me the honor to invite me
to it. I got a very fine seat, and the ladies were served 650
with refreshments between the ceremonies. I was seized
with horror at seeing them burn the two Jews, and the
honest Biscayan who married his godmother; but how
great was my surprise, my consternation, my anguish,
when I saw in a sanbenito and mitre, a person that
somewhat resembled Pangloss! I rubbed my eyes, I
looked upon him very attentively, and I saw him hanged. I
fell into a swoon, and scarce had I recovered my senses,
when I saw you stripped stark naked; this was the height
of horror, consternation, grief, and despair. I will frankly 660
own to you, that your skin is still whiter, and of a better
complexion than that of my Bulgarian captain. This sight
increased all the sensations that oppressed and
distracted my soul. I cried out, I was going to say stop,
barbarians; but my voice failed me, and all my cries
would have been to no purpose. When you had been
severely whipped: How is it possible, said I, that the
amiable Candide, and the sage Pangloss, should both be
at Lisbon;—the one to receive a hundred lashes and the
other to be hanged by order of my Lord the Inquisitor, by 670
whom I am so greatly beloved? Pangloss certainly
deceived me most cruelly, when he said that everything
was for the best in this world.

"Agitated, astonished, sometimes beside myself, and
sometimes ready to die with weakness; my head filled
with the massacre of my father, my mother, and my
brother, the insolence of the vile Bulgarian soldier, the
stab he gave me with his hanger, my abject servitude,
and my acting as a cook to the Bulgarian captain; the
rascal Don Issachar, my abominable inquisitor; the 680
execution of Dr. Pangloss, the grand music on the organ
while you were whipped, and especially the kiss I gave
you behind the screen, the last day I saw you. I praised
the Lord for having restored you to me after so many
trials. I charged my old woman to take care of you, and to
bring you hither as soon as she could. She has executed
her commission very well; I have tasted the inexpressible
pleasure of seeing you, hearing you, and speaking to you.
You must have a ravenous appetite, by this time; I am
hungry myself, too; let us, therefore, sit down to supper." 690

On this, they both sat down to table; and after supper,
they seated themselves on the fine couch before
mentioned. They were there, then Signor Don Issachar,
one of the masters of the house, came in. It was his
Sabbath day, and he came to enjoy his right, and to
express his tender love.

*[Candide, Cunegonde and the old woman travel to Cadiz. The
old woman recounts her past misfortunes. They sail to America,
where Candide finds a South American paradise, El Dorado,
filled with kind and reasonable people; however, he loses*

*Cunegonde to a Spanish colonial nobleman. On his way back
to Europe, Candide meets the disillusioned pessimist, Martin,
who opens Candide's eyes to the evil in the world. Following
various adventures in Europe, Candide travels to Turkey and
encounters Pangloss, whom he had thought dead.]*

Chapter 29

How Candide Found Cunegonde and the Old Woman Again

While Candide, the Baron, Pangloss, Martin, and
Cacambo were relating their adventures to each other,
and disputing about the contigent and non-contigent
events of this world, and while they were arguing upon 700
effects and causes, on moral and physical evil, on liberty
and necessity, and on the consolations a person may
experience in the galleys in Turkey, they arrived on the
banks of the Propontis, at the house of the Prince of
Transylvania. The first objects which presented
themselves were Cunegonde and the old woman, hanging
out some table-linen on the line to dry.

The Baron grew pale at this sight. Even Candide, the
affectionate lover, on seeing his fair Cunegonde awfully
tanned, with her eye-lids reversed, her neck withered, 710
her cheeks wrinkled, her arms red and rough, was seized
with horror, jumped near three yards backwards, but
afterwards advanced to her, but with more politeness than
passion. She embraced Candide and her brother, who,
each of them, embraced the old woman, and Candide
ransomed them both.

There was a little farm in the neighborhood, which the
old woman advised Candide to hire, till they could meet
with better accommodations for their whole company.
As Cunegonde did not know that she had grown ugly, 720
nobody having told her of it, she put Candide in mind of
his promise to marry her, in so peremptory a manner, that
he durst not refuse her. But when this thing was intimated
to the Baron, "I will never suffer," said he, "such
meanness on her part, nor such insolence on yours. With
this infamy I will never be reproached. The children of my
sister shall never be enrolled in the chapters[25] of Germany.
No; my sister shall never marry any but a Baron of the
empire." Cunegonde threw herself at her brother's feet,
and bathed them with her tears, but he remained 730
inflexible. "You ungrateful puppy, you," said Candide to
him, "I have delivered you from the galleys; I have paid
your ransom; I have also paid that of your sister, who was
a scullion here, and is very homely; I have the goodness,
however, to make her my wife, and you are fool enough to
oppose it; I have a good mind to kill you again, you make
me so angry." "You may indeed kill me again," said the
Baron; "but you shall never marry my sister, while I
have breath."

Chapter 30

Conclusion

Candide had no great desire, at the bottom of his heart, 740
to marry Cunegonde. But the extreme impertinence of the
Baron determined him to conclude the match, and

---

[25]Noble assemblies.

Cunegonde pressed it so earnestly, that he could not retract. He advised with Pangloss, Martin, and the trusty Cacambo. Pangloss drew up an excellent memoir, in which he proved, that the Baron had no right over his sister, and that she might, according to all the laws of the empire, espouse Candide with her left hand.[26] Martin was for throwing the Baron into the sea: Cacambo was of opinion that it would be best to send him back again to the Levant captain, and make him work at the galleys. This advice was thought good; the old woman approved it, and nothing was said to his sister about it. The scheme was put in execution for a little money, and so they had the pleasure of punishing the pride of a German Baron.

It is natural to imagine that Candide, after so many disasters, married to his sweetheart, living with the philosopher Pangloss, the philosopher Martin, the discreet Cacambo, and the old woman, and especially as he had brought so many diamonds from the country of the ancient Incas, must live the most agreeable life of any man in the whole world. But he had been so cheated by the Jews,[27] that he had nothing left but the small farm; and his wife, growing still more ugly, turned peevish and insupportable. The old woman was very infirm, and worse humored than Cunegonde herself. Cacambo, who worked in the garden, and went to Constantinople to sell its productions, was worn out with labor, and cursed his fate. Pangloss was ready to despair, because he did not shine at the head of some university in Germany. As for Martin, as he was firmly persuaded that all was equally bad throughout, he bore things with patience. Candide, Martin, and Pangloss disputed sometimes about metaphysics and ethics. They often saw passing under the windows of the farmhouse boats full of effendis, bashaws, and cadis,[28] who were going into banishment to Lemnos, Mitylene, and Erzerum. They observed that other cadis, other bashaws, and other effendis succeeded in the posts of those who were exiled, only to be banished themselves in turn. They saw heads nicely impaled, to be presented to the Sublime Porte. These spectacles increased the number of their disputations; and when they were not disputing, their *ennui* was so tiresome that the old woman would often say to them, "I want to know which is the worst;—to be ravished an hundred times by negro pirates, to run the gauntlet among the Bulgarians, to be whipped and hanged, to be dissected, to row in the galleys; in a word, to have suffered all the miseries we have undergone, or to stay here, without doing anything?" "That is a great question," said Candide.

This discourse gave rise to new reflections, and Martin concluded upon the whole, that mankind were born to live either in the distractions of inquietude, or in the lethargy of disgust. Candide did not agree with that opinion, but remained in a state of suspense. Pangloss confessed, that he had always suffered dreadfully; but having once maintained that all things went wonderfully well, he still kept firm to his hypothesis, though it was quite opposed to his real feelings.

What contributed to confirm Martin in his shocking principles, to make Candide stagger more than ever, and

to embarrass Pangloss, was, that one day they saw Paquetta and Girofflee, who were in the greatest distress, at their farm. They had quickly squandered away their three thousand piastres,[29] had parted, were reconciled, quarrelled again, had been confined in prison, had made their escape, and Girofflee had at length turned Turk. Paquetta continued her trade wherever she went, but made nothing by it. "I could easily foresee," said Martin to Candide, "that your presents would soon be squandered away, and would render them more miserable. You and Cacambo have spent millions of piastres, and are not a bit happier than Girofflee and Paquetta." "Ha! ha!" said Pangloss to Paquetta, "has Providence then brought you amongst us again, my poor child? Know, then, that you have cost me the tip of my nose, one eye, and one of my ears, as you see. What a world this is!" This new adventure set them a philosophizing more than ever.

There lived in the neighborhood a very famous dervish, who passed for the greatest philosopher in Turkey. They went to consult him. Pangloss was chosen speaker, and said to him, "Master, we are come to desire you would tell us, why so strange an animal as man was created."

"What's that to you?" said the dervish; "is it any business of yours?" "But, my reverend father," said Candide, "there is a horrible amount of evil in the world." "What does it matter," said the dervish, "whether there be good or evil? When his Sublime Highness sends a vessel to Egypt, does it trouble him, whether the mice on board are at their ease or not?" "What would you have one do then?" said Pangloss. "Hold your tongue," said the dervish. "I promised myself the pleasure," said Pangloss, "of reasoning with you upon effects and causes, the best of possible worlds, the origin of evil, the nature of the soul, and the pre-established harmony."— The dervish, at these words, shut the door in their faces.

During this conference, news was brought that two viziers and a mufti were strangled at Constantinople, and a great many of their friends impaled. This catastrophe made a great noise for several hours. Pangloss, Candide, and Martin, on their way back to the little farm, met a good-looking old man, taking the air at his door, under an arbor of orange trees. Pangloss, who had as much curiosity as philosophy, asked him the name of the mufti who was lately strangled. "I know nothing at all about it," said the good man; "and what's more, I never knew the name of a single mufti, or a single vizier, in my life. I am an entire stranger to the story you mention; and presume that, generally speaking, they who trouble their heads with state affairs, sometimes die shocking deaths, not without deserving it. But I never trouble my head about what is doing at Constantinople; I content myself with sending my fruits thither, the produce of my garden, which I cultivate with my own hands!" Having said these words, he introduced the strangers into his house. His two daughters and two sons served them with several kinds of sherbet, which they made themselves, besides caymac, enriched with the peels of candied citrons, oranges, lemons, bananas, pistachio nuts, and Mocha coffee, unadulterated with the bad coffee of Batavia and the isles. After which, the two daughters of this good Muslim perfumed the beards of Candide, Pangloss, and Martin.

[26]A marriage that denies noble status to the party of the lower rank.
[27]Voltaire's antisemitism seems to have been the result of financial losses he suffered from the bankruptcies of Jewish moneylenders.
[28]Highranking members of the Turkish nobility.

[29]Spanish dollars; pieces of eight.

"You must certainly," said Candide to the Turk, "have a very large and very opulent estate!" "I have only twenty acres," said the Turk; "which I, with my children, cultivate. Labor keeps us free from three of the greatest evils; boredom, vice, and need."

As Candide returned to his farm, he made deep reflections on the discourse of the Turk. Said he to Pangloss and Martin, "The condition of this good old   870 man seems to me preferable to that of the six kings with whom we had the honor to dine." "The grandeurs of royalty," said Pangloss, "are very precarious, in the opinion of all philosophers. For, in short, Eglon, king of the Moabites, was assassinated by Ehud; Absalom was hung by the hair of his head, and pierced through with three darts; King Nadab, the son of Jeroboam, was killed by Baasha; King Elah by Zimri; Ahaziah by Jehu; Athaliah by Jehoiadah; the kings Joachim, Jechonias, and Zedekias, were carried into captivity. You know the   880 fates of Croesus, Astyages, Darius, Dionysius of Syracuse, Pyrrhus, Perseus, Hannibal, Jugurtha, Ariovistus, Caesar, Pompey, Nero, Otho, Vitellius, Domitian, Richard II, Edward II, Henry VI, Richard III, Mary Stuart, Charles I of England, the three Henrys of France, and the Emperor Henry IV.[30] You know—" "I know very well," said Candide, "that we ought to look after our garden." "You are in the right," said Pangloss, "for when man was placed in the garden of Eden, he was placed there, *ut operatur cum*, to cultivate it; which   890 proves that mankind are not created to be idle." "Let us work," said Martin, "without disputing; it is the only way to render life supportable."

All their little society entered into this laudable design, according to their different abilities. Their little piece of ground produced a plentiful crop. Cunegonde was indeed very homely, but she became an excellent pastry cook. Paquetta worked at embroidery, and the old woman took care of the linen. There was no idle person in the company, not excepting even Girofflee; he made a very   900 good carpenter, and became a very honest man.

As to Pangloss, he evidently had a lurking consciousness that his theory required unceasing exertions, and all his ingenuity, to sustain it. Yet he stuck to it to the last; his thinking and talking faculties could hardly be diverted from it for a moment. He seized every occasion to say to Candide, "All the events in this best of possible worlds are admirably connected. If a single link in the great chain were omitted, the harmony of the entire universe would be destroyed. If you had not been   910 expelled from that beautiful castle, with those cruel kicks, for your love to Miss Cunegonde; if you had not been imprisoned by the inquisition; if you had not travelled over a great portion of America on foot; if you had not plunged your sword through the baron; if you had not lost all the sheep you brought from that fine country, Eldorado, together with the riches with which they were laden, you would not be here to-day, eating preserved citrons, and pistachio nuts."

"That's very well said, and may all be true," said   920 Candide; "but let's cultivate our garden."

———————◆———————

[30] All rulers who came to a bad end.

Satire in Chinese Literature

While the satires of Voltaire and Swift drew enthusiastic audiences in the West, satire came into vogue as an important genre elsewhere in the world. Following the Manchu conquest of China in the mid-seventeenth century, Chinese writers indulged in writing bitter fictional tales which satirized a wide variety of contemporary social practices, including Buddhist rituals, commercial banditry, and homosexual unions. One of the cruelest satires of the eighteenth century consisted of a collection of stories attacking the absurdities of China's traditional civil service examination system by which talented individuals were brought into government service. *The Scholars*, as the novel is titled, written around 1750 by Wu Jingzi (1701–1754), reflects Wu's own failure to pass the highly competitive exams, which often brought pseudo-scholars to positions of great wealth and power in China. The satire emphasized the unpopular and anti-Confucian truth that the morally unscrupulous often gain great prizes in the world, while the virtuous do not always flourish.

Chinese satire was also effective in attacking some of the more socially inhibiting practices of traditional Chinese culture, such as female footbinding. Beginning in the eleventh century, upper-class Chinese parents bound the feet of their young daughters (thus breaking the arch and stunting the feet to half the normal size) in order to exempt them from common labor, hence make them more physically attractive as marriage partners to wealthy men. Toward the end of the great age of Chinese prose fiction, the philologist Li Ruzhen (1763–1830) boldly attacked this practice in a satire entitled *Flowers in the Mirror*. An adventure story on the model of *Gulliver's Travels* or *Candide, Flowers* is a series of loosely woven stories which recount the travels of a hero to many strange lands, including the Country of Two-Faced People, the Country of Long-Armed People, and the Country of Women. In the last of these fictional lands, the traditional roles of the sexes are reversed, and the ruling women of the country set upon the hero to prepare him as "royal concubine": They plait his hair, apply lipstick and powder to his face, pierce his ears, and, to his ultimate dismay, they bind his feet in the traditional Chinese manner. Li Ruzhen's blunt social criticism and his bold assertion of equal rights for women fell on deaf ears, for despite the fact that Manchu rulers censured the old Chinese custom, footbinding continued in many parts of China until the early twentieth century.

READING 4.24

From Li Ruzhen's *Flowers in the Mirror*

When Tang Ao heard that they had arrived at the Country of Women, he thought that the country was populated entirely by women, and was afraid to go ashore. But Old Tuo said, "Not at all! There are men as well as women, only they call men women, and women men. The men wear the skirts and take care of the home, while the women wear hats and trousers and manage affairs outside. If it were a country populated solely by women, I doubt that even Brother Lin here would dare to venture ashore, although he knows he always makes a good profit from sales here!"

"If the men dress like women, do they use cosmetics and bind their feet?" asked Tang Ao.

"Of course they do!" cried Lin, and took from his pocket a list of the merchandise he was going to sell, which consisted of huge quantities of rouge, face powder, combs and other women's notions. "Luckily I wasn't born in this country," he said. "Catch me mincing around on bound feet!"

When Tang Ao asked why he had not put down the price of the merchandise, Lin said, "The people here, no matter rich or poor, from the 'King' down to the simplest peasant, are all mad about cosmetics. I'll charge them what I can. I shall have no difficulty selling the whole consignment to rich families in two or three days."

Beaming at the prospect of making a good profit, Lin went on shore with his list.

Tang Ao and Old Tuo decided to go and see the city. The people walking on the streets were small of stature, and rather slim, and although dressed in men's clothes, were beardless and spoke with women's voices, and walked with willowy steps.

"Look at them!" said Old Tuo. "They are perfectly normal-looking women. Isn't it a shame for them to dress like men?"

"Wait a minute," said Tang Ao. "Maybe when they see us, they think, 'Look at them, isn't it a shame that they dress like women'?"

"You're right. 'Whatever one is accustomed to always seems natural,' as the ancients say. But I wonder what the men are like?"

[Invited to sell his wares at the court of the "King," Lin visits the Palace.]

In a little time, Merchant Lin was ushered to a room upstairs where victuals of many kinds awaited him. As he ate, however, he heard a great deal of noise downstairs. Several palace "maids" ran upstairs soon, and calling him "Your Highness", kowtowed to him and congratulated him. Before he knew what was happening, Merchant Lin was being stripped completely bare by the maids and led to a perfumed bath. Against the powerful arms of these maids, he could scarcely struggle. Soon he found himself being anointed, perfumed, powdered and rouged, and dressed in a skirt. His big feet were bound up in strips of cloth and socks, and his hair was combed into an elaborate braid over his head and decorated with pins. These male "maids" thrust bracelets on his arms and rings on his fingers, and put a phoenix headdress on his head. They tied a jade green sash around his waist and put an embroidered cape around his shoulders.

Then they led him to a bed, and asked him to sit down.

Merchant Lin thought that he must be drunk, or dreaming, and began to tremble. He asked the maids what was happening, and was told that he had been chosen by the "King" to be the Imperial Consort, and that a propitious day would be chosen for him to enter the "King's" chambers.

Before he could utter a word, another group of maids, all tall and strong and wearing beards, came in. One was holding a threaded needle. "We are ordered to pierce your ears," he said, as the other four "maids" grabbed Lin by the arms and legs. The white-bearded one seized Lin's right ear, and after rubbing the lobe a little, drove the needle through it.

"Ooh!" Merchant Lin screamed.

The maid seized the other ear, and likewise drove the needle through it. As Lin screamed with pain, powdered lead was smeared on his earlobes and a pair of "eight-precious" earrings was hung from the holes.

Having finished what they came to do, the maids retreated, and a black-bearded fellow came in with a bolt of white silk. Kneeling down before him, the fellow said, "I am ordered to bind Your Highness's feet."

Two other maids seized Lin's feet as the black-bearded one sat down on a low stool, and began to rip the silk into ribbons. Seizing Lin's right foot, he set it upon his knee, and sprinkled white alum powder between the toes and the grooves of the foot. He squeezed the toes tightly together, bent them down so that the whole foot was shaped like an arch, and took a length of white silk and bound it tightly around it twice. One of the others sewed the ribbon together in small stitches. Again the silk went around the foot, and again, it was sewn up.

Merchant Lin felt as though his feet were burning, and wave after wave of pain rose to his heart. When he could stand it no longer, he let out his voice and began to cry. The "maids" had hastily made a pair of soft-soled red shoes, and these they put on both his feet.

"Please, kind brothers, go and tell Her Majesty that I'm a married man," Lin begged. "How can I become her Consort? As for my feet, please liberate them. They have enjoyed the kind of freedom which scholars who are not interested in official careers enjoy! How can you bind them? Please tell your 'King' to let me go. I shall be grateful, and my wife will be very grateful."

But the maids said, "The King said that you are to enter his chambers as soon as your feet are bound. It is no time for talk of this kind."

When it was dark, a table was laid for him with mountains of meat and oceans of wine. But Merchant Lin only nibbled, and told the "maids" they could have the rest.

Still sitting on the bed, and with his feet aching terribly, he decided to lie down in his clothes for a rest.

At once a middle-aged "maid" came up to him and said, "Please, will you wash before you retire?"

No sooner was this said than a succession of maids came in with candles, basins of water and spittoon, dressing table, boxes of ointment, face powder, towels, 120 silk handkerchiefs, and surrounded him. Lin had to submit to the motions of washing in front of them all. But after he had washed his face, a maid wanted to put some cream on it again.

Merchant Lin stoutly refused.

"But night time is the best time to treat the skin," the white-bearded maid said. "This powder has a lot of musk in it. It will make your skin fragrant, although I dare say it is fair enough already. If you use it regularly your skin will not only seem like white jade, but will give off a 130 natural fragrance of its own. And the more fragrant it is, the fairer it will become, and the more lovely to behold, and the more lovable you will be. You'll see how good it is after you have used it regularly."

But Lin refused firmly, and the maids said, "If you are so stubborn, we will have to report this, and let Matron deal with you tomorrow."

Then they left him alone. But Lin's feet hurt so much that he could not sleep a wink. He tore at the ribbons with all his might, and after a great struggle succeeded 140 in tearing them off. He stretched out his ten toes again, and luxuriating in their exquisite freedom, finally fell asleep.

The next morning, however, when the black-bearded maid discovered that he had torn off his foot-bandages, he immediately reported it to the "King", who ordered that Lin should be punished by receiving twenty strokes of the bamboo from the "Matron". Accordingly, a white-bearded "Matron" came in with a stick of bamboo about eight feet long, and when the others had stripped him 150 and held him down, raised the stick and began to strike Lin's bottom and legs.

Before five strokes had been delivered, Lin's tender skin was bleeding, and the Matron did not have the heart to go on. "Look at her skin! Have you ever seen such white and tender and lovable skin? Why, I think indeed her looks are comparable to Pan An and Sung Yu!" the Matron thought to himself. "But what am I doing, comparing her bottom and not her face to them? Is that a compliment?" 160

The foot-binding maid came and asked Lin if he would behave from now on.

"Yes, I'll behave," Lin replied, and they stopped beating him. They wiped the blood from his wounds, and special ointment was sent by the "King" and ginseng soup was given him to drink.

Merchant Lin drank the soup, and fell on the bed for a rest. But the "King" had given orders that his feet must be bound again, and that he should be taught to walk on them. So with one maid supporting him on each 170 side, Merchant Lin was marched up and down the room all day on his bound feet. When he lay down to sleep that night, he could not close his eyes for the excruciating pain.

But from now on, he was never left alone again. Maids took turns to sit with him. Merchant Lin knew that he was no longer in command of his destiny. . . .

———————◆———————

The Visual Satires of William Hogarth

Like Li Ruzhen in China and his European forebears Goldsmith, Swift, and Voltaire, the English artist William Hogarth (1697–1764) was a master of satire. Hogarth's paintings and prints are a record of the ills of eighteenth-century British society. He illustrated the novels of Defoe and Swift, including *Gulliver's Travels*, and executed a series of paintings based on John Gay's *Beggar's Opera*—a mock-heroic comedy that equated low-class crime with high-class corruption. Popular novels and plays provided inspiration for what Hogarth called his "modern moral subjects"; while the theater itself prompted many of the devices he used for pictorial representation: boxlike staging, lighting from below, and a wealth of "props." "I have endeavored," he wrote, "to treat my subjects as a dramatic writer: my picture is my stage, and men and women my actors."

Hogarth made engraved versions of his paintings and sold them, just as Diderot sold the volumes of the *Encyclopédie*, by subscription. So popular were these prints that they were pirated and sold without his authorization (a practice that continued even after Parliament passed the first copyright law in 1735). Especially successful were two series of prints based on his paintings. The first ("The Harlot's Progress") illustrate the misfortunes of a young woman who becomes a London prostitute; the second ("The Rake's Progress") reports the comic misadventures of an antihero and ne'er-do-well named Tom Rakewell. Following these, Hogarth published a series of six engravings entitled "Marriage à la Mode" (1742–1764), which depicts the tragic consequences of a marriage of convenience between the son of a poverty-stricken nobleman and the daughter of a wealthy and ambitious merchant. The first print in the series, *The Marriage Transaction*, shows the two families transacting the terms of the matrimonial union (Figure **25.4**). The scene unfolds as if upon a stage: The corpulent Lord Squanderfield, victim of the gout (an ailment traditionally linked with rich food and drink), sits pompously in his ruffled velvet waistcoat, pointing to his family tree, which springs from the loins of William the Conqueror. Across the table, the wealthy merchant and father of the bride carefully peruses the financial terms of the marriage settlement. On a settee in the corner of the room, the pawns of this socially expedient match turn away from each other in attitudes of mutual dislike. The earl's son, young Squanderfield, sporting a beauty patch, opens his snuffbox and vainly gazes at himself in a mirror, while his bride-to-be idly dangles her betrothal ring on a kerchief. She leans

Figure 25.4 William Hogarth, *The Marriage Transaction*, from the "Marriage à la Mode" series, 1742–1746. Engraving. Reproduced by courtesy of the Trustees of the British Museum, London.

forward to hear the honeyed words of her future seducer, a lawyer named Lord Silvertongue. A combination of **caricature** (exaggeration of peculiarities or defects), comic irony, and symbolic detail, Hogarth's "stylish marriage" is drawn with a stylus every bit as sharp as Voltaire's pen.

Like Voltaire's Paris, Hogarth's London was not yet an industrial city, but it was plagued by some of the worst urban conditions of the day. It lacked sewers, streetlights, and adequate law enforcement. A city of vast contrasts between rich and poor, it was crowded with thieves, drunks, and prostitutes, all of whom threatened the jealously guarded privileges of the rich. Hogarth represented mid-eighteenth-century London at its worst in the famous engraving *Gin Lane* (Figure 25.5). This devastating attack on the combined evils of urban poverty and alcoholism portrays poor, ragged, and drunk men and women in various stages of depravity. Some pawn their possessions to support their expensive addictions (lower left); others commit suicide (upper right corner); and one pours gin down the throat of a babe-in-arms, following the common practice of using liquor and other drugs to quiet noisy infants (far right). In the center of the print is the figure of a besotted mother—her leg covered with syphilitic sores—who carelessly allows her child to fall over the edge of the stair rail. Hogarth's visual satirization of gin addiction was a heroic attack on the social conditions of his time and on drug abuse in general. But even Parliament's passage of the Gin Law in 1751, which more than doubled the gin tax, did little to reduce the widespread use of gin in eighteenth-century England. While Hogarth's prints failed to reduce the ills and inequities of his society, they remain an enduring condemnation of human hypocrisy, cruelty, vanity, and greed.

Figure 25.5 William Hogarth, *Gin Lane*, 1751. Engraving.
Reproduced by courtesy of the Trustees of the British Museum, London.

Rousseau's Revolt Against Reason

Jean Jacques Rousseau, introduced in chapter 24 as a contributor to Diderot's *Encyclopédie*, was one of the Enlightenment's most outspoken critics. A playwright, composer, and educator, Rousseau took issue with some of the basic precepts of Enlightenment thought, including the idea that the progress of the arts and sciences might improve human conduct. Human beings may be good by nature, argued Rousseau, but they are ultimately corrupted by society and its institutions. "God makes all things good," wrote Rousseau; "man meddles with them and they become evil." Rousseau condemned the artificiality of civilized life and, although he did not advocate that humankind should return to a "state of nature," he exalted the "noble savage" as the model of the uncorrupted individual. Rousseau's philosophy of the heart elevated the role of instinct over reason and encouraged a new appreciation of nature and the natural—principles that underlay the romantic movement of the early nineteenth century (see chapters 27 to 29). In the following excerpt from the *Discourse on the Origin of Inequality among Men* (1755), Rousseau gives an eloquent account of how, in his view, human beings came to lose their freedom and innocence.

READING 4.25

From Rousseau's *Discourse on the Origin of Inequality among Men*

The first man who, having enclosed a piece of land, thought of saying "This is mine" and found people simple enough to believe him, was the true founder of civil society. How many crimes, wars, murders; how much misery and horror the human race would have been spared if someone had pulled up the stakes and filled in the ditch and cried out to his fellow men: "Beware of listening to this impostor. You are lost if you forget that the fruits of the earth belong to everyone and that the earth itself belongs to no one!" But it is highly probable that by this time things had reached a point beyond which they could not go on as they were; for the idea of property, depending on many prior ideas which could only have arisen in successive stages, was not formed all at once in the human mind. It was necessary for men to make much progress, to acquire much industry and knowledge, to transmit and increase it from age to age, before arriving at this final stage of the state of nature. Let us therefore look farther back, and try to review from a single perspective the slow succession of events and discoveries in their most natural order. 20

Man's first feeling was that of his existence, his first concern was that of his preservation. The products of the earth furnished all the necessary aids; instinct prompted him to make use of them. While hunger and other appetites made him experience in turn different modes of existence, there was one appetite which urged him to perpetuate his own species; and this blind impulse, devoid of any sentiment of the heart, produced only a purely animal act. The need satisfied, the two sexes recognized each other no longer, and even the child meant nothing to the mother, as soon as he could do without her. 30

Such was the condition of nascent[1] man; such was the life of an animal limited at first to mere sensation; and scarcely profiting from the gifts bestowed on him by nature, let alone was he dreaming of wresting anything from her. But difficulties soon presented themselves and man had to learn to overcome them. The height of trees, which prevented him from reaching their fruits; the competition of animals seeking to nourish themselves on the same fruits; the ferocity of animals who threatened his life—all this obliged man to apply himself to bodily exercises; he had to make himself agile, fleet of foot, and vigorous in combat. Natural weapons—branches of trees and stones—were soon found to be at hand. He learned to overcome the obstacles of nature, to fight when necessary against other animals, to struggle for his subsistence even against other men, or to indemnify[2] himself for what he was forced to yield to the stronger. 40

[Rousseau then describes how people devised a technology for hunting and fishing, invented fire, and developed superiority over other creatures.]

Instructed by experience that love of one's own wellbeing is the sole motive of human action, he found 50 himself in a position to distinguish the rare occasions when common interest justified his relying on the aid of his fellows, and those even rarer occasions when competition should make him distrust them. In the first case, he united with them in a herd, or at most in a sort of free association that committed no one and which lasted only as long as the passing need which had brought it into being. In the second case, each sought to grasp his own advantage, either by sheer force, if he believed he had the strength, or by cunning and subtlety 60 if he felt himself to be the weaker. . . .

. . . the habit of living together generated the sweetest sentiments known to man, conjugal love and paternal love. Each family became a little society, all the better united because mutual affection and liberty were its only bonds; at this stage also the first differences were established in the ways of life of the two sexes which had hitherto been identical. Women became more sedentary and accustomed themselves to looking after the hut and the children while men went out to seek their common 70 subsistence. The two sexes began, in living a rather softer life, to lose something of their ferocity and their strength; but if each individual became separately less able to fight wild beasts, all, on the other hand, found it easier to group together to resist them jointly. . . .

To the extent that ideas and feelings succeeded one another, and the heart and mind were exercised, the human race became more sociable, relationships became more extensive and bonds tightened. People grew used to gathering together in front of their huts or around a large 80 tree; singing and dancing, true progeny[3] of love and leisure, became the amusement, or rather the occupation, of idle men and women thus assembled. Each began to look at the others and to want to be looked at himself; and public esteem came to be prized. He who sang or danced the best; he who was the most handsome, the strongest, the most adroit[4] or the most eloquent became the most highly regarded, and this was the first step toward inequality and at the same time toward vice. From those first preferences there arose, on the one side, 90 vanity and scorn, on the other, shame and envy, and the fermentation produced by these new leavens[5] finally produced compounds fatal to happiness and innocence.

As soon as men learned to value one another and the idea of consideration was formed in their minds, everyone claimed a right to it, and it was no longer possible for anyone to be refused consideration without affront. This gave rise to the first duties of civility, even among savages: and henceforth every intentional wrong became an outrage, because together with the hurt which might 100 result from the injury, the offended party saw an insult to his person which was often more unbearable than the hurt itself. Thus, as everyone punished the contempt shown him by another in a manner proportionate to the esteem he accorded himself, revenge became terrible, and men grew bloodthirsty and cruel. This is precisely the stage reached by most of the savage peoples known to us; and it is for lack of having sufficiently distinguished between different ideas and seen how far those peoples

---

[1]Early, developing.
[2]Compensate.

[3]Offspring.
[4]Skillful.
[5]Significant changes.

already are from the first state of nature that so many authors have hastened to conclude that man is naturally cruel and needs civil institutions to make him peaceable, whereas in truth nothing is more peaceable than man in his primitive state. Placed by nature at an equal distance from the stupidity of brutes[6] and the fatal enlightenment of civilized man, limited equally by reason and instinct to defending himself against evils which threaten him, he is restrained by natural pity from doing harm to anyone, even after receiving harm himself: for according to the wise Locke: "Where there is no property, there is no injury." 120

But it must be noted that society's having come into existence and relations among individuals having been already established meant that men were required to have qualities different from those they possessed from their primitive constitution. . . .

As long as men were content with their rustic huts, as long as they confined themselves to sewing their garments of skin with thorns or fishbones, and adorning themselves with feathers or shells, to painting their 130 bodies with various colors, to improving or decorating their bows and arrows; and to using sharp stones to make a few fishing canoes or crude musical instruments; in a word, so long as they applied themselves only to work that one person could accomplish alone and to arts that did not require the collaboration of several hands, they lived as free, healthy, good and happy men. . . .

. . . but from the instant one man needed the help of another, and it was found to be useful for one man to have provisions enough for two, equality disappeared, 140 property was introduced, work became necessary, and vast forests were transformed into pleasant fields which had to be watered with the sweat of men, and where slavery and misery were soon seen to germinate and flourish with the crops.

◆

Rousseau was haunted by contradictions within the social order and within his own mind (he suffered acute attacks of paranoia during the last fifteen years of his life). The opening words of his treatise, *The Social Contract* (1762), "Man is born free, and everywhere he is in chains," reflect his apprehension concerning the inhibiting role of institutional authority. In order to safeguard individual liberty, said Rousseau, people should form a contract among themselves. Unlike Hobbes, whose social contract involved transferring absolute authority from the citizens to a sovereign ruler, or Locke, whose social contract gave limited power to the ruler, Rousseau defined the state as nothing more than "the general will" of its citizens. Sovereignty, for Rousseau, was nothing but the exercise of the general will. "The general will alone," he explained, "can direct the State according to the object for which it was

instituted, that is, the common good." Rousseau insisted, moreover, that whoever refused to obey the general will should be constrained to do so by the whole society; that is, all humans should "be forced to be free." "As nature gives each man absolute power over all his members," wrote Rousseau, "the social compact gives the body politic absolute power over all its members also." Such views might have contributed to newly developed theories of democracy, but they were equally effective in justifying totalitarian constraints leveled in the name of the people.

Rousseau's wish to preserve the natural also led him to propose revolutionary changes in education. If society is indeed hopelessly corrupt, then let children grow up in accord with nature, argued Rousseau. In *Emile* (1762), his treatise on education, Rousseau advanced the hypothesis—unheard of in his time—that the education of a child begins at birth. He divided childhood development into five stages over a twenty-five-year span and outlined the type of rearing desirable for each stage. "Hands-on" experience was essential to education, according to Rousseau, especially in the period just prior to the development of reason and intellect, which he placed between the ages of twelve and fifteen. "Nature provides for the child's growth in her own fashion, and this should never be thwarted. Do not make him sit still when he wants to run about, nor run when he wants to be quiet." Rousseau also made a clear distinction between the education of men and that of women. Arguing that a woman's place was in the home and beside the cradle, he proposed for her a domestic education that cultivated modesty, obedience, and other virtues agreeable to her mate. Thus Rousseau's views on women's education were not radically different from those advanced by Castiglione some two hundred years earlier in *The Book of the Courtier* (see chapter 16). Nevertheless, *Emile* became a landmark in educational theory, and Rousseau's new approach to education—particularly his emphasis on the cultivation of natural inquisitiveness over and above rote learning—influenced modern teaching methods such as those developed by the Italian educator Maria Montessori (1870–1952). Ironically, however, Rousseau saw fit to put all five of his own children in a foundling hospital rather than raise them himself.

Kant's Mind/World Revolution

The German philosopher Immanuel Kant (1724–1804) was "awakened from his slumber," as he put it, when he read the treatises of the Scottish philosopher David Hume (1711–1776). Hume had maintained that genuine knowledge was limited to two sorts: statements of logical relationships ("Bachelors are unmarried") and statements of sense perception ("This chalk is yellow").

---

[6]Beasts.

Hume concluded that all other statements described belief, not true knowledge. Provoked by the arguments of "the gentle skeptic," as Hume was called, Kant rejected Hume's conclusions. Offering his own analysis of the relationship between the perceiver and the perceived, Kant explained the mind *not* as a passive recipient of information (Locke's "blank slate") but, rather, as a participant in the knowledge process. As Kant put it, "though our knowledge begins *with* experience, it does not follow that [all knowledge] arises *out of* experience." Concepts such as time, space, and causality are not (as Hume had it) mere habits of the mind, but the innate conditions of experience itself. The forms of intuition (space and time) and the categories of thought (quantity, quality, relationship, and modality) exist in the mind from birth; they shape the data of the senses into a consistent picture of the world.

Kant's argument altered the relationship between mind and world as radically as Copernicus had changed the relationship between earth and sun. Shifting the focus of philosophic debate from the nature of objective reality to the question of cognition itself—the process by which the mind comprehends experience—Kant described the mind as not merely reflecting experience, but as organizing experience into a coherent pattern. Knowledge, argued Kant, is a synthetic product of the logical self. In 1781, in the *Critique of Pure Reason*, Kant unfolded his revolutionary view of mind and world. The preeminence Kant gave to the role of the mind in constructing our idea of the world laid the basis for transcendental **idealism**, the doctrine that holds that reality consists of the mind and its forms of perception and understanding.

Human reason also plays an important role in Kant's system of ethics. In contrast with Hume, who had argued that values were a matter of sentiment or feeling, but not reason, Kant made reason the keystone for human conduct. Recognizing that notions of good and evil varied widely among different groups of people, Kant sought an absolute ethical system that transcended individual circumstances. In the *Critique of Practical Reason* (1788), he proposed a general moral law called the "categorical imperative": namely, that we should act as if we could will that the maxim of our actions should become the law for all humankind. The

basis of this moral law is the recognition of our duty to act rationally, that is, to act in ways justified by reasons so universal that they are good for all people at all times. It is not enough that our acts have good effects; it is necessary that we *will* the good. Kant's notion of "good will" is not, however, identical with Christian charity. Nor is it the same as Jesus' commandment to "Do to others as you would wish them do to you," since for Kant ethical conduct is based not on love for humankind (which, after all, one may lack), but on respect for the imperative to act rationally, a condition essential to human dignity.

The Revolutions of the Late Eighteenth Century

The American and French Revolutions drew inspiration from the Enlightenment faith in the reforming power of reason. Both, however, demonstrated the limits of reason in achieving social change. As early as 1776, America's thirteen colonies had rebelled against the longstanding political control of the British government. In the Declaration of Independence (see chapter 24), Jefferson restated Locke's assertion that government must protect its citizens' rights to life, liberty, and property. The British government, however, in making unreasonable demands for revenues, threatened colonial liberty, igniting the passions of fervent populists who sought democratic reform. In 1783, following some seven years of armed conflict, several thousand battle deaths, and a war expense estimated at over $100 million, the thirteen North American colonies achieved their independence. And, in 1789, they began to function under the Constitution of the United States of America. The British political theorist Thomas Paine (1737–1809) observed that the Revolution had done more to enlighten the world and diffuse a spirit of freedom among humankind than any event that had preceded it.

The American Revolution did not go unnoticed in France. French intellectuals followed its every turn; the French government secretly aided the American cause and eventually joined in the war against Great Britain. However, the revolution that began on French soil in 1789 involved circumstances that were quite different from those in America. In France, the lower classes sought to overturn longstanding social and political institutions and end upper-class privilege. The French Revolution was, in the main, the product of two major sets of problems: class inequality and a serious financial crisis, brought about by some five hundred years of costly wars and royal extravagances (see chapter 23). With his nation on the verge of bankruptcy, King Louis XVI sought new measures for raising revenue.

1752	Benjamin Franklin proves that lightning is a form of electricity
1769	James Watt patents the steam engine
1783	the first parachute is used in France
1783	the French make the first manned hot-air balloon flight
1795	the Springfield flintlock musket is developed in the United States

Figure 25.6 Briffault de la Charprais and Mme. Esclapart, *The Siege of the Bastille, July 14, 1789*. 1791–1796. Engraving, 18¼ × 12 in. Pierpont Morgan Library, New York. Bequest of Gordon N. Ray, GNR 78 (plate #16).

Throughout French history, taxes had fallen exclusively on the shoulders of the lower and middle classes, the so-called Third Estate. Almost four-fifths of the average peasant's income went to pay taxes, which supported the privileged upper classes. In a population of some twenty-five million people, the First Estate (the clergy) and the Second Estate (the nobility)—a total of only two hundred thousand citizens—controlled nearly half the land in France; yet they were exempt from paying taxes. Peasant grievances were not confined to matters of taxation: Population growth and rising prices led to severe shortages of bread, the principal food of the lower classes. When, in 1789, in an effort to obtain public support for new taxes, King Louis XVI called a meeting of the Estates General—its first meeting in 175 years—the Third Estate withdrew and, declaring itself representative of the general will of the people, formed a separate body claiming the right to approve or veto all taxation. This daring act set the Revolution in motion. No sooner had the Third Estate declared itself a national assembly than great masses of peasants and laborers began to riot throughout France.

The crowds that stormed the Bastille destroyed the visible symbol of the old French regime (Figure 25.6). Less than one month later, on August 4, the National Assembly—as the new body established by the Third Estate called itself—issued decrees that abolished the last remnants of medieval feudalism, including manorial courts, feudal duties, and church tithes. It also made provisions for a limited monarchy and an elected legislative assembly. The decrees of the National Assembly became part of the Constitution of 1791. It was prefaced by the 1789 Declaration of the Rights of Man and Citizen, which was modeled on the American Declaration of Independence. A Declaration of the Rights of Woman and Citizen, drafted in 1791 by a butcher's daughter, Olympe de Gouges, demanded equal rights for women, the sex de Gouges described as "superior in beauty and courage." (Indeed, in October of 1789 six thousand courageous women had marched on Versailles to protest the lack of bread in Paris.) For the first time in history women constituted a collective revolutionary force, making demands for equal property rights, government employment for women, and equal educational opportunities—demands guaranteed by the Constitution of 1793 but lost less than two years later by the terms of a new Constitution.

Enlightenment idealism, summed up in Rousseau's slogan "Liberty, Equality, Fraternity," had inflamed popular passions and inspired armed revolt. Nevertheless, from the time of the storming of the Bastille through the rural revolts and mass protests that followed, angry, unreasoning mobs controlled the course of the Revolution. Divisions among the revolutionaries themselves led to a more radical phase of the Revolution, called the Reign of Terror. This phase ensured the failure of the government established in 1793 and sent Louis XVI and his queen to the guillotine. Between 1793 and 1794, over forty thousand people (including Olympe de Gouges) met their death at the guillotine. In 1794, a National Convention devised a system of government run by two legislative chambers and a five-man executive body of directors, one of whom, Napoleon Bonaparte, would turn France into a military dictatorship some five years later. If, indeed, the French Revolution defended the Enlightenment bastions of liberty and equality, its foundations of reason and rationality ultimately crumbled under the forces of extremism and violence. The radicals of this and many other world-historical revolutions to follow rewrote the words of the *philosophes* in blood.

SUMMARY

The Enlightenment faith in the promise of reason, the cornerstone of eighteenth-century optimism, was tempered by an equally enlightened examination of the limits of reason. Olaudah Equiano's autobiography protested the inhumane trade in African slaves that persisted throughout the eighteenth century. In England, the keenest critic of Enlightenment idealism was Jonathan Swift, while in France, the acerbic writings of Voltaire described human folly as a universal condition. These three masters of satire found their Asian counterpart in Li Ruzhen, whose witty prose attacked long-standing Chinese traditions. Voltaire's *Candide* remains the classic statement of comic skepticism in Western literature. Voltaire's contemporary, William Hogarth, brought the bitter invective of the satirist to the visual arts. His engravings exposed the social ills and class discrepancies of British society, even as they mocked universal human pretensions.

Questioning the value of reason for the advancement of the human condition, Jean Jacques Rousseau argued that society itself corrupted the individual. He rejected the artificiality of the wig-and-silk-stocking culture in which he lived and championed "man in his primitive state." Rousseau's treatises on social history, government, and education explored ways in which

individuals might retain their natural goodness and remain free and self-determining. In Germany, the philosopher Immanuel Kant examined the limits of the mind in the process of knowing. He argued that human beings have knowledge of the world through certain innate capabilities of mind. Kant appealed to "good will" as the basis for moral action.

While Enlightenment ideals fueled armed revolt in both America and France, the revolutions themselves blazed with antirational sentiment. In France especially, the men and women who fired the cannons of revolt abandoned reason as inadequate to the task of effecting social and political reform. Operating according to the dictates of their passions and their will, they gave dramatic evidence of the limits of reason to create a heaven on earth. The shift away from reason and the rational was to have major repercussions in the centuries to follow.

GLOSSARY

caricature exaggeration of peculiarities or defects to produce comic or burlesque effects

idealism/ideas in philosophy, the theory that holds that reality consists of the mind and its ideas; transcendental (or critical) idealism is Kant's name for the doctrine that knowledge is a synthetic product of the logical self

SUGGESTIONS FOR READING

Adams, F. D. and Barry Sanders, eds. *Three Black Writers in Eighteenth-Century England*. Belmont, Calif.: Wadsworth, 1971.

Babbitt, Irving. *Rousseau and Romanticism*. New York: Meridian, 1957.

Bernier, Olivier. *Words of Fire, Deeds of Blood: The Mob, the Monarchy, and the French Revolution*. Boston: Little, Brown, 1989.

Durant, Will and Ariel. *The Age of Voltaire*. Vol. IX of *The Story of Civilization*. New York: Simon and Schuster, 1965.

Gershoy, Leo. *From Despotism to Revolution, 1763–1789*. Westport, Conn.: Greenwood Press, 1983.

Jarrett, Derek. *England in the Age of Hogarth*. London: Hart-Davis MacGibbon, 1974.

Leith, James A. *The Idea of Art as Propaganda in France 1750–1799: A Study in the History of Ideas*. Toronto: University of Toronto Press, 1965.

Lindsay, Jack. *Hogarth: His Art and His World*. New York: Taplinger, 1979.

Richter, Peyton, and Ilona Ricardo. *Voltaire*. Boston: Twayne, 1980.

26
Eighteenth-Century Art, Music, and Society

The dynamics of class and culture had a shaping influence on the arts of eighteenth-century Europe. European aristocrats of the period between 1715 and 1750 found pleasure in an elegant and refined style known as the *rococo*. Toward the end of the century, middle-class bonds to Enlightenment idealism and revolutionary reform, along with a new archeological appreciation of ancient Greece and Rome, ushered in the *neoclassical* style. In music, too, the era witnessed notable turns: from the ponderous baroque to the more delicate and playful rococo, and then, in the 1780s, to the formal and measured sounds of the *classical* symphony and the string quartet. An increased demand for secular entertainment called forth new genres in instrumental music and a wide range of subject matter in the visual arts. Despite their stylistic diversity, the arts shared a spirit of buoyant optimism and vitality that ensured their endurance beyond the Age of the Enlightenment.

The Rococo Style

The rococo style was born in France among members of the leisured nobility who had outlived Louis XIV. At Versailles and in the elegant urban townhouses (or *hôtels*, as they were called) of Paris, where the wealthy gathered to enjoy the pleasures of dancing, dining, and conversing, the rococo provided an atmosphere of elegant refinement (Figure **26.1**). The word "rococo" derives from a combination of *rocailles* and *coquilles* (French for "pebbles" and "seashells")—objects that were commonly used to ornament aristocratic gardens

Figure 26.1 *The Grand Ball.* © The Bettmann Archive, New York.

Figure 26.2 Germain Boffrand, Salon de la Princesse, Hôtel de Soubise, Paris, ca. 1740. Oval, 33 ft. × 26 ft.
Scala/Art Resource, New York.

Figure 26.3 Martin Carlin (master 1766–1785), Lady's desk, ca. 1775. Decorated with Sèvres porcelain plaques; tulipwood, walnut, and hardwood veneered on oak, height 31⅞ in., width 25⅞ in., diameter 16 in. The Metropolitan Museum of Art, New York. Gift of Samuel H. Kress Foundation, 1958 (58.75.49).

and grottoes. Rococo interiors display the organic vitality of seashells, plants, and flowers. And while rococo artists preserved the ornate and luxuriant features of the baroque style, they favored elements of play and intimacy that were best realized in works of a small scale, such as porcelain figurines, furniture, and paintings suitable for domestic quarters.

The Salon de la Princesse in the Hôtel de Soubise in Paris typifies the rococo style (Figure 26.2): Its interior is airy and fragile by comparison with a Louis XIV *salon* (see Figure 23.9). Brilliant white walls accented with pastel tones of rose, pale blue, and lime replace the ruby reds and royal blues of the baroque *salon*. The geometric regularity of the baroque interior has given way to an organic medley of curves and countercurves, echoed in elegant mirrors and chandeliers. The walls, ornamented with gilded tendrils, playful cupids, and floral garlands, melt into sensuously painted ceiling vaults crowned with graceful moldings.

Rococo furnishings are generally more delicate than baroque furnishings, and chairs are often fully upholstered—an innovation of the eighteenth century. Bureaus and tables may be fitted with panels of porcelain (Figure 26.3)—a Chinese technique that Marie Antoinette, the consort of Louis XVI, introduced at

Versailles. Aristocratic women, especially such notable females as Marie Antoinette in France, Catherine the Great in Russia, and Maria Theresa in Austria, eagerly embraced the rococo style. Indeed, the rococo, whose widespread commercialization made it popular throughout most of Europe, may be said to reflect the distinctive influence of eighteenth-century women of taste.

Beyond the *salon*, the garden was the favorite setting for the leisured elite. Unlike the geometrically ordered garden parks at Versailles, rococo gardens imitated the calculated naturalism of Chinese gardens. They featured undulating paths that gave false impressions of scale and distance. They also often included artificial lakes, small colonnaded temples, ornamental pagodas, and other architectural "follies." Both outdoors and in, the fascination with Chinese objects and motifs, which began as a fashion in Europe around 1720, promoted the cult of *chinoiserie* (see chapter 23).

Although the rococo style originated in France, it reached spectacular heights in the courts of secular princes at Würzburg, Munich, Salzburg, and Vienna. In Austria and in the German states, it became the favorite style for the ornamentation of rural pilgrimage churches. In the Benedictine Church of Ottobeuren in Bavaria, designed by the eighteenth-century German architect Johann Michael Fischer, walls seem to disappear beneath a riot of stucco "frosting" as rich and sumptuous as any wedding cake. The more restrained elegance of French rococo interiors here gives way to a dazzling array of organic forms that sprout from the moldings and cornices like unruly flora (Figure 26.4). Shimmering light floods into the white-walled interior

Figure 26.4 Cherubs, Benedictine abbey, Ottobeuren, Bavaria, 1736–1766. Stucco. Foto Marburg/Art Resource, New York.

Figure 26.5 Johan Michael Fischer, interior, Benedictine abbey, Ottobeuren, Bavaria, 1736–1766. Painted and gilded wood and stucco. Vanni/Art Resource, New York.

through oval windows, and pastel-colored frescoes turn ceilings and walls into heavenly ante-chambers. Illusionism reigns: Wooden columns and stucco cornices are painted to look like marble; angels and cherubs, tendrils and leaves, curtains and clouds—all made of wood and stucco that have been painted and gilded—come to life as props in a theater of miracles (Figure **26.5**). At Ottobeuren, the somber majesty of the Roman baroque church has given way to a sublime vision of paradise that is as well a feast for the senses.

Rococo Painting in France

The pursuit of pleasure—a major eighteenth-century theme—dominates the paintings of the four great rococo masters: Antoine Watteau (1684–1721), François Boucher (1703–1770), Marie-Louise-Elisabeth Vigée-Lebrun (1775–1842), and Jean-Honoré Fragonard (1732–1806). The first of these artists, the Flemish-born Watteau, began his career by painting theatrical scenes. In 1717, he submitted to the French Academy *Departure from the Island of Cythera* (Figure **26.6**), a painting that pays tribute to the fleeting nature of romantic love. The painting shows a group of fashionable men and women preparing to board a golden boat

by which they will depart the island of Cythera. According to legend, the island of Cythera was the birthplace of Venus, and on this outing—a *fête galante* (literally, "elegant entertainment")—aristocrats pay homage to the Goddess of Love, whose rose-bedecked shrine appears at the far right. Amidst fluttering cupids, the pilgrims of love linger in pairs as they wistfully take leave of their florid hideaway. Watteau repeats the serpentine line formed by the figures in the delicate arabesques of the trees and rolling hills. And he bathes the entire panorama in a misty, golden light. Not since the sixteenth-century artists Giorgione and Titian had any painter indulged so deeply in the pleasures of nature or the voluptuous world of the senses.

Watteau's fragile forms and delicate colors, painted with feathery brushstrokes reminiscent of Rubens, evoke a mood of reverie and nostalgia. His doll-like men and women provide sharp contrast with Rubens' physically powerful figures (see Figure 23.16) or, for that matter, with Poussin's idealized heroes (see Figure 23.13). Watteau's art conveys no noble message; rather, it explores the world of familiar but transitory pleasures.

If Watteau's world was wistful and poetic, that of his contemporary François Boucher was sensual and indulgent. Boucher, a specialist in designing

Figure 26.6 Antoine Watteau, *Departure from the Island of Cythera*, 1717. Oil on canvas, 4 ft. 3 in. × 6 ft. 4 in. Louvre, Paris. Photo: © R.M.N., Paris.

mythological scenes, became head of the Gobelins tapestry factory in 1755 and director of the Royal Academy ten years later. He was First Painter to King Louis XV and a good friend of the king's favorite mistress, Jeanne Antoinette Poisson, the Marquise de Pompadour (1721–1764). A woman of remarkable beauty and intelligence—she owned two telescopes, a microscope, and a lathe that she installed in her apartments in order to carve cameos—Madame de Pompadour influenced state policy and dominated fashion and the arts at Versailles for almost twenty years. In the idyllic *Venus Consoling Love*, Boucher flattered his patron by portraying her as Goddess of Love (Figure **26.7**). Surrounded by attentive doves and cupids, the nubile Venus reclines on a bed of sumptuous rose and satin draperies laid amidst a bower of leafy trees and windswept grasses. Boucher delighted in sensuous contrasts of flesh, fabric, feathers, and flowers. And his girlish women, with their unnaturally tiny feet, rosebud-pink nipples, and wistful glances, were coy symbols of erotic pleasure.

Boucher also designed sets and costumes for the Royal Opera and motifs for tapestries and porcelains. From the Sèvres porcelain factory, located near Paris and founded by Madame de Pompadour, came magnificent porcelains ornamented with gilded wreaths, arabesque cartouches, and playful cupids floating on fleecy clouds (Figure **26.8**). Outside of France, in Germany and Austria, porcelain figurines of shepherds and shepherdesses advertised the eighteenth-century enthusiasm for the pastoral life.

Fashion and fashionableness—clear expressions of self-conscious materialism—were major themes of rococo art. Marie-Louise Elisabeth Vigée-Lebrun, the most famous of a number of eighteenth-century female artists, produced refined portrait paintings for an almost exclusively female clientele. Vigée-Lebrun's travels in the Low Countries allowed her to study the works of Rubens and van Dyck, whose painterly style she admired. Her glamorous likeness of Marie Antoinette is a tribute to the European fashion industry (Figure

Figure 26.8 Sèvres porcelain potpourri vase, mid-eighteenth century. Gondola-shaped body, scrolled handles, 4-lobed cover, height 14⅛ in., length 14½ in., width 8 in. This vase, purchased by Madame de Pompadour, is one of the finest products of the Sèvres porcelain factory which she sponsored and patronized. The Metropolitan Museum of Art, New York. Gift of Samuel H. Kress Foundation, 1958 (58.75.88 a, b, c).

26.9). Plumed headdresses and low-cut gowns bedecked with lace, ribbons, and tassels turned the aristocratic female into a conspicuous ornament; the size of her billowing skirt required that she turn sideways to pass through open doors. In response to the upper-class infatuation with pastoral and idyllic themes, Vigée-Lebrun also painted portraits of more modestly dressed women in muslin skirts and straw hats. Unlike Boucher,

Vigée-Lebrun did not cast her subjects as goddesses, but she imparted to them a chic sweetness and artless simplicity. These talents earned her the equivalent of over $200,000 a year and allowed her an independence uncommon among eighteenth-century women.

Jean-Honoré Fragonard, the last of the great rococo artists, was the undisputed master of translating the art of seduction into paint. In the works he completed

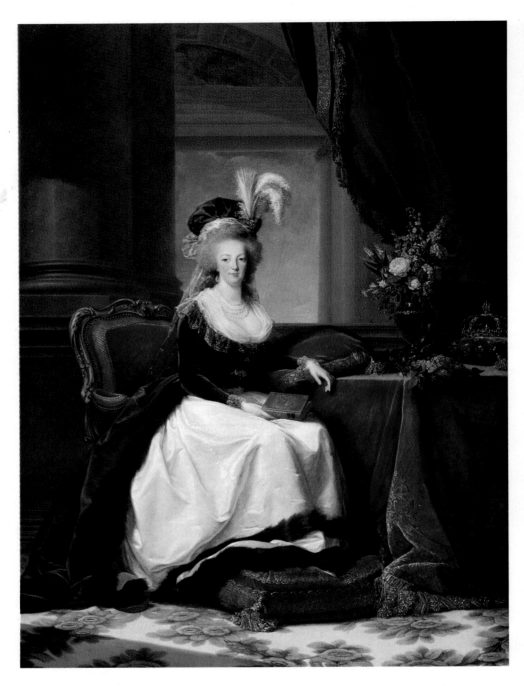

Figure 26.9 Marie-Louise Elisabeth Vigée-Lebrun, *Marie Antoinette*, 1788. Oil on canvas, 12 ft. 1½ in. × 6ft. 3½ in. Musée de Versailles. Giraudon/Art Resource, New York.

shortly before the French Revolution, he captured the pleasures of a waning aristocracy, including and especially the pleasures of courtship and romantic love. In 1766, a wealthy aristocrat commissioned Fragonard to paint a scene that showed the patron's mistress seated on a swing being pushed by a friendly old clergyman. *The Swing* depicts a flirtatious encounter that takes place in a garden bower filled with frothy trees, classical statuary, and delicate light. The young woman, dressed in yards of satin and lace, kicks her tiny shoe into the air in the direction of a statue of Cupid, while her lover, hiding in the bushes below, peers delightedly beneath her billowing skirts (Figure **26.10**). Whether or not the young lady is aware of her lover's presence, her coy gesture and the irreverent behavior of the *ménage à trois* (lover, mistress, and cleric) create a mood of erotic intrigue similar to that found in the comic operas of this period. Fragonard's deft brushstrokes caress the figures and render the surrounding foliage in delicate pastel tones. Although Fragonard immortalized the union of wealth, privilege, and pleasure enjoyed by the upper classes of the eighteenth century, he captured a spirit of sensuous abandon that has easily outlived the particulars of time, place, and social class.

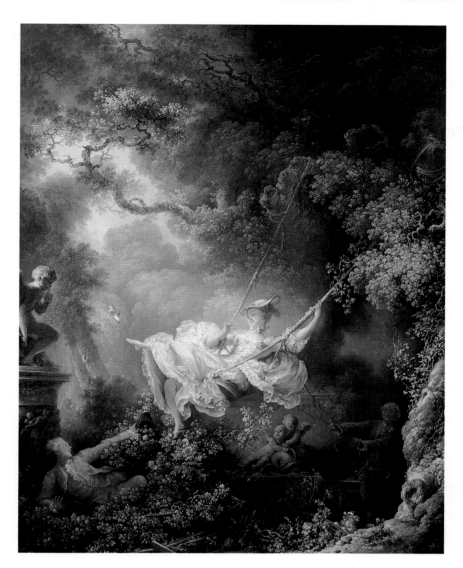

Figure 26.10 Jean-Honoré Fragonard, *The Swing*, 1768. Oil on canvas, 32 × 35 in. The Wallace Collection, London.

Figure 26.11 (below) Clodion (Claude Michel), *The Intoxication of Wine*, ca. 1775. Terra-cotta, height 23¼ in. The Metropolitan Museum of Art, New York. Bequest of Benjamin Altman, 1913 (14.40.687).

Rococo Sculpture

The finest examples of eighteenth-century sculpture are small in scale, intimate in mood, and almost entirely lacking in the dramatic urgency and religious fervor of baroque art. Intended for the boudoir or the drawing room, rococo sculpture usually depicted elegant dancers, wooing couples, and other lighthearted subjects. The French sculptor Claude Michel, known as Clodion (1738–1814), who worked almost exclusively for private patrons, was among the favorite rococo artists of the late eighteenth century. His *Intoxication of Wine* revived a classical theme—a celebration honoring Dionysus, the Greek god of wine and fertility (Figure 26.11). Flushed with wine and revelry, the **satyr** (a semi-bestial woodland creature symbolic of Dionysus) embraces a **bacchante**, an attendant of Dionysus. Clodion made the piece in terra-cotta, a clay medium that requires rapid modeling, thus inviting the artist to capture a sense of spontaneity. Rococo painters sought similar effects through the use of loose and rapid brushstrokes and by sketching with pastels. The expressive impact of *The Intoxication of Wine* belies its tiny size—it is just under 2 feet high.

Eighteenth-Century French Genre Painting

Many of the *philosophes* found the works of Boucher, Clodion, and other rococo artists trivial and morally degenerate. Diderot, for example, denounced rococo boudoir imagery and demanded an art that made "virtue attractive and vice odious." The French artists Jean-Baptiste Greuze (1725–1805) and Jean-Baptiste-Siméon Chardin (1699–1779) heeded the plea for art with a moral purpose. These artists abandoned the indulgent sensuality and frivolity of the rococo; instead they painted realistic scenes of everyday life among the middle and lower classes.

Greuze, Diderot's favorite artist, exalted the simple life and natural virtues of ordinary people. He painted such moralizing subjects as *The Father Reading the Bible to His Children*, *The Well-Beloved Mother*, and *The Effects of Drunkenness*. In the manner of Hogarth (whose works

Greuze admired), he chose engaging narratives that might require a series of paintings. Greuze's *Village Betrothal* of 1761 tells the story of an impending matrimony among hardworking, simple-living rustics: The father, who has just given over the dowry to the humble groom, blesses the couple; the mother laments losing a daughter; while the other members of the household, including the hen and chicks (possibly a symbol of the couple's prospective progeny), look on approvingly (Figure **26.12**). Greuze's painting could easily have been an illustration of a scene from a popular eighteenth-century novel. Greuze shunned the intellectualism of Poussin, the sensuality of Fragonard, and the satirical acrimony of Hogarth. His melodramatic representations appealed to common emotion and sentiment. Understandably, they were among the most popular images of the eighteenth and nineteenth centuries.

The art of Greuze's contemporary Chardin was less steeped in sentimentality. Chardin painted humble still lifes and genre scenes showing nurses, governesses, and

Figure 26.12 Jean-Baptiste Greuze, *Village Betrothal*, 1761. Oil on canvas, 3 ft. 10½ in. × 3 ft. Louvre, Paris. Alinari/Art Resource, New York.

Figure 26.13 Jean-Baptiste-Siméon Chardin, *The Kitchen Maid*, 1738. Oil on canvas, 18⅛ x 14¾ in. © 1998 Board of Trustees, National Gallery of Art, Washington, D.C. Samuel H. Kress Collection.

kitchen maids at work (Figure **26.13**). Unlike Greuze, who illustrated his moral tales as literally as possible, Chardin avoided both explicit moralizing and anecdotal themes. Yet Chardin's paintings bear a deep concern for commonplace humanity, and they carry an implicit message—that of the ennobling dignity of work and the virtues of domesticity. The forthright qualities of Chardin's subjects are echoed in his style: His figures are simple and monumental, and his compositions reveal an uncanny sense of balance reminiscent of the works of de Hooch and Vermeer. Each object in the spatial field seems to assume its proper and predestined place. Executed in mellow, creamy tones, Chardin's paintings evoke a mood of gentility and gravity.

Greuze and Chardin brought painting out of the drawing room and into the kitchen. Their canvases had popular appeal and were in such high demand that they were sold widely in engraved copies. Ironically, while Chardin's subjects were humble and commonplace, his patrons were often bankers, foreign ambassadors, and royalty itself—Louis XV owned at least two of Chardin's paintings.

1775	the flush toilet is patented in England	
1777	steam heat is used in France for the first time since the Roman era	
1779	the first bicycles appear in Paris	

Eighteenth-Century Neoclassicism

Neoclassicism—the self-conscious revival of Greco-Roman culture—belonged to a tradition that stretched at least from the early Renaissance through the age of Louis XIV. During the seventeenth century, Poussin and other artists of the European Academies (see chapter 23) had resurrected the classical ideals of clarity, simplicity, balance, and restraint, following the model of Raphael, the High Renaissance standard-bearer of the Greco-Roman style. The neoclassicism of the eighteenth century was inspired for the most part by archeological excavations of Greek and Roman sites—most specifically, the scientific investigation of two Roman towns, Herculaneum and Pompeii. Greek and Roman artifacts, which had previously been seen only by the nobility and rulers, became available to the general public. Study of these works enabled artists and antiquarians, for the first time in history, to make clear distinctions between the artifacts of Greece and those of Rome. The result was a more austere and archeologically correct neoclassicism than any that had flourished previous to the eighteenth century.

Rome had been a favorite attraction for well-educated tourists and students of art since Renaissance times. But during the eighteenth century, Rome and its monuments came under new scrutiny. Architects studied the monuments of antiquity (see chapter 7), and artists made topographic sketches, often reproduced in copper engravings that were sold cheaply—in the manner of modern-day postcards. In 1740 the Venetian architect and engineer Giovanni Battista Piranesi (1720–1778) established himself in Rome as a printmaker. Piranesi's engravings of Rome were widely bought and appreciated (see chapter 9), while his studies of Roman monuments, with their precisely rendered technical details and inscriptions, exerted considerable influence on French and English architects of his time (Figure **26.14**). Piranesi's later works—nightmarish visions of dungeons inspired by the Roman sewer system—abandoned all classical canons of objectivity and emotional restraint. Nevertheless, with European artists more eager than ever to rediscover antiquity through the careful study of its remains, the neoclassical revival was under way.

Figure 26.14 Giovanni Battista Piranesi, *View of the Forum*, #15, from *Views of Rome*, ca. 1748–1778. Etching. The Metropolitan Museum of Art, New York, Rogers Fund, 1941 (41.7.1[16]).

Figure 26.15 Giovanni Paolo Panini (copy after), *Picture Gallery (Roma Antica)*, Italian (Roman), 1691–1765. Pen and black ink with brush and gray wash and watercolor over graphite on ivory laid paper, 17¼ × 27³⁄₁₆ in. © 1998 The Art Institute of Chicago. All Rights Reserved. Emily Crane Chadbourne Collection (1955.7.45).

A major factor for the widespread interest in antiquity, and one that made eighteenth-century neoclassicism unique, was the scientific uncovering of ancient classical ruins. In 1738, the king of Naples sponsored the first archeological excavations at Herculaneum, one of the two Roman cities in Southern Italy buried under volcanic ash by the eruption of Mount Vesuvius in 79 C.E. The excavations at Pompeii would follow in 1748. These enterprises, followed by European archeological expeditions to Greece and Asia Minor in 1750, inspired scholars to assemble vast collections of Greek and Roman artifacts (Figure **26.15**). Both the Louvre and the Vatican became museum repositories that housed the treasures of these expeditions. Shortly after the first English expeditions to Athens, the German scholar Johann Joachim Winckelmann (1717–1768) began to study Greek and Roman antiquities. He published an eloquent assessment of these objects in his magnificently illustrated *History of Ancient Art* (1764). These and other of Winckelmann's widely circulated texts, which offered a critical analysis of art objects (rather than a biographical history of artists), established Winckelmann as the father of modern art historical scholarship.

Although Winckelmann himself never visited Greece, he was infatuated with Hellenic and Hellenistic sculpture. He argued that artists of his time could become great only by imitating the ancient Greeks, whose best works, he insisted, betrayed "a noble simplicity and a quiet grandeur." Of his favorite ancient statue, the *Apollo Belvedere* (see Figure 26.18, left), Winckelmann proclaimed, "In the presence of this miracle of art, I forget the whole universe and my soul acquires a loftiness appropriate to its dignity." Winckelmann's reverence for antiquity typified the eighteenth-century attitude toward classicism as a vehicle for the elevation of human consciousness. Here, finally, was a style that mirrored the Enlightenment program of reason, clarity, and order—a style that equated Beauty with Goodness, Virtue, and Truth. Winckelmann's publications became an inspiration for artists and aesthetes all over Europe. In Britain, Sir Joshua Reynolds (1723–1792), the painter and founder of the British Royal Academy of Art, lectured on the Grand Manner; his *Discourses* were translated into French, German, and Italian. The lofty vision of a style that captured the nobility and dignity of the Greco-Roman past fired the imagination of intellectuals across Western Europe and America.

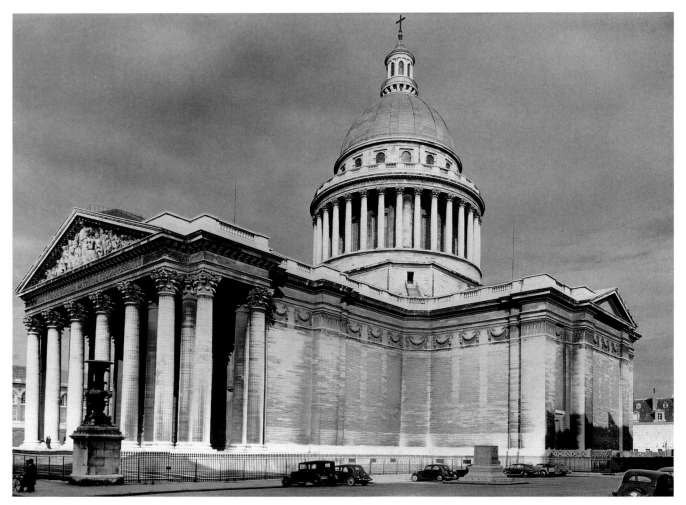

Figure 26.16 Jacques-Germain Soufflot, Sainte Geneviève (renamed the "Panthéon" during the French Revolution), Paris, 1757–1792. Photo: A. F. Kersting, London.

Neoclassical Architecture

The classical revival of the eighteenth century was unique in its accuracy of detail and its purity of design. Neoclassical architects made careful distinctions between Greek and Roman buildings and between the various Renaissance and post-Renaissance styles modeled upon antiquity. Simple geometric masses—spheres, cubes, and cylinders—became the bases for a new, more abstract and austere classicism. Neoclassical architects rejected the illusionistic theatricality of the baroque style with its broken pediments, cartouches, and ornamental devices. They also turned their backs on the stucco foliage, cherubic angels, and "wedding-cake" fantasies of the rococo. The ideal neoclassical exterior was free of frivolous ornamentation, while its interior consisted of clean and rectilinear wall planes, soberly accented with engaged columns or pilasters, geometric motifs, and shallow niches that housed copies of antique statuary (see Figure 26.18).

In France, the leading architect of the eighteenth century was Jacques-Germain Soufflot (1713–1780). Soufflot's Church of Sainte Geneviève (Figure **26.16**), the patron saint of Paris, follows a strict central plan with four shallow domes covering each of the arms. A massive central dome, supported entirely on pillars, rises over the crossing (compare Saint Paul's in London; Figure 21.2). The facade of Sainte Geneviève resembles the portico of the Pantheon in Rome (see chapter 7), while the interior of the church (Figure **26.17**)—which entombs, among others, Voltaire and Rousseau—recalls the grandeur of Saint Peter's in Rome. As the "Panthéon" illustrates, Soufflot did not slavishly imitate any single classical structure; rather, he selected specific features from a variety of notable sources and combined them with clarity and reserve. In contrast with its baroque and rococo ancestors, the Church of Sainte Geneviève was no theater of miracles but rather a rationally ordered, this-worldly shrine.

EIGHTEENTH-CENTURY ART, MUSIC, AND SOCIETY ◆ 153

Figure 26.17 Jacques-Germain Soufflot, interior of Sainte Geneviève ("Panthéon"), Paris, 1757–1792. Photo: A. F. Kersting, London.

Some of the purest examples of the classical revival are found in late eighteenth-century English country homes. The interiors of these sprawling symbols of wealth and prestige reflect close attention to archeological drawings of Greek and Roman antiquities. Kedleston Hall in Derbyshire, England, designed by the Scottish architect Robert Adam (1728–1792), reflects a pristine taste for crisp contours and the refined synthesis of Greco-Roman motifs (Figure **26.18**). In such estates as this, the neoclassical spirit touched everything from sculpture (Figure **26.19**) and furniture to tea services and tableware. Among the most popular items of the day were the ceramics of the English potter Josiah Wedgwood (1730–1795). Wedgwood's wares were modeled on Greek and Roman vases and embellished with finely applied, molded white clay surface designs (Figure **26.20**).

The austerity and dignity of neoclassicism made it the ideal style for public monuments and offices of state. In Paris, Berlin, and Washington D.C., neoclassical architects borrowed Greek and Roman temple designs for public and private buildings, including and especially banks, where the modern-day gods of money and materialism took the place of the ancient

Figure 26.18 Robert Adam, Marble Hall, Kedleston Hall, Derbyshire, England, 1763–1777. (Note copy of the *Apollo Belvedere* in niche at left.) 67 ft. × 42 ft., height 40 ft. Photo: A. F. Kersting, London.

Figure 26.19 (above) Antonio Canova, *Pauline Borghese as Venus*, 1808. Marble, life-sized. Galleria Borghese, Rome. Alinari/Art Resource, New York.

deities. In some instances, the spirit of revival produced daring architectural hybrids. In England, for instance, the Scottish architect James Gibbs (1682–1754) designed churches that combined a classical portico with a Gothic spire (Figure **26.21**). This scheme, which united the baroque love of contrast with the neoclassical rule of symmetry, became extremely popular in America, especially in the congregational churches built across New England.

Neoclassicism in America

A tour of the city of Washington in the District of Columbia will convince any student of the impact of neoclassicism on the architecture of the United States. The neoclassical movement in America did not originate, however, in the capital city, whose major buildings date only from the nineteenth century, but, rather, among the Founding Fathers. One of the most passionate devotees of Greco-Roman art and life was the Virginia lawyer and statesman Thomas Jefferson

Figure 26.20 Wedgwood and Sons, Copy of Portland Vase (#7) with stand, ca. 1790. Black and white jasperware, height 10 in. Courtesy Museum of Fine Arts, Boston. Gift of Dr. Lloyd E. Hawes.

Figure 26.21 James Gibbs, Saint Martin-in-the-Fields, London, 1721–1726. Photo: A. F. Kersting, London.

Figure 26.22 Jean-Antoine Houdon, *Thomas Jefferson*, 1789. Marble, height 21½ in. Library of Congress, Washington, D.C.

(1743–1826), whose Declaration of Independence was discussed in chapter 24. Farmer, linguist, educator, inventor, architect, musician, and politician, the man who served as third president of the United States was an eighteenth-century *uomo universale* (Figure **26.22**). Jefferson was a student of ancient and Renaissance treatises on architecture and an impassioned apostle of neoclassicism. In 1786, he designed the Virginia State Capitol (see chapter 7) modeled on the Maison Carrée (see Figure 26.30). For the design of his own country estate in Monticello and for the University of Virginia—America's first state university—he drew on the Pantheon in Rome, which he greatly admired. Jefferson reconstructed this ancient temple at two-thirds its original size in the Rotunda, which housed the original library of the University of Virginia (Figure **26.23**). Considerably smaller than Soufflot's "Panthéon," the stripped-down Rotunda is also purer in form. Jefferson's tightly organized and geometrically correct plan for the campus of the University of Virginia reflects the basic sympathy between neoclassical design and the rationalist ideals of the Enlightenment. The "academical village," as Jefferson described it, was a community of the free-thinking elite—exclusively white, wealthy, and male, yet it provided both a physical and a spiritual model for non-sectarian education in the United States.

The young American nation drew on the heritage of the ancients (and especially the history of the Roman Republic) to symbolize its newly forged commitment to the ideals of liberty and equality. The leaders of the American Revolution regarded themselves as

Figure 26.23 Thomas Jefferson, Rotunda, University of Virginia, Charlottesville, Virginia, 1822–1826. Prints Collection, Special Collections Department, University Archives, University of Virginia Library.

Figure 26.24 Great Seal of the United States. Courtesy of the Bureau of Printing and Engraving, U.S. Treasury Department.

Figure 26.25 Jean-Antoine Houdon, *George Washington*, 1786–1796. Marble, height 6 ft. 2 in. State capitol, Richmond, Virginia. Virginia State Library and Archives.

descendants of ancient Roman heroes and some even adopted Latin names, much as the Italian Renaissance humanists had done. On the Great Seal of the United States, as on the earliest American coins and paper currency, the Latin phrase "E pluribus unum" ("out of many, one") and the *fasces* (the ancient Roman badge of authority consisting of a bundle of rods and an ax) identified America as heir to republican Rome (Figure **26.24**).

Neoclassical Sculpture

Neoclassical sculptors heeded the Enlightenment demand for an art that perpetuated the memory of illustrious men. Jean-Antoine Houdon (1741–1828), the leading portrait sculptor of Europe, immortalized in stone the features of his contemporaries. His portrait busts, which met the popular demand for achieving a familiar likeness, revived the realistic tradition in sculpture that had reached its high-water mark among the Romans. Houdon had a special talent for catching characteristic gestures and expressions: Diderot, shown without a wig, surveys his world with inquisitive candor (see Figure 24.3), while the aging Voltaire addresses us with a grim and knowing smile (see Figure 25.3). While visiting America, Houdon carved portraits of Jefferson (see Figure 26.22), Franklin, and other "virtuous men" of the republic. His life-sized statue of George Washington renders the first president of the United States as country gentleman and eminent statesman (Figure **26.25**). Resting his hand on a columnar *fasces*, the poised but slightly potbellied Washington recalls (however faintly) the monumental dignity of the Greek gods and the Roman emperors.

While Houdon invested neoclassicism with a strong taste for realism, most of his contemporaries followed the Hellenic impulse to idealize the human form. Such was the case with the Italian-born sculptor Antonio Canova (1757–1822). Canova's life-sized portrait of Napoleon Bonaparte's sister, Pauline Borghese, is a sublime example of neoclassical refinement and restraint (see Figure 26.19). Canova casts Pauline in the guise of a reclining Venus. Perfectly proportioned and flawless, she shares the cool elegance of classical statuary and Wedgwood reliefs. In contrast to the vigorously carved surfaces of baroque sculpture (recall, for instance, Bernini's *Ecstasy of Saint Teresa*, Figure 20.2), Canova's figure is smooth and neutral—even stark. A comparison of Canova's *Pauline Borghese as Venus* with Clodion's *Intoxication of Wine* (see Figure 26.11) is also revealing: Both depend on classical themes and models, but whereas Clodion's piece is intimate, sensuous, and spontaneous, Canova's seems remote, controlled, and calculated. Its aesthetic distance is intensified by the ghostlike whiteness of the figure and its "blank" eyes— eighteenth-century sculptors seem to have been unaware that classical artists painted parts of their statues to make them look more lifelike.

Neoclassical Painting and Politics: The Art of David

During the last decades of the eighteenth century, as the tides of revolution began to engulf the indulgent lifestyles of the French aristocracy, the rococo style in painting gave way to a soberminded new approach to picturemaking. The pioneer of the new style was the French artist Jacques-Louis David (1748–1825). David's early canvases were executed in the rococo style of his teacher and distant cousin, Boucher. But after winning

the coveted Prix de Rome, which sent him to study in the foremost city of antiquity, David found his place among the classicists. In 1782 he completed one of the most influential paintings of the late eighteenth century: *The Oath of the Horatii* (Figure **26.26**). The painting was commissioned by the French king some eight years before the outbreak of the Revolution; ironically, however, it became a symbol of the very spirit that would topple the royal crown.

The Oath of the Horatii illustrates a dramatic event recorded by Livy in his *History of Rome*. It depicts the moment when the three sons of the noble patriarch Horatius Proclus swear to oppose the treacherous Curiatii family in a win-or-die battle that would determine the future of Rome. In France, Livy's story had become especially popular as the subject of a play by the French dramatist Pierre Corneille (1606–1684). David captured the spirit of the story in a single potent image: Resolved to pursue their destiny as defenders of liberty, the Horatii lift their arms in a dramatic military salute. Bathed in golden light, the sculpturesque figures stand along the strict horizontal line of the picture plane. The body of the leftmost warrior forms a rigid triangular

Figure 26.26 Jacques-Louis David, *The Oath of the Horatii*, 1782. Oil on canvas, 10 ft. 10 in. × 14 ft. Louvre, Paris. Photo: © R.M.N., Paris.

Figure 26.27 Jacques-Louis David, *The Death of Socrates*, 1787. Oil on canvas, 4 ft. 3 in. × 6 ft. 5¼ in. The Metropolitan Museum of Art, New York. Catharine Lorillard Wolfe Collection. Wolfe Fund, 1931 (31.45).

shape that is subtly repeated throughout the composition—in the arches of the colonnade, for instance, and in the group of grieving women (one of whom represents the fiancée of a Curiatius). According to the tale, her victorious brother, the sole survivor of the combat, returned home to find her mourning for her dead lover and murdered her in a fit of rage.

David's painting was an immediate success: People lined up to see it while it hung in the artist's studio in Rome, and the city of Paris received it enthusiastically when it arrived there in 1785. The huge canvas (over 10 by 14 feet) came to be perceived as a clear denunciation of aristocratic pastimes. In place of the lace cuffs, silk suits, and powdered wigs of the rococo drawing room, David had detailed the trappings of war. His painting presented life as serious drama: It proclaimed the importance of reason and the intellect over and above feeling and sentiment, and it defended the ideals of male heroism and self-sacrifice in the interest of one's country. Stylistically, too, the painting was revolutionary: David rejected the luxuriant sparkle of rococo art for sober simplicity. He replaced the pliant forms, sensuous textures, and pastel tones of the rococo with rectilinear shapes, hard-edged contours, and somber

colors—features that recalled the art of Poussin (whom David deeply admired). His technique was austere, precise, and realistic—witness the archeologically correct Roman helmets, sandals, and swords.

Three years after painting *The Oath of the Horatii*, David conceived the smaller but equally popular *Death of Socrates* (Figure **26.27**; see also Part Opener, p. 96). The scene is a fifth-century B.C.E. Athenian prison. It is the moment before Socrates, the father of Greek philosophy, drinks the fatal hemlock. Surrounding Socrates are his students and friends, posed in various expressions of lament, while the apostle of reason himself—illuminated in the style of Caravaggio—rhetorically lifts his hand to heaven. Clarity and intellectual control dominate the composition: Figures and objects are arranged as if plotted on a grid of lines horizontal and vertical to the picture plane. This ideal geometry, a metaphor for the ordering function of reason, complements the grave and noble message of the painting: Reason guides human beings to live and, if need be, to die for their moral principles. In *The Death of Socrates*, as in *The Oath of the Horatii*, David put neoclassicism at the service of a morality based on Greco-Roman Stoicism, self-sacrifice, and stern patriotism.

Ingres and the Neoclassical Line

David's most talented pupil was the draftsman Jean-Auguste-Dominique Ingres (1780–1867). Ingres was famous for his polished depictions of classical history and myth and for his accomplished portraits. He worshiped, as he himself admitted, "Raphael, his century, the ancients, and above all the divine Greeks." But Ingres departed from academic dictums in certain matters of style. He abandoned the weighty realism of David in favor of a purity of line similar to that found in Greek vase paintings. Drawing, he insisted, is the true basis of art, while color "is no more than a handmaiden."

Intrigued by the exoticism of Turkish culture (publicized by Napoleon's campaigns in North Africa), Ingres painted his greatest work, *La Grande Odalisque* (Figure **26.28**), in 1814. The languorous harem slave, a distant kin of Titian's reclining *Venus of Urbino* (see chapter 17), is the quintessential image of the seductive female. Ingres rejected neoclassical canons of proportion and elongated the limbs of his nude in ways reminiscent of the Italian mannerist Parmigianino's *Madonna of the Long Neck* (see Figure 20.4). The flatness and "incorrect" anatomy of the figure drew strong criticism from Ingres' colleagues, who claimed his subject had three too many vertebrae and called his style "primitive" and "Gothic." However, the *Odalisque* remains one of the most arresting images of womanhood in Western art.

Neoclassicism under Napoleon

While neoclassicism was the "official" style of the French Revolution, it soon became the vehicle of French imperialism. Under the leadership of Napoleon Bonaparte (1769–1821), the imagery of classical Greece and republican Rome was abandoned for the more appropriate imagery of Augustan Rome. Like the Roman emperors, Napoleon used the arts to magnify his greatness. He appointed David to commemorate his military achievements and he commissioned architects to redesign Paris in the spirit of ancient Rome. Paris became a city of straight, wide avenues and huge, impressive squares. Imaginary axes linked the various monuments raised to honor the emperor, and older buildings were remodeled in the new Empire style. Alexandre-Pierre Vignon (1763–1828) redesigned the Church of Saint Mary Magdalene (called "La Madeleine") as a Roman temple dedicated to the glory of the French army (Figure **26.29**). Fifty-two Corinthian columns, each 66 feet tall, surround the temple, which rises on a 23-foot-high podium, like a gigantic version of the Maison Carrée in Nîmes (Figure **26.30**). Vignon's gloomy interior—a nave crowned with three domes—falls short of reflecting the majesty of the exterior, despite his use of the Corinthian and Ionic orders in the decorative scheme.

Elsewhere, Napoleon's neoclassicism was more

Figure 26.28 Jean-Auguste-Dominique Ingres, *La Grande Odalisque*, 1814. Oil on canvas, 2 ft. 11¼ in. × 5 ft. 3¾ in. Louvre, Paris. Photo: © R.M.N., Paris.

Figure 26.29 Alexandre-Pierre Vignon, Church of Mary Magdalene ("La Madeleine"), Paris, 1807–1842. Length 350 ft., width 147 ft., height of podium 23 ft. Photo: A. F. Kersting, London.

Figure 26.30 Maison Carrée, Nîmes, France, 16 B.C.E. Foto Marburg/Art Resource, New York.

precise. The Arc du Carrousel, which stands adjacent to the Louvre, is faithful to its Roman model, the Arch of Constantine in Rome. And the grandest of Paris' triumphal arches, which occupies the crossing of twelve avenues at the end of the famous Avenue des Champs-Elysées (Figure 26.31), closely resembles the Arch of Titus in the Roman Forum (see chapter 7). The 164-foot-high commemorative monument—which was dedicated to the French army—was larger than any arch built in ancient times. Napoleon would become one of the nineteenth century's most celebrated romantic heroes (see chapter 28), but the monuments he commissioned for Paris were stamped unmistakably with the classical spirit.

Figure 26.31 Jean-François Thérèse Chalgrin and others, Arc de Triomphe, Paris, 1806–1836. Height 164 ft. J. Feuillie/© DACS 1998.

Eighteenth-Century Western Music

The eighteenth century was as rich in music as it was in the visual arts. Music filled the courts and concert halls. The eighteenth-century concert hall was small by modern standards. Its lights were rarely dimmed during performances and audiences were not expected to wait until the end of each piece to applaud. Often they showed their enthusiasm by applauding after a movement, insisting that it be repeated. Religious compositions were still very much in demand, but church music was overshadowed by the vast amounts of music composed for secular entertainment. Composers sought the patronage of wealthy aristocrats, at whose courts they often served. At the same time, composers wrote music for amateur performance and for the public concert hall. While opera remained the favorite type of vocal music, new forms of instrumental music emerged. Social constraints still determined specific types of music, but, inevitably, music began to free itself from religious and ceremonial functions.

During the eighteenth century certain distinctive characteristics of Western music converged. These characteristics included the idea that harmony was proper and essential to music, that a piece of music should be thoughtfully (and individually) composed, and that it should be studiously rehearsed and performed in much the same manner each time it is played. These traits, which stressed control and formality over spontaneity and improvisation, set Western musical culture apart from that of Africa, Asia, and the rest of the world.

Rococo Music

By the middle of the eighteenth century, the rococo (or *galant*) style began to replace the music of Bach and Handel. Rococo composers abandoned the intricate counterpoint and dense textures of the baroque in favor of light and graceful melodies organized into short, distinct phrases. As with rococo art, rococo music was delicate in sound, thin in texture, and natural in feeling. These qualities dominated the works of the French composer François Couperin (1668–1733).

Couperin, a contemporary of Bach, wrote in both the baroque and rococo styles, as did many composers of the early eighteenth century. In 1716, Couperin published one of the most important musical treatises of the

| 1680s | the earliest form of the clarinet is invented in Germany |
| 1700 | the French coin the term *acoustics* to describe the science of sound |

period, *The Art of Playing the Clavecin*, which offers precise instructions for keyboard fingering and for the execution of musical ornaments known as *agréments*. The rococo preference for intimate forms of expression cast in miniature is reflected in Couperin's suites for harpsichord (in French, *clavecin*). The individual sections of these suites often bear playful titles based on women's names, parlor games, or human attributes, such as Languor, Coquetry, and Jealousy. "Le Croc-en-jambe"♪ (*donner un croc-en-jambe* means "to trip up" or "to play a dirty trick"), for example, is itself a tripping, lighthearted piece. Couperin's suites were written for solo instruments or for ensembles and accompanied such dances as the courante, the minuet, and the sarabande, all of which were performed in fashionable eighteenth-century *salons*. Embroidered with florid *agréments*, Couperin's music shares the lighthearted spirit and fragile elegance of the rococo style in the visual arts.

Classical Music

The word *classical*, when used in reference to music, has two principal meanings. In its broadest sense, it describes that which is enduring and authoritative (see "The Classical Legacy," in Book 1); hence "classical" is commonly used to distinguish serious (or "art") music from the more ephemeral "popular" (or "folk") music. "Classical" is also employed, however, to describe a specific musical style that prevailed in the West between approximately 1760 and 1820—one that shares the essential features of Greco-Roman art: symmetry, balance, and formal restraint. Unlike neoclassical art and architecture, classical music had little to do with the heritage of Greece and Rome, for European composers had no surviving evidence of Greek and Roman music and, therefore, no antique musical models to imitate. Nevertheless, classical music was unique in its clarity of form and purity of design. Classical composers, most of whom came from Germany and Austria, completed the liberation of melody from baroque polyphony, a process clearly anticipated in rococo music. They wrote homophonic compositions that featured easy-to-grasp melodies, which were repeated or developed according to a definitive formal structure.

Although classical composers retained the fast/slow/fast contrasts of baroque instrumental forms, they rid their compositions of many baroque features. They replaced, for instance, the abrupt changes from loud to soft with more gently graduated contrasts. They eliminated the unflagging rhythms and ornate embellishments of baroque polyphony in favor of clear-cut musical phrases. Although counterpoint continued to

♪See Music Listening Selections at end of chapter.

Figure 26.32 The classical symphony orchestra. From Carter Harmon, *A Popular History of Music.* Copyright © 1956 by Carter Harmon. Used by permission of Dell Books, a division of Bantam Doubleday Dell Publishing Group, Inc.

play an important role in classical music, the intricate webs of counterpoint typical, for instance, of a Bach fugue, gave way to a new harmonic clarity. In short, classical music reflects an infatuation with formal structure which parallels the neoclassical artist's quest for reasoned clarity, balance, and purity of design.

The Birth of the Orchestra

Eighteenth-century instrumental music served as secular entertainment in public theaters and in the *salons* of courtly residences. The most important instrumental grouping to emerge at this time was the orchestra. The eighteenth-century Bohemian composer Johann Stamitz (1717–1757), who settled in the South German town of Mannheim in the 1740s, organized what is thought to have been one of the earliest forms of the classical orchestra. It consisted of groups of related instruments, each with its own character or personality. The **strings**, made up of violins, violas, cellos, and double basses, formed the nucleus of the orchestra, since they were the most melodious and most lyrical of the instrumental families. The **woodwinds**, consisting of flutes, oboes, clarinets, and bassoons, specialized in mellow harmonies. The **brass** section, made up of French horns and trumpets (and, at the end of the

century, trombones), added volume and resonance. And the **percussion** section, comprised of kettledrums (or tympani), functioned as rhythm markers (Figure **26.32**). Stamitz's orchestra was small by modern-day standards. It included some thirty-five pieces, many of which were still rudimentary: Brass instruments lacked valves, and the clarinet was not perfected until roughly 1790. The piano, which was invented around 1720, remained until 1775 more closely related to the clavichord than to the modern grand piano. During the last quarter of the century, however, as the piano underwent technical refinement, it came to be the favorite solo instrument.

As musical instruments became more sophisticated, the orchestra, capable of an increasingly expressive and subtle range of sounds, grew in size and popularity. The eighteenth-century orchestra was led by a musician (often the composer himself) who played part of the composition on the clavier or keyboard instrument located at the place now occupied by the conductor's podium. The string section was seated to the right and left, while the other instruments were spread across the middle distance, in a pattern that has persisted to this day.

To facilitate the conductor's control over the music, the Mannheim orchestra used a **score**, that is, a record of musical notation that indicated every sound to be played by each instrument. Each musical part appeared in groups of five-line staffs which enabled the conductor to "view" the composition as a whole. Separate parts were written out for each instrument as well. In the eighteenth century, both instrumentation and methods of scoring became standardized. Scores included a time signature, which indicated the number of beats per measure, a key signature, which noted the number of sharps or flats in the specified key, and abbreviations of the Italian words that indicated the dynamics of specific passages: *f* for *forte* ("loud") and *p* for *piano* ("soft"). Interpretive directions, such as *scherzando* ("sprightly") and *affettuoso* ("with feeling"), signified the intentions of the composer as to how a musical passage should be performed. All these notational devices served the principle of formality that governed eighteenth-century music and Western musical composition in general.

Classical Instrumental Compositions

Classical composers wrote music for a variety of instrumental groupings. The most challenging of these was the orchestral form known as the **symphony**. The Italian word *sinfonia* was used during the seventeenth century to describe various kinds of instrumental pieces; but, by the mid-eighteenth century, the word came to mean an independent instrumental composition for full orchestra. In addition to the symphony, three other instrumental genres dominated the classical era: the **string quartet**, a composition for four stringed instruments—two violins, a viola, and a cello; the **concerto**, a composition featuring one or more solo instruments and an orchestra; and the **sonata**, a composition for an unaccompanied keyboard instrument or for another instrument with keyboard accompaniment.

Although the concerto and the sonata originated earlier (see chapter 22), they now took on a new formality. Indeed, all four instrumental forms—the symphony, the string quartet, the classical concerto, and the classical sonata—assumed a singular formal structure: They were divided into three or four sections, or movements, each of which followed a specific tempo, or musical pace. The first movement was played *allegro* or in fast tempo; the second *andante* or *largo*, that is, in moderate or slow tempo; the third movement (usually omitted in concertos) was written in dance tempo (usually in three-quarter time); and the fourth was again *allegro*.

Classical composers used a special form for the organization of the first and fourth movements of classical symphonies, string quartets, concertos, and sonatas. This form, known as **sonata form** (or **sonata allegro form**; Figure 26.33), calls for the division of the movement into three parts: the exposition, the development, and the recapitulation. In the exposition, the composer "exposes," or introduces, a theme in the "home" key, then contrasts it with a second theme in a different key. Musical effect is based on the tension of two opposing key centers. In the development, the composer moves to contrasting keys, expanding and altering the themes stated in the exposition. Finally, in the recapitulation, the themes from the exposition are restated, both now in the home key, resolving the

Figure 26.33 Sonata form.

SECTION	EXPOSITION	DEVELOPMENT	RECAPITUALTION	CODA
THEME	second theme / bridge / first theme	first and second themes developed	first theme / bridge / second theme	
TONALITY	home key / second key	contrasting keys	home key	

earlier tension. A coda ("tail") is often added as a definitive end piece.

Although classical composers frequently deviated from sonata form, they looked to it to provide the "rules" of musical design—the architectural guidelines, so to speak, for musical composition. Just as neoclassical artists and writers favored clear definitions and an Aristotelian "beginning, middle, and end," so classical composers delighted in the threefold balance of the sonata form, the repetition of simple harmonies, and the crisp phrasing of appealing melodies.

The Development of the Classical Style: Haydn

Whether a symphony, string quartet, sonata, or concerto, classical music is usually bright, melodic, and free-flowing. These features characterize the works of the Austrian composer Franz Joseph Haydn (1732–1809). Of peasant birth, Haydn was recruited at the age of eight to sing in the choir of Saint Stephen's Cathedral in Vienna. As a young man, he taught music and struggled to make a living. In 1761, at the age of twenty-nine, Haydn became musical director to the court of the powerful and wealthy Hungarian nobleman Prince Paul Anton Esterházy, who was also an accomplished musician. The magnificent Esterházy country estate (modeled on Versailles) included two theaters—one for opera and one for puppet plays—and two richly appointed concert halls. There, for almost thirty years, Haydn took charge of all aspects of musical entertainment: He composed music, trained choristers, oversaw the repair of instruments, and rehearsed and conducted an orchestra of some twenty-five musicians. At the princely court, Haydn produced music for various instrumental groups. Tailoring his creative talents to suit special occasions and the tastes of his wealthy patron, he wrote operas, oratorios, solo concertos, sonatas, overtures, and liturgical music. But his most original works were those whose forms he himself helped to develop: the classical symphony and the string quartet. The Father of the Symphony, as Haydn is often called, wrote 104 symphonies and 84 string quartets. The string quartet, a concentrated instrumental form, met the need for elite entertainment in a small room or chamber—hence the term "chamber music." Unfortunately, such works are today often performed in huge music halls, rather than in the intimate surroundings for which they were intended.

After the death of Prince Esterházy in 1790, Haydn was invited to perform in London, where he composed his last twelve symphonies. In the London symphonies, which Haydn wrote for an orchestra of some sixty players, he explored an expanded harmonic range and a wealth of dramatic effects. For some of the symphonies he used folk melodies as basic themes, inventively repeating key fragments in different parts of the piece. Among the most memorable of the London symphonies is Symphony No. 94,♪ nicknamed "The Surprise," because Haydn introduced an unexpected *fortissimo* ("very loud") instrumental crash on a weak beat in the second movement of the piece. Tradition has it that the blaring chord was calculated to waken a drowsy audience—London concerts often lasted well past midnight—and entice them to anticipate the next "surprise" which never does occur. Haydn brought a lifetime of musical experience to his last works. Their witty phrasing and melodic effects made these symphonies enormously popular—so popular, in fact, that eighteenth-century music publishers often sold compositions that they falsely attributed to Haydn. A celebrity in his old age, "Papa Haydn" (as he was affectionately called) was one of the first musicians to attain the status of a culture hero during his own lifetime.

The Genius of Mozart

The foremost musical genius of the eighteenth century—and for some critics, of all time—was Haydn's younger contemporary and colleague, Wolfgang Amadeus Mozart (1756–1791). A child prodigy, Mozart wrote his first original composition at the age of six. During his brief (thirty-five-year) life, he produced a total of some 650 works, including 41 symphonies, 60 sonatas, 23 piano concertos, and 20 operas. (These were catalogued and numbered in the late nineteenth century by Ludwig von Köchel, hence the "K." numbers used to identify Mozart compositions.)

Wolfgang, the son of a prominent composer, was born in Salzburg, Austria. With his father, he toured Europe, performing hundreds of public and private concerts before he was thirteen (Figure **26.34**). He often performed his own pieces, particularly his piano concertos, which constitute some of the most important contributions of his musical career. Unlike Haydn, Mozart did not invent any new forms. However, he brought to the instrumental genres of his time unparalleled melodic inventiveness. He borrowed melodies from popular dance tunes and transformed them into elegant compositions appropriate for garden parties, weddings, and balls. One such piece is the Serenade in G Major, K. 525, also known as "Eine kleine Nachtmusik" ("A Little Nightmusic"), a work for small string orchestra.♪ He incorporated popular melodies into his symphonies as well, three of which (K. 543, K. 550, and K. 551) were written in a six-week period in 1788.

♪See Music Listening Selections at end of chapter.

Figure 26.34 Louis Carmontelle, *The Mozarts in Concert: Leopold, Wolfgang (age seven), and Nannerl*, 1764. Reproduced by courtesy of the Trustees of the British Museum, London.

These pieces remain among the most eloquent examples of the classical symphonic form.

After leaving the service of the Archbishop of Salzburg in 1781, Mozart sought appointments in the aristocratic courts of Europe, but he never received adequate patronage and had difficulty supporting himself and his family. When he died in Vienna in 1791, he was buried in a pauper's grave.* During the last six years of his life, Mozart wrote four of his finest operas, receiving commissions for all but the first. These works are among the best loved in the Western operatic repertory: *Le nozze di Figaro* (*The Marriage of Figaro*, 1786), *Don Giovanni* (1787), *Così fan tutte* (*Thus Do All Women*, 1790), and *Die Zauberflöte* (*The Magic Flute*, 1791).

The Marriage of Figaro is an example of **opera buffa**, a type of comic opera that developed during the eighteenth century as a short, humorous entertainment formerly inserted between the acts of a serious play or opera. Such intermezzos made use of stock, comic types such as the clever servant, the miser, and the fool. Like the playwright Molière (see chapter 23), Mozart transformed the stock characters of the Italian *opera buffa* into psychologically penetrating studies of human nature. At the same time, he leveled a pointed attack on the decadence of the European aristocracy. The central intrigue of *Figaro* features the maid Susanna and her fiancé, the valet Figaro, in a plot to outwit their master Count Almaviva, who seeks to seduce Susanna. In an era dominated by aristocratic privilege, and one that still honored the feudal claim to "first-night rights" over a female servant, *The Marriage of Figaro* was sharp satire: It championed the wit and ingenuity of the lower class over the self-serving arrogance of the nobility. And while such a theme might seem less than controversial today, it stirred heated debate in Mozart's time— Napoleon called the play by Pierre-Augustin Beaumarchais (1732–1799), on which the opera was based, "revolution already in action." Certainly Mozart was more interested in music than in political reform—he even agreed to temper Beaumarchais' scolding satire by way of Lorenzo da Ponte's Italian libretto. But his scorn for the upper classes—perhaps stemming from his own personal difficulties with aristocratic patrons—is readily apparent in the piece.

Politics aside, the enduring beauty of *The Marriage of Figaro* lies in its lyrical force and its expressive ingenuity. Mozart had a special talent for shaping personalities by way of music. While the characters in the operas of Monteverdi and Lully were allegorical stick figures, Mozart's appeal to us as real human beings. They convey a wide range of human expression, from grief and despair to hope and joy. Mozart's vocal music is never sentimental; it retains the precision and clarity of the classical style and invests it with melodic grace. Only by listening to his music can one appreciate the reason why Haydn called Mozart "the greatest composer known to me either in person or by name."

SUMMARY

Eighteenth-century European art and music reflected the changing character and tastes of its various social classes. The fashionable rococo style reflected the aristocratic affection for ornamental delicacy, intimacy, and playful elegance. The rococo style dominated the *salons* of Paris and the courts and churches of Austria and Germany. In France, Watteau, Boucher, Vigée-Lebrun, Fragonard, and Clodion produced art that evoked a world of physical pleasure and sensuous delight.

By mid-century, a reaction against the rococo style occurred among members of a growing middle class, who identified their interests with the rational ideals of the European Enlightenment. Encouraged by the *philosophes*' demand for an art of moral virtue, Greuze and Chardin produced genre paintings that gave dignity to the life and work of ordinary individuals. At the same time, archeological investigations in Greece and Southern Italy encouraged new interest in the classical past. The neoclassical style swept away the rococo in the same way that the French Revolution swept away the Old Regime. David's stirring pictorial recreations of Greek and Roman history invoked a message of self-sacrifice and moral purpose.

The neoclassical style symbolized the Enlightenment ideals of reason and liberty. In America neoclassicism was best expressed in the architectural achievements of Thomas Jefferson. In Europe, neoclassicism influenced all the arts, from Adam's English country houses and Soufflot's "Panthéon" to the portraits of Houdon and the ceramics of Wedgwood. During the reign of Napoleon, neoclassicists drew on the arts of imperial Rome to glorify Paris and the emperor himself.

The period between 1760 and approximately 1820 witnessed the birth of the orchestra and the development of the classical forms of Western instrumental music. Classical music was characterized by balance, symmetry and intellectual control—features similar to those admired by neoclassical writers, painters, sculptors, and architects. Composers used the sonata form to govern the composition of the symphony, the string quartet, the sonata, and the concerto. Haydn shaped the character of the classical symphony and the string quartet; Mozart moved easily between rococo and classical styles, investing both with extraordinary melodic grace. In his operas, as well as in his symphonies,

---

*For a fascinating interpretation of Mozart's life, see the play *Amadeus* by Peter Shaffer (New York: Harper and Row, 1981) and the Academy Award-winning film version of the play produced in 1984.

Mozart achieved a balance between lyrical invention and technical control that brought the classical style to its peak. In the decades to follow, the polite formalism of the European Enlightenment would yield to the seductive embrace of the Romantic Era.

GLOSSARY

allegro (Italian, "cheerful") a fast tempo in music

andante (Italian, "going," i.e., a normal walking pace) a moderate tempo in music

bacchante a female attendant or devotee of Dionysus

brass a family of wind instruments that usually includes the French horn, trumpet, trombone, and tuba

coda (Italian, "tail") a passage added to the closing section of a movement or musical composition in order to create the sense of a definite ending

concerto see Glossary, chapter 22; the classical concerto, which made use of *sonata form*, usually featured one or more solo instruments and orchestra

fête galante (French, "elegant entertainment") a festive diversion enjoyed by aristocrats, a favored subject in rococo art

fortissimo (Italian, "very loud") a directive indicating that the music should be played very loud; its opposite is *pianissimo* ("very soft")

largo (Italian, "broad") a very slow tempo; the slowest of the conventional tempos in music

opera buffa a type of comic opera usually featuring stock characters

percussion a group of instruments that are sounded by being struck or shaken, used especially for rhythm

satyr a semi-bestial woodland creature symbolic of Dionysus

score the musical notation for all of the instruments or voices in a particular composition; a composite from which the whole piece may be conducted or studied

sonata a composition for an unaccompanied keyboard instrument or for another instrument with keyboard accompaniment; see also Glossary, chapter 22

sonata form (or **sonata allegro form**) a structural form commonly used in the late eighteenth century for the first and fourth movements of symphonies and other instrumental compositions

string quartet a composition for four stringed instruments, each of which plays its own part

strings a family of instruments that usually includes the violin, viola, cello, and double bass (which are normally bowed); the harp, guitar, lute, and zither (which are normally plucked) can also be included, as can the viol, a bowed instrument common in the sixteenth and seventeenth centuries and a forerunner of the violin family

symphony an independent instrumental composition for orchestra

woodwinds a family of wind instruments, usually consisting of the flute, oboe, clarinet, and bassoon

SUGGESTIONS FOR READING

Bernier, Olivier. *The Eighteenth-Century Woman.* New York: Doubleday, 1981.
Conisbee, Philip. *Painting in Eighteenth-Century France.* Ithaca, N.Y.: Cornell University Press, 1981.
Harries, Karsten. *The Bavarian Rococo Church: Between Faith and Aestheticism.* New Haven: Yale University Press, 1983.
Hawley, Henry. *Neoclassicism: Style and Motif.* New York: Abrams, 1964.
Honour, Hugh. *Neoclassicism.* New York: Harper, 1979.
Jones, Stephen. *The Eighteenth Century.* Cambridge: Cambridge University Press, 1985.
Kalnein, Wend G., and Michael Levey. *Art and Architecture of the Eighteenth Century in France.* New York: Penguin, 1972.
Levey, Michael. *From Rococo to Revolution: Major Trends in Eighteenth-Century Painting.* New York: Praeger, 1966.
Messing, Scott. *Neoclassicism in Music.* Ann Arbor, Mich.: UMI Research Press, 1988.
Park, William. *The Idea of Rococo.* Cranbury, N.J.: University of Delaware Press, 1992.
Pauly, Reinhard. *Music in the Classic Period.* Englewood Cliffs, N.J.: Prentice-Hall, 1965.
Sheriff, Mary D. *The Exceptional Woman: Elizabeth Vigée-LeBrun and the Cultural Politics of Art.* Chicago: University of Chicago Press, 1996.
Solomon, Maynard. *Mozart.* New York: Harper, 1995.
Till, Nicolas, ed. *Mozart and the Enlightenment: Truth, Virtue, and Beauty in Mozart's Operas.* New York: Norton, 1993.

MUSIC LISTENING SELECTIONS

Cassette II Selection 8 Couperin, Ordre No. 22, "Le Croc-en-jambe," 1730.
Cassette II Selection 9 Haydn, Symphony No. 94 in G Major, "Surprise," second movement, 1791.
Cassette II Selection 10 Mozart, Serenade No. 3 in G Major, K. 525, "Eine kleine Nachtmusik," first movement, 1787.

Selected General Bibliography

Anderson, Bonnie S., and Judith P. Zinsser. *A History of Their Own: Women in Europe from Prehistory to the Present.* Vol. 2. New York: Harper, 1988.

Artz, F. B. *From the Renaissance to Romanticism: Trends in Style in Art, Literature, and Music, 1300–1830.* Chicago: University of Chicago Press, 1962.

Bridenthal, Renate, and Claudia Koonz, eds. *Becoming Visible: Women in European History.* Boston: Houghton Mifflin, 1977.

Bronowski, Jacob, and Bruce Mazlish. *The Western Intellectual Tradition: From Leonardo to Hegel.* New York: Harper, 1960.

Brown, Calvin S. *Music and Literature: A Comparison of the Arts.* Hanover, N.H.: University Press of New England, 1987.

Bugner, Ladislas, ed. *The Image of the Black in Western Art.* Vol. 3, *From Sixteenth-Century Europe to Nineteenth-Century America.* Cambridge, Mass.: Harvard University Press, 1986.

Chadwick, Whitney. *Women, Art and Society.* New York: Norton, 1991.

Chang, H. C. *Chinese Literature: Popular Fiction and Drama.* New York: Columbia University Press, 1973.

Clark, Kenneth. *Civilisation: A Personal View.* New York: Harper, 1970.

Clarke, Mary, and Clement Crisp. *The History of Dance.* New York: Crown, 1981.

Copland, Aaron. *What to Listen for in Music,* rev. ed. New York: New American Library, 1963.

Craven, Roy C. *Indian Art.* London: Thames and Hudson, 1976.

Fitzgerald, C. P. *The Horizon History of China.* New York: American Heritage, 1969.

Fleming, William. *Concerts of the Arts: Their Interplay and Modes of Relationship.* Gainesville, Fla.: University of West Florida Press, 1990.

—— *Musical Arts and Styles.* Gainesville, Fla.: University of West Florida Press, 1990.

Harman, Carter. *A Popular History of Music,* rev. ed. New York: Dell, 1973.

Held, Julius S., and Donald Posner. *Seventeenth- and Eighteenth-Century Art.* Englewood Cliffs, N.J.: Prentice-Hall, 1972.

Hsia, C. T. *The Classic Chinese Novel: A Critical Introduction.* Bloomington: Indiana University Press, 1980.

Kitson, Michael. *The Age of the Baroque.* New York: McGraw-Hill, 1967.

Kostoff, Spiro. *A History of Architecture: Settings and Rituals.* New York: Oxford University Press, 1985.

Million, Henry A. *Baroque and Rococo Architecture.* New York: Braziller, 1965.

Nelson, Lynn H., and Patrick Peebles, eds. *Classics of Eastern Thought.* San Diego: Harcourt, 1991.

Orrey, Leslie. *Opera: A Concise History.* London: Thames and Hudson, 1968.

Pevsner, Nikolaus. *An Outline of European Architecture,* 6th ed. Baltimore, Md.: Penguin, 1960.

Raynor, Henry. *A Social History of Music: From the Middle Ages to Beethoven.* New York: Schocken Books, 1972.

Russell, Bertrand. *A History of Western Philosophy,* 2nd ed. New York: Simon and Schuster, 1984.

Sadie, Stanley, ed. *The New Grove Dictionary of Music and Musicians.* New York: Macmillan, 1980.

Schirokauer, Conrad. *A Brief History of Chinese and Japanese Civilizations.* San Diego: Harcourt, 1978.

Sorrell, Walter. *The Dance Through the Ages.* New York: Grosset and Dunlap, 1967.

Spence, Jonathan D. *The Search for Modern China.* New York: Norton, 1990.

Sterling, Charles. *Still Life Painting from Antiquity to the Twentieth Century,* 2nd rev. ed. New York: Harper, 1981.

Sypher, Wyle. *Rococo to Cubism in Art and Literature.* New York: Random House, 1960.

Tapie, Victor L. *The Age of Grandeur: Baroque Art and Architecture,* translated by A. Ross Williams. New York: Praeger, 1960.

Weiss, Piero, and Richard Taruskin. *Music in the Western World. A History in Documents.* New York: Schirmer, 1984.

Wiener, Philip P., ed. *Dictionary of the History of Ideas.* New York: Scribners, 1973.

Wu, Qingyun. *Female Rule in Chinese and English Literary Utopias.* Syracuse, N.Y.: Syracuse University Press, 1995.

BOOKS IN SERIES

Great Ages of Man: A History of the World's Cultures. New York: Time-Life Books, 1965–1969.

Library of Art Series. New York: Time-Life Books, 1967.

Time-Frame. 25 vols. (projected). New York: Time-Life Books, 1990–.

Credits

The author and publishers wish to thank the following for permission to use copyright material. Every effort has been made to trace the copyright holders but if any have been inadvertently overlooked the publishers will be pleased to make the necessary arrangement at the first opportunity.

Reading 4.1 (p. 6) Loyola Press for material from *The Spiritual Exercises of St. Ignatius,* trs. Louis J. Puhl, SJ (1951), pp. 32–33, 157–158, 160

Reading 4.19 (p. 109) The Orion Publishing Group Ltd. for material from Antoine Nicolas de Condorcet, *Sketch for a Historical Picture of the Progress of the Human Mind,* trs. June Barraclough (1955), Weidenfeld & Nicolson, pp. 173, 179, 182–184

Reading 4.21 (p. 114) Heinemann Publishers, Oxford, for material from *Equiano's Travels,* ed. Paul Edwards, Heinemann Educational Books (1969), pp. 1, 15–17, 24–32

Reading 4.24 (p. 130) Peter Owen Ltd. for material from Li Ruzhen, *Flowers in the Mirror,* trs. Lin Tai-yi (1965), pp. 107, 110–112

Reading 4.25 (p. 134) Sterling Lord Literistic, Inc., on behalf of the author, for material from Jean Jacques Rousseau, *A Discourse on the Origin of Inequality,* trs. Maurice Cranston (1984), Viking, pp. 109–116. Translation copyright © 1984 by Maurice Cranston

Index

**Numbers in bold refer to figure numbers.
Text excerpts are indicated by (quoted).**

A

Abbas, Shah 83
absolutism 61, 63, 82
academies:
    French 69, 75, 76, 143
    Royal Academy of Art, London 151
a cappella style 24
acoustics 162
Adam, Robert: Kedleston Hall, Derbyshire
    153, **26.18**
Adams, Abigail 103
Adams, John, US President 103
Addison, Joseph 110
Advancement of Learning, The (Bacon) 45
African slaves 113–17
Agony in the Garden, The (El Greco) 13,
    20.7
Agra, India: Taj Mahal 86–87, **23.26**
agréments 162
Akbar, Mogul emperor 84, 86, **23.21**
Alba Madonna (Raphael) 26
Alberti, Leon Battista xvi, 1
    Santa Maria Novella 20, **20.17**
Alceste (Lully) **23.7**
Alembert, Jean Le Rond d' 106
allegro 164, 168
Amadeus (Shaffer) 167n
Amati family 58
America *see* United States of America
American Revolution 136, 156–57
Americas, the 34
    Jesuit missionaries in 5, 7
Amsterdam, Netherlands 36, 48, 56
Anabaptism 36
anatomical studies 42
Anatomy Lesson of Dr. Nicolaes Tulp
    (Rembrandt) 57, **22.14**
andante 164, 168
anthropology 98
Apollo Attended by the Nymphs (Girardon)
    70, **23.12**
Apollo Belvedere 151, **26.18**
Apotheosis of Saint Ignatius (Pozzo) 3, 22,
    20.20
aquatints **21.5**
Arcadian Shepherds (Poussin) 71–72,
    23.13
architecture:
    American 154, 156
    baroque 18–22, 27, 34, 141
    British 34, 153–54

Chinese 89–90
French 152, 160–61
German 141, 143
Italian 18, 20–22, 27, 34
Mogul 84, 85–87
neoclassical 152–54, 156–57, 160–61
Persian (Safavid) 83, **23.20**
rococo 141, 143
Argis, Antoine-Gaspart Boucher d' 106
arias 25, 26
Aristotle 42, 43, 44, 51, 76
art *see* painting; sculpture
Art of the Fugue, The (Bach) 59
Art of Playing the Clavecin, The
    (Couperin) 162
Asoka, Emperor 84
Assembly in a Salon (Dequevauviller)
    24.2
astronomy 22, 42, 43–44, 50–51, 98
Augustinians 7
Austria:
    music *see* Haydn; Mozart
    see also Vienna

B

bacchantes 147
Bach, Johann Sebastian 38, 39–40, 58,
    163, **21.9**
    The Art of the Fugue 59
    Brandenburg Concertos 59
    Cantata No. 80 40
    Passion According to Saint Matthew 40
    Well-Tempered Keyboard 58
Bacon, Francis 44, 47
    The Advancement of Learning 45
    Novum Organum 44–45 (quoted)
    Of Studies 45, 46 (quoted)
ballet 76, 77
Ballet de la Nuit 76, **23.17**
balloons, hot-air 136
baroque style 3, 5, 14, 63
    architecture 18–22, 27, 34, 141
    music 24–25, 38–40, 58–59, 162
    painting in Italy 14–16, 22
    painting in the North 35–36, 51–52,
    72–73, 74
    sculpture 17–18, 70
Basho, Matsuo: *haiku* poem 95 (quoted)
Bastille, the 119, 137, 138
    The Siege of the Bastille (La Charprais and
    Esclapart) **25.6**
Bavaria: Ottobeuren Benedictine abbey
    141, 143, **26.4**, **26.5**

Beaumarchais, Pierre-Augustin:
    The Marriage of Figaro 167
Beccaria, Cesare de: *On Crimes and
    Punishments* 109
Beggar's Opera, The (Gay) 131
Beijing (Peking), China 92
    Forbidden City 88, 89, 90, **23.27–23.29**
    Summer palace 92
Bernini, Gianlorenzo 17, 70
    Baldacchino, Saint Peter's, Rome 18,
    20.14
    The Ecstasy of Saint Teresa 9, 17–18, **20.2**
    Fountain of the Four Rivers, Piazza
    Navona, Rome 17, **20.11**
    Louis XIV 70, **23.11**
    Saint Peter's (Rome) colonnades 18,
    20.13
Bernstein, Leonard: *Candide* 121
Bible, the 27, 43
    Douay 29 (quoted)
    King James 29 (quoted)
    and the *philosophes* 105
    and the pietists 27
Bichitr: *Jahangir Preferring a Sufi Shaikh to
    Kings* 85, **23.22**
bicycles 149
Bill of Rights (English Parliament) 27
Bodin, Jean 98
Boffrand, Germain: Salon de la Princesse,
    Hôtel de Soubise 141, **26.2**
Book of the Courtier, The (Castiglione) 135
Borch, Gerard ter: *The Suitor's Visit* 52,
    22.7
Borghese, Pauline 157
    Pauline Borghese as Venus (Canova)
    157–58, **26.19**
Borromini, Francesco 21
    San Carlo alle Quattro Fontane, Rome
    21, **20.18**, **20.19**
Bosch, Hieronymus xvii, 52
botanical studies 108
Boucher, François 143–44, 145, 158
    Venus Consoling Love 144, **26.7**
Bourgeois Gentilhomme, Le (Molière) 77–82
    (quoted)
Bramante, Donato 1
Brandenburg Concertos (Bach) 59
brass instruments 163, 168
Britain:
    architecture 34, 153–54
    Civil War 27, 31, 98
    "Glorious Revolution" 27, 100
    literature 29–33, 110–11, 117–19,
    see also political theory; scientific
    literature (*below*)

music 58
  painting 75, 131
  Parliament 27, 132
  philosophy 49–50, 135–36
  political theory 98–102, 136
  prints 131–32
  scientific literature 44–46, 50–51
Brueghel, Pieter 54
Brunelleschi, Filippo xvi, 1
Bruno, Giordano 44
Buddhism 7, 93
Buffon, Georges Leclerc, Comte de 108
burins 36, 41, **21.5**

C

Calvinism 27, 35, 36, 102
camera obscura 54, 55, **22.8**
Candide (Voltaire) 120, 121–29 (quoted)
Canova, Antonio 157
  Pauline Borghese as Venus 157–58, **26.19**
Cantata No. 80 (Bach) 40
cantatas 40, 41
Cao Xueqin: *The Dream of the Red Chamber* (*The Story of the Stone*) 92
Caravaggio (Michelangelo Merisi) 14
  The Crucifixion of Saint Peter 15, **20.9**
  The Supper at Emmaus 14–15, **20.8**
caricature 132, 138
Carlin, Martin: lady's desk 141, **26.3**
Carmelites 7–8
Carmontelle, Louis: *The Mozarts in Concert* **26.34**
carpets, Asian 84
  Persian **23.19**
Cartesianism 47, *see* Descartes, René
cartouches 21, 26
Castiglione, Baldassare xvi
  The Book of the Courtier 135
Catherine II ("the Great"), Empress of Russia 100, 120, 141
Catholic church/Catholicism 5
  and mysticism 5, 7–9, 14, 27
  and the *philosophes* 105
  and science and astronomy 43–44
  see also Catholic Reformation; Inquisition; Jesuits
Catholic Reformation (Counter-Reformation) 5–6, 25
  and architecture 18–22
  and literature 7–9
  and music 24–25
  and painting 9–16
  and sculpture 17–18
cellos 58, 163, 164
ceramics:
  Chinese 90–91, **23.30**, **23.31**
  Sèvres porcelain 144, **26.3**, **26.8**
  Wedgwood 153, **26.20**
Cremona, Italy 58
Chalgrin, Jean-François Thérèse: Arc de Triomphe, Paris 161, **26.31**
Chambers' *Encyclopedia* 105
Chardin, Jean-Baptiste-Siméon 148–49
  The Kitchen Maid **26.13**
Charles I, King of England 27, 99
  Charles I on Horseback (van Dyck) 75, **21.1**
Charlottesville, Virginia: Rotunda, University of Virginia 156, **26.23**
chemistry, study of 108

child labor 113
China 5, 7, 61, 92, 110, 129
  architecture 89–90
  ceramics 90–91
  literature 92, 108, 110, 129–31
  Manchu dynasty 3, 88–89, 90, 92, 129
  Ming dynasty 3, 63, 88, 90
  opera 92
  painting 55, 90
  Qing dynasty 63, 89, 90, 91, 108
  tapestries 92
  theater 92
chinoiserie 92, 95, 141
choreography 76, 95
Christ Preaching (Rembrandt) 37, **21.6**, **21.7**
chromatic scale 24, 26, 58
Cervantes, Miguel de 1, 110
Civil Government, Of (Locke) 100, 101–102 (quoted)
Civil War, English 27, 31, 98
clarinets 162, 163
classical music (18th century) 139, 162–65, 167
Claude Lorrain 72
  The Marriage of Isaac and Rebekah (*The Mill*) 72, **23.14**
clavecins see harpsichords
clocks, pendulum 47
Clodion (Claude Michel) 147
  The Intoxication of Wine 147, 158, **26.11**
coda, musical 165, 168
comédie-ballet 77, 95
commedia dell'arte 77
Cicero xvi
"Commonwealth" 27
"conceits" 30
concertato 24, 26
concerto grosso 59, 60
concertos 58, 60, 164, 168
concerts, public 39, 162, 165
Condorcet, Antoine Nicolas de 109
  Sketch for a Historical Picture of the Progress of the Human Mind 109–10 (quoted)
Confucius and Confucianism 7, 90, 120
Constantinople (Istanbul) 83
context x–xi
continuo 39, 41
Copernicus, Nicolas 42, 44, 50
  On the Revolution of the Heavenly Spheres 42
copyright law 131
Cornaro Chapel, Santa Maria della Vittoria, Rome **20.12**
  see also Bernini: *Ecstasy of Saint Teresa*
Corneille, Pierre 158
Così fan tutte (Mozart) 167
Couchet, Johannes: harpsichord **22.15**
counterpoint (music) 162–63
Counter-Reformation *see* Catholic Reformation
Couperin, François 58, 162
  The Art of Playing the Clavecin 162
courante (dance) 162
Crashaw, Richard 9
  The Flaming Heart 9 (quoted)
  A Hymn to the Name and Honor of the Admirable Saint Teresa 9
cloisonné vessels 92, **23.32**
Crimes and Punishments, On (Beccaria) 109
Critique of Practical Reason (Kant) 136
Critique of Pure Reason (Kant) 136
Cromwell, Oliver 27
Crucifixion of Saint Peter, The (Caravaggio) 15, **20.9**

D

d'Alembert *see* Alembert, Jean Le Rond d'
dances x, 58, 75–76, 162; *see also* ballet
Dante Alighieri: *Divine Comedy* 31, 42
David, Jacques-Louis 158, 160
  The Death of Socrates 97, 159, **26.27**
  The Oath of the Horatii 158–59, **26.26**
Death of Socrates, The (David) 97, 159, **26.27**
Declaration of Independence 102–103 (quoted), 136
Decline and Fall of the Roman Empire (Gibbon) 108
deductive reasoning 47, 60
Defoe, Daniel 131
  Robinson Crusoe 110
de Gouges *see* Gouges, Olympe de
de Heem *see* Heem, Jan de
de Hooch *see* Hooch, Pieter de
deism and deists 48, 60, 111, 120
Delhi, India: Shahjahanabad ("The Red Fort") 86, **23.23–23.25**
Departure from the Island of Cythera (Watteau) 143, **26.6**
Dequevauviller, François: *Assembly in a Salon* **24.2**
Derbyshire, England: Kedleston Hall 153, **26.18**
Descartes, René 47, 48, **22.2**
  Discourse on Method 47–48 (quoted)
Dialogue Concerning the Two Principal Systems of the World (Galileo) 44
Diderot, Denis 105, 106, 148
  ed. *Encyclopédie* 105–106, 107–108 (quoted), 131, **24.4**
  Houdon portrait sculpture 157, **24.3**
Discourse on Method (Descartes) 47–48 (quoted)
Discourse on the Origin of Inequality among Men (Rousseau) 133–35 (quoted)
Discourses (Reynolds) 151
Divine Comedy (Dante Alighieri) 31, 42
Dominicans 7
Donatello (Donato Bardi) xvi
Don Giovanni (Mozart) 167
Donne, John 29
  Holy Sonnets 30–31 (quoted)
  Meditation 17 29–30 (quoted)
Douay Bible 29 (quoted)
drama *see* theater
Dream of the Red Chamber, The (Cao Xueqin) 92
dualism 47
du Châtelet, Gabrielle-Emilie Le Tonnelier de Breteuil, Marquise 106, **24.5**
Dürer, Albrecht 1
Dutch art:
  landscape paintings 54–55
  portraiture 56–57, 72
  still lifes 51–52
  see also Rembrandt van Rijn
Dutch Courtyard, A (Hooch) ii, 52, **22.5**
Dyck, Anthony van 75, 144
  Charles I on Horseback 75, **21.1**
dynamics (music) 24, 26, 164

E

economics 3, 98, 103–104, 112
Ecstasy of Saint Teresa (Bernini) 9, 17–18, **20.2**
Edo (Tokyo), Japan 93
education:
  Condorcet on 110, 111

and Roman Catholics 111
Rousseau on 135
and sex discrimination 102, 106, 135
"Eine Kleine Nachtmusik" (Mozart) 165
Elementary Treatise of Chemistry (Lavoisier) 108
El Greco *see* Greco, El
Elizabeth I, Queen of England 27
Emile (Rousseau) 135
Encyclopédie (ed. Diderot) 105–106, 107–108 (quoted), 131, **24.4**
England *see* Britain
English Civil War 27, 31, 98
engravings 131–32, 149, 150, **25.4**, **25.5**
Enlightenment, the 97, 98, 106, 110, 111, 112, 113, 117, 156
equal temperament (music) 58, 60
Equiano, Olaudah 113, **25.2**
Travels 113–17 (quoted)
Erasmus of Rotterdam 1, 117
Escalapart, Mme. *see* La Charprais
Essay Concerning Human Understanding (Locke) 49–50 (quoted)
Essay on Man (Pope) 111 (quoted), 113
Essay on Manners (Voltaire) 120
essays, journalistic 110
Estates General, France 63, 137
Esterházy, Prince Paul Anton 165
etchings 36–37, 41, 150, **21.5–21.7**, **26.14**
ethics, Kantian 136
exposition (music) 164, **26.33**
Eyck, Jan van 52, 55

F

famille verte porcelain 91, **23.31**
fêtes galantes 143, 168
Feuillet, Raoul Auget: choreographic notation 76
Ficino, Marsilio xvi
Fielding, Henry 110
figured bass (music) 39, 41
Fischer, Johann Michael: Benedictine abbey, Ottobeuren 141, 143, **26.4**, **26.5**
Flaming Heart, The (Crashaw) 9 (quoted)
Flemish painters, 17th-century 74–75
Florence, Italy xvi
Santa Maria Novella 20, **20.17**
Flowers in the Mirror (Li Ruzhen) 129–31 (quoted)
Forbidden City, Beijing 88, 89, 90, **23.27–23.29**
foreshortening (perspective) 14, 26
forte 24, 164
fortissimo 168
Fountain of the Four Rivers, Piazza Navona, Rome (Bernini) 17, **20.11**
Four Seasons, The (Vivaldi) 59
Fragonard, Jean-Honoré 143, 145–46
The Swing 146, **26.10**
France 82
academies 69, 75, 76, 143
architecture *see* Paris; Versailles, palace of
Estates General 63, 137
Gobelins tapestries 68, 144
literature and drama 76–82, 119–29
music and dance 58, 75–76, 162
painting 71–73, 143–46, 148–49, 158–60
philosophes 104–105, 106, 108–109, 113, 119, 148
philosophy 47–48, 49, 133–35
political theory 102, 109–10
Revolution *see* French Revolution
sculpture 70, 147, 157

Sèvres porcelain 144
Francis I, King of France 82
Franciscans 7
Franklin, Benjamin 136, 156
Frederick II ("the Great"), king of Prussia 100
French Revolution 105, 109, 136–38, 160
frescoes 9–10, 11–12, 22, **20.3**, **20.6**, **20.20**
Frost, Robert x
fugues (music) 59, 60, 163

G

Gabler, Joseph: organ **21.10**
Gabrieli, Giovanni 24
In Ecclesiis 24
Galileo Galilei 42, 43–44, 50
Dialogue Concerning the Two Principal Systems of the World 44
gardens:
Chinese 90
Mogul 86
rococo 141
at Versailles 66
Gay, John: *The Beggar's Opera* 131
Gellée, Claude *see* Claude Lorrain
genre paintings:
Dutch 52
French 148–49
Gentileschi, Artemisia 15–16
Judith Slaying Holofernes 16, **20.10**
geocentric theory (astronomy) 42
Geographer, The (Vermeer) 55, **22.1**
geometry 42, 44, 47
George II, King of England 39
George III, King of England 102
Germany 27
architecture 141, 143
astronomy 42–43
music 162, 163, *see also* Bach, Johann Sebastian
philosophy 108, 135–36
Gibbon, Edward: *The Decline and Fall of the Roman Empire* 108
Gibbs, James 154
Saint Martin-in-the-Fields, London 154, **26.21**
gigues 58
Gin Lane (Hogarth) 132, **25.5**
Girardon, François 70, 71
Apollo Attended by the Nymphs 70, **23.12**
"Glorious Revolution" (England, 1688) 27, 100
Gobelins tapestries 68, 144
Goldsmith, Oliver 131
Góngora y Argote, Luis de 9
Gouges, Olympe de 137, 138
Grand Ball, The (anon.) **26.1**
Grande Odalisque, La (Ingres) 160, **26.28**
Great Seal of the United States 157, **26.24**
Greco, El (Domenikos Theotokopoulos) 13, 24
The Agony in the Garden 13, **20.7**
Greeks, ancient xvi, 111, 150, 151, 152, 153, 159
Greenhill, John: *Portrait of John Locke* **24.1**
Greuze, Jean-Baptiste 148, 149
Village Betrothal 148, **26.12**
Grotius, Hugo 98
Grünewald, Matthias (Mathis Neithardt) 1
Guadalupe, Virgin of 7, **20.1**
Guarneri family 58
Gulliver's Travels (Swift) 117, 131
Gutenberg, Johannes 1

H

haikus 94–95
Hakuin Ekaku 93
Two Blind Men Crossing a Log Bridge 93, **23.25**
Halley, Edmund: comet 98
Hals, Frans 56
Portrait of René Descartes 56, **22.2**
Portrait of a Member of the Haarlem Civic Guard 56, **22.11**
Handel, George Frederick 38, 39
Messiah 39
Samson 39
hanging scrolls, Japanese 93, **23.35**
Hardouin-Mansart, Jules: palace of Versailles 66, 68, **23.4**, **23.9**, **23.10**
"Harlot's Progress" (Hogarth) 131
harpsichords 58, 162, **22.15**
Harvey, William 42
Haussman, Elias Gottlob: *Bach* **21.9**
Haydn, Franz Joseph 165, 167
Symphony No. 94 ("The Surprise") 165
Heavenly Joys Come to Earth for Akbar (Mogul miniature) 84, **23.21**
Heem, Jan Davidsz de: *Still Life with View of the Sea* 51, **22.3**
heliocentric theory (astronomy) 42, 43
Herculaneum, excavations at 151
heroic couplets 111, 112
History of Rome (Livy) 158–59
Hobbes, Thomas 98–99, 111*n*, 135
Leviathan 99–100 (quoted)
Hogarth, William 131, 148
Gin Lane 132, **25.5**
"The Harlot's Progress" 131
"Marriage à la Mode" 131–32, **25.4**
"The Rake's Progress" 131
Hold of a Slave Ship, The (Rugendas) **25.1**
Holland *see* Netherlands
Holy Sonnets (Donne) 30–31 (quoted)
Homer: *Iliad* and *Odyssey* 111
homophonic music 39, 41
Hooch, Pieter de 52
A Dutch Courtyard ii, 52, **22.5**
Portrait of a Family Making Music 52, **22.6**
Horace (Quintus Horatius Flaccus) 110
Houdon, Jean-Antoine 157
Diderot 157, **24.3**
Thomas Jefferson 157, **26.22**
Voltaire in Old Age 157, **25.3**
George Washington 157, **26.25**
humanism xvi
Hume, David 135–36
"Hundred-Guilder Print" (Rembrandt) *see Christ Preaching*
Huygens, Christian 47
Hymn to the Name and Honor of the Admirable Saint Teresa, A (Crashaw) 9

I

idealism:
Enlightenment 138
transcendental (Kantian) 136, 138
Ignatius, Saint *see* Loyola, Saint Ignatius
illusionism 21, 22, 34
immunology, science of 84, 108
impasto 36, 41
Index Expurgatorius 6
India 5, 34, 61
Mogul Empire in 84–87
inductive reasoning 44, 60
Industrial Revolution 113

In Ecclesiis (Gabrieli) 24
Ingres, Jean-Auguste-Dominique 160
    La Grande Odalisque 160, **26.28**
inoculations 84, 108
*Inquiry into the Nature and Causes of the
    Wealth of Nations, An* (Smith) 103–104
    (quoted)
Inquisition, the 5, 6, 44, 120
intaglio printing processes **21.5**
Intoxication of Wine, The (Clodion) 147,
    158, **26.11**
inventions *see under* science
Ireland 117, *see also* Swift, Jonathan
Irises at Yatuhashi (Ogata Korin) 93, **23.34**
Isfahan, Iran: Imperial Mosque 83, **23.20**
Islam see Muslims
Istanbul (Constantinople) 83
Italy:
    architecture 18, 20–22, 27, 34;
        see also Rome
    astronomy 43–44
    literature xvi, 31, 42, 98, 135
    music and opera 18, 24–25, 58, 59
    painting 14–16, 22
    sculpture 17–18, 157–58
    social reform 109

J

Jahan, Shah 86–87
Jahangir, Mogul emperor 85
    Jahangir Preferring a Sufi Shaikh to Kings
        (Bichitr) 85, **23.22**
James I, King of England 27, 28, 85
    King James Bible 29 (quoted)
James II, King of England 27
Japan 5, 7
    haikus 94–95
    ink scrolls 93
    Kabuki theater 94
    literature 92, 94–95, 110
    screens 93
    tea ceremony 93
    Tokugawa dynasty 7, 63, 92–93
    woodblock prints 94
jasperware, Wedgwood 153, **26.20**
Jefferson, Thomas 102, 103, 154, 156
    Declaration of Independence 102–103
        (quoted), 136
    Houdon portrait sculpture of 157, **26.22**
    Rotunda, University of Virginia 156,
        26.23
Jerome, Saint 29
Jerusalem 83
Jesuits (Society of Jesus) 5–6, 7, 48, 92,
    119, 120
jigs 58
John of the Cross, Saint 9
Johnson, Dr. Samuel 108
Judith Slaying Holofernes (Gentileschi)
    16, **20.10**
Juvenal 117

K

Kabuki theater 94, **23.26**
Kangxi, Manchu Emperor 92
Kant, Immanuel 135, 136, 138
    Critique of Practical Reason 136
    Critique of Pure Reason 136
Kedleston Hall, Derbyshire, England
    153, **26.18**
Kepler, Johannes 42–43, 50

Kitchen Maid, The (Chardin) 149, **26.13**
Köchel, Ludwig von 165
Koran *see* Qur an
Korin, Ogata: *Irises at Yatuhashi* 93, **23.34**

L

labor:
    child 113
    division of (Smith) 103–104
    exploitation 113
La Charprais, Briffault de, and
    Mme Esclapart: *The Siege of
    the Bastille* **25.6**
lacquerware, oriental 90, 93
landscape painting:
    Chinese 55, 90
    Dutch (17th-century) 54–55
    ideal (17th-century) 72
Largillière, Nicolas de: *Marquise du
    Châtelet* **24.5**
largo 164
La Rochefoucauld, François de 76
    Maxims 76 (quoted)
Last Judgment, The (Michelangelo) 9–10,
    20.3
Last Supper, The (Leonardo) 11–12, **20.6**
Last Supper, The (Tintoretto) 11–13, **20.5**
Lavoisier, Antoine: *Elementary Treatise of
    Chemistry* 108
Le Brun, Charles
    The Louvre **23.5**
    Palace of Versailles 68, **23.10**
Leeuwenhoek, Anton van 47
Leibniz, Gottfried Wilhelm 51, 108,
    111, 120
Le Nôtre, André: gardens of Versailles 66
Leonardo da Vinci ix, xvii
    The Last Supper 11–12, **20.6**
Le Pautre, Jean: *Marble Court,
    Versailles* **23.7**
Le Romain: "Negroes" (*Encyclopédie* article)
    107–108 (quoted)
Le Vau, Louis:
    The Louvre 66, **23.5**
    Palace of Versailles 63, 66, **23.2**, **23.4**
Leviathan (Hobbes) 99–100 (quoted)
Leyster, Judith 56
    Self-Portrait 56, **22.12**
Li Ruzhen: *Flowers in the Mirror* 129–31
    (quoted)
Linnaeus, Carolus 108
Lisbon earthquake (1755) 120
literature x
    British 29–33, 110–111, 117–19
    and the Catholic Reformation 7–9
    Chinese 92, 108, 110, 129–31
    French 76–82, 119–29, *see also
        philosophes*
    Italian xvi, 31, 42, 98, 135,
    Japanese 92, 94–95, 110
    scientific 44–46, 50–51
    see also philosophy; political theorists
Livy: *History of Rome* 158–59
Locke, John 49, 98, 99, 102, 103, 119, 135,
    136, **24.1**
    Essay Concerning Human Understanding
        49–50 (quoted)
    First Treatise on Government 100
    Of Civil Government 100, 101–102
        (quoted)
London 34, 113, 132, 165
    Globe Theatre 34
    Royal Society of London for Improving

Natural Knowledge 34, 45
    Royal Academy of Art 151
    Saint Martin-in-the-Fields, London 154,
        26.21
    Saint Paul's Cathedral 29, 30, 34, **21.2**,
        21.3
Louis XIII, King of France 69, 75, 76
Louis XIV, King of France xi, 63, 66, 68,
    69–70, 72, 75, 76, 83, 84, 102, 104,
    23.17
    bust (Bernini) 70, **23.11**
    portrait (Rigaud) 73, **23.1**
Louis XV, King of France 105, 144, 149
Louis XVI, King of France 136, 137, 138,
    141
Louvre, The, Paris 63, 66, 69, 70, **23.5**
Loyola, Saint Ignatius 5, 20
    Spiritual Exercises 6 (quoted)
Lully, Jean-Baptiste 75, 77, 167
    Alceste **23.7**
Luther, Martin xvii, 39
    "A Mighty Fortress is Our God" 40
Lutheran chorales 1, 39, 40

M

Machiavelli, Niccolò xvi, 98
"Madeleine, La", Paris 160, **26.29**
Maderno, Carlo: Saint Peter's, Rome **20.13**
Madonna of the Long Neck (Parmigianino)
    10–11, 160, **20.4**
Magic Flute, The (Mozart) 167
Maids of Honor, The (Velásquez)
    see Meninas, Las
Maison Carrée, Nîmes, France 156, 160,
    26.30
Manchu dynasty (China) 3, 88–89, 90, 92,
    129
mannerist painting 9–13
Mannheim orchestra 163–64
Mansart *see* Hardouin-Mansart, Jules
manuscripts, illuminated (Mogul) 84,
    23.21
maps xi
    empires (16th–17th century) **23.1**
    intellectual revolution **22.1**
Marble Court, Versailles (Le Pautre) **23.7**
Maria Theresa, Empress of Austria 141
Marie Antoinette 141
    Vigée-Lebrun's portrait of 144–45, **26.9**
marquetry 68, 95
Marquise du Châtelet (Largillière) **24.5**
"Marriage à la Mode" (Hogarth) 131–32,
    25.4
Marriage of Figaro, The (Mozart) 167
Marriage of Isaac and Rebekah, The (Claude
    Lorrain) 72, **23.14**
Marriage Transaction, The (Hogarth) 131,
    25.4
Masaccio (Tommaso di Giovanni di Mone)
    xvi
mathematics 42, 44
maxims 76
Maxims (La Rochefoucauld) 76 (quoted)
Mecca 83
medical advances 42, 84, 108, 110
Meditation 17 (Donne) 29–30 (quoted)
Meninas, Las (Maids of Honor) (Velásquez)
    73–74, **23.15**
Mesmer, Franz 110
Messiah (Handel) 39
metaphysical poetry 29–31
Mexico City: shrine of Virgin of

Guadalupe 7, **20.1**
Mexico, Jesuits in 5, 7
Michelangelo Buonarroti xvii
   The Last Judgment 9–10, **20.3**
   Saint Peter's, Rome **20.13**
microscopes 42, 51
"Mighty Fortress is Our God, A" (Luther) 40
Mill, The (Claude Lorrain) *see Marriage of Isaac and Rebekah, The*
Milton, John 31, 39
   Paradise Lost 31–33 (quoted), 111
Ming dynasty (China) 3, 63, 88, 90
   cloisonné vessels 92, **23.32**
   literature and theater 92
   tapestries 92, **23.33**
mining industry 113
minuets 58, 75, 162
missionaries, Christian 5, 7, 82
Modest Proposal, A (Swift) 117–19 (quoted)
Mogul Empire 3, 63, 84
   architecture 84, 85–87
   painting 84, 85
Molière (Jean-Baptiste Poquelin) 77
   Le Bourgeois Gentilhomme 77–82 (quoted)
Mongols 3, 88
Montaigne, Michel de xvii
Montesquieu, Charles Louis de Secondat 102, 103, 106
   The Spirit of the Laws 102
Montessori, Maria 135
Monteverdi, Claudio 24–25, 167
   Orfeo 25
More, Thomas 1
movements (music) 58, 164
Mozart, Leopold 165, **26.34**
Mozart, Wolfgang Amadeus 165, 167, **26.34**
   Così fan tutte 167
   Don Giovanni 167
   "Eine Kleine Nachtmusik" 165
   The Magic Flute 167
   The Marriage of Figaro 167
   symphonies 165
Mozarts in Concert, The (Carmontelle) **26.34**
Mughal Empire *see* Mogul Empire
Mumtaz Mahal 87
Murasaki, Lady Shikibu: *The Tale of Genji* 110
music and musical instruments x, 108
   baroque 24–25, 38–41, 58–59, 162
   Chinese 92
   classical 139, 162–65, 167–68
   Lutheran 1, 39, 40
   rococo 139, 162
   see also opera
muskets, flintlock 136
Muslims 82–83, 84
mysticism, Catholic 5, 7–9, 14, 27

N

Napoleon Bonaparte 138, 157, 160, 161, 167
natural law 97, 98
   Encyclopédie article on 106, 107 (quoted)
"Negroes" (Le Romain) 107–108 (quoted)
neoclassicism 70, 110, 139, 150–51
   in architecture 152–54, 156–57, 160–61
   in literature 76
   in painting 71–72, 158–60
   in sculpture 70, 153, 157–58

Netherlands, the 27, 35–36
   etching 36–37
   music making 52
   painting 35, 36, 51–57, 72
New England, USA: churches 154
newspapers 110
Newton, Sir Isaac 50, 97
   Principia 50–51, 98, 108
Nîmes, France: Maison Carrée 156, 160, **26.30**
Nō plays, Japanese 94
novels:
   British 110
   Chinese 92
   Japanese 92, 110
Novum Organum (Bacon) 44–45 (quoted)

O

Oath of the Horatii, The (David) 158–59, **26.26**
oboes 58, 163
Odalisque see Grande Odalisque, La
Of Civil Government (Locke) 100, 101–102 (quoted)
Of Studies (Bacon) 45, 46 (quoted)
Olivier, P.D.: *The Teatro Regio* **20.21**
On the Revolution of the Heavenly Spheres (Copernicus) 42
Oosterwyck, Maria van: *Vanitas Still Life* 51–52, **22.4**
opera:
   Chinese 92
   French 75
   Italian 18, 24–25, **20.21**
   see also Handel; Mozart
opera buffa 167
optics, science of 44
"optimism, philosophic" 108
Oration on the Dignity of Man (Pico della Mirandola) xvi
oratorios 38–39, 40, 41, **21.8**
orchestras 25, 163–64, **20.21**, **26.32**
Orfeo (Monteverdi) 25
organs 39–40, 58, **21.10**
Ottobeuren, Bavaria: Benedictine abbey 141, 143, **26.4**, **26.5**
Ottoman Empire 82–83, 84
   ceremonial canteen **23.18**
overtures 25, 26
   French 75

P

Paine, Thomas 136
painting:
   baroque 14–16, 22, 35–36, 51–52, 72–73, 74
   in Britain 75, 131
   and the Catholic Reformation 9–16
   Chinese 55, 90
   Dutch 35, 36, 51–52, 54–57, 72
   French 71–73, 143–46, 148–49, 158–60
   Japanese 93
   mannerist 9–13
   Mogul 84, 85
   neoclassical 71–72, 158–60
   Renaissance xvi–1, 9
   rococo 143–46, 147, 148
   Spanish 9, 73–74, *see also* Greco, El
Palestrina, Giovanni di 24
   Pope Marcellus Mass 24
Palladio, Andrea xvi

Panini, Giovanni Paolo (after): *Picture Gallery (Roma Antica)* **26.15**
"Panthéon" (Sainte Geneviève), Paris 152, **26.16**, **26.17**
Paracelsus, Philippus Ambrosius 42
parachute, first 136
Paradise Lost (Milton) 31–33 (quoted), 111
Paris 104, 113, 139, 149, 159
   Arc du Carrousel 161
   Arc de Triomphe 161, **26.31**
   Church of Mary Magdalene ("La Madeleine") 160, **26.29**
   Hôtel de Soubise 141, **26.2**
   The Louvre 63, 66, 69, 70, **23.5**
   Luxembourg Palace 74
   Royal Opera 144
   Sainte Geneviève ("Panthéon") 152, **26.16**, **26.17**
   salons 141
Parliament, English 27, 132
Parmigianino: *Madonna of the Long Neck* 10–11, 160, **20.4**
Pascal, Blaise 49
   Pensées 49
Passion According to Saint Matthew (Bach) 40
Pauline Borghese as Venus (Canova) 157–58, **26.19**
pavanes 58
Peking *see* Beijing
Pensées (Pascal) 49
percussion instruments 163, 168
periodicals 110
Perrault, Claude: The Louvre, Paris 66, 70, **23.5**
Persia 82, 84
   architecture 83
   carpets 83, **23.19**
perspective: and foreshortening 14, 26
Petrarch (Francesco Petrarca) xvi
Phèdre (Racine) 76
Philip II, King of Spain 13, 24, 35
Philip IV, King of Spain 73, 75
philosophes, the 104–105, 106, 108–109, 113, 119, 148
philosophy and philosophers x
   British *see* Hume; Locke
   Buddhism 7, 93
   Confucianism 7, 90, 120
   French 47–48, 49, 108–10, 133–35
   German 108, 135–36
   Renaissance humanism xvi
pianissimo 168
piano 24, 164
pianos 163
Pico della Mirandola 111*n*
   Oration on the Dignity of Man xvi
Picture Gallery (after Panini) **26.15**
pietism 27
pietra dura 86, 95, **23.25**
Piranesi, Giovanni Battista 150
   View of the Forum 150, **26.14**
pizzicato 25, 26
Plato 1, 48
poetry x
   British 30, 111
   Japanese *haikus* 94–95
   metaphysical 30
   religious 9
   see also Milton; Pope
political theorists 98–103, 136
Pollaiuolo, Antonio del xvi
polychoral music 24, 26
Pompadour, Jeanne Antoinette Poisson, Marquise de 144, **26.8**
Pompeii, excavations at 151

Ponte, Lorenzo da 167
Pope, Alexander 110–11, 117, 120
　　Essay on Man 111 (quoted), 113
Pope Marcellus Mass (Palestrina) 24
porcelain 144
　　Chinese 90–91, **23.31**
　　Sèvres 144, **26.3**, **26.8**
Porta, Giacomo della:
　　Il Gesù, Rome 20, **20.15**, **20.16**
　　Saint Peter's, Rome (dome) **20.13**
Portland Vase (Wedgwood) 153, **26.20**
Portrait of a Family Making Music (Hooch)
　　52, **22.6**
*Portrait of a Member of the Haarlem Civic
　　Guard* (Hals) 56, **22.11**
portraiture:
　　American 73
　　aristocratic 72–74, 75
　　Dutch 56–57, 72
　　in England 75
　　French 72–73, 144–45
　　Mogul 85
　　rococo 144–45
Poussin, Nicolas 71, 72, 159
　　Arcadian Shepherds 71–72, **23.13**
Pozzo, Andrea: *Apotheosis of Saint Ignatius 3*,
　　22, **20.20**
preludes 40, 41
Principia (Newton) 50–51, 98, 108
prints:
　　British engravings 131–32
　　etchings 41, **21.5**
　　woodblock 94, **23.36**
prison reform 109
programmatic music 59
Protestantism/Protestant Reformation 1, 3,
　　5, 27, 43, *see also* Calvinism
protozoa, discovery of 47
Psalm, Twenty-Third 29
Ptolemy 42
Purcell, Henry 58
Puritans, the 27, 31, 34

Q

Qing dynasty 63, 89, 108
　　ceramics 90–91, **23.30**, **23.31**
Quesnay, François 106
Quran 86

R

Rabelais, François 1, 110
Racine, Jean 76
　　Phèdre 76
"Rake's Progress, The" (Hogarth) 131
Rape of the Daughters of Leucippus (Rubens)
　　74–75, **23.16**
Raphael (Raffaello Sanzio) xvii, 71, 150, 160
　　Alba Madonna 26
realism: in Dutch painting 51–52
reasoning: deductive 47, 60
　　inductive 44, 60
recapitulation (music) 164–65, **26.33**
recitatives 25, 26
"Red Fort" (Shahjahanabad), Delhi, India
　　86, **23.23–23.25**
Reformation *see* Catholic (Counter)
　　Reformation; Protestant Reformation
refrigeration experiments 47
religion(s) *see* Anabaptists; Calvinism;
　　Catholic Church; Protestantism;
　　see also deism

Rembrandt van Rijn 35, 36, 56–57
　　Anatomy Lesson of Dr. Nicolaes Tulp 57,
　　　22.14
　　Christ Preaching ("The Hundred-Guilder
　　　Print") 37, **21.6**, **21.7**
　　The Return of the Prodigal Son 36, **21.4**
　　Self-Portrait 57, **22.13**
Renaissance:
　　architecture 21
　　art xvi–1, 9, 42
　　humanists xvi
　　"Republicanism" 103
Return of the Prodigal Son, The (Rembrandt)
　　36, **21.4**
revolutions:
　　American 136, 156–57
　　French 105, 109, 136–38, 160
　　"Glorious" (1688) 27, 100
　　Industrial 113
　　intellectual (map) **22.1**
　　"Scientific" 42*ff.*
Reynolds, Sir Joshua 151
　　Discourses 151
Richardson, Samuel 110
Rigaud, Hyacinthe: *Portrait of Louis XIV* 73,
　　23.1
Robinson Crusoe (Defoe) 110
rococo style 139, 141
　　architecture 141, 143
　　music 162
　　painting 143–46, 147, 148
　　sculpture 147
Romans, ancient xvi, 150, 151, 152, 153
Rome 9, 17, 18, 150, 158
　　Baldacchino, Saint Peter's 18, **20.14**
　　Cornaro Chapel, Santa Maria della
　　　Vittoria **20.12**, *see also* Bernini: *Ecstasy
　　　of Saint Teresa*
　　Fountain of the Four Rivers, Piazza
　　　Navona 17, **20.11**
　　Il Gesù 20–21, **20.15**, **20.16**
　　San Carlo alle Quattro Fontane 21,
　　　20.18, **20.19**
　　Sant'Ignazio *opp. 3*, 22, **20.20**
　　Saint Peter's 18, 34, **20.13**
　　Sistine Chapel, Vatican (*Last Judgment*)
　　　9–10, **20.3**
　　View of the Forum (Piranesi) 150, **26.14**
Rotunda, University of Virginia 156, **26.23**
Rousseau, Jean-Jacques 106, 108, 113,
　　133, 135, 138, 152
　　*Discourse on the Origin of Inequality among
　　　Men* 133–35 (quoted)
　　Emile 135
　　The Social Contract 135
Royal Academy of Art, London 151
Royal Society of London for Improving
　　Natural Knowledge 34, 45
Rubens, Peter Paul 74, 144
　　Rape of the Daughters of Leucippus 74–75,
　　　23.16
Rugendas, Johann Moritz: *The Hold of a
　　Slave Ship* **25.1**
Russia 120

S

Safavid dynasty 63, 83
　　architecture 83
　　carpet 83, **23.19**
Sainte Geneviève ("Panthéon"), Paris 152,
　　26.16, **26.17**
Saint Martin-in-the-Fields, London 154,
　　26.21

Saint Paul's Cathedral, London 29, 30, 34,
　　21.2, **21.3**
Saint Peter's, Rome 18, 34, **20.13**
　　Baldacchino (Bernini) 18, **20.14**
salons, French 68, 95, 104, 110, 119, 141,
　　162, **23.9**, **24.2**, **26.2**
Samson (Handel) 39
samurai 92
sarabande 162
satire 97, 117
　　in Chinese literature 129–31
　　in English art 131–32
　　in English literature 117–19
　　in French literature 119–29
satyrs 147
scale, chromatic 24, 26, 58
Scholars, The (Wu Jingzi)
science and the Scientific Revolution
　　42–44, 59
　　and art 51–52
　　discoveries and inventions 42, 43, 47,
　　　84, 108, 113, 136
　　and religion 42–44, 48–49
scores, musical 163–64, 168
screens, Japanese 93, **23.34**
scrolls, Japanese 93, **23.35**
sculpture:
　　baroque 17–18, 70
　　French 70, 147, 157, 158
　　Italian 17–18, 157–58
　　neoclassical 70, 153, 157–58
　　rococo 147
Self-Portrait (Leyster) 56, **22.12**
Self-Portrait (Rembrandt) 57, **22.13**
Sèvres porcelain 144, **26.3**, **26.8**
sexual discrimination 102, 103, 106, 110,
　　135, 137–38
Shaffer, Peter: *Amadeus* 167*n*
Shahjahanabad ("Red Fort"), Delhi 86,
　　23.23–23.25
Shakespeare, William xvii, 29, 34
Sharaku, Toshusai: *Segawa Tomisaburo as
　　Yadorigi* **23.36**
Siege of the Bastille, The (La Charprais and
　　Mme Esclapart) **25.6**
sinfonia 164
Sistine Chapel, Vatican, Rome: *The Last
　　Judgment* (Michelangelo) 9–10, **20.3**
*Sketch for a Historical Picture of the Progress
　　of the Human Mind* (Condorcet)
　　109–10 (quoted)
slave trade, transatlantic 113–17
smallpox, inoculation against 84, 108
Smith, Adam 103
　　*An Inquiry into the Nature and Causes of the
　　　Wealth of Nations* 103–104 (quoted)
social contract 98–99, 112, 135
Social Contract, The (Rousseau) 135
Society of Jesus *see* Jesuits
sociology 98
Socrates 159
sonata (sonata allegro) form 164–65, 168,
　　26.33
sonatas 58, 60, 164
Soufflot, Jacques-Germain: church of
　　Sainte Geneviève, Paris 152, **26.16**,
　　26.17
Spain 24, 35
　　painting 9, 73–74, *see also* Greco, El
　　religious literature 7–9, *see
　　also* Loyola, Saint Ignatius
Spectator (periodical) 110
Spinoza, Baruch 48–49
Spirit of the Laws, The (Montesquieu) 102
Spiritual Exercises (Loyola) 6 (quoted)

Stamitz, Johann 163
steam engines 113, 136
Steele, Richard 110
still lifes, Dutch 51–52
Still Life with View of the Sea (Heem) 51, **22.3**
Story of the Stone, The see Dream of the Red Chamber, The
Stradivari family 58
Striggio, Alessandro 25
stringed instruments 25, 58, 163, 168
string quartets 139, 164, 168
stucco 18, 26
Studies, Of (Bacon) 45, 46 (quoted)
style x
subtext xi
suites, musical 58, 60
Suitor's Visit, The (Borch) 52, **22.7**
Suleiman the Magnificent 63, 82–83
Supper at Emmaus, The (Caravaggio) 14–15, **20.8**
Swift, Jonathan 117
    Gulliver's Travels 117, 131
    A Modest Proposal 117–19 (quoted)
Swing, The (Fragonard) 146, **26.10**
symphonies, classical 139, 164, 165
Symphony No. 94 ("The Surprise") (Haydn) 165

T

Taj Mahal, Agra 86–87, **23.26**
Tale of Genji, The (Murasaki) 110
tapestries:
    Chinese (Ming) 92, **23.33**
    French (Gobelins) 68, 144
Tatler (periodical) 110
tea ceremony, Japanese 93
Teatro Regio, The (Olivier) **20.21**
technological progress *see under* science
telescopes 42, 43, 51
ter Borch, Gerard *see* Borch, Gerard ter
Teresa of Avila, Saint 7–8
    Visions 9 (quoted)
textile industry 113
theater:
    Chinese 92
    British 34, 131
    French 76, 77–82
    Japanese 94
thermometers 110
Thirty Years' War (1618–48) 3, 5
Tintoretto, Jacopo 74
    The Last Supper 11–13, **20.5**
Titian (Tiziano Vecelli) xvii, 74
toilets, flush 149
Tokugawa dynasty (Japan) 7, 92–93
    poetry 94–95
Tokyo, Japan *see* Edo
Tomisaburo, Segawa **23.36**
tonality (music) 24, 26
Travels (Equiano) 113–17 (quoted)

Trent, Council of 6, 24
trombones 163
Turin: Teatro Regio **20.21**
Turks *see* Ottoman Empire
Two Blind Men Crossing a Log Bridge (Hakuin) 93, **23.25**

U

ukiyo prints 94
United States of America:
    Constitution 102, 103
    Declaration of Independence 102–103 (quoted), 136
    Great Seal 157, **26.24**
    neoclassical architecture 154, 156
    see also American Revolution
universities, English: sectarianism 111

V

van Dyck *see* Dyck, Anthony van
van Eyck *see* Eyck, Jan van
vanitas paintings 51–52, 60
Vanitas Still Life (Oosterwyck) 51–52, **22.4**
van Oosterwyck *see* Oosterwyck, Maria van
Vatican, Rome: Sistine Chapel (*The Last Judgment*) 9–10, **20.3**
Velásquez, Diego 73
    Las Meninas (The Maids of Honor) 73–74, **23.15**
Venice, Italy 9, 24
    Saint Mark's Cathedral 24, 59
Venus Consoling Love (Boucher) 144, **26.7**
Vermeer, Jan 54
    The Geographer 55, **22.1**
    View of Delft 54–55, **22.9**
    Woman Holding a Balance 55, **22.10**
Versailles, palace of 63, 66, 68–69, 75, 82, 83, 104, 137, 139, 141, **23.2–23.4**, **23.6–23.10**
Vesalius, Andreus 42
Vesuvius, Mount 151
Victoria, Tomás Luis de 24
Vienna 141, 167
    Saint Stephen's Cathedral 165
View of Delft (Vermeer) 54–55, **22.9**
View of the Forum (Piranesi) 150, **26.14**
Vigée-Lebrun, Marie-Louise-Elisabeth 143, 144, 145
    Marie Antoinette 144–45, **26.9**
Vignola, Giacomo da: Il Gesù, Rome 20–21, **20.15**, **20.16**
Vignon, Alexandre-Pierre: Church of Mary Magdalene ("La Madeleine"), Paris 160, **26.29**
Village Betrothal (Greuze) 148, **26.12**
violas 58, 163, 164
violins 58, 163, 164
viols 168

Virgil 110
Virginia, USA:
    Rotunda, University 156, **26.23**
    State Capitol 156
Virgin of Guadalupe 7, **20.1**
Visions (Saint Teresa of Avila) 9 (quoted)
Vivaldi, Antonio 59
    The Four Seasons 59
Voltaire (François-Marie Arouet) 106, 108, 119–20, 152
    Candide 120, 121–29 (quoted)
    Essay on Manners 120
Voltaire in Old Age (Houdon) 157, **25.3**

W

wars:
    English Civil War 27, 31, 98
    Thirty Years' War (1618–48) 3, 5
Washington, D.C. 153, 154
Washington, George: Houdon's portrait sculpture 157, **26.25**
Watt, James: steam engine 113, 136
Watteau, Antoine 143
    Departure from the Island of Cythera 143, **26.6**
Wealth of Nations (Smith) 103–104 (quoted)
Wedgwood, Josiah/Wedgwood & Co. 153
    copy of *Portland Vase* **26.20**
Well-Tempered Keyboard (Bach) 58
Westphalia, Treaty of (1648) 3
wigs, men's **24.4**
Wilber, Richard: *Candide* 121
William and Mary, of England 27
Winckelmann, Johann Joachim 151
    History of Ancient Art 151
Woman Holding a Balance (Vermeer) 55, **22.10**
women:
    in America 103
    artists *see* Gentileschi; Leyster; Oosterwyck; Vigée-Lebrun
    in China 110, 129
    discrimination against 102, 103, 106, 110, 137–38
    in France 106, 135, 137–38
woodblock prints, Japanese 94, **23.36**
woodcuts **21.8**
woodwind instruments 163, 168
Wren, Sir Christopher 34
    Saint Paul's Cathedral 34, **21.2**, **21.3**
Wu Jingzi 129
    The Scholars 129

Z

Zauberflöte, Die see Magic Flute
Zen Buddhism 93